CONSOLIDATION
of FINANCIAL STATEMENTS
under IFRS

A Visual Approach

- Comprehensive Illustration of the Basics of Consolidation
- Practical Guide

Third Edition

Richard Bozec Ph.D.

Consolidation of Financial Statements under IFRS: A Visual Approach
Richard Bozec Ph.D.
www.richardbozec.com

Editor: Parmitech
Interior and cover design: Parmitech
Proofreading: With One Stone Educational Services

Copyright © 2011, Parmitech, Ottawa.
Parmitech. All rights reserved.

This publication is protected by copyright, and permission should be obtained from the publisher prior to any prohibited reproduction, storage in a retrieval system, or transmission in any form or by any means, electronic, mechanical, photocopying, recording, or otherwise.

Printed and bound in Canada

ISBN 978-0-9739225-9-2

Abbreviations Used in this Book

Abbreviations	Concepts
BV	Book Value
COGS	Cost of Goods Sold
CU	Currency Unit
FV	Fair Value
FVI	Fair Value Increment
I/S	Income Statement
NBV	Net Book Value
NCI	Non-Controlling Interest
RE	Retained Earnings
SC	Share Capital

Contents

ABBREVIATIONS III
PREFACE IX
INTRODUCTION 1

Part I Controlling Ownership

CHAPTER 1
PARENT FOUNDED SUBSIDIARIES 13
1.1 Consolidation as of the Date of Creation 14
1.2 Consolidation Following the Creation 22
    1.2.1 Consolidation of the Statement of Financial Position 25
    1.2.2 Consolidation of the Income Statement 29
Comprehensive Illustration 30
Summary of the Consolidation Adjustments in Journal Entry Form 34

CHAPTER 2
WHOLLY OWNED SUBSIDIARIES 37
2.1 Consolidation as of the Date of Acquisition 38
2.2 Consolidation Following the Date of Acquisition 49
    2.2.1 Consolidation of the Statement of Financial Position 53
    2.2.2 Consolidation of the Income Statement 61
    2.2.3 Price Differential: Additional Considerations 65
Comprehensive Illustration 69
Summary of the Consolidation Adjustments in Journal Entry Form 81

CHAPTER 3
NON-WHOLLY OWNED SUBSIDIARIES 85
3.1 Consolidation as of the Date of Acquisition 87
3.2 Consolidation Following the Date of Acquisition 97
    3.2.1 Consolidation of the Statement of Financial Position 99
    3.2.2 Consolidation of the Income Statement 108

Comprehensive Illustration 112
Summary of the Consolidation Adjustments in Journal Entry Form 128

Part II Intercompany Transactions

Chapter 4

Intercompany Dividends 133

4.1 Consolidation in Period of Intercompany Dividends 134
4.2 Consolidation in Period Subsequent to the Year of Intercompany Dividends 138

Summary of the Consolidation Adjustments in Journal Entry Form 139

Chapter 5

Intercompany Sales of Land 141

5.1 Consolidation in Period of Intercompany Sale of Land 142
    5.1.1 The Land is Held by the Purchasing Affiliate 145
    5.1.2 The Land Has Been Resold to an Outsider 146
5.2 Consolidation in Period Subsequent to the Year of Intercompany Sale of Land 149
    5.2.1 The Land is Still Held by the Purchasing Affiliate 150
    5.2.2 The Land Has Been Resold to an Outsider 151

Summary of the Consolidation Adjustments in Journal Entry Form 156

Chapter 6

Intercompany Sales of Inventory 159

6.1 Consolidation in Period of Intercompany Sale of Inventory 160
    6.1.1 All the Inventory is Held by the Purchasing Affiliate 163
    6.1.2 All the Inventory Has Been Resold to External Parties 166
    6.1.3 Only a Portion of the Inventory Has Been Resold to External Parties 168
6.2 Consolidation in Period Subsequent to the Year of Intercompany Sale of Inventory 172

Summary of the Consolidation Adjustments in Journal Entry Form 175

Chapter 7

Intercompany Sales of Depreciable Assets 177

7.1 Consolidation in Period of Intercompany Sale of Asset 178
7.2 Consolidation in Periods Subsequent to the Year of Intercompany Sale of Asset 183

Summary of the Consolidation Adjustments in Journal Entry Form 188

Part III Summary

CHAPTER 8

PRACTICAL GUIDE **193**

    8.1 Worksheet Approach 194
        8.1.1 Summary of the Consolidation Adjustments at the Date of Creation or Acquisition 194
        8.1.2 Summary of the Consolidation Adjustments Following the Date of Creation or Acquisition 197
    8.2 Direct Approach 207

CHAPTER 9

COMPREHENSIVE ILLUSTRATION **211**

    9.1 Basic Information 212
    9.2 Preliminary Analysis 214
        9.2.1 Controlling Ownership 216
        9.2.2 Intercompany Transactions 218
    9.3 Consolidation of Financial Statements 219
        9.3.1 Worksheet Approach 220
        9.3.2 Direct Approach 227
    9.4 Investment Account on Equity Basis 233

Part IV Cases and Solutions

CASE 1 FAST INC **241**

CASE 2 PRIME INC **255**

CASE 3 GLOBAL INC **269**

CASE 4 MOTHER INC **275**

CASE 5 PARENT INC **289**

CASE 6 BIG INC **311**

CASE 7 PLUS INC **333**

CASE 8 LARGE INC **353**

CASE 9 TOTAL INC **361**

CASE 10 GIANT INC **379**

KEY CONCEPTS **401**

Preface

The third edition of "Consolidation of Financial Statements under IFRS: A Visual Approach" continues to provide a clear illustration of the basics of consolidation. The second edition was based on the 2005 Exposure Draft on Business Combinations, this new edition, on the revised IAS 27 (Consolidated and Separate Financial Statements) and IFRS 3 (Business Combinations) as of September 2010. As a result, chapters 3 and 9 have been updated to account for changes made to the measurement basis for non-controlling interest. The solutions to the cases presented in part IV have also been revised accordingly.

The supplemental material for the third edition includes "Advanced Accounting: Student Manual". Based on a building-block approach, the manual presents, in slide format, an overview of the basics of intercorporate investments, business combinations, consolidation, and foreign currency translation under IFRS. For each module, the fundamental concepts are introduced before advancing to the procedures. The manual includes approximately 700 slides logically organized and integrated so as to provide a quick and easy to follow review of current advanced accounting topics. The manual contains comprehensive illustrations, a test bank, end-of-module review questions, quizzes and exercises.

Introduction

What this Book is About

This book focuses exclusively on the consolidation of financial information. Consolidation of financial statements is required whenever a corporation gains *control* over another. This situation is typical in today's business as most major corporations, and many smaller ones, have control over an array of corporations. Control is the power to govern the financial and operating policies of an entity so as to obtain benefits from its activities. In most cases, control is presumed if a corporation, *the parent*, holds a majority (50 percent and more) of the outstanding voting shares of another corporation, *the subsidiary*. Control gives the right to elect the majority of the members of the other corporation's board of directors, hence, the power to determine its strategic operating, investing, and financing policies. When a majority of voting stock is held, the investor-investee relationship has become so closely connected that the two corporations, which continue to exist as separate legal entities, are viewed as a single entity for external reporting purposes. Therefore, consolidated financial statements must be prepared by the parent company with all the assets, liabilities, revenues and expenses of the group brought together. Consolidated information will account for the overall resources of the parent and all its subsidiaries, also known as the *economic entity* (Figure 1).

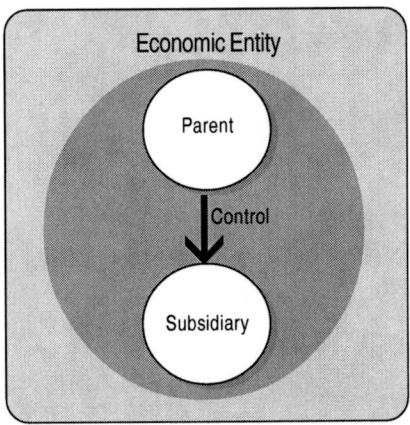

Figure 1 • The Economic Entity

In practical terms, consolidation refers to the mechanical process of bringing together the financial records of the affiliated companies to form a single set of financial statements. More precisely, consolidation consists of cross-adding the accounts of the parent to those of the subsidiaries, after proper eliminations and adjustments are made. This book provides a comprehensive coverage of the basic procedural steps and consolidation adjustments involved in most common yet simple situations. The rationale underlying such adjustments is emphasized.

Objectives of this Book

The main objectives of this book are to illustrate the basics of consolidation and to provide a practical guide to students and practitioners. The book also fully complies with the International Financial Reporting Standards. The following explains in more detail each of these objectives.

❒ *Provide a Thorough Understanding of the Basics of Consolidation*

Consolidation of financial information is certainly one of the most complex procedures in all accounting. This topic is generally perceived as unfriendly by most of our accounting students. It is in fact quite easy to be overwhelmed by the detailed numbers. Students also have difficulty explaining why some adjustments and eliminations are necessary in preparing consolidated financial statements. They can however overcome these difficulties by memorizing consolidation entries, thanks to the recurrent and mechanical nature of consolidation procedures. The first objective of this book is to provide a thorough understanding as to why basic consolidation entries are required.

❒ *Provide a Practical Guide*

The second objective of the book is to provide a guide to those preparing consolidated financial information. Students can refer to the summary presented in chapter 8 as a reference when testing themselves with exercises and problems from their textbooks. Practitioners can also use the summary from chapter 8 when dealing with real life consolidations. Each chapter is devoted to one specific scenario which together form the building-blocks of common consolidations. Thus, anyone can have quick access to any section of the book to refresh his or her memory or to learn more about specific consolidation concepts and procedures.

❒ *Provide an Up-To-Date Summary of the Accounting Standards on Business Combinations and Consolidated Financial Statements*

More and more countries around the globe have either adopted or plan to adopt the International Financial Reporting Standards (IFRS). The objective is to achieve global convergence in financial reporting. By fully complying with the International Accounting Standards including IAS 27 (Consolidated and Separate Financial Statements) and IFRS 3 (Business Combinations), this book provides guidance to accountants regarding these new or upcoming standards.

Approaches Introduced in this Book

Three successive approaches are used in this book to illustrate the consolidation process, namely the visual approach, the worksheet approach, and the direct approach.

❒ *The Visual Approach*

The visual approach presents the overall consolidation process while keeping a close watch on the individual financial statements of the affiliated companies as we progressively go through their transformation. This approach is used for pedagogical purposes only. Visualization of the impact of intercompany transactions on the financial statements of the units involved reinforces understanding of the required consolidation adjustments.

❒ *The Worksheet Approach*

The worksheet approach consists of listing on a worksheet all the account balances from the books of the consolidating companies. Consolidation entries are then entered onto the worksheet before cross-adding the accounts of both companies. This approach provides an organized structure for consolidation by keeping track of all the adjustments. Therefore, it will most likely be used in practice.

❒ *The Direct Approach*

The direct approach consists of an independent computation of each consolidated account balance.

Who Should Use this Book

❒ *Students in Advanced Financial Accounting Courses*

This book can be used to build the foundations required to get to more complex consolidation cases. Because it is concise, it can also be used for quick review when preparing for academic or professional examinations.

❒ *Non-Accounting Students*

Non-accounting students can use this book to learn the basics of consolidation as a precondition to analyzing and discussing cases dealing with consolidation at a more general level.

☐ *Practitioners*

Accountants can use this book as a practical guide or reference while working through consolidations under IFRS. Moreover, by providing knowledge and understanding of the foundations of consolidation, this book can be of interest to consolidated financial statement users such as lenders, investors, and financial analysts.

How this Book is Organized

The book is organized into four parts, as shown in Figure 2. The first part deals with different types of controlling ownership including ownership in a parent founded subsidiary, a wholly owned subsidiary, and a non-wholly owned subsidiary. The second part of the book examines several intercompany transactions and illustrates their impact on the preparation of consolidated financial statements. The third part of the book summarizes the different consolidation scenarios while the last part represents a variety of consolidation cases with their detailed solutions. The following describes in more detail the content of the book.

Part 1 : Controlling Ownership

Chapter 1 deals with the consolidation of a parent founded subsidiary. Many business enterprises create other business units to meet their goals. Consolidation entries for created subsidiaries are straightforward because of the equality between the investment account of the parent and the equity account of the subsidiary as of the date of creation. We take advantage of this simple yet common case to illustrate the *double-counting issue* that arises in the consolidation of the statement of financial position. The elimination entry that is required to get rid of the double-counting forms the core of consolidation adjustments.

Chapter 2 examines the case of a wholly owned subsidiary and illustrates the additional consolidation entries required to account for the *purchase price differential*. More precisely, in a business combination, the price paid by the investor to acquire the outstanding voting shares of the investee is based on the market price of these shares rather than the book value of the investee's assets and liabilities. As a result, there often is a difference between the purchase price and the proportionate share of the investee's net book value. This difference is referred to as a purchase price differential. Positive price differential usually appears when the fair value of the investee's net identifiable assets is greater than the book value, and when other items, most likely intangibles such as *goodwill*, are not accounted for by the subsidiary.

Chapter 3 completes the discussion of consolidated reporting by presenting the case of a non-wholly owned subsidiary. Special consolidation problems from partial ownership are highlighted including those related to *non-controlling interest*. In essence, the chapter reflects the view of the *entity theory* which considers the parent and the subsidiary as constituting a

Introduction 5

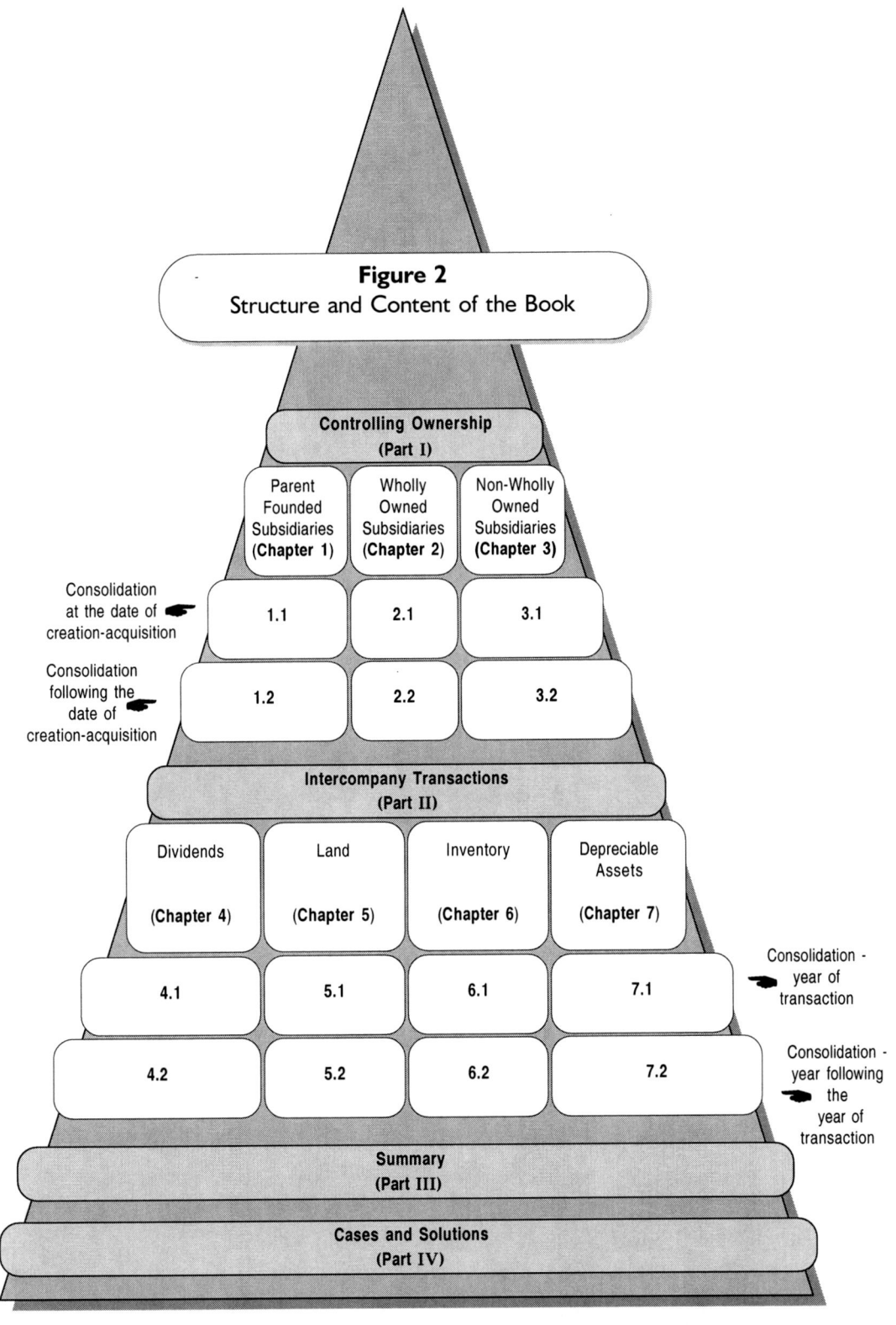

single entity.

Consolidation of financial statements is illustrated as of the date of creation-acquisition, and in a year subsequent to the date of creation-acquisition. In the latter, we assume that there is no intercompany transaction, a topic covered in Part 2 of the book.

Part 2 : Intercompany Transactions

Consolidated financial statements report the underlying activities of the consolidating affiliates as if the separate affiliates constituted a single company, an economic entity on its own. Thus, only transactions realized at arm's length or with interests outside the consolidated group should be accounted for in the consolidated financial statements (see Figure 3). When parent companies and their subsidiaries engage in transactions among themselves, which is often the case, *intercompany transactions* could lead to account overstatements and *unrealized profits or losses.* Adjustments required in such a case will depend on the year the intercompany transaction occurred (current or prior years), the type of asset being transferred (dividends, merchandise or capital assets), and the direction of the transaction (upstream or downstream transfers).

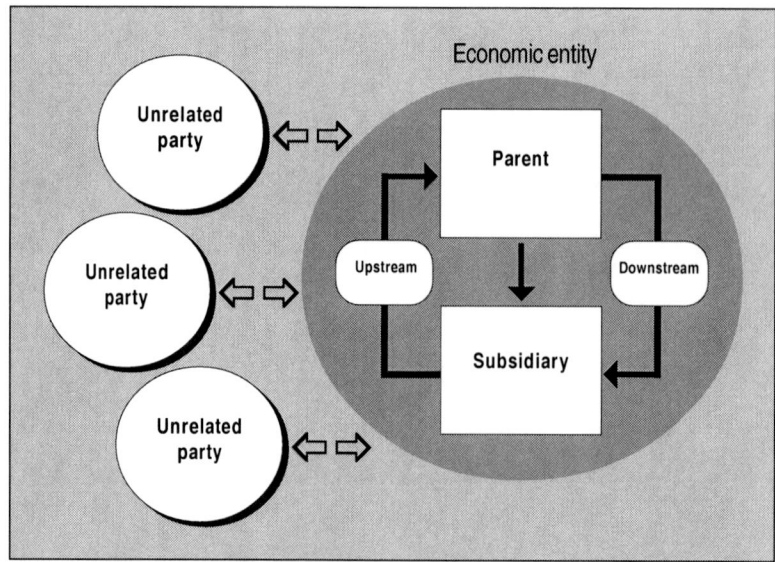

Figure 3 • Transactions of the Economic Entity

These different scenarios are analyzed in Part 2 of the book while dealing with the following intercompany transactions:
> Intercompany dividends (**chapter 4**).

Introduction 7

> Transfer of non-depreciable capital assets such as land (**chapter 5**).
> Transfer of inventory (**chapter 6**).
> Transfer of depreciable assets (**chapter 7**).

The building-block approach used in this book is summarized below.

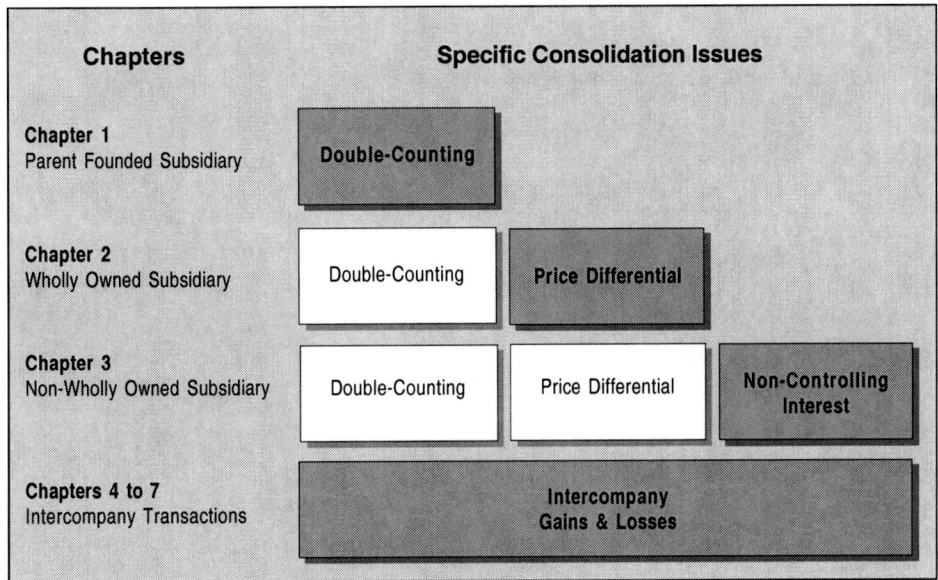

Part 3 : Summary

Part 3 of the book summarizes the previous chapters (chapter 1 through chapter 7, inclusive). **Chapter 8** classifies consolidation entries introduced throughout the book and presents a user-friendly guide that should apply to a wide range of consolidation cases. **Chapter 9** shows how to use the guide in a comprehensive case involving a non-wholly owned subsidiary and several intercompany transactions.

Throughout the book, we assume that the investment of the parent company in its subsidiary is accounted for using the *cost method*. This recording method is almost always used internally for bookkeeping convenience. This is also the method that can be employed when an entity elects, or is required by local regulations, to present separate financial statements. More precisely, in this situation, the parent company must account for its investments in subsidiaries either at cost or in accordance with IAS 39 (Financial Instruments). The alternative method, the *equity method*, will therefore rarely be used. However, this method is discussed and illustrated in chapter 9. The equity method is also introduced in the solutions of the cases presented in Part 4 of the book.

Part 4 : Cases and Solutions

The last part of the book offers ten comprehensive consolidation cases along with their detailed solutions. The cases deal with the consolidation of parent-founded subsidiaries (Cases 1 and 2), the consolidation of wholly owned subsidiaries (Cases 3 to 7), and the consolidation of non-wholly owned subsidiaries (Cases 8 to 10). For each case, the solution offers a balance between the worksheet approach and the direct approach and between the cost method and the equity method. The solutions are carefully explained, logically presented and closely coordinated with the first three parts of the book to ensure consistency.

How to Use this Book

As a practical guide, the book can be used while working the problems either from a textbook or with real organizations. The first step is to determine the type of subsidiary to be included in the consolidation : parent founded, wholly owned or non-wholly owned subsidiary, and the year the consolidation is taking place: date of creation-acquisition or a year subsequent to the date of creation-acquisition. If the consolidation happens to be in a year subsequent to the date of creation-acquisition, the second step would consist of identifying the intercompany transactions that occurred in the current and prior years. Each scenario is accounted for and examined in a specific section of the book. All the adjustments required for the consolidation can easily be selected from the summary reported in Chapter 8, thus providing a customized walk-through solution format.

The Pedagogy Used in this Book

❒ *Visual Approach*

To improve the pedagogy of teaching consolidations, the visual approach is privileged throughout the book so as to make the learning process more efficient.

❒ *Simplified Approach*

Illustrations are purposely straightforward and aim at only one objective: to help the reader to better understand the fundamental concepts and procedures involved in consolidations. Once this objective is successfully achieved, technical complexities can easily be introduced.

❒ *Building-Block Approach*

The book is designed to lead the reader through the essential knowledge and skills necessary to consolidate financial statements. All the building-blocks of common consolidations are presented in the first two parts of the book, with the complete picture set out in part

3. The complexities are layered gradually throughout the book.

 Layout of the Book

The following special elements are included in the text to set off different types of information and to ease the reading.

Effect on Income Tax Allocation

Income tax implications related to business combinations and intercompany transactions are analyzed in special notes throughout the book.

 Note...

Special notes augment the material in each chapter to clarify concepts and procedures.

What If...

Specific cases are introduced along with the corresponding consolidation entries.

Part I

Controlling Ownership

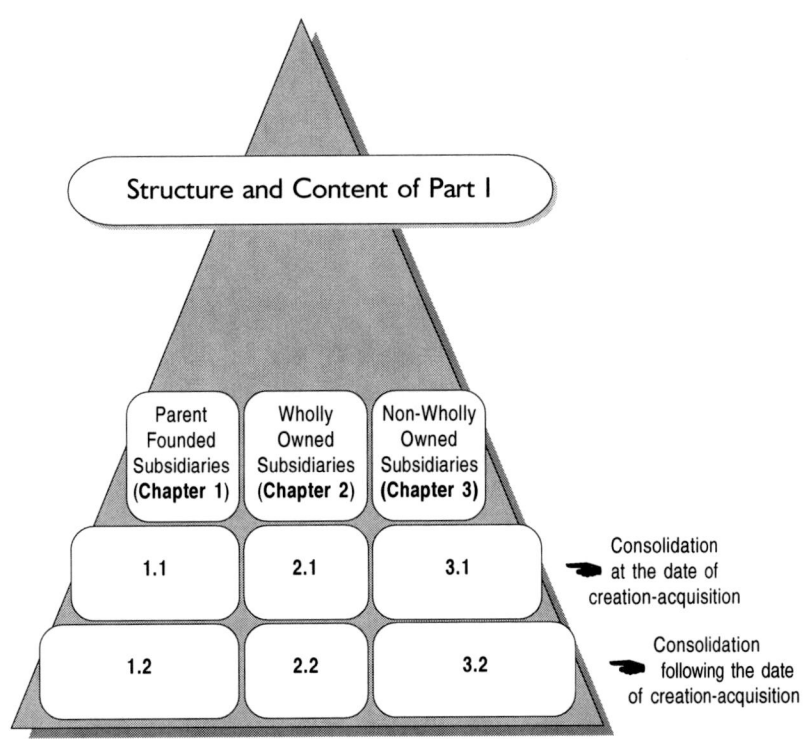

Chapter 1

Parent Founded Subsidiaries

Double-Counting

In this chapter

1.1 Consolidation as of the Date of Creation 14

1.2 Consolidation Following the Creation 22
    1.2.1 Consolidation of the Statement of Financial Position 25
    1.2.2 Consolidation of the Income Statement 29

✎ Comprehensive Illustration 30
✎ Summary of the Consolidation Adjustments in Journal Entry Form 34

Key Concepts: Parent Founded Subsidiary; Double-Counting; Visual Approach; Worksheet Approach; Direct Approach; Working Paper Entry; Cost Method for Strategic Investments; Economic Entity

Most subsidiaries are founded by a parent corporation. The establishment of a separate legal entity enables an organization to carry out its business in different provinces or countries. Such a strategy is often conducted for legal, regulatory, or tax reasons. *Parent founded subsidiaries* are usually wholly owned by the parent leading to a sustained control relationship. Therefore, for external reporting purposes, the parent company must prepare consolidated financial information which will combine the financial statements of the affiliated companies.

The purpose of this chapter is to provide an overview of the consolidation process of a parent founded subsidiary. In the first part, we examine the consolidation as of the date of creation. Despite being overly simple, this scenario helps to illustrate more clearly the double-counting issue that needs to be resolved in order to consolidate the affiliated companies. The elimination required to avoid double-counting is then introduced. This elimination forms the core of consolidation adjustments and, as such, will have to be repeated in subsequent year consolidations. This scenario is explored in the second part of the chapter.

1.1 Consolidation as of the Date of Creation

Assume that Company A established a subsidiary on January 1, X1, by creating a new corporation named Company B. Company B issued common shares to Company A in return for CU10,000 cash paid by Company A. The following presents the journal entries reported respectively by Company A and Company B at the date of creation.

Books of A

Investment in B	10,000	
Cash		10,000

Books of B

Cash	10,000	
Common Shares		10,000

The affiliation structure of Company A and Company B following the creation of Company B is diagrammed next.

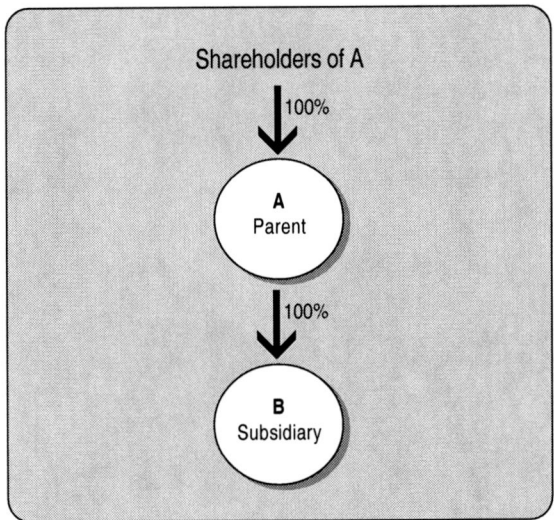

Company A now owns 100 percent of the outstanding voting shares of Company B creating a parent-subsidiary relationship. For consolidation purposes, Company A and Company B are viewed as a single reporting entity also known as the *economic entity*. For the economic entity to provide information regarding its operations, the financial statements of the affiliated companies must be combined or consolidated. In this regard, note that the statement of financial position of Company B following its creation is made up of only two accounts: Cash and Common Shares. The balance of both accounts equals CU10,000. This value reflects the amount initially invested by Company A at the establishment of Company B.

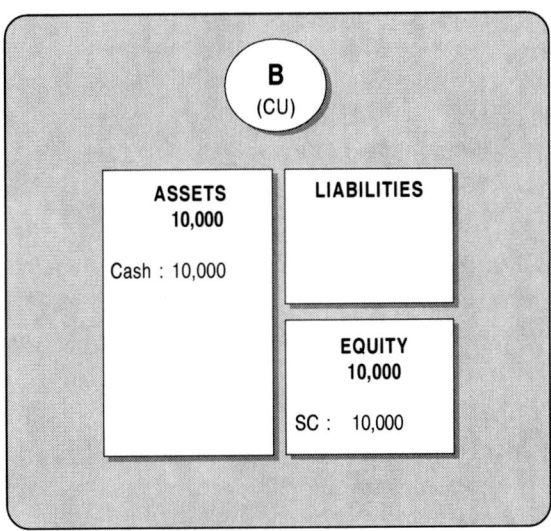

In order to start its operations, assume that Company B engaged in different transactions including the purchase of capital assets via a CU15,000 bank loan. Exhibit 1.1 presents the summarized individual statements of financial position of Company A and Company B following these transactions.

Exhibit 1.1 • Statements of Financial Position of Company A and Company B Following the Creation of Company B

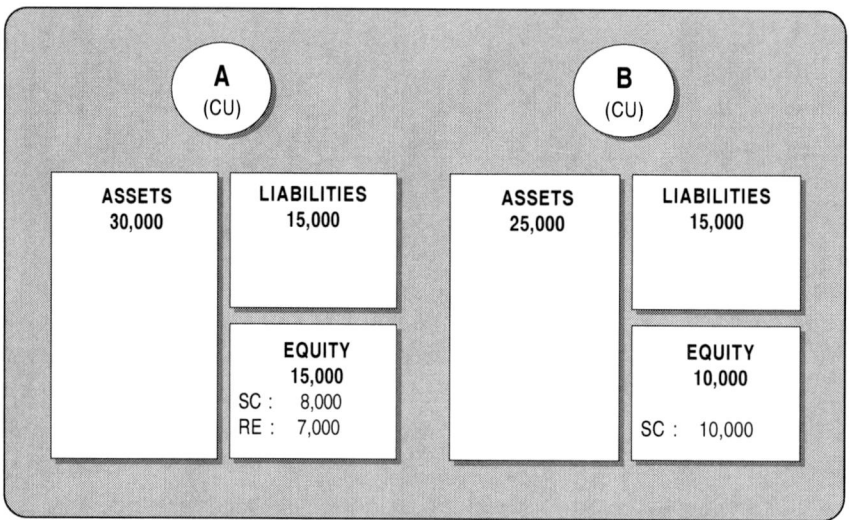

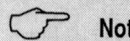 **Note...**

The statements of financial position shown in Exhibit 1.1 will be used to illustrate the consolidation as of the date of creation. The asset and liability accounts of both companies are condensed so as to simplify the presentation of the consolidation process. A comprehensive illustration is, however, introduced at the end of the chapter.

The creation of a subsidiary leads to a unique situation where the balance of the investment account of the parent company is equal to the net book value or the equity section of the subsidiary at the date of creation. Such a situation is expected as the parent company receives from the subsidiary new shares in return for its initial cash investment. More precisely, the cost of the investment carried on the books of Company A (CU10,000) is represented by the equity section of Company B (Common Shares of CU10,000) which in turn is represented by Company B's identifiable assets (CU25,000) less liabilities assumed (CU15,000). Therefore, cross-adding the affiliated companies accounts at the date of creation will give rise to *double-counting* of CU10,000 as potrayed next.

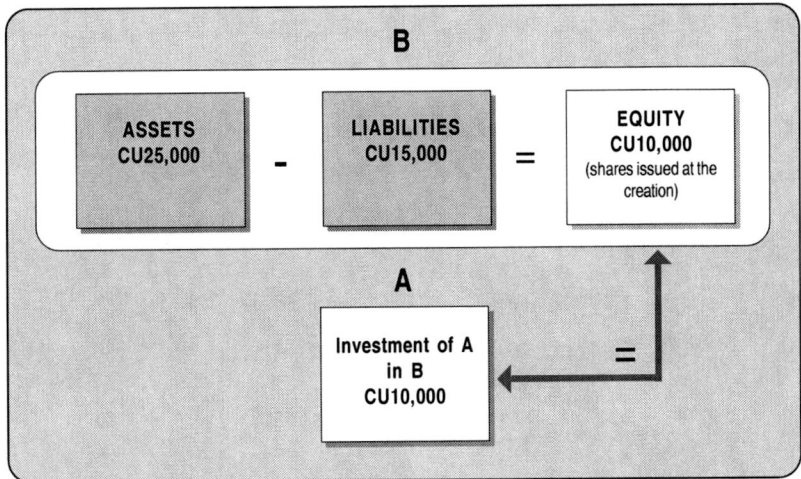

The asset and liability accounts of Company B being the ones to be combined with those of Company A, reciprocal investment and equity accounts must be eliminated for consolidation purposes. Since double-counting is recurrent, such elimination will be required not only at the date of creation but in post-creation consolidations as well.

In the next sections, we illustrate the consolidation process of Company A as of the date of creation using the following three approaches:

① The Visual Approach;

② The Worksheet Approach;

③ The Direct Approach.

① The Visual Approach

The *visual approach* is used only for pedagogical purposes and is first introduced to provide an overall view of the consolidation process. With this approach, a close watch can be kept on the condensed statement of financial position of both the parent and the subsidiary as we adjust them along the way. The four figures below show the step by step consolidation process of Company A's statement of financial position immediately following the creation of Company B.

18 Part I Controlling Ownership

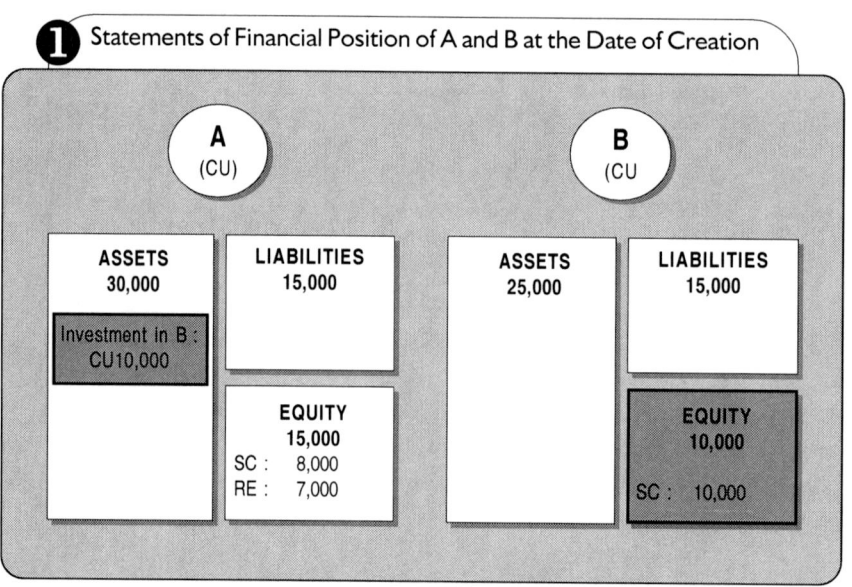

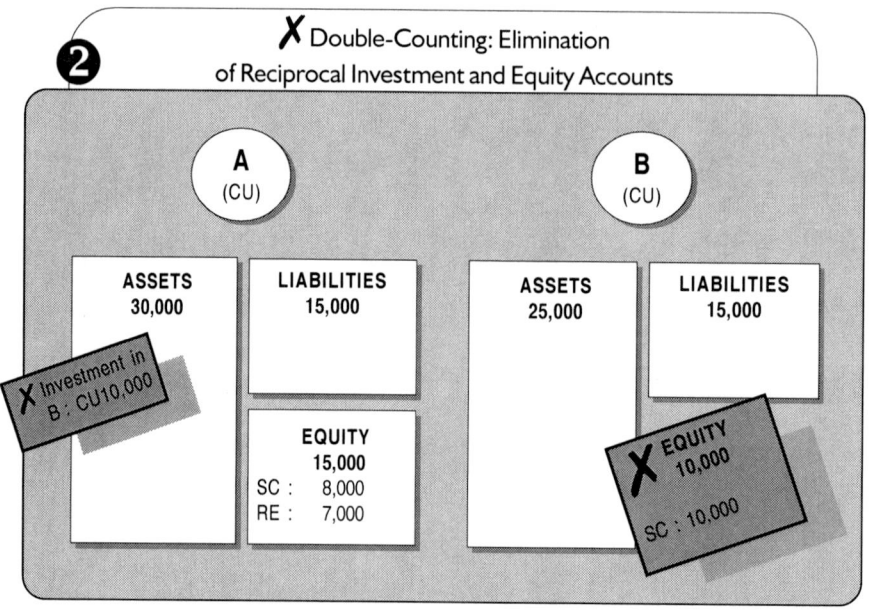

Chapter 1 Parent Founded Subsidiaries 19

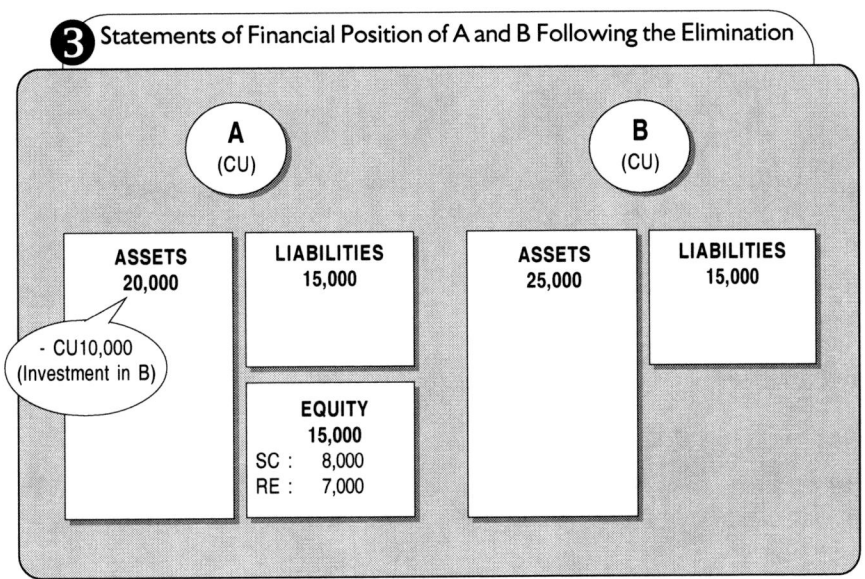

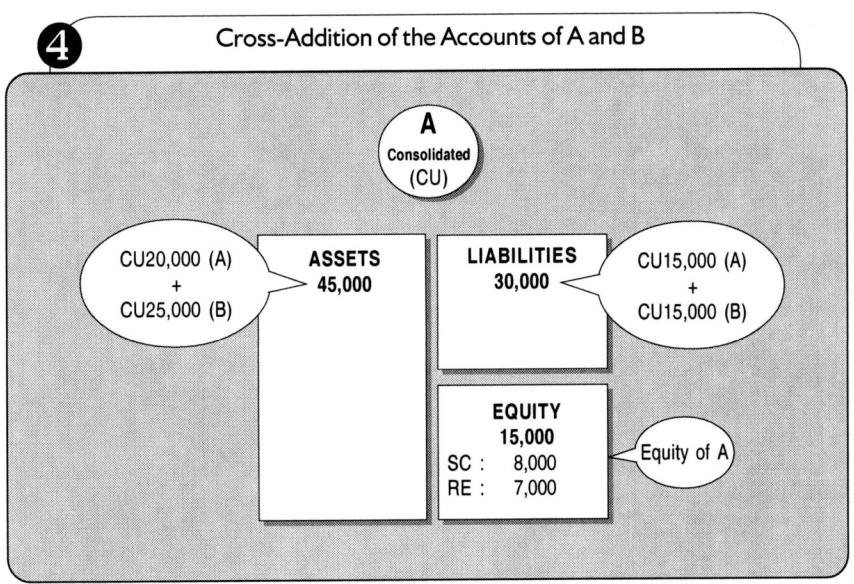

The simultaneous elimination of the investment account (CU10,000) and the equity section of Company B (Common Shares of CU10,000) is required before adding, line by line, all the asset and liability accounts of Company A to those of Company B. For consolidation purposes, such elimination is necessary to avoid double-counting of CU10,000.

Overall, consolidation at the date of creation consists of replacing the investment account of Company A (CU10,000) with the book value of all the asset and liability accounts of Company B (CU25,000 - CU15,000 = CU10,000). Consolidated assets and liabilities consist of the sum of the parent and subsidiary assets and liabilities. Since the equity section of Company B is eliminated in the process, consolidated equity at the date of creation (CU15,000) is made up of only Company A's accounts and includes Common Shares of CU8,000 and Retained Earnings of CU7,000.

② The Worksheet Approach

The *worksheet approach* uses a multi-columnar worksheet to enter the statements of financial position of Company A and Company B. After reporting the required eliminations onto the worksheet, the accounts are then cross-added to determine the consolidated balance sheet. The consolidation worksheet of Company A is reproduced below.

Consolidation Worksheet

	A (CU)	B (CU)	Elimination (CU)	Consolidated (CU)
ASSETS				
Investment in B	10,000		(10,000) (1)	-
Other identifiable assets	20,000	25,000		45,000
	30,000	25,000		45,000
LIABILITIES	15,000	15,000		30,000
EQUITY				
Common shares	8,000	10,000	(10,000) (1)	8,000
Retained earnings	7,000			7,000
	30,000	25,000		45,000

Chapter 1 Parent Founded Subsidiaries

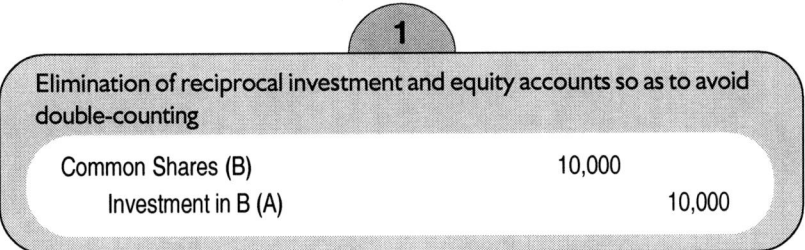

Only one *working paper entry* is needed to consolidate the statement of financial position of Company A at the date of creation. The entry is reproduced in general journal form for convenient reference. The parentheses indicate the company on whose statements the accounts being eliminated appear. The purpose of this elimination is to facilitate completion of the working paper to consolidate Company A. This elimination is not recorded on either the parent or the subsidiary's books and, as such, would have to be repeated in subsequent consolidation periods. Notice that the consolidated entity is a fictitious reporting entity that does not maintain a ledger of accounts.

The elimination of reciprocal investment and equity accounts is required in order to avoid double-counting. Once this core elimination is completed, accounts of Company A and Company B can be cross-added to obtain the amounts that will be used to prepare the consolidated statement of financial position at the date of creation. Since a worksheet keeps track of the consolidation adjustments and provides an organized structure, it will most likely be used by accountants.

③ The Direct Approach

The *direct approach* consists of an independent computation of each balance account. Each account is separately calculated and entered into the consolidated statement of financial position. The following provides such calculation for the consolidated total assets, total liabilites and equity balances of Company A as of the date of creation.

Assets	CU
• Parent (A) (excluding the investment account)	20,000
• Subsidiary (B)	25,000
Total	**45,000**

Liabilities	CU
• Parent (A)	15,000
• Subsidiary (B)	15,000
Total	**30,000**

Common Shares	CU
Parent (A) balance only as of January 1, X1	**8,000**

Retained Earnings	CU
Parent (A) balance only as of January 1, X1	**7,000**

With the direct approach, the equity accounts of Company B at the date of creation are ignored. Only accounts that should be included in the consolidated statement of financial position are considered. Consolidated information is computed through an *additive approach*. By contrast, with the worksheet approach, the equity accounts of Company B must be eliminated (as all the account balances from the books of the affiliated companies are first entered in the consolidation workpaper). Consolidated information is determined using a *residual approach*. Despite these mechanical differences, the two approaches obviously yield the same results.

1.2 Consolidation Following the Creation

In this section, we continue the development of Company A and Company B through the first five years of combined operations. The separate financial statements of Company A and Company B for the year ended December 31, X5, are shown in Exhibit 1.2.

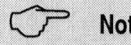 **Note...**

The selection of a five year period subsequent to the date of creation is arbitrary. In fact, the time factor does not introduce additional complications into the consolidation process of a parent founded subsidiary, assuming no intercompany transactions have occurred.

Exhibit 1.2 • Financial Statements of Company A and Company B for the Year Ended December 31, X5

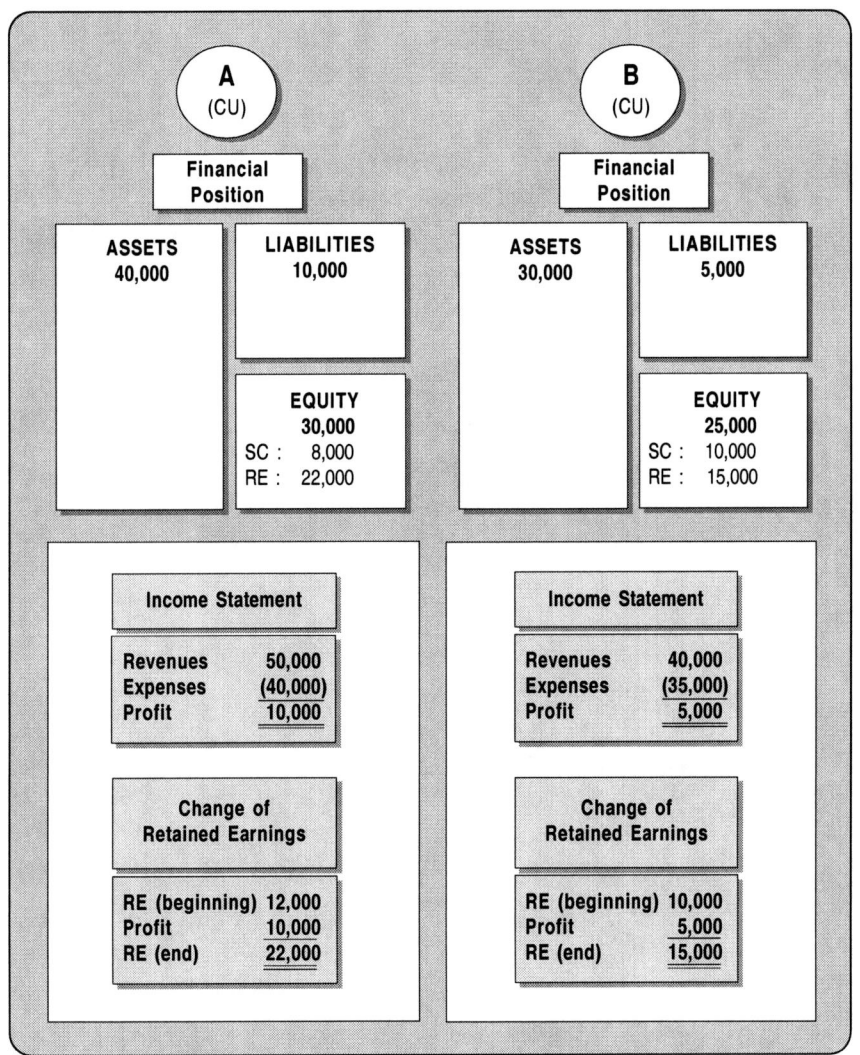

Exhibit 1.3 shows the change of the net book value of Company B since creation, that is, from January 1, X1 (date of creation) to December 31, X5 (end of the current year).

Exhibit 1.3 • Net Book Value Increase of Company B Since Creation

Equity of B	Balance at Jan. 1, X1 (CU)	Change (CU)	Balance at Dec. 31, X5 (CU)
Common Shares	10,000	–	10,000
Retained Earnings	–	15,000	15,000
Total	10,000	15,000	25,000

The net book value of Company B has increased by CU15,000 since the date of creation. Because there is no transaction involving the capital stock and no retained earnings were recorded at the date of creation, the positive change of the net book value of Company B over the past five years is equivalent to the balance of Company B's Retained Earnings at December 31, X5 (CU15,000).

Because the investment balance is eliminated as part of every recurring consolidation, the selection of a particular method for internal record-keeping does not affect the consolidated information. However, as a matter of corporate bookkeeping convenience, the *cost method* will usually be used. The cost method is also one of the methods that can be employed when separate financial statemets are prepared. More precisely, when an entity elects, or is required by local regulations, to present separate financial statements, investments in subsidiaries must be accounted for at cost or in accordance with IAS 39 (Financial Instruments). Consequently, one should expect the use of the cost method to be prevalent. On the cost basis, the investment account is not revised over time, but remains on the parent company's statement of financial position at original cost. The only income reported is dividend when declared by the investee.

Assume that Company A applies the cost method for its investment in Company B. Therefore, the investment account remains at CU10,000 on the books of Company A at the end of X5. This amount reflects the initial cash investment made by Company A to establish Company B. To simplify, assume also that the affiliated companies have not engaged in transactions among themselves since the date of creation.

Chapter 1 Parent Founded Subsidiaries

> ☞ **Note...**
>
> The alternative recording method to report controlling ownership, the *equity method*, is explored in chapter 9 and in the solutions of the cases presented in part 4. Application of the equity method to account for strategic investments will change slightly the consolidation working paper procedures in time periods subsequent to the year of creation (or acquisition) as additional consolidation entries are needed in order to eliminate the investment account of the parent company.

The next sections illustrate the consolidation process of Company A's statement of financial position at December 31, X5, using the three following approaches:

① The Visual Approach;

② The Worksheet Approach;

③ The Direct Approach.

Coverage of the consolidation of the income statement is provided in a separate section.

1.2.1 Consolidation of the Statement of Financial Position

① The Visual Approach

The following figures illustrate the consolidation process of Company A at December 31, X5.

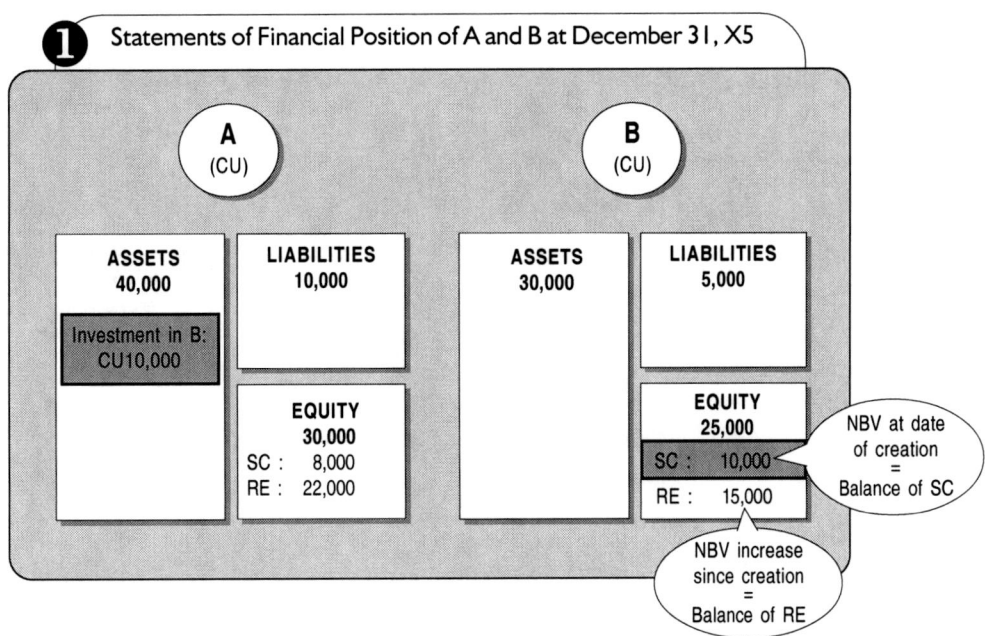

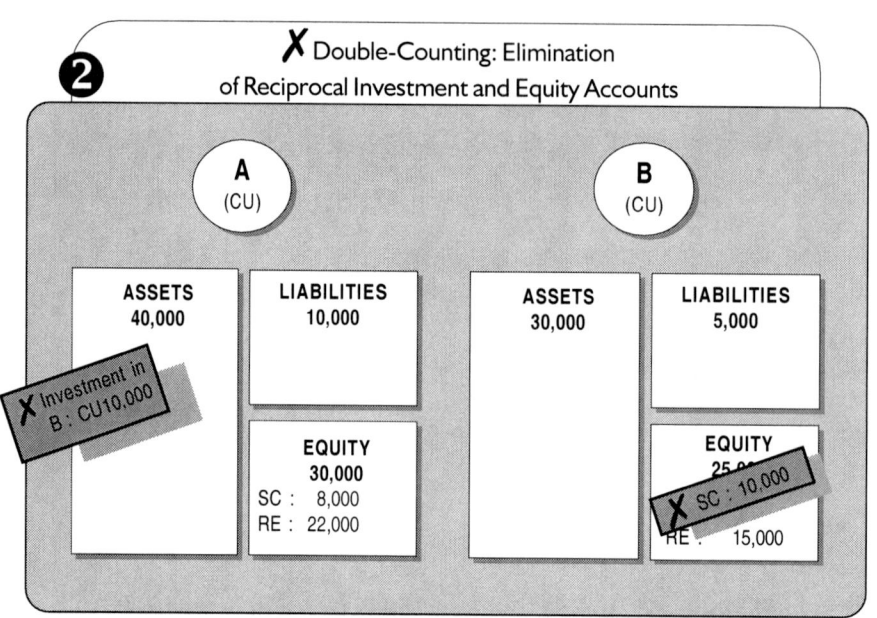

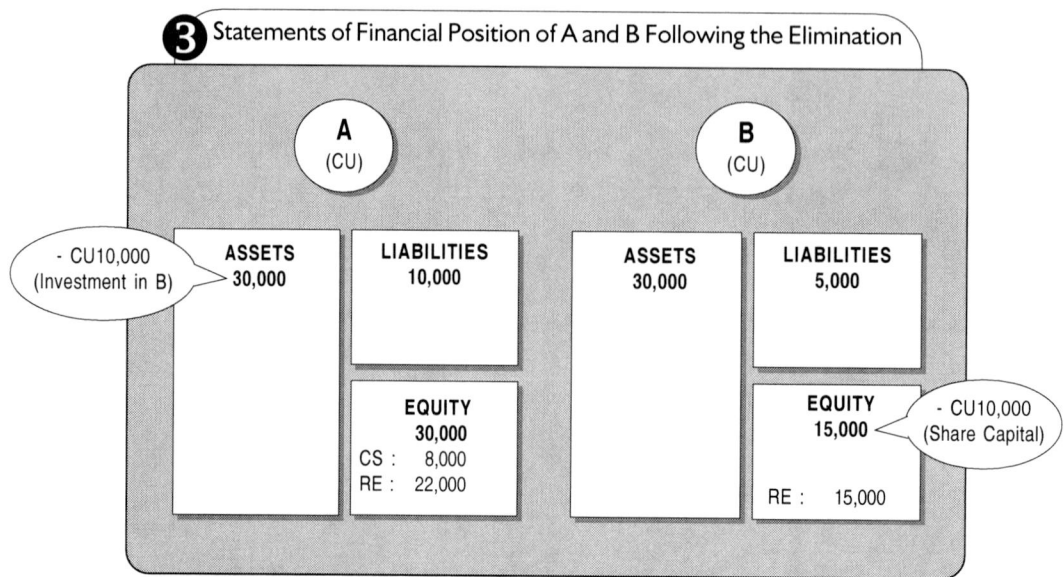

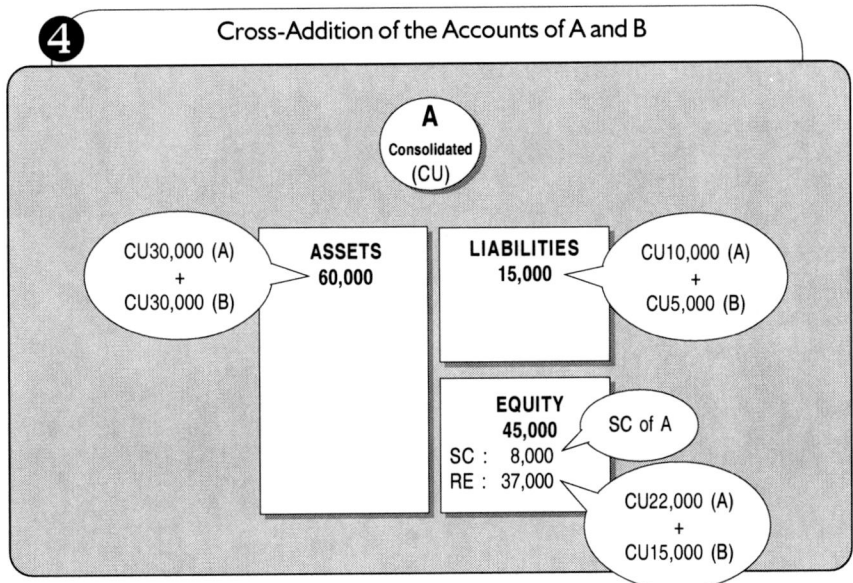

The double-counting of CU10,000 at the date of creation remains an issue in post-creation consolidations. The elimination of reciprocal investment and equity accounts of CU10,000 that was required at the date of creation must be repeated (figure #2). Since the investment in Company B is accounted for by Company A on the cost basis, the balance of that account has not been revised since creation and, as such, is entirely eliminated in the process.

Consolidated assets and liabilities still consist of the sum of the parent and subsidiary assets and liabilities. However, once the elimination of reciprocal investment and equity accounts has been carried out, the cross-addition of both companies' accounts leads to a transfer of Company B's net book value increase since acquisition (CU15,000) to Company A. Such a value increase is reflected in the balance of Company B's Retained Earnings. Therefore, consolidated Retained Earnings (CU37,000) can easily be obtained by summing the balance of Retained Earnings from the books of the affiliated companies at December 31, X5 (CU22,000 + CU15,000 = CU37,000). Note that consolidated Share Capital is the same as the parent company's Share Capital.

② The Worksheet Approach

The consolidation worksheet of Company A at December 31, X5, is presented below along with the consolidation entry stated in a general journal format.

Consolidation Worksheet

	A (CU)	B (CU)	Elimination (CU)	Consolidated (CU)
ASSETS				
Investment in B	10,000		(10,000) (1)	–
Other identifiable assets	30,000	30,000		60,000
	40,000	**30,000**		**60,000**
LIABILITIES	10,000	5,000		15,000
EQUITY				
Common shares	8,000	10,000	(10,000) (1)	8,000
Retained earnings	22,000	15,000		37,000
	40,000	**30,000**		**60,000**

1

Elimination of reciprocal investment and equity accounts as of the date of creation so as to avoid double-counting

Common Shares (B)	10,000	
Investment in B (A)		10,000

The eliminations and adjustments required for the consolidation are made on a working paper. As a result, although reciprocal investment and equity accounts have been eliminated while consolidating Company A at the date of creation, the same elimination has to be entered onto the worksheet in order to consolidate Company A five years later.

③ The Direct Approach

Direct computations of Company A's consolidated assets, liabilities and equity balances as of December 31, X5, are presented below.

Assets	CU
• Parent (A) (excluding the investment in B)	30,000
• Subsidiary (B)	30,000
Total	**60,000**

Liabilities	CU
• Parent (A)	10,000
• Subsidiary (B)	5,000
Total	**15,000**

Common Shares	CU
Parent (A) balance only as of December 31, X5	**8,000**

Retained Earnings	CU
• Parent (A)	22,000
• Subsidiary (B)	15,000
Total	**37,000**

1.2.2 Consolidation of the Income Statement

Since Company B has been established by Company A and no intercompany transaction has occurred between the two corporations, consolidation of the income statement is straightforward and consists of combining the revenue and expense accounts of the affiliated companies as shown next.

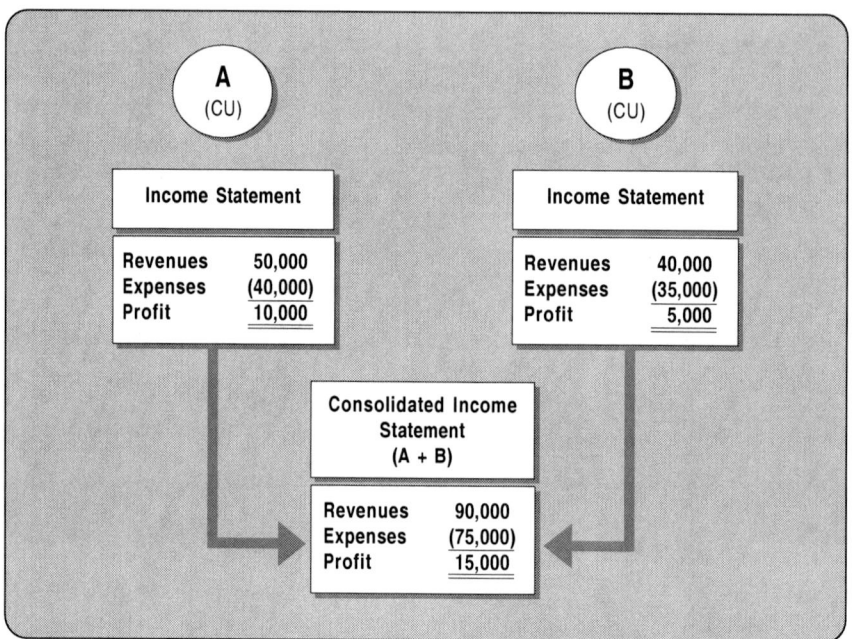

In sum, consolidated profit for the year is computed by adding the profits of the affiliated companies as follows: CU10,000 (A) + CU5,000 (B) = **CU15,000**.

Comprehensive Illustration

Basic Information

On December 31, X6, Para Corporation established a subsidiary by creating a new corporation named Rain Enterprise. Rain issued common shares to Para for CU100,000 cash paid by Para. For bookeeping convenience, Para applies the cost method to report its investment in Rain.

We are now on December 31, X10, four years subsequent to the date of creation of Rain. Since Para still owns 100 percent of the capital stock of Rain, you are asked to prepare the consolidated financial statements of Para. Assume that Para and Rain never engaged in transactions among themselves.

Exhibit 1.4 presents the separate financial statements of both companies at December 31, X10.

Chapter 1 Parent Founded Subsidiaries

Exhibit 1.4 • Financial Statements of Para Corporation and Rain Enterprise for the Year Ended December 31, X10

Statements of Financial Position
December 31, X10
(in CU)

	Para	Rain
Assets		
Cash	40,000	15,000
Accounts receivable	12,000	
Buildings (net)	200,000	130,000
Investment in Rain	100,000	
Total assets	352,000	145,000
Liabilities and equities		
Bank loan	25,000	10,000
Accounts payable	10,000	15,000
Bonds payable	75,000	
Share capital	150,000	100,000
Retained earnings	92,000	20,000
Total liabilities and equities	352,000	145,000

Income Statements
Year Ended December 31, X10
(in CU)

	Para	Rain
Sales	500,000	230,000
Sales expenses	250,000	90,000
Administration expenses	200,000	130,000
Profit for the year	50,000	10,000

	Para			Rain		
	Share Capital	Retained Earnings	Total	Share Capital	Retained Earnings	Total
Balance at January 1, X10	150,000	42,000	192,000	100,000	10,000	110,000
Profit for the year		50,000	50,000		10,000	10,000
Balance at December 31, X10	150,000	92,000	242,000	100,000	20,000	120,000

Statements of Changes in Equity
Year Ended December 31, X10
(in CU)

Rain's Share Capital of CU100,000 reflects the amount initially invested by Para to establish Rain whereas Retained Earnings of CU20,000 reflects Rain's net book value increase since creation. This positive change in value will be assigned entirely to Para in the consolidation process.

Consolidation of Financial Statements

In order to consolidate Para and Rain, reciprocal investment and equity accounts of CU100,000 at the date of creation must be eliminated. Since Para uses the cost method to report its investment in Rain, the balance of the investment account is still shown on the books of Para at its original cost (CU100,000) and thus will be entirely eliminated in the process. Because no intercompany transaction has occurred, no further consolidation entries are required. The double-counting problem being resolved via the elimination of reciprocal investment and equity accounts, the remaining balances from the books of Para and Rain can be cross-added.

We illustrate the consolidation process of Para at December 31, X10, following:

① The Worksheet Approach;

② The Direct Approach.

① The Worksheet Approach

The consolidation worksheet required to combine Para and Rain at December 31, X10, is shown next.

Chapter 1 Parent Founded Subsidiaries 33

Consolidation Worksheet

	Para (CU)	Rain (CU)	Eliminations (CU)	Consolidated (CU)
ASSETS				
Cash	40,000	15,000		55,000
Accounts receivable	12,000			12,000
Buildings (net)	200,000	130,000		330,000
Investment in Rain	100,000		(100,000)(1)	-
	352,000	**145,000**		**397,000**
LIABILITIES				
Bank loan	25,000	10,000		35,000
Accounts payable	10,000	15,000		25,000
Bonds payable	75,000			75,000
EQUITY				
Common shares	150,000	100,000	(100,000)(1)	150,000
Retained earnings	92,000	20,000		112,000
	352,000	**145,000**		**397,000**
Sales	500,000	230,000		730,000
Sales expenses	250,000	90,000		340,000
Admin. expenses	200,000	130,000		330,000
Profit	**50,000**	**10,000**		**60,000**

(1) Elimination of reciprocal investment and equity accounts as of the date of creation so as to avoid double-counting

Common Shares (Rain)	100,000	
Investment in Rain (Para)		100,000

② The Direct Approach

Para's consolidated financial statements at December 31, X10, are shown in Exhibit 1.5. The consolidation process consists of adding the balance of the accounts from each company's records. In a relatively uncomplicated task such as this, consolidated financial information can be carried out easily without the use of a worksheet. The balances from the books of each affiliated company are shown in brackets.

Exhibit 1.5 • Consolidated Financial Statements of Para Corporation for the Year Ended December 31, X10

Consolidated Statement of Financial Position of Para Corporation
December 31, X10
(in CU)

Assets
Cash (CU40,000 + CU15,000)	55,000
Accounts receivable (Para)	12,000
Buildings (net) (CU200,000 + CU130,000)	330,000
Total assets	**397,000**

Liabilities and equities
Bank loan (CU25,000 + CU10,000)	35,000
Accounts payable (CU10,000 + CU15,000)	25,000
Bonds payable (Para)	75,000
Share capital (Para)	150,000
Retained earnings (CU92,000 + CU20,000)	112,000
Total liabilities and equities	**397,000**

Rain's Retained Earnings (CU20,000) is assigned entirely to Para.

Consolidated Income Statement of Para Corporation
Year Ended December 31, X10
(in CU)

Sales (CU500,000 + CU230,000)	730,000
Sales expenses (CU250,000 + CU90,000)	340,000
Administration expenses (CU200,000 + CU130,000)	330,000
Profit for the year	**60,000**

Consolidated Statement of Changes in Equity of Para Corporation
Year Ended December 31, X10
(in CU)

	Share Capital	Retained Earnings	Total
Balance at January 1, X10	150,000	52,000	202,000
Profit for the year		60,000	60,000
Balance at December 31, X10	**150,000**	**112,000**	**262,000**

Summary of the Consolidation Adjustments in Journal Entry Form

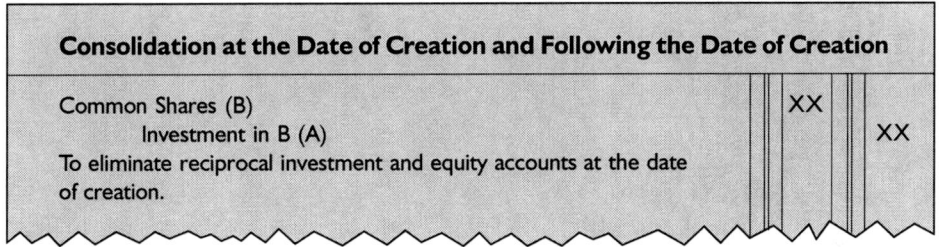

Consolidation at the Date of Creation and Following the Date of Creation

Common Shares (B)   XX
    Investment in B (A)   XX
To eliminate reciprocal investment and equity accounts at the date of creation.

Chapter 2

Wholly Owned Subsidiaries

Price Differential

In this chapter

2.1 Consolidation as of the Date of Acquisition 38

2.2 Consolidation Following the Date of Acquisition 49
    2.2.1 Consolidation of the Statement of Financial Position 53
    2.2.2 Consolidation of the Income Statement 61
    2.2.3 Price Differential : Additional Considerations 65

Comprehensive Illustration 69
Summary of the Consolidation Adjustments in Journal Entry Form 81

Key Concepts: Business Combinations; Wholly Owned Subsidiary; Acquisition Method; Price Differential; Price Differential Amortization; Fair Value Increments-Decrements; Goodwill; Goodwill Impairment; Subsidiary's Net Adjusted Value; Negative Goodwill

A *business combination* is a transaction in which a corporation obtains control of one or more businesses. From a legal point of view, a business combination can take different forms. The acquirer might either purchase the aquiree's net assets, acquire a majority (more than 50 percent) of the acquiree's outstanding voting shares or merge with the acquiree (statutory amalgamation). In return, the acquirer might transfer cash, cash equivalents, net assets or issue equity interests. Regardless of the legal option selected and the nature of the consideration given by the acquirer, only one accounting method must be used to account for all business combinations, namely the *acquisition method*. According to the acquisition method, each identifiable asset and liability is measured at its acquisition-date fair value.

When a business combination is consummated as an asset acquisition, the books of the acquired company are closed out and the acquisition is recorded on the books of the acquirer. When a business combination is effected through merger, all the companies involved are dissolved, except one. However, when a business combination involves an open-market acquisition of shares, the affiliated companies, that is the parent company and its subsidiary, continue to exist as separate legal enties and, as such, maintain independent accounting systems. In this case, the acquirer, the parent company, must prepare consolidated financial statements for external reporting purposes. Contrary to a parent founded subsidiary, when a subsidiary is acquired, the cost of the investment to the investor will be different from the investor's proportionate share of the net book value of the investee. Such a difference, referred to as *price differential* or *price discrepancy*, adds a new complexity to the process of consolidating financial information apart from the double-counting issue examined in chapter 1 which is recurrent.

The objective of this chapter is to provide background material necessary for preparing consolidated financial statements of a *wholly owned subsidiary*. First, consolidation techniques and procedures as of the date of acquisition are covered. We then carry this process one step further by examining the consolidation procedures that must be followed in time periods subsequent to the date of acquisition.

2.1 Consolidation as of the Date of Acquisition

Assume that on January 1, X1, Company A acquired all the outstanding voting shares of Company B for CU22,000 cash paid. The following presents the entry on the books of Company A at the date of the combination.

| Investment in B | 22,000 | |
| Cash | | 22,000 |

No entry is reported on the books of Company B as the transaction only engaged Company A and the shareholders of Company B. Moreover, the consideration given being cash, the shareholders of Company A do not share control with the shareholders of Company B in the post-acquisition period. The affilation structure of Company A and Company B following the acquisition is reported below.

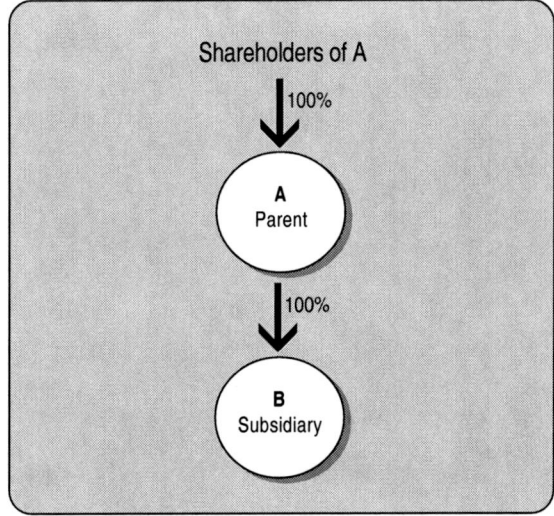

The condensed statements of financial postion of Company A and Company B as of the date of acquisition appear in Exhibit 2.1.

Recall that when a subsidiary is created, the investment of the parent company equals the equity section (Common Shares) of the subsidiary as of the date of creation. However, in a business combination, such equality rarely exists, the price paid by the investor being based on the fair market value of the investee's outstanding shares at the date of combination. Price differential generally occurs because the investee's assets and liabilities may be worth more or less than their underlying book value at the date of acquisition. More precisely, when the fair value of an asset or a liability is greater than its underlying book value, the difference is referred to as a *fair value increment* (FVI). When such fair value is lower, a *fair value decrement* (FVD) will be considered.

Exhibit 2.1 • Statements of Financial Position of Company A and Company B at the Date of Acquisition

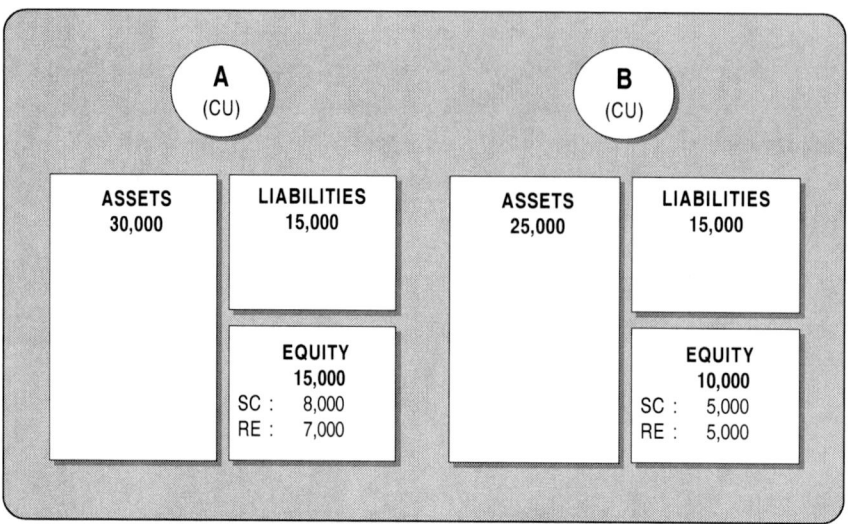

Excess price could also be paid for *goodwill*. Goodwill is an unrecorded account by the investee that represents its excess earning power or the premium paid to acquire control. Goodwill exists only through a business combination and is computed by subtracting the net fair value of the acquiree from the purchase price. To summarize, the purchase price can be allocated as follows:

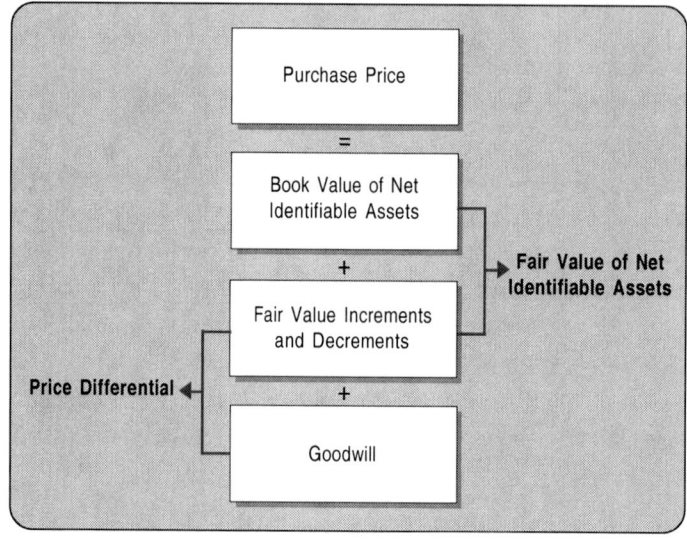

In our illustration, the price paid by Company A to acquire all the voting stock of Company B (CU22,000) is CU12,000 higher than Company B's net book value at the date of combination (CU10,000) as depicted in the following diagram.

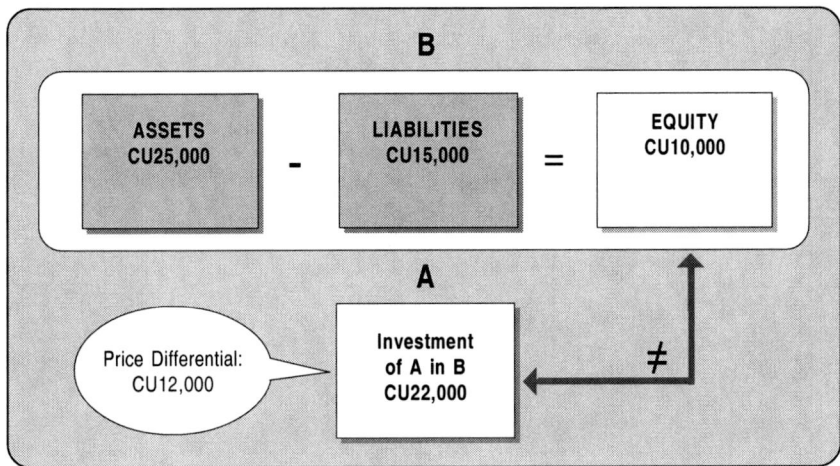

Assume that the positive price differential of CU12,000 paid by Company A to acquire Company B is related to a fair value increment on capital assets. In other words, Company A paid an excess price of CU12,000 over Company B's net book value because Company B had capital assets that had a fair value of CU12,000 greater than book value at the date of the combination.

Exhibit 2.2 presents the allocation of the purchase price as of January 1, X1. The information conveyed in this exhibit will be used to form the consolidation entries necessary to combine Company A and Company B at the date of acquisition.

Since the price paid by Company A equals the fair value of Company B's identifiable net assets at the date of acquisition (CU22,000), there is no residual or goodwill.

Exhibit 2.2 Wholly Owned Subsidiary - Allocation of the Purchase Price as of January 1, X1

		CU
Cost of investment in B		22,000
Shareholders' equity of B at the date of acquisition:		
Share capital	5,000	
Retained earnings	5,000	10,000
Price differential		12,000
Fair value increment - Capital assets		(12,000)
Goodwill		–

In the next sections, we illustrate the consolidation process of Company A as of the date of acquisition using the following three approaches:

① The Visual Approach;

② The Worksheet Approach;

③ The Direct Approach.

① The Visual Approach

The figures below summarize the different steps involved in the consolidation of Company A's statement of financial position as of January 1, X1.

Chapter 2 Wholly Owned Subsidiaries 43

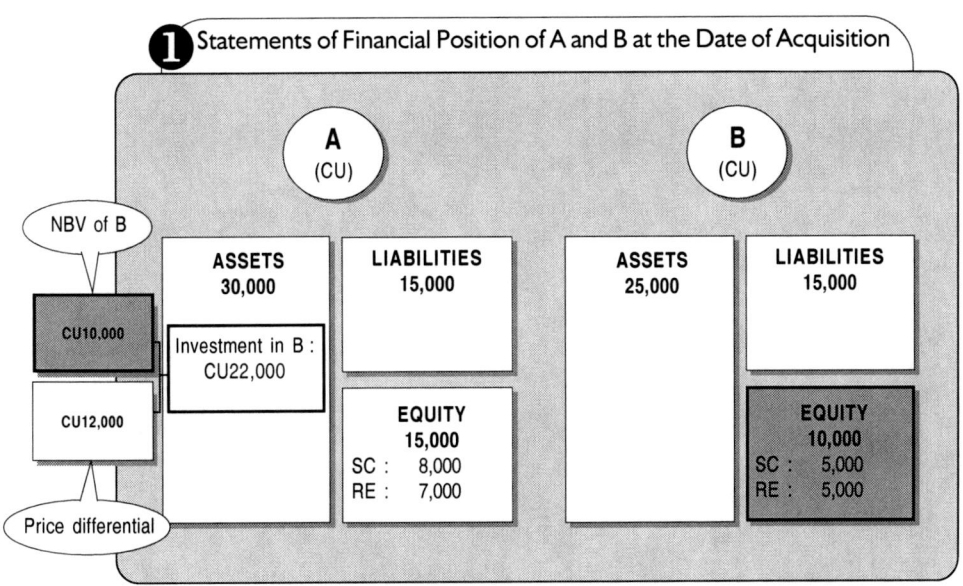

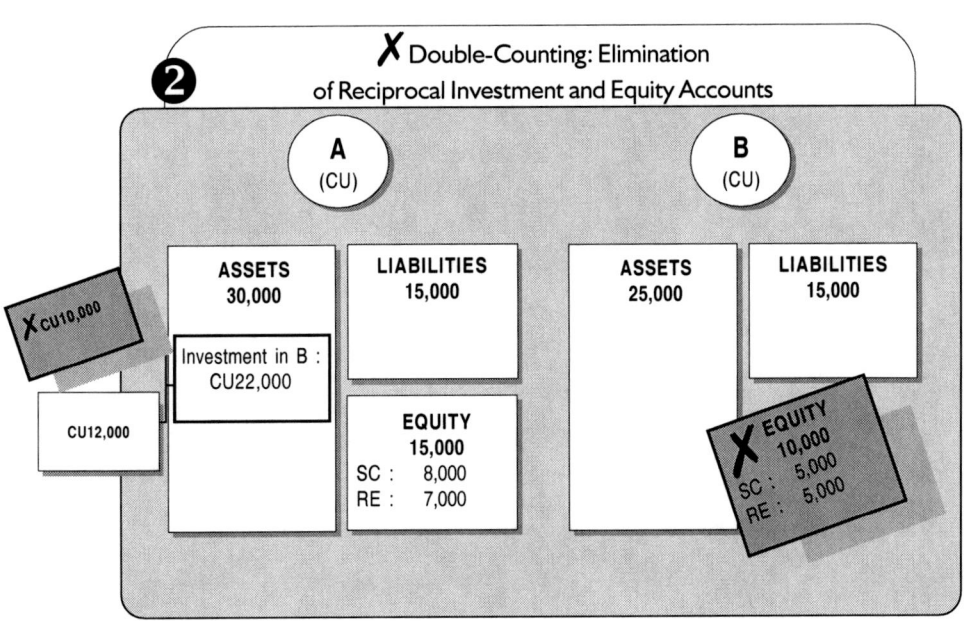

44 Part I Controlling Ownership

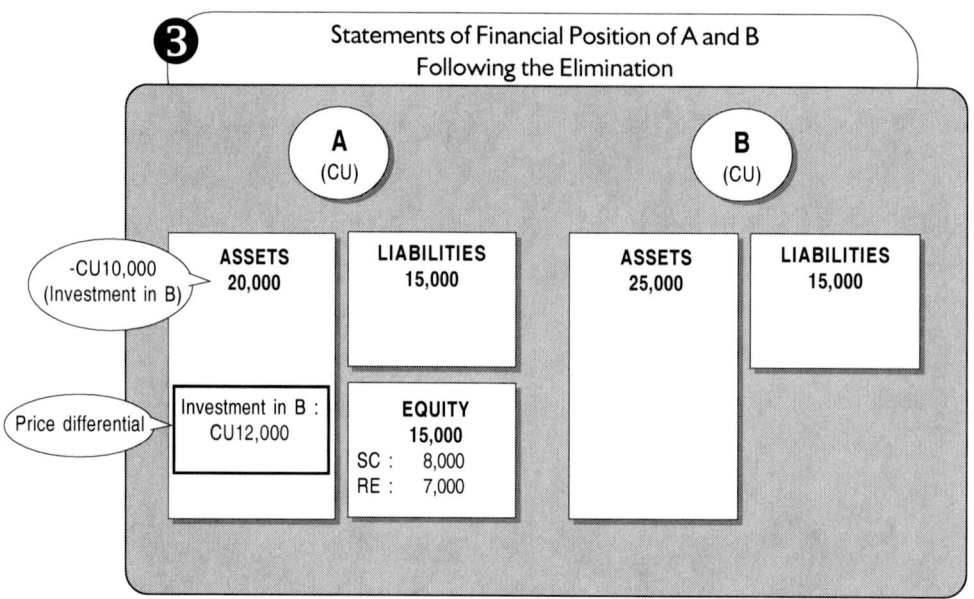

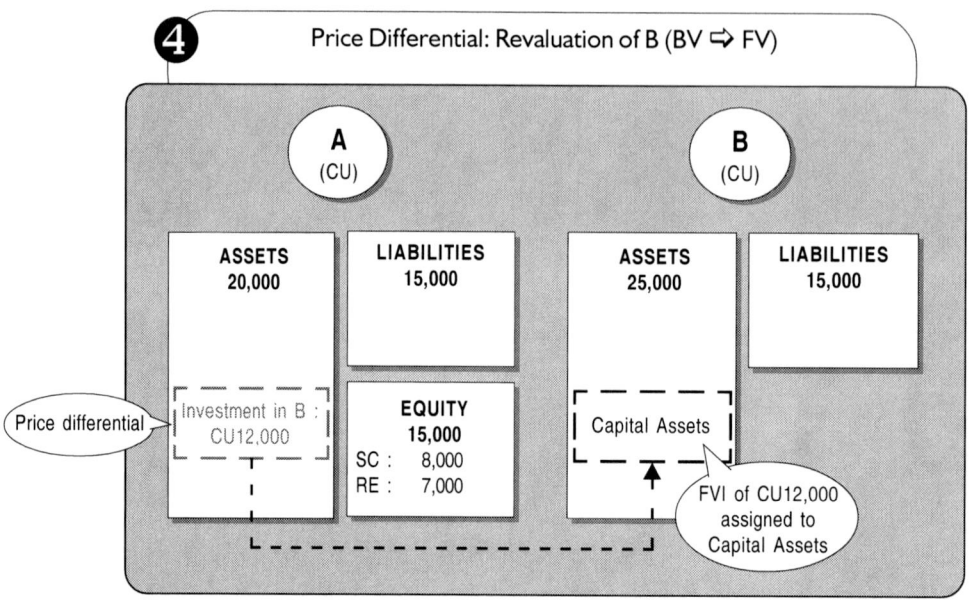

Chapter 2 Wholly Owned Subsidiaries

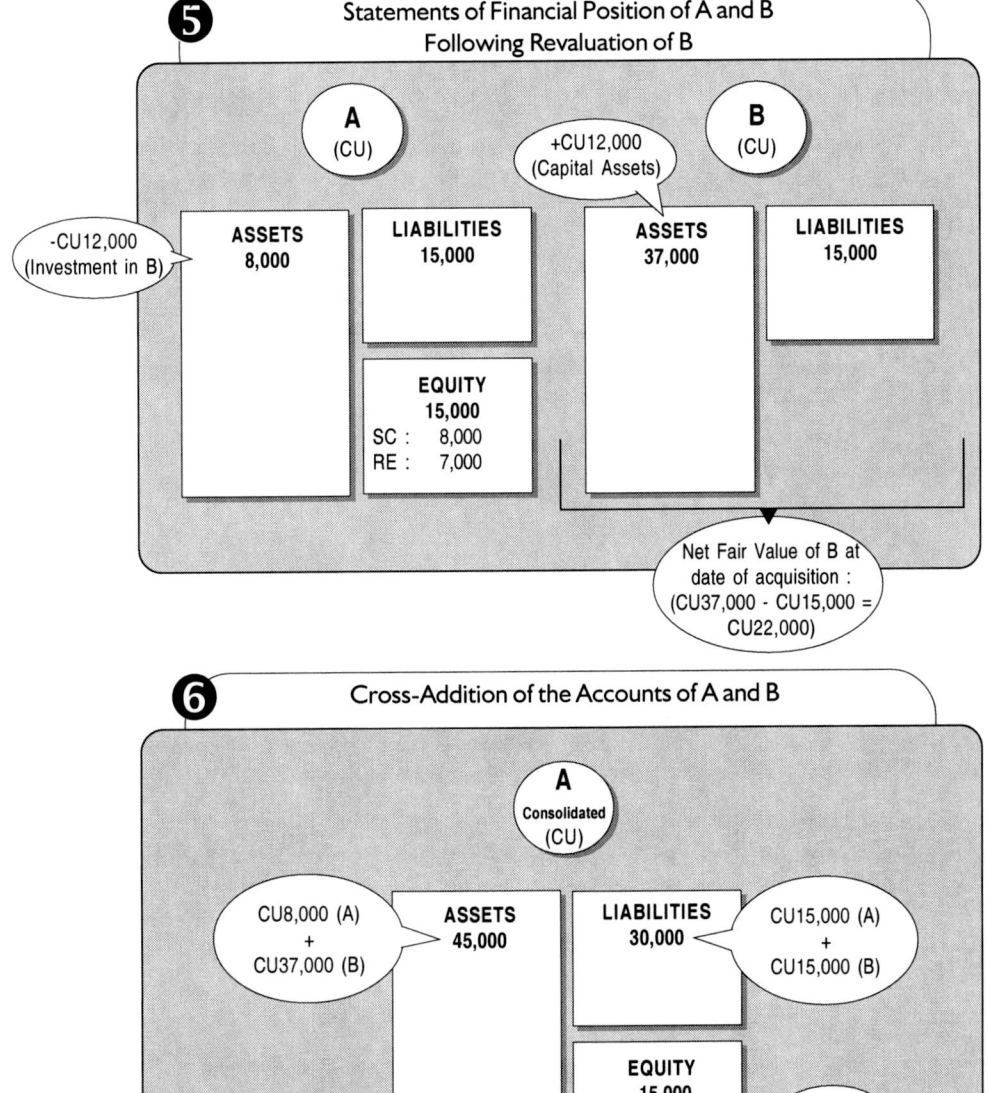

As one can see, the investment account of CU22,000 has been eliminated in a two step process. First, the equity account of Company B at the date of acquisition (Common Shares of CU5,000 + Retained Earnings of CU5,000 = CU10,000) has been eliminated to avoid double-counting (figure #2). Second, the positive price differential (CU12,000) has been allocated to capital assets so as to reflect the acquisition-date full fair value of Company B (figure #4). The consolidation process of Company A at the date of combination consists of replacing the investment account (CU22,000) with the fair value of Company B which is composed of identifiable assets of CU37,000 and liabilities of CU15,000 (CU37,000 - CU15,000 = CU22,000). This approach is consistent with the *acquisition method* which follows the rationale usually applicable to the initial recognition and measurement of assets acquired and liabilities assumed.

The consolidated value can be computed by adding the fair value of Company B to the book value of Company A. Since the shareholders' equity of Company B is eliminated in the process, only Company A's equity accounts are shown on the consolidated statement of financial position at the date of acquisition. This includes Common Shares of CU8,000 and Retained Earnings of CU7,000 (figure #6).

> **Note...**
>
> **Bargain Purchase**
> Sometimes, in a *bargain purchase*, the price paid could be less than the fair value of the net identifiable assets acquired. This situation might happen if the sale is forced, that is, when the seller is acting under compulsion. In such a case, the difference, referred to as *negative goodwill*, should be reduced to zero and recognized in income as a gain.
>
> **Direct Costs**
> *Direct costs* incurred to establish a business combination, such as advisory, legal, accounting, valuation and other professional or consulting fees, are not regarded as assets and must be excluded from the measurement of the consideration transferred for the acquiree. Instead, direct costs engaged in connection with a business combination must be expensed in the periods in which the costs are incurred and the services are received.
>
> **Goodwill versus Intangible Assets**
> It is important to recognize apart from goodwill intangible assets that arise from legal rights, such as trademarks and tradenames, and from contractual rights, such as royalties, lease and franchise agreements. Moreover, intangible assets that can be separated from the acquired entity and transferred to another entity, such as customer lists and databases, must also be recognized apart from goodwill.

② The Worksheet Approach

The consolidation worksheet of Company A at the date of acquisition is shown below along with the consolidation entries reproduced in a general journal form.

Consolidation Worksheet

	A (CU)	B (CU)	Eliminations Adjustments (CU)	Consolidated (CU)
ASSETS				
Investment in B	22,000		(10,000) (1a) (12,000) (1b)	–
Other identifiable assets	8,000	25,000	12,000 (1b)	45,000
	30,000	**25,000**		**45,000**
LIABILITIES	15,000	15,000		30,000
EQUITY				
Common shares	8,000	5,000	(5,000) (1a)	8,000
Retained earnings	7,000	5,000	(5,000) (1a)	7,000
	30,000	**25,000**		**45,000**

1a

Elimination of reciprocal investment and equity accounts so as to avoid double-counting

Common Shares (B)	5,000	
Retained Earnings (B)	5,000	
Investment in B (A)		10,000

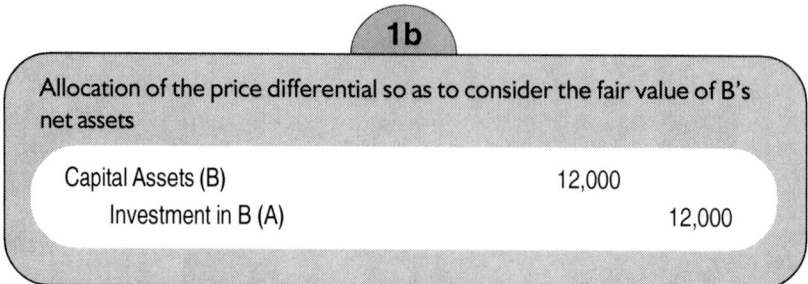

Consistent with the visual approach, the investment account (CU22,000) is eliminated following two consolidation entries. The first, consolidation entry #1a, is based on the net book value of Company B at the date of acquisition (CU10,000) and aims at avoiding double-counting. The second, consolidation entry #1b, consists of allocating the positive price differential (CU12,000) so as to establish Company B's net fair value at the date of acquisition.

③ The Direct Approach

The independent computations of Company A's consolidated total assets, total liabilities and equity balances as of the date of combination are shown below.

Assets	CU
• Parent (A) (excluding the investment in B)	8,000
• Subsidiary (B)	25,000
• Fair value increment on Capital Assets at the date of acquisition	12,000
Total	**45,000**

Liabilities	CU
• Parent (A)	15,000
• Subsidiary (B)	15,000
Total	**30,000**

Common Shares	CU
Parent (A) balance only as of January 1, X1	**8,000**

Retained Earnings	CU
Parent (A) balance only as of January 1, X1	**7,000**

Effect on Income Tax Allocation

The tax basis of an asset is usually different from its carrying value, a situation that gives rise to temporary differences. Temporary differences between accounting income and taxable income must be accounted for by companies in their own records. These effects show up as Deferred Tax in the statement of financial position. When temporary differences are related to amortizable assets, they are usually consumed over the remaining useful life of the relevant asset.

Business combinations are prone to create additional temporary differences because the acquisition-date full fair market value of the subsidiary's identifiable assets and liabilities assumed are considered for consolidation purposes. These temporary differences correspond to the fair value increments and decrements established at the date of acquisition. Note that no deferred tax is recorded in relation to goodwill because goodwill is merely a residual.

In the case of Company B's acquisition, a temporary difference of CU12,000 is created which consists of the fair value increment on capital assets. Assuming a corporate tax rate of 30 percent, Deferred Tax Liability related to the fair value increment amounts to CU3,600 at the date of acquisition (CU12,000 X 30%). Therefore, had the income tax related to business combinations been considered, Company B's Deferred Tax Liability should have been increased by CU3,600 at the date of acquisition. This procedure would have had an offsetting increase in goodwill.

2.2 Consolidation Following the Date of Acquisition

The passage of time introduces additional complexities into the consolidation process mainly due to the initial recognition of price differential. To explore these new complications, let's continue the development of Company A and Company B through the first five years following the date of acquisition. The condensed financial statements of both companies for the year ended December 31, X5, are shown in Exhibit 2.3.

Exhibit 2.3 • Financial Statements of Company A and Company B for the Year Ended December 31, X5

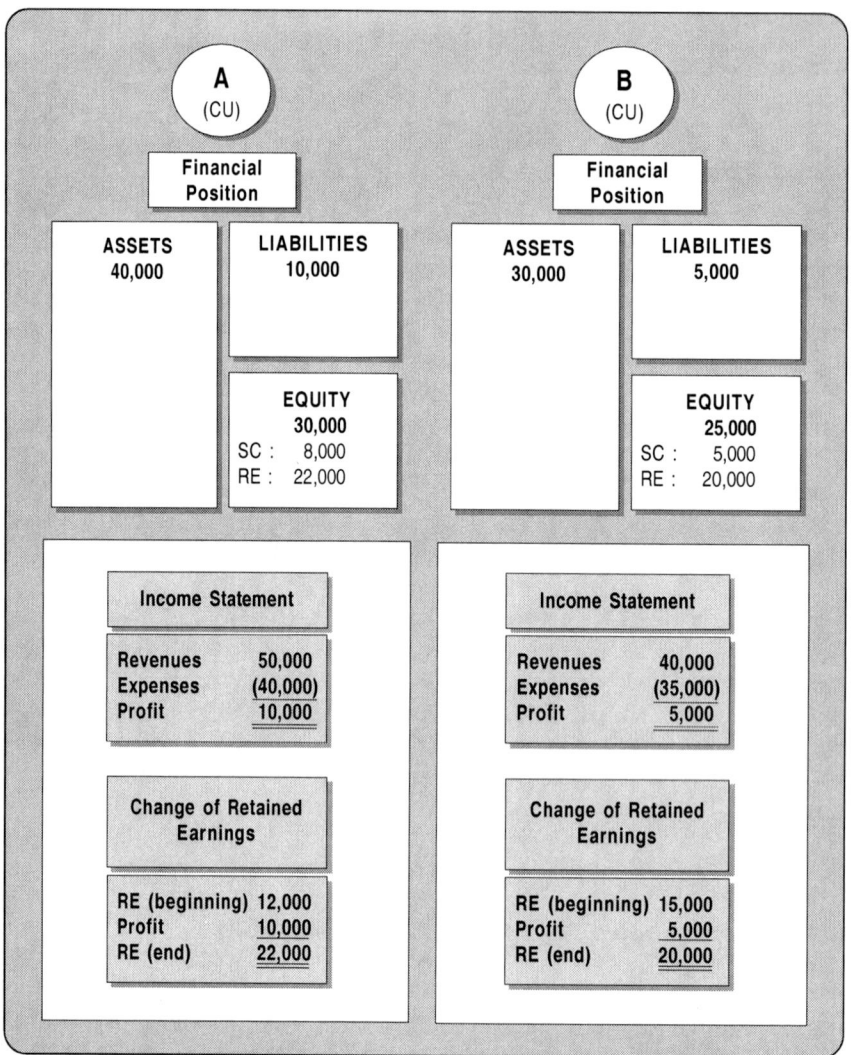

Exhibit 2.4 presents the change of the net book value of Company B since acquisition. As no transaction involved the capital stock since the date of acquisition, the net book value increase of CU15,000 consists of Company B's Retained Earnings increase from X1 through X5, inclusive (CU20,000 - CU5,000 = CU15,000).

Exhibit 2.4 • Net Book Value Increase of Company B Since Acquisition

Equity of B	Balance at Jan. 1, X1 (CU)	Change (CU)	Balance at Dec. 31, X5 (CU)
Common Shares	5,000	–	5,000
Retained Earnings	5,000	15,000	20,000
Total	10,000	15,000	25,000

For internal record-keeping, assume that Company A employs the cost method to account for its investment in Company B. Recall that under the cost method, the cost of the investment is not revised over time. Therefore, the balance of the investment account carried on the books of Company A remains at CU22,000 at December 31, X5. This value reflects the price paid by Company A five years ago to purchase all the outstanding voting stock of Company B.

Company A paid an excess price of CU12,000 over the net book value of Company B at the date of acquisition. This positive price differential has been assigned entirely to Capital Assets in the consolidation process so as to establish the fair value of Company B at the date of combination. Since consolidation entries are made on a worksheet rather than on the books of the affiliated companies, depreciation expense on capital assets carried on Company B's records continues to be based on the book value of the capital assets instead of the fair market value. From a consolidated viewpoint, such inconsistency gives rise to underdepreciation. Therefore, consolidation adjustment is required to correct the undervalued depreciation expense on capital assets.

To proceed with such adjustment, assume that Company B's capital assets had a remaining useful life of 12 years from the date of combination and that Company B is using the straight-line method to calculate all depreciation and amortization. Furthermore, assume that the net book value of Capital Assets at the date of acquisition equals CU6,000. Computation of the annual underdepreciation on capital assets is provided in Exhibit 2.5.

Exhibit 2.5 • Consolidation of the Financial Statements of Company A - The Annual Underdepreciation on Capital Assets

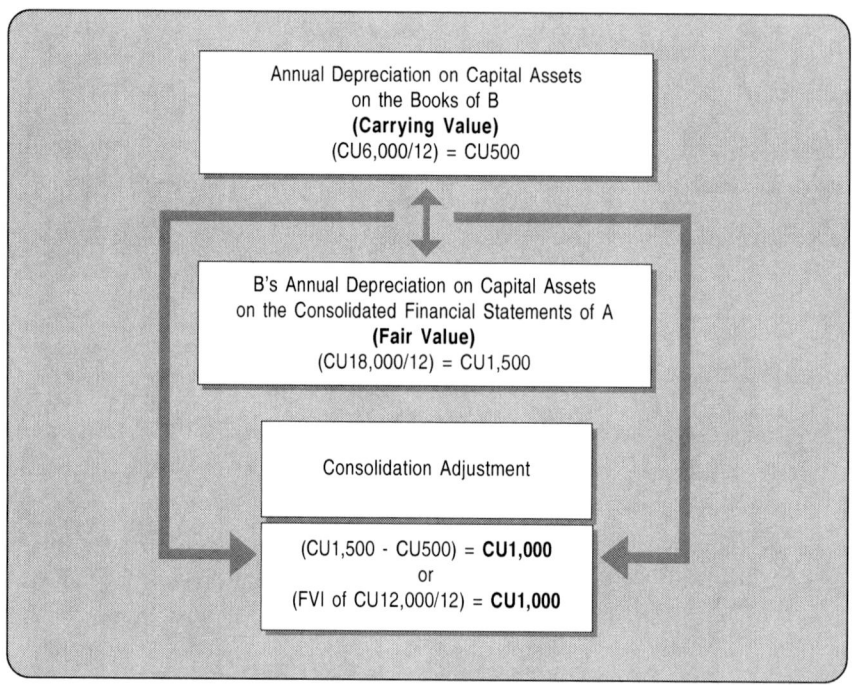

The acquisition-date fair value of capital assets (CU18,000) is determined by summing the carrying value (CU6,000) and the fair value increment (CU12,000). For consistency purposes, since the fair value of Company B's capital assets is considered in the consolidated process, consolidated depreciation expense on capital assets must be based on the fair value as well.

In order to achieve this, depreciation expense on capital assets taken from Company B's records must be increased by CU1,000 every year (over a 12 year period subsequent to acquisition). This amount consists of the difference between the annual depreciation expense recorded by Company B (CU500), which is based on the carrying value of the assets (CU6,000), and the depreciation expense to be reflected in the consolidated income statement (CU1,500), which is based on the fair market value of the assets at the date of acquisition (CU18,000). The annual underdepreciation expense can also be computed more directly by dividing the fair value increment on capital assets at the date of acquisition over the remaining useful life of the relevant assets from the date of acquisition (CU12,000/12 years = CU1,000). This process is referred to as *price differential amortization*.

Consolidated information should reflect the realization of the fair value change on the capital assets since combination. The cumulative underdepreciation on capital assets at December 31, X5, is equal to CU5,000 which consists of an annual underdepreciation of CU1,000 over five years, that is, from X1 through X5, inclusive.

The following sections present the consolidation process of the statement of financial position of Company A at December 31, X5 using:

① The Visual Approach;

② The Worksheet Approach;

③ The Direct Approach.

The consolidation of the income statement is illustrated in a separate section.

2.2.1 Consolidation of the Statement of Financial Position

① The Visual Approach

The following figures depict the successive transformation of the affiliated companies' statements of financial position through the consolidation process of Company A at December 31, X5.

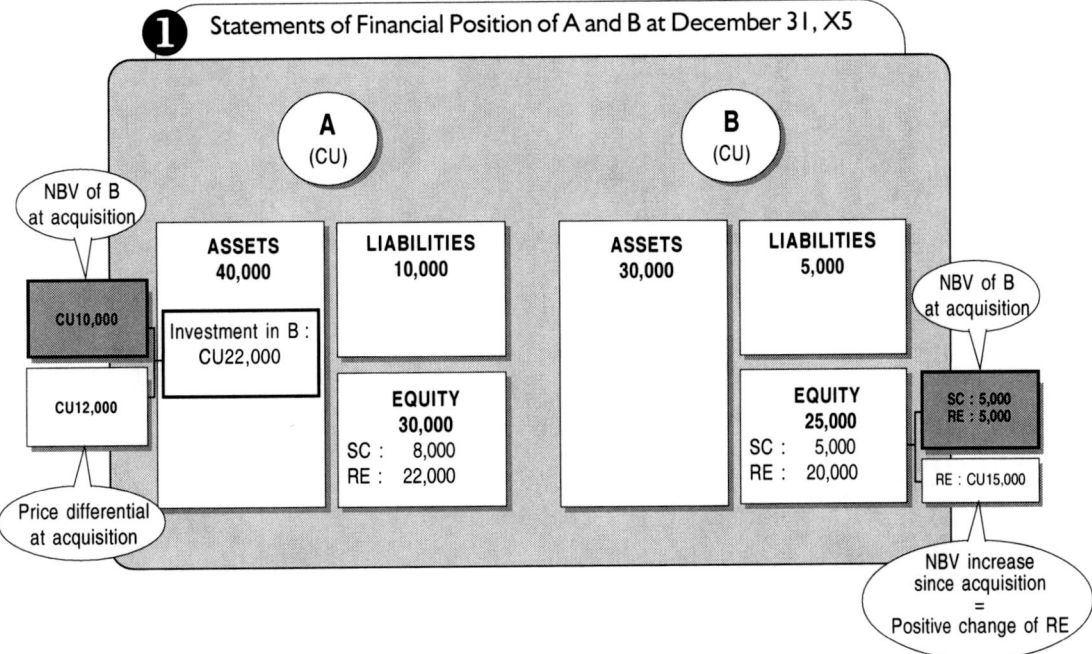

54 Part I Controlling Ownership

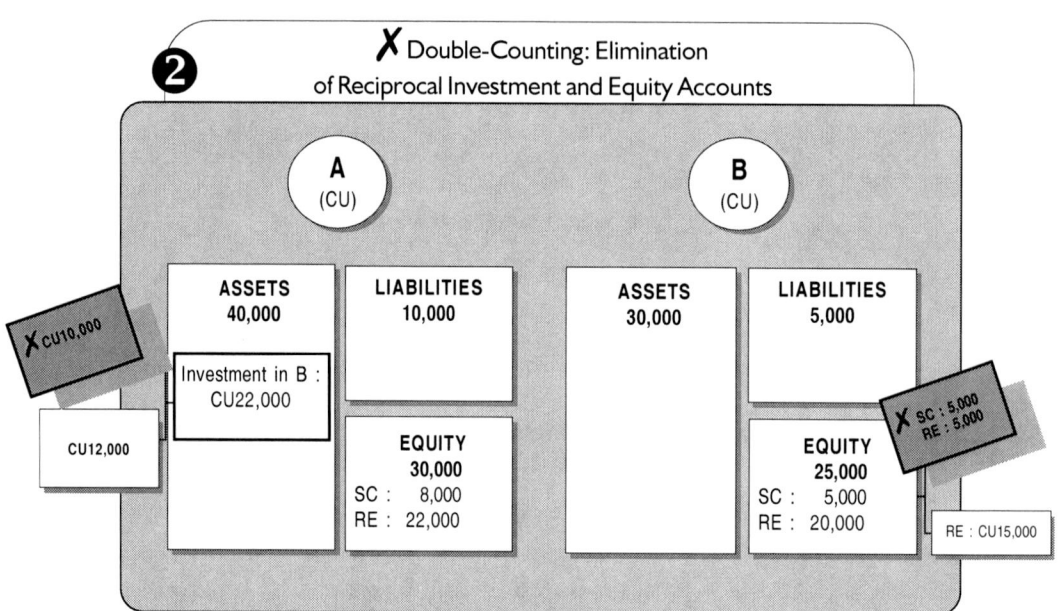

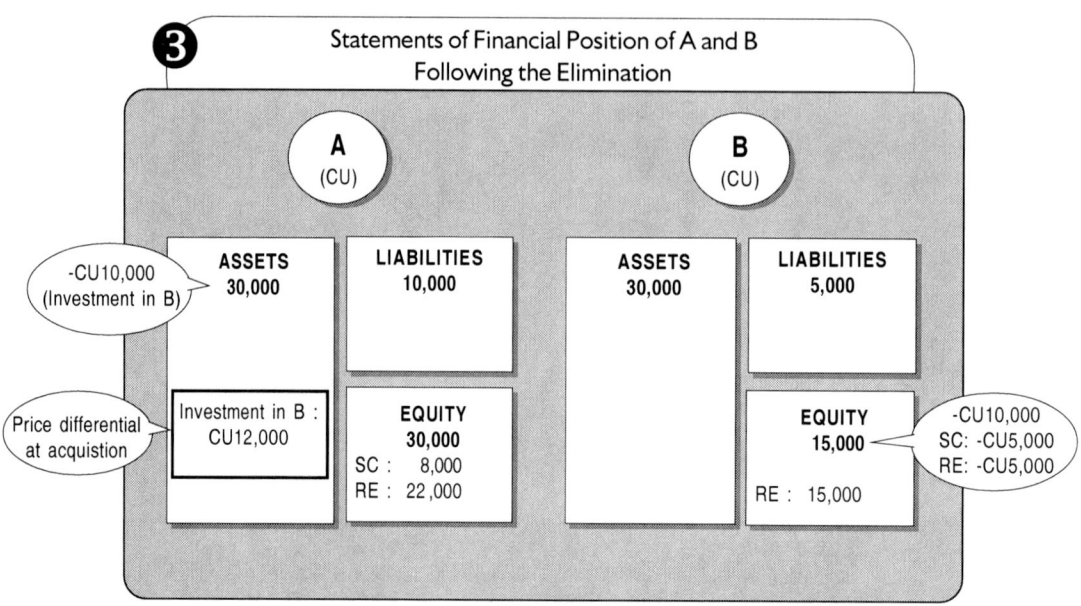

Chapter 2 Wholly Owned Subsidiaries 55

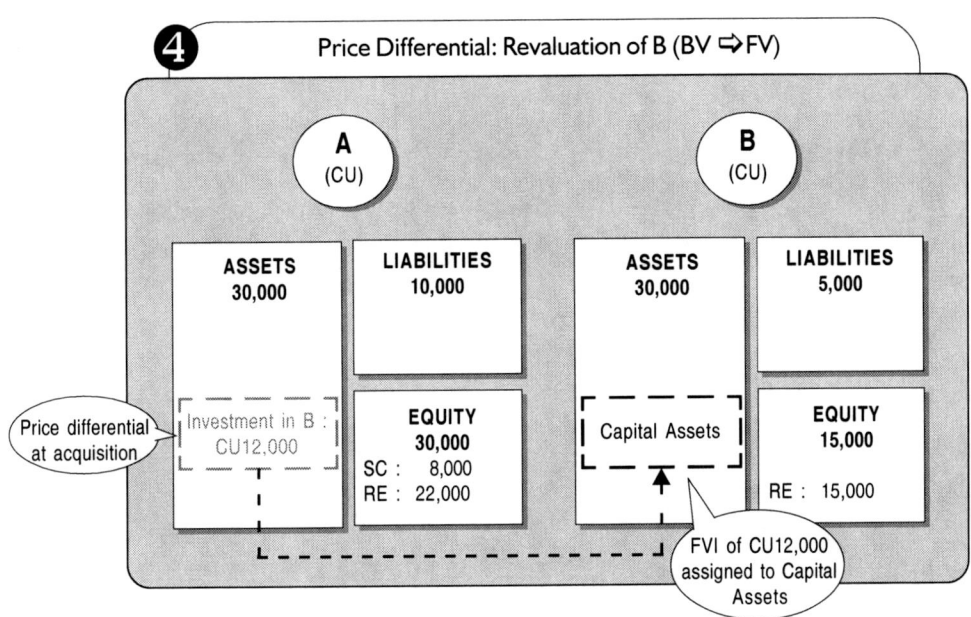

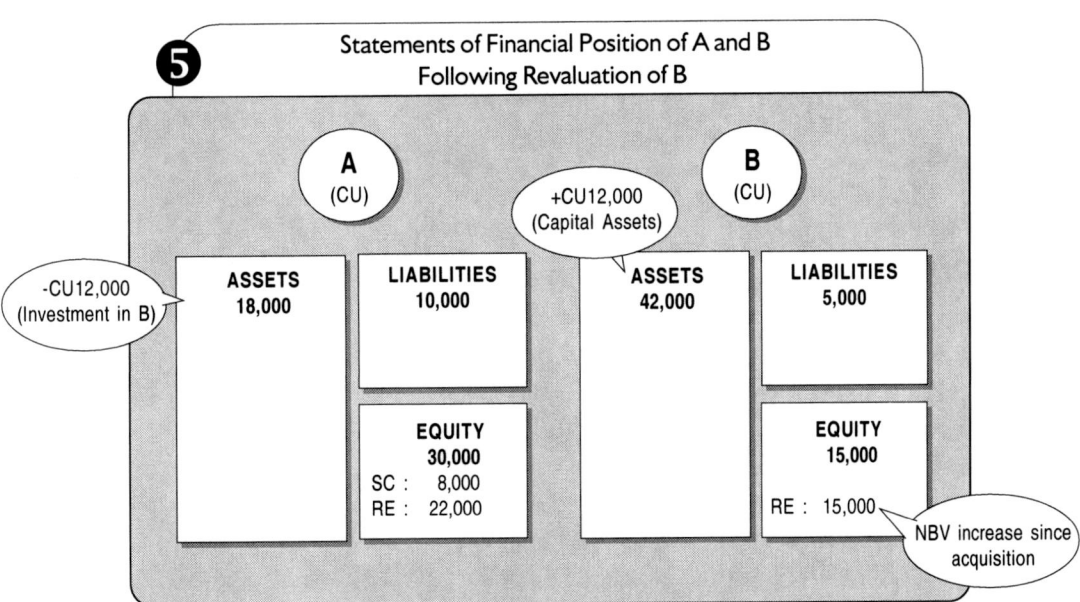

56 Part I Controlling Ownership

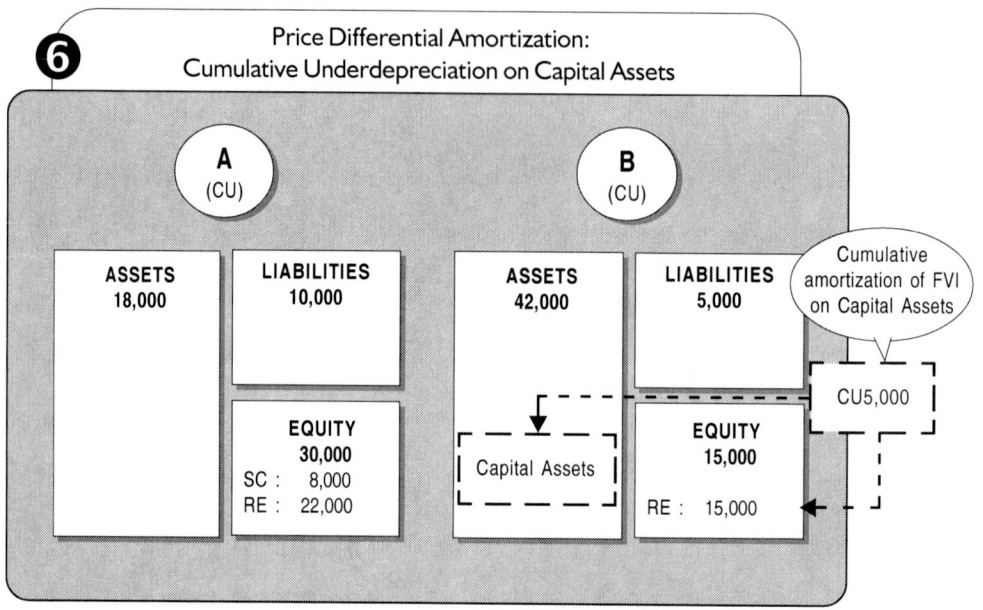

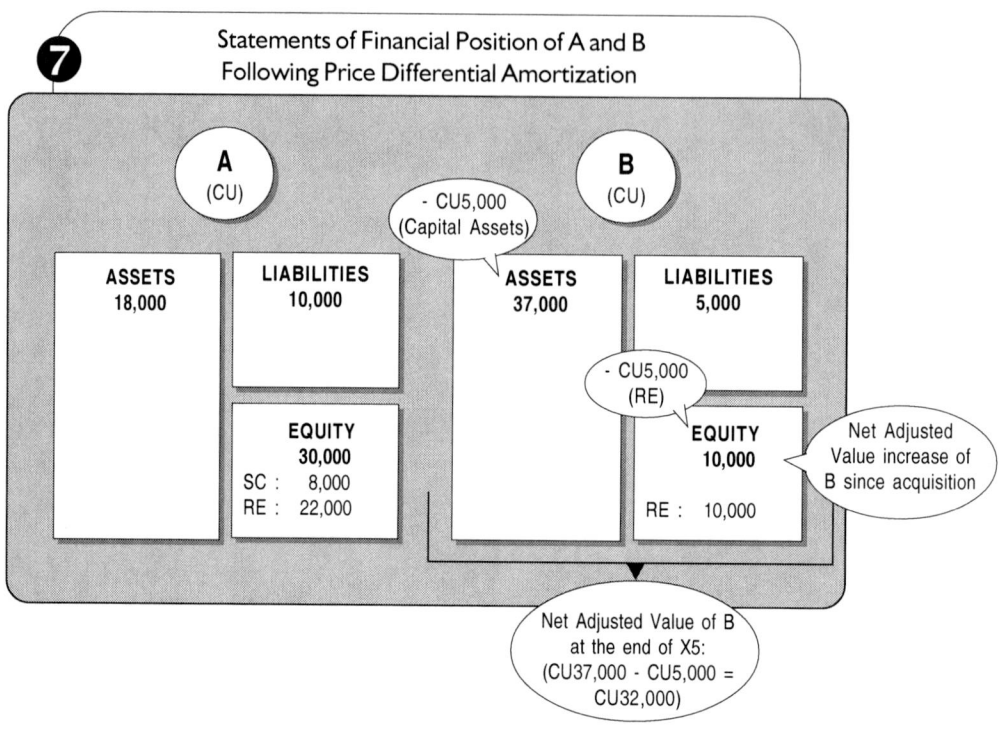

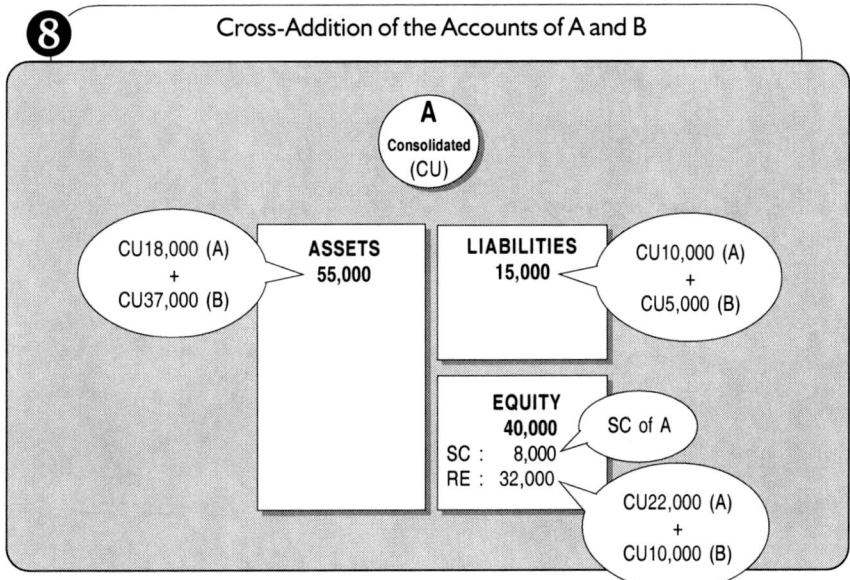

The procedure used in adjusting to the proper consolidated balances follows a consistent pattern. Adjustments in each case involve the elimination of the investment account (CU22,000), first, by eliminating Company B's equity accounts at the date of acquisition (CU10,000) (figure #2), and second, by allocating the purchase price differential (CU12,000) (figure #4). In sum, the investment account is replaced by the fair value of Company B at the date of acquisition.

In addition, adjusting for the cumulative underdepreciation on capital assets since acquisition (CU5,000) decreases simultaneously Company B's capital assets and Company B's retained earnings increase since acquisition (figure #6). As a result, only the *net adjusted value* of Company B since acquisition (CU15,000 - CU5,000 = CU10,000) is transferred to Company A in the consolidation process. Consolidated Retained Earnings at December 31, X5 (CU32,000) consist of the balance of Company A's Retained Earnings as of December 31, X5 (CU22,000) and the net adjusted value increase of Company B since combination (CU10,000) (figure #7).

Figure 2.1 presents the different components of Company B's net adjusted value or consolidated value at the end of the current period, that is, the net value of Company B after proper consolidation adjustments are made.

As portrayed in Figure 2.1, Company B's net adjusted value as of December 31, X5

(CU32,000) can be segregated into the following four basic components:

> Company B's net book value at the date of acquisition (CU10,000).
> Plus the purchase price differential (CU12,000).
> Plus Company B's net book value or retained earnings increase since acquisition (CU15,000).
> Less price differential amortization since acquisition (CU5,000).

These four components can be combined either horizontally or vertically to arrive at the same adjusted figures. More precisely, Company B's net adjusted value at the end of the current period (CU32,000) is comprised of the purchase price (CU22,000) plus Company B's net adjusted value increase since acquisition (CU10,000). Company B's net adjusted value is also equivalent to Company B's net book value at December 31, X5 (CU25,000) plus the unamortized portion of the price differential at the end of the accounting period (CU7,000). Recall that consolidation adjustments relating to price differential and price differential amortization are made on a working paper and, therefore, do not affect Company B's individual records.

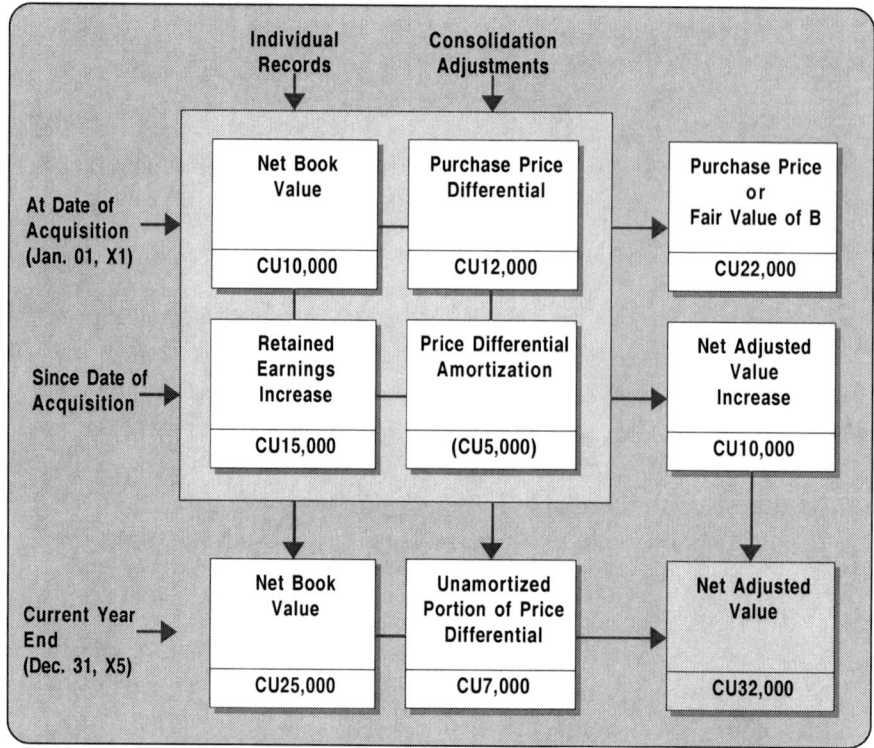

Figure 2.1 • Company B's Net Adjusted Value as of December 31, X5

Company B's net adjusted value (CU32,000) is assigned entirely to Company A in the consolidation process. In particular, consolidated assets and liabilities consist of the sum of the book value of the parent and the adjusted value of the subsidiary assets and liabilities. Once the elimination of the investment account has been carried out or replaced by the fair value of Company B at date of acquisition (CU22,000), the combination of both companies leads to a transfer of Company B's net adjusted value increase since acquisition (CU10,000) to Company A.

② The Worksheet Approach

The following presents the consolidation entries with the accompanying consolidation worksheet that combines Company A and Company B at December 31, X5.

1a

Elimination of reciprocal investment and equity accounts as of the date of acquisition so as to avoid double-counting

Common Shares (B)	5,000	
Retained Earnings (B)	5,000	
Investment in B (A)		10,000

1b

Allocation of the price differential so as to consider the fair value of B's net assets at the date of acquisition

Capital Assets (B)	12,000	
Investment in B (A)		12,000

2

Price differential amortization since acquisition: Amortization of the fair value increment on Capital Assets since acquisition

Retained Earnings (B)	5,000	
Accumulated Depreciation - Capital Assets (B)		5,000

(CU12,000 X 5/12) = CU5,000

Consolidation Worksheet

	A (CU)	B (CU)	Eliminations Adjustments (CU)	Consolidated (CU)
ASSETS				
Investment in B	22,000		(10,000)(1a) (12,000)(1b)	–
Other identifiable assets	18,000	30,000	12,000 (1b) (5,000)(2)	55,000
	40,000	30,000		55,000
LIABILITIES	10,000	5,000		15,000
EQUITY				
Common shares	8,000	5,000	(5,000)(1a)	8,000
Retained earnings	22,000	20,000	(5,000)(1a) (5,000)(2)	32,000
	40,000	30,000		55,000

Note...

At one point, consolidation entries may be combined. However, to be consistent with the building-block approach privileged in the book and to help the reader to better grasp the fundamental concepts and procedures involved in consolidation, we purposely avoid combining consolidation eliminations/adjustments. Consolidation entries #1a and #1b reflect adjustments relating to the date of acquisition, and consolidation entry #2, to the five year period post-acquisition.

③ The Direct Approach

The independent computation of the consolidated balance of total assets, total liabilities and equity accounts is shown next.

Assets	CU
• Parent (A) (excluding the investment in B)	18,000
• Subsidiary (B)	30,000
• Unamortized balance of the fair value increment on Capital Assets (CU12,000 X 7/12)	7,000
Total	**55,000**

Liabilities	CU
• Parent (A)	10,000
• Subsidiary (B)	5,000
Total	**15,000**

Common Shares	CU
Parent (A) balance only at December 31, X5	**8,000**

Retained Earnings		CU
• Parent (A)		22,000
• Subsidiary (B)'s net adjusted value since acquisition		
- Retained earnings increase since acquisition	15,000	
- Price differential amortization since acquisition: Cumulative amortization of the fair value increment on Capital Assets (CU12,000 X 5/12)	(5,000)	
	10,000	10,000
Total		**32,000**

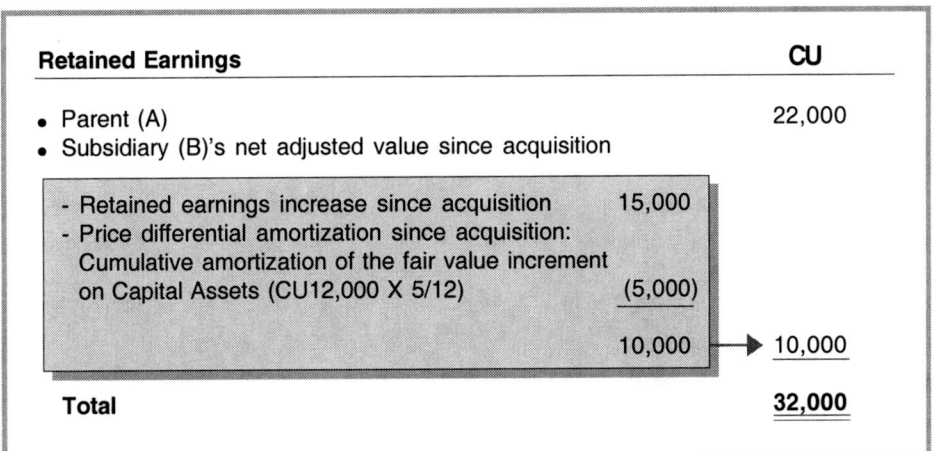

2.2.2 Consolidation of the Income Statement

The consolidation of the income statement consists of cross-adding the revenue and expense accounts of the affiliated companies. Recall that the depreciation expense on capital assets carried on the books of Company B is computed based on the original cost rather than the fair value of the assets estimated at the date of combination. The latter value is the one that is reflected on the consolidated balance sheet, not the carrying value. The fair value being greater than the book value at the date of combination (fair value increment of CU12,000), the current year undervalued depreciation expense (CU1,000) must be corrected (see exhibit 2.5).

To illustrate, let's return to figure 6 from the visual approach. Then, let's add the income statement and the change of retained earnings of Company A and Company B for the year ended December 31, X5. The full set of condensed financial statements are shown on the next page.

Notice that the cumulative underdepreciation of CU5,000 since acquisition (X1- X5) has been allocated to:
› Prior years (X1-X4) while decreasing the opening balance of Retained Earnings by CU 4,000 (CU1,000 X 4 years).
› Current year (X5) while increasing Depreciation Expense by CU1, 000.

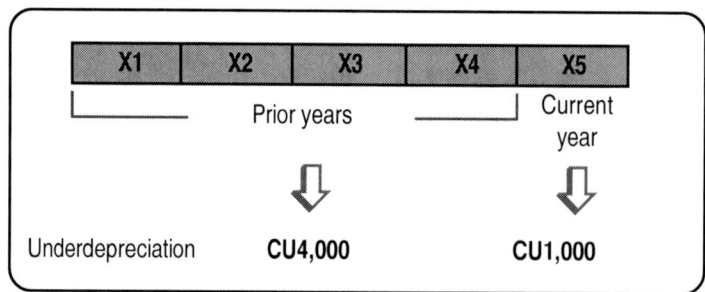

The worksheet adjustment #2 previously introduced when preparing the consolidated statement of financial position of Company A at December 31, X5, was based on the cumulative underdepreciation since acquisition (X1 through X5, inclusive). Only the statement of financial position accounts were thus affected. This consolidation entry is reproduced below.

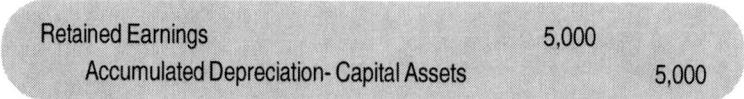

In order to report the consolidated income statement of Company A, the current-period underdepreciation on capital assets must be adjusted. Therefore, the following consolidation entry must be considered instead.

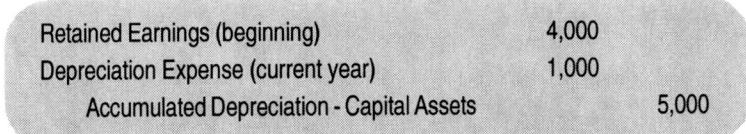

Retained Earnings (beginning)	4,000
Depreciation Expense (current year)	1,000
Accumulated Depreciation - Capital Assets	5,000

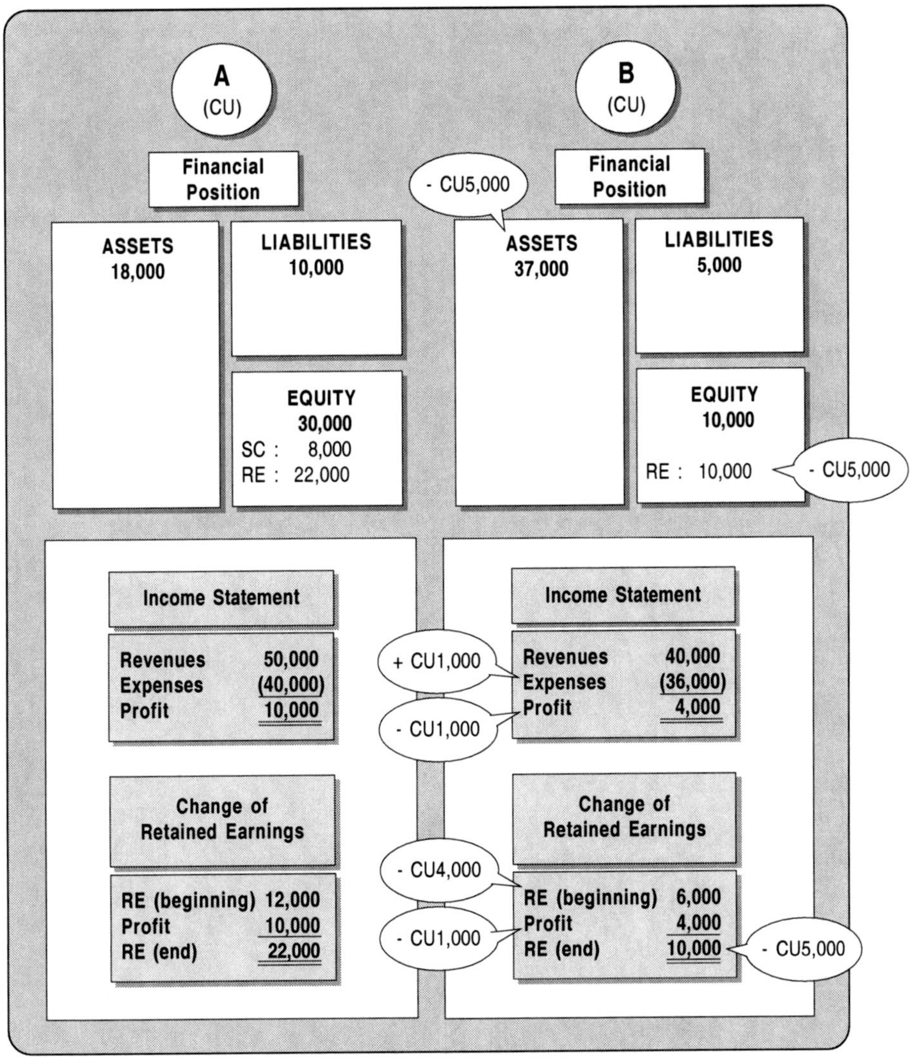

A (CU)

Financial Position

ASSETS 18,000 | LIABILITIES 10,000

EQUITY 30,000
SC : 8,000
RE : 22,000

− CU5,000

B (CU)

Financial Position

ASSETS 37,000 | LIABILITIES 5,000

EQUITY 10,000
RE : 10,000 − CU5,000

Income Statement (A)

Revenues 50,000
Expenses (40,000)
Profit 10,000

+ CU1,000
− CU1,000

Income Statement (B)

Revenues 40,000
Expenses (36,000)
Profit 4,000

Change of Retained Earnings (A)

RE (beginning) 12,000
Profit 10,000
RE (end) 22,000

− CU4,000
− CU1,000

Change of Retained Earnings (B)

RE (beginning) 6,000
Profit 4,000
RE (end) 10,000 − CU5,000

The underdepreciation on capital assets being corrected, we can complete the consolidation of the income statement by cross-adding the revenue and expense accounts of Company A and Company B. The consolidated income statement for the year ended December 31, X5, is reproduced next.

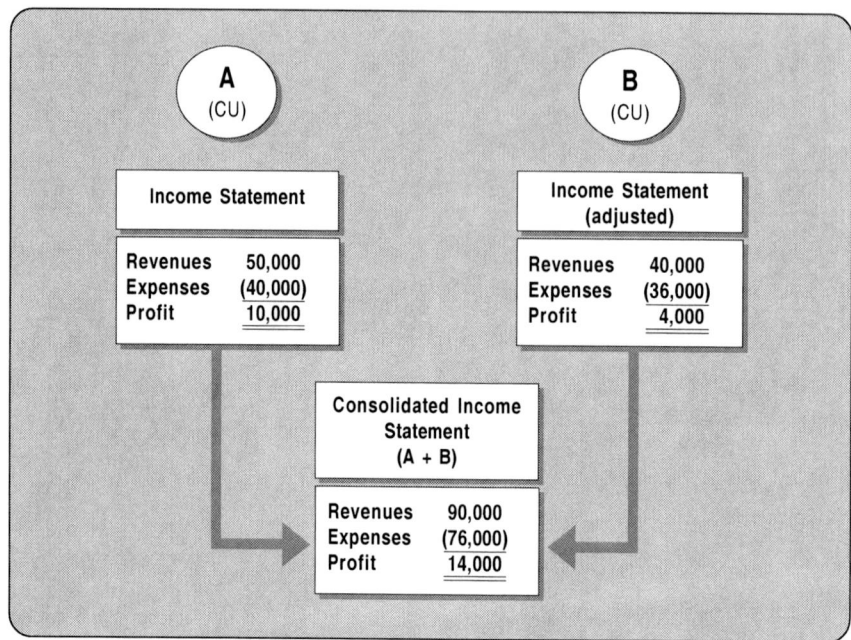

Computation of the consolidated profit for X5 is shown below.

◆ Consolidated Profit for the Year		CU
• A's profit		10,000

• B's adjusted profit:
 - B's profit
 - Current-year price differential amortization:
   Underdepreciation on Capital Assets
   (CU12,000/12)
	5,000
	
	 (1,000)
		
		 4,000

Total		14,000

> **Effect on Income Tax Allocation**
>
> As the fair value increment on Capital Assets (CU12,000) is being amortized, the temporary difference that must have been recognized at the date of acquisition (Deferred Tax Liability of CU3,600) decreases. More precisely, the annual amortization of the fair value increment is CU1,000 (CU12,000/12 years). Therefore, Deferred Tax Liability must be reduced by CU300 every year (CU1,000 X 30% tax rate or CU3,600/12 years) with an offsetting decrease in Income Tax Expense. The cumulative impact of this tax allocation since acquisition amounts to CU1,500 (CU300 X 5 years), that is, CU1,200 for prior-periods (X1 through X4, inclusive) and CU300 for the current period (X5). The following presents the additional consolidation entry that would have been required had the income tax allocation related to business combinations been considered.
>
> | | | |
> |---|---|---|
> | Deferred Tax Liability | 1,500 | |
> | Income Tax Expense | | 300 |
> | Retained Earnings | | 1,200 |

2.2.3 Price Differential: Additional Considerations

Fair Value Increments and Decrements

As previously illustrated, when a positive price differential is assigned to a depreciable asset, the asset-related fair value increment must be amortized over the remaining useful life of the asset so as to adjust the undervalued depreciation expense carried on the subsidiary's records. The same approach would apply had a fair value decrement been considered. In such a case, the amortization of the fair value decrement would be necessary to correct the excess depreciation expense.

If a price differential is assigned to a *non-depreciable asset* such as land or inventory, the asset-related fair value increment or decrement must be added to the asset balance in the consolidation process. Such adjustment must be repeated in subsequent consolidation periods for as long as the asset is not sold by the subsidiary to an unrelated party.

When an asset to which a differential is assigned is sold to an external party, the unamortized portion of the asset-related fair value increment or decrement at the date of the sale should be fully recognized in the year of the asset disposal and the gain or loss recognized by the selling affiliate should be adjusted accordingly.

As a basis for this coverage, assume that a subsidiary sold land to an outsider for CU25,000. The original cost of the land was CU10,000. Therefore, a gain of CU15,000 is recognized by the subsidiary as the following.

Cash	25,000	
Land (Book Value)		10,000
Gain on Sale of Land		15,000

If a positive price differential of CU5,000 has been assigned to the land in the consolidation process (fair value increment at the date of acquisition), the gain on sale of land recognized by the subsidiary will be overvalued by CU5,000. Thus, the following consolidation adjustment would be required.

Gain on Sale of Land	5,000	
Land		5,000

In sum, the gain on sale of land reported on the consolidated income statement will be based on the fair value of the land (CU15,000) rather than its book value (CU10,000). The transaction that will be reflected on the consolidated financial statements is reproduced below.

Cash	25,000	
Land (Fair Value)		15,000
Gain on Sale of Land		10,000

The following table provides a summary of the additional consolidation adjustments required when a price differential has already been assigned to a non-depreciable asset such as inventory or land and when the relevant asset is subsequently sold to external parties.

Fair Value Increment

If the asset to which a fair value increment is assigned is sold to an outsider:
- In the current year

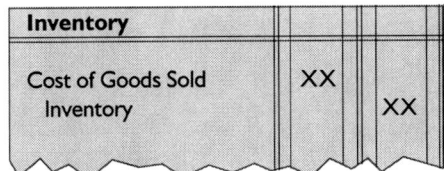
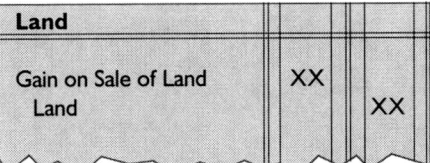

- In a prior year

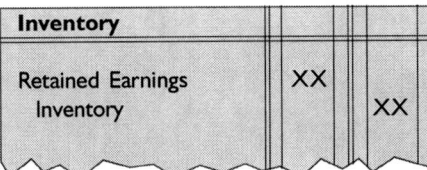
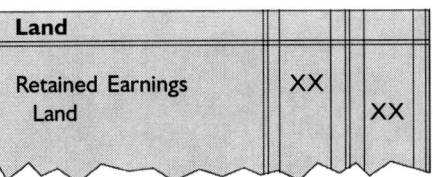

Fair Value Decrement

If the asset to which a fair value decrement is assigned is sold to an outsider:
- In the current year

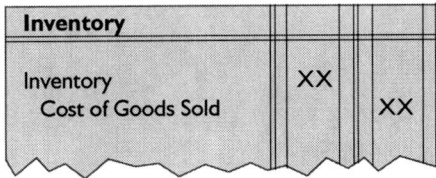

- In a prior year

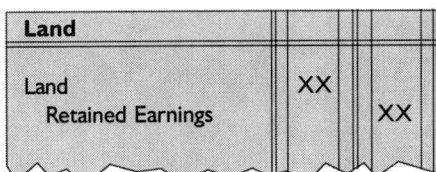

Goodwill

Goodwill will be carried forward on the consolidated balance sheet at the original amount, without amortization, unless it becomes impaired. Goodwill must be tested for impairment annually. It is only upon the recognition of an impairment loss that goodwill will decline from one period to the next.

A two-step testing procedure must be followed to detect any potential *goodwill impairment*. More precisely, if the entire subsidiary is designated as a reporting unit, the first test consists of comparing the fair value of the subsidiary, including the allocated goodwill, with its carrying value. If the total fair value exceeds the carrying value, goodwill is not considered impaired and no further analysis is needed. However, if the fair value of the subsidiary or reporting unit has fallen below its carrying value, goodwill could have been impaired. In this case, a second test must be performed.

The second test consists of comparing the fair value of goodwill with its carrying value. The implied fair value of goodwill can be computed in a similar manner to the determination of goodwill in a business combination. More precisely, the fair value of the subsidiary estimated at the time the impairment test is conducted is treated as the purchase price. The fair value of goodwill is thus obtained while working through a purchase price allocation as seen previously in this chapter. If it appears that the implied fair value of goodwill has declined below its carrying value, an impairment loss must be recognized for the excess carrying value over fair value.

The following consolidation entries would be required had an impairment loss been computed.

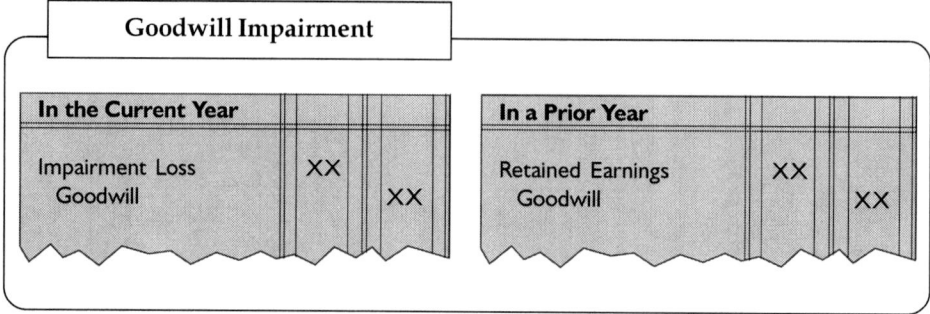

Comprehensive Illustration

Basic Information

On January 1, X6, Para Corporation acquired all the outstanding voting stock of Rain Enterprise for CU100,000 cash. You are asked to prepare the consolidated financial statements of Para Corporation for the year ended December 31, X10, that is, five years subsequent to the date of combination. Assume that the affiliated companies never engaged in transactions among themselves.

Exhibit 2.6 reproduces the statement of financial postion of Rain at the date of acquisition.

Exhibit 2.6 • Statement of Financial Position of Rain Enterprise at January 1, X6

Assets	(CU)
Cash	10,000
Land	55,000
Buildings (net)	50,000
Total assets	**115,000**
Liabilities and equities	
Bank loan	45,000
Accounts payable	5,000
Share capital	55,000
Retained earnings	10,000
Total liabilities and equities	**115,000**

On the date of acquisition, the identifiable assets and liabilities of the Rain Enterprise had fair values that were equal to their carrying values except for land and buildings, which had a fair value CU10,000 and CU15,000, respectively, greater than their carrying values. From the date of acquisition, buildings had a remaining useful life of ten years. Both companies use the straight-line method to calculate all depreciation and amortization.

Exhibit 2.7 presents the financial statements of Para Corporation and Rain Enterprise for the year ended December 31, X10.

Exhibit 2.7 • Financial Statements of Para Corporation and Rain Enterprise for the Year Ended December 31, X10

Income Statements
Year Ended December 31, X10
(in CU)

	Para	Rain
Sales	500,000	230,000
Sales expenses	250,000	90,000
Administration expenses	200,000	130,000
Profit for the year	**50,000**	**10,000**

Statements of Financial Position
December 31, X10
(in CU)

	Para	Rain
Assets		
Cash	40,000	15,000
Accounts receivable	12,000	50,000
Land		55,000
Buildings (net)	200,000	25,000
Investment in Rain	100,000	
Total assets	**352,000**	**145,000**
Liabilities and equities		
Bank loan	25,000	10,000
Accounts payable	10,000	15,000
Bonds payable	75,000	
Share capital	150,000	55,000
Retained earnings	92,000	65,000
Total liabilities and equities	**352,000**	**145,000**

Note that the investment account of Para in Rain is still shown at CU100,000 (purchase price) on the books of Para as of December 31, X10. This signals the use by Para of the cost method of accounting for its strategic investments.

Statements of Changes in Equity
Year Ended December 31, X10
(in CU)

	Para			Rain		
	Share Capital	Retained Earnings	Total	Share Capital	Retained Earnings	Total
Balance at January 1, X10	150,000	42,000	192,000	55,000	55,000	110,000
Profit for the year		50,000	50,000		10,000	10,000
Balance at December 31, X10	150,000	92,000	242,000	55,000	65,000	120,000

In addition, note that the net book value of Rain has increased by CU55,000 since acquisition. This amount is reflected in the change of Retained Earnings from January 1, X6 (CU10,000) to December 31, X10 (CU65,000). This positive change in Rain's value since acquisition will be assigned to Para in the consolidation process after proper adjustments are made.

Preliminary Analysis

Exhibit 2.8 reproduces the allocation of the purchase price as of the date of acquisition.

Exhibit 2.8 • Acquisition of All the Outstanding Voting Stock of Rain by Para on January 1, X6 - Allocation of the Purchase Price

		CU
Cost of investment in Rain		100,000
Shareholders' equity of Rain at the date of acquisition:		
Share capital	55,000	
Retained earnings	10,000	65,000
Price differential		35,000
Fair value increments:		
- Land		(10,000)
- Buildings		(15,000)
Goodwill		10,000

The excess of investment cost over book value acquired is CU35,000. This positive price differential is allocated first to Land (CU10,000) and Buildings (CU15,000), and the remainder to Goodwill (CU10,000). In this regard, assume that goodwill has not been impaired since acquisition.

The consolidated balance of Land and Buildings must be increased by CU10,000 and CU15,000, respectively, to account for Rain's acquisition-date full fair value. Since the land is retained by Rain at the end of the current period, no further adjustments are required. However, the buildings being used by Rain to generate revenue, the fair value increment on buildings must be amortized over the remaining useful life of the asset from the date of acquisition (ten years). Amortization of the fair value increment on buildings aims at adjusting the annual underdepreciation of CU1,500. Exhibit 2.9 provides the details of this adjustment.

Exhibit 2.9 • Consolidation of the Financial Statements of Para Corporation - The Annual Underdepreciation on Buildings

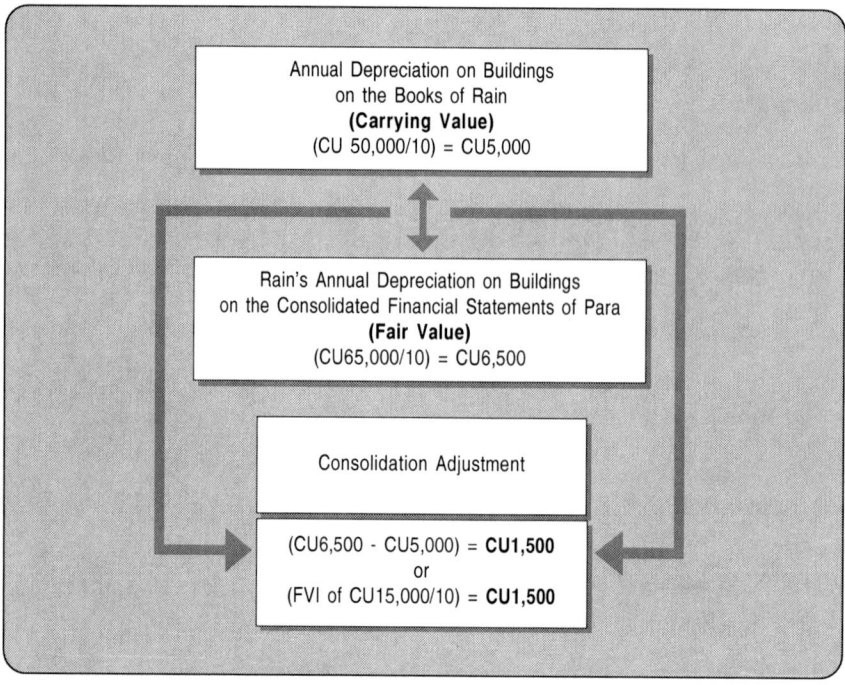

Exhibit 2.10 presents the price differential amortization schedule. This schedule summarizes the information regarding the change of fair value increments and goodwill since acquisition. This information will form the basis for post-acquisition consolidation adjustments.

Exhibit 2.10 • Consolidation of the Financial Statements of Para Corporation - Price Differential Amortization Schedule

Items	Price Differential Balance at Acquisition (CU)	Amortization Prior Years (X6-X9) (CU)	Amortization Current Year (X10) (CU)	Unamortized Excess at Dec. 31, X10 (CU)
Land	10,000	-	-	10,000
Buildings	15,000	6,000	1,500	7,500
Goodwill	10,000	-	-	10,000
Total	**35,000**	**6,000**	**1,500**	**27,500**

The cumulative underdepreciation on buildings since acquisition is CU7,500. Of that amount, CU6,000 relates to prior years (X6 through X9, inclusive) and CU1,500 to the current year (X10). The unamortized balance of the fair value increment on buildings as of December 31, X10, is CU7,500. The fair value increment on land (CU10,000) and the original amount assigned to goodwill at the date of acquisition (CU10,000) remain unchanged.

Consolidation of Financial Statements

The following sections present the consolidation process of Para Corporation as of December 31, X10, using:

① The Worksheet Approach;

② The Direct Approach.

① The Worksheet Approach

The following reports the basic consolidation entries required for the preparation of the consolidated information of Para Corporation as of December 31, X10.

1a

Elimination of reciprocal investment and equity accounts as of the date of acquisition so as to avoid double-counting

Common Shares (Rain)	55,000	
Retained Earnings (Rain)	10,000	
Investment in Rain (Para)		65,000

1b

Allocation of the price differential so as to consider the fair value of Rain's net assets including goodwill at the date of acquisition

Land (Rain)	10,000	
Buildings (Rain)	15,000	
Goodwill (Rain)	10,000	
Investment in Rain (Para)		35,000

2

Price differential amortization since acquisition: Amortization of the fair value increment on Buildings since acquisition

Retained Earnings (Rain)	6,000	
Depreciation Expense (Rain)	1,500	
Accumulated Depreciation - Buildings (Rain)		7,500

(CU15,000 X 5/10) = CU7,500

The overall underdepreciation of CU7,500 on buildings since acquisition (X6-X10) has been allocated to:

> Prior years (X6-X9) while decreasing the opening balance of Retained Earnings by CU6,000 (CU1,500 X 4 years).
> Current year (X10) while increasing Depreciation Expense by CU1,500.

Chapter 2 Wholly Owned Subsidiaries

The consolidation worksheet that combines Para Corporation and Rain Enterprise at December 31, X10, is shown below.

Consolidation Worksheet

	Para (CU)	Rain (CU)	Eliminations Adjustments (CU)	Consolidated (CU)
ASSETS				
Cash	40,000	15,000		55,000
Accounts receivable	12,000	50,000		62,000
Land		55,000	10,000 (1b)	65,000
Buildings (net)	200,000	25,000	15,000 (1b) (7,500) (2)	232,500
Investment in Rain	100,000		(65,000) (1a) (35,000) (1b)	–
Goodwill			10,000 (1b)	10,000
	352,000	**145,000**		**424,500**
LIABILITIES				
Bank loan	25,000	10,000		35,000
Accounts payable	10,000	15,000		25,000
Bonds payable	75,000			75,000
EQUITY				
Common shares	150,000	55,000	(55,000) (1a)	150,000
Retained earnings	92,000	65,000	(17,500)	139,500
	352,000	**145,000**		**424,500**
Revenues	500,000	230,000		730,000
Sales expenses	250,000	90,000	1,500 (2)	341,500
Administration expenses	200,000	130,000		330,000
Profit	**50,000**	**10,000**		**58,500**
Retained earnings (beginning)	42,000	55,000	(10,000) (1a) (6,000) (2)	81,000
Retained earnings (end)	**92,000**	**65,000**	**(17,500)**	**139,500**

Net impact on the ending balance of RE

What If...

Land

If the land were sold by Rain outside the affiliated grouping, the asset-related fair value increment of CU10,000 should have been fully written down and the gain or loss on disposal adjusted accordingly. More precisely, the following additional entry would have been required for the consolidation of Para at December 31, X10:

‣ If the sale of the land occurred in the current year (X10):

Gain on Sale of Land	10,000	
Land		10,000

‣ If the sale of the land occurred in a prior year (between X6 and X9):

Retained Earnings	10,000	
Land		10,000

Negative Goodwill

If the purchase price were CU80,000 instead of CU100,000, the cost of the acquisition would have been lower than the fair value of Rain's net assets. The excess of fair value or negative goodwill would have been CU10,000 (CU90,000 - CU80,000). Negative goodwill must be reduced to zero and recognized as a gain. Therefore, consolidation entry #1b would have been the following:

‣ At date of acquisition (X6):

Land (Rain)	10,000	
Buildings (Rain)	15,000	
Investment in Rain (Para)		15,000
Gain on acquisition (Para)		10,000

‣ In periods subsequent to acquisition:

Land (Rain)	10,000	
Buildings (Rain)	15,000	
Investment in Rain (Para)		15,000
Retained Earnings (Para)		10,000

Notice that in the event of a bargain acquisition leading to negative goodwill, we still account for the full market value of the subsidiary's net assets at date of combination.

What If...

If goodwill were impaired (let's assume an impairment loss of CU 4,000), the following entry would have been added to the consolidation workpaper of Para as of December 31, X10:

▸ If the impairment occurred in the current year (X10):

Impairment Loss	4,000	
Goodwill		4,000

▸ If the impairment occurred in a prior year (between X6 and X9):

Retained Earnings	4,000	
Goodwill		4,000

Effect on Income Tax Allocation

Assuming a corporate tax rate of 30 percent, additional entries would have been required to account for the income tax related to Rain's acquisition. More precisely, temporary differences created by the fair value increments on Land (CU10,000) and Buildings (CU15,000) should have been translated into a Deferred Tax Liability of CU7,500 (CU25,000 X 30%) at the date of acquisition. In post-acquisition periods, a portion of these temporary differences would have been consumed via the amortization of the fair value increment on Buildings. The change of temporary differences in prior-years (X6 through X9, inclusive) amounts to CU6,000 (see Exhibit 2.10) which would have been equivalent to a reduction of Deferred Tax Liability of CU1,800 (CU6,000 X 30%). The change of temporary differences in the current year (X10) equals CU1,500 which would have been equivalent to a reduction of Income Tax Expense of CU450 (CU1,500 X 30%). Had Deferred Tax Liability been increased by CU7,500 at the date of acquisition, the following additional consolidation entry would have been required for X10.

Deferred Tax Liability	2,250	
Income Tax Expense		450
Retained Earnings		1,800

② The Direct Approach

Exhibit 2.11 presents the consolidated financial statements of Para Corporation as of December 31, X10. The balance of the account from the books of the affiliated companies is shown in brackets. More sophisticated computations are shown in a note.

Exhibit 2.11 • Consolidated Financial Statements of Para Corporation for the Year Ended December 31, X10

Consolidated Income Statement of Para Corporation
Year Ended December 31, X10
(in CU)

Revenues (CU500,000 + CU230,000)	730,000
Sales expenses **(1)**	341,500
Administration expenses (CU200,000 + CU130,000)	330,000
Profit for the year	**58,500**

Consolidated Statement of Financial Position of Para Corporation
December 31, X10
(in CU)

Assets	
Cash (CU40,000 + CU15,000)	55,000
Accounts receivable (CU12,000 + CU50,000)	62,000
Land **(2)**	65,000
Buildings (net) **(3)**	232,500
Goodwill (at acquisition)	10,000
Total assets	**424,500**
Liabilities and equities	
Bank loan (CU25,000 + CU10,000)	35,000
Accounts payable (CU10,000 + CU15,000)	25,000
Bonds payable (Para)	75,000
Share capital (Para)	150,000
Retained earnings **(4)**	139,500
Total liabilities and equities	**424,500**

Consolidated Statement of Changes in Equity of Para Corporation
Year Ended December 31, X10
(in CU)

	Share Capital	Retained Earnings	Total
Balance at January 1, X10	150,000	81,000	231,000
Profit for the year		58,500	58,500
Balance at December 31, X10	**150,000**	**139,500**	**289,500**

---

(1) Sales Expenses — CU

- Parent (Para) — 250,000
- Subsidiary (Rain) — 90,000
- Current-year underdepreciation on Buildings (CU15,000/10) — 1,500

Total — 341,500

---

(2) Land — CU

- Subsidiary (Rain) — 55,000
- Fair value increment at the date of acquisition — 10,000

Total — 65,000

---

(3) Buildings (net) — CU

- Parent (Para) — 200,000
- Subsidiary (Rain) — 25,000
- Unamortized balance of the fair value increment (CU15,000 × 5/10) — 7,500

Total — 232,500

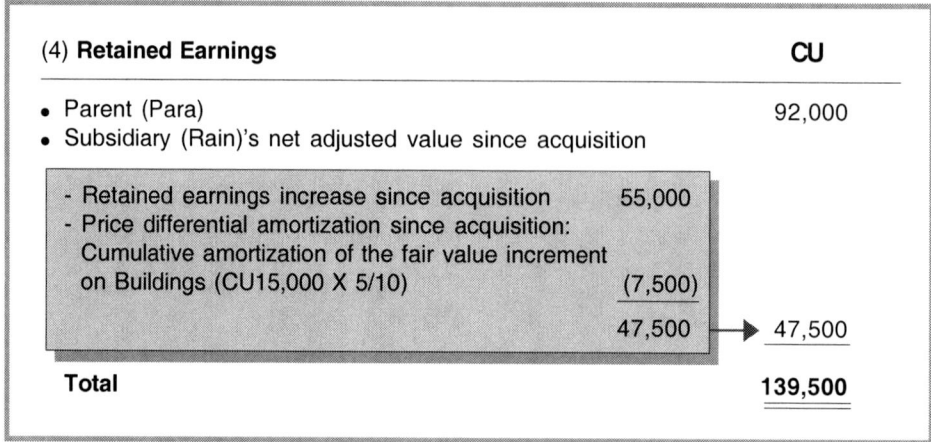

To summarize, Figure 2.2 presents the net adjusted value of Rain as of December 31, X10.

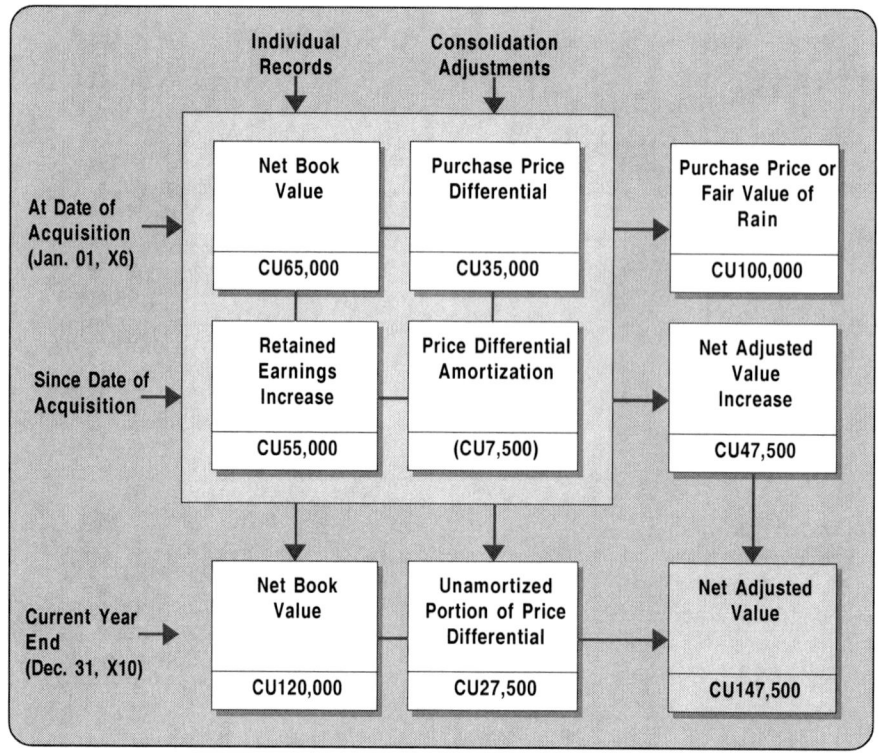

Figure 2.2 • Rain's Net Adjusted Value as of December 31, X10

Summary of the Consolidation Adjustments in Journal Entry Form

At the Date of Acquisition

Elimination of the Investment Account in the Subsidiary

a) Common Shares (B) XX
   Retained Earnings (B) XX
       Investment in B (A) XX
   To eliminate reciprocal investment and equity accounts.

b) Asset-Related Fair Value Increments (B) XX
   Liability-Related Fair Value Decrements (B) XX
   Goodwill (B) XX
   Other assets not recorded by B (B) XX
       Liability-Related Fair Value Increments (B) XX
       Asset-Related Fair Value Decrements (B) XX
       Investment in B (A) XX
   To allocate the price differential so as to account for the subsidiary's fair value at the date of acquisition.

Effect on Income Tax Allocation

Deferred Tax related to fair value increments and decrements must be accounted for at the date of acquisition. Adding this account in the purchase price allocation will have an offsetting effect on Goodwill.

Following the Date of Acquisition		
1. Elimination of the Investment Account in the Subsidiary (Cost Basis)		
a) Common Shares (B)	XX	
Retained Earnings (B)	XX	
Investment in B (A)		XX
To eliminate reciprocal investment and equity accounts at the date of acquisition.		
b) Asset-Related Fair Value Increments (B)	XX	
Liability-Related Fair Value Decrements (B)	XX	
Goodwill (B)	XX	
Other assets not recorded by B (B)	XX	
Liability-Related Fair Value Increments (B)		XX
Asset-Related Fair Value Decrements (B)		XX
Investment in B (A)		XX
To allocate the price differential so as to account for the subsidiary's fair value at the date of acquisition.		
2. Price Differential Amortization/Realization Since Acquisition		
a) Retained Earnings (prior-period amortization)	XX	
Depreciation Expense (current-year amortization)	XX	
Accumulated Depreciation		XX
To amortize any fair value increment (decrement) on depreciable asset (liability).		
Accumulated Depreciation	XX	
Depreciation Expense (current-year amortization)		XX
Retained Earnings (prior-period amortization)		XX
To amortize any fair value decrement (increment) on depreciable asset (liability).		
b) Retained Earnings (if disposal in a prior year)	XX	
Gain or Loss (if disposal in the current year)	XX	
Asset (or liability)		XX
To recognize any unamortized portion of fair value increment (decrement) when related asset (liability) is disposed of.		
Asset (or liability)	XX	
Gain or Loss (if disposal in the current year)		XX
Retained Earnings (if disposal in a prior year)		XX
To recognize any unamortized portion of fair value decrement (increment) when related asset (liability) is disposed of.		
c) Retained Earnings (if impairment in prior years)	XX	
Impairment Loss (if impairment in the current year)	XX	
Goodwill		XX
To account for any goodwill impairment.		

Following the Date of Acquisition (continued...)

Effect on Income Tax Allocation
Deferred Tax related to fair value increments and decrements must be accounted for at the date of acquisition. Following the date of acquisition, any change in temporary differences arising from price differential amortization or realization must be recognized for consolidation purposes. Assuming that a Deferred Tax Liability has been considered at the date of acquisition, the adjustment required in post-acquisition periods to account for the change in temporary differences is journalized below.

Deferred Tax Liability   XX
    Income Tax Expense (current-year)   XX
    Retained Earnings (prior-years)   XX

Chapter 3

Non-Wholly Owned Subsidiaries

Non-Controlling Interest

In this chapter

3.1 Consolidation as of the Date of Acquisition 87

3.2 Consolidation Following the Date of Acquisition 97
    3.2.1 Consolidation of the Statement of Financial Position 99
    3.2.2 Consolidation of the Income Statement 108

✎ Comprehensive Illustration 112
✎ Summary of the Consolidation Adjustments in Journal Entry Form 128

Key Concepts: Non-Wholly Owned Subsidiary; Non-Controlling Interest; Entity Theory; Economic Entity Concept; Implied Purchase Price; Full Fair Value Increments-Decrements; Full Goodwill; Full Goodwill Approach; Partial Goodwill Approach

There is a presumption of control whenever a corporation owns more than 50 percent of the outstanding voting stock of another corporation. Thus, control of all the resources of a corporation can be obtained with less than 100 percent ownership. Lack of total ownership is frequently encountered with foreign subsidiaries as laws of many countries often prohibit outsiders from gaining full control of domestic enterprises. Partial ownership is also inevitable if a few stockholders of the subsidiary have elected to retain their ownership. Business combination achieved under partial ownership has the potential to reduce substantially the consideration given by the acquirer. However, such a situation leads to a new configuration of the combined entity since the controlling shareholder, the parent company, has to come to terms with the minority or the non-controlling shareholders of the subsidiary. On the consolidation front, a *non-wholly owned subsidiary* adds a new complexity as the *non-controlling interest* must be fully recognized in the process.

This chapter illustrates techniques and procedures involved in establishing non-controlling interest in consolidated financial statements. The first part presents the consolidation as of the date of combination. The second part continues the development of the same affiliated companies in a post-acquisition period. In addition to avoiding double-counting and allocating price differential (see prior chapters), treating non-controlling interests represents an extra challenge when consolidating non-wholly owned subsidiaries.

The chapter endorses the view of the economic entity which conceptualizes the parent and subsidiary companies as a single entity for reporting purposes. Accordingly, acquisition-date full fair values of the subsidiary must be recognized for consolidation purposes even though the parent company owns less than 100 percent of the subsidiary's voting stock. Observable full market value of identifiable assets acquired and liabilities assumed are then assigned proportionally between controlling and non-controlling shareholders.

The recording of goodwill under the *economic entity concept* is one of the most controversial of the topics addressed by IASB in the recent years. The 2005 Exposure Draft on Business Combinations supported the view of the *entity theory*. Accordingly, the amount of goodwill had to be determined as if the parent company had acquired 100 percent of the subsidiary's outstanding voting shares. This approach resulted in the consideration of the full fair market value of the subsidiary at date of combination. Full goodwill was then estimated and allocated proportionally between the parent company and the non-controlling interest. This approach is referred to as the *full goodwill approach*.

However, the revised IFRS #3 introduces a choice of measurement basis for non-controlling interest. The non-controlling interest can be measured as the minority shareholders' share of the fair value of the subsidiary's net assets. Since only the parent's share of the subsidiary's goodwill is brought onto the consolidated financial statements, no goodwill is assigned to non-controlling interest. IFRS #3 also allows non-controlling interest to be measured at its fair value at date of acquisition. Fair value might be estimated on the basis of an active market prices for the equity shares not held by the acquirer. Hence, an amount of goodwill might be allocated to non-controlling interest if the fair value of the equity share of the minority shareholders is higher than their share of the fair value of the subsidiary's net assets. The approach adopted by IASB is referred to as the *partial goodwill approach*.

Despite differences regarding the amount of goodwill to be assigned to non-controlling interest, full goodwill and partial goodwill approaches are consistent with the ecomomic entity concept in so far as they both fully represent the full fair market value of the subsidiary's net assets at date of combination. Therefore, to illustrate more clearly the fundamentals underlying the economic entity concept, we first examine a case that does not involve any goodwill. Next, we present a comprehensive illustration that highlights consolidation procedures under the full goodwill and partial goodwill alternatives respectively.

3.1 Consolidation as of the Date of Acquisition

Assume that on January 1, X1, Company A acquired 70 percent of the outstanding voting shares of Company B for CU15,400 cash. The following presents the journal entry on the books of Company A to account for the acquisition.

Company A controls Company B with less than 100 percent ownership. Under the economic entity concept, non-controlling shareholders are viewed as part of the economic entity because the parent company, Company A, controls the decision-making process of the subsidiary, Company B, regardless of the ownership percentage. The affiliation structure of Company A and Company B is diagrammed as follows.

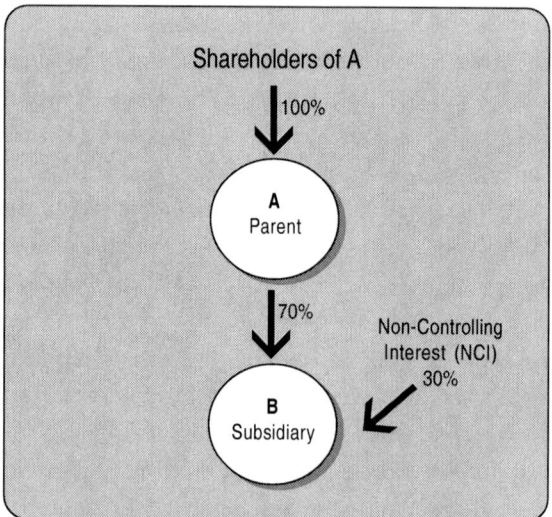

The condensed statements of financial position of the affiliated companies as of the date of combination are reproduced in Exhibit 3.1

Exhibit 3.1 • Statements of Financial Position of Company A and Company B at the Date of Acquisition

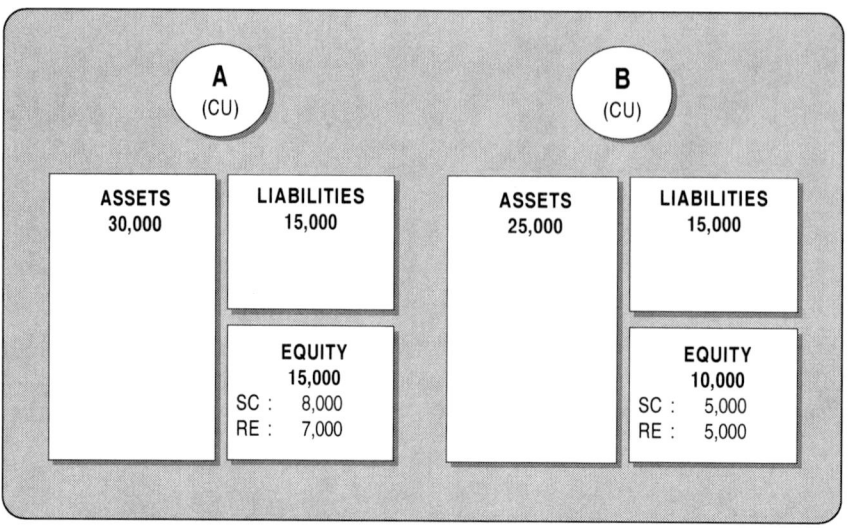

On the date of combination, the identifiable assets and liabilities of Company B had fair values that were equal to their carrying values except for capital assets which had a fair value CU12,000 greater than their net book value.

Note...

The basic information for this illustration is the same as the one provided in chapter 2, except that Company A now only acquired 70 percent of Company B's voting stock instead of 100 percent. Consequently, the consideration given is lower, that is, CU15,400 instead of CU22,000.

Under the economic entity concept, consolidated statements are prepared from the standpoint of the consolidated entity. As a result, controlling and non-controlling shareholders are considered as two separate groups, each having an equity in the combined entity. Consistent with this view, the full market value of the subsidiary must be estimated and included in the consolidated statement of financial position.

In the case of Company A, the process of imputing the total market value can simply be accomplished by dividing the price paid (CU15,400) by the percentage acquired (70 percent). Therefore, the *implied purchase price* for all Company B's voting stock would be CU22,000 (CU15,400/0.70). Once the total market value has been calculated, the implied purchase price can be allocated to *full fair value increments-decrements* and *full goodwill* as follows:

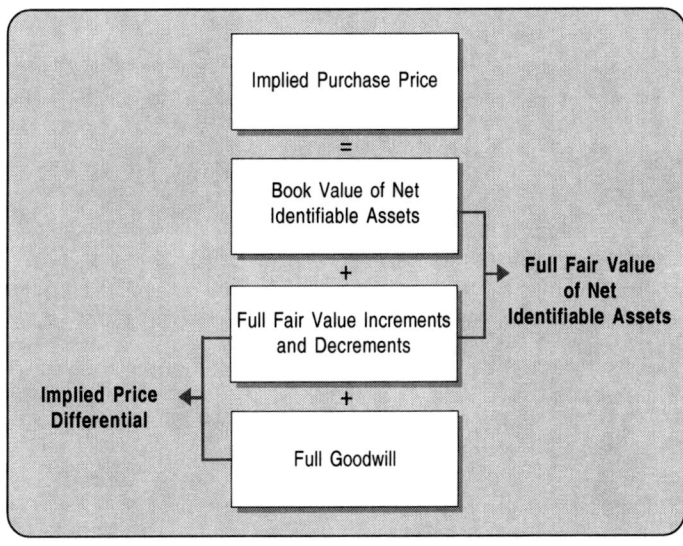

Exhibit 3.2 presents the allocation of the implied purchase price of CU22,000.

Exhibit 3.2 • Non-Wholly Owned Subsidiary - Allocation of the Implied Purchase Price as of January 1, X1

	Implied (100%) CU	A (70%) CU	Minority (30%) CU
Cost of investment in B	22,000	15,400	6,600
Shareholders' equity of B at the date of acquisition:			
Share capital 5,000			
Retained earnings 5,000	10,000	7,000	3,000
Price differential	12,000	8,400	3,600
Fair value increment - Capital assets	(12,000)	(8,400)	(3,600)
Goodwill	—	—	—

 Note...

The implied purchase price (CU22,000) is the same as the price paid by Company A to acquire 100 percent of the outstanding voting stock of Company B, a case illustrated in Chapter 2. In both scenarios, a positive price differential of CU12,000 has been computed and assigned to Capital Assets so as to reflect the full fair value of Company B at the date of combination. However, now that Company B is partially owned by Company A, the implied purchase price must be allocated proportionally between Company A (CU22,000 X 70% = CU15,400) and the non-controlling shareholders (CU22,000 X 30% = CU6,600).

Since there is no goodwill, the implied purchase price is equal to the full fair value of the subsidiary's identifiable net assets at the date of acquisition.

Procedures involved in the consolidation of Company A as of the date of combination are illustrated in the next sections under the following approaches :

①   The Visual Approach;

②   The Worksheet Approach;

③   The Direct Approach.

Chapter 3 Non-Wholly Owned Subsidiaries

① The Visual Approach

The figures below portray the transformation of the affiliated companies' statements of financial position through the consolidation process of Company A as of January 1, X1.

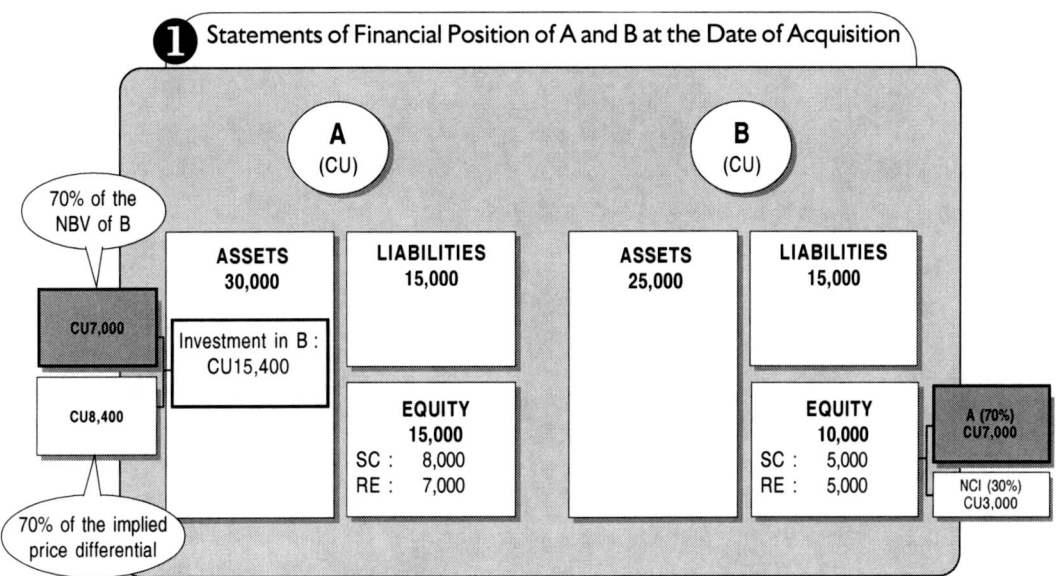

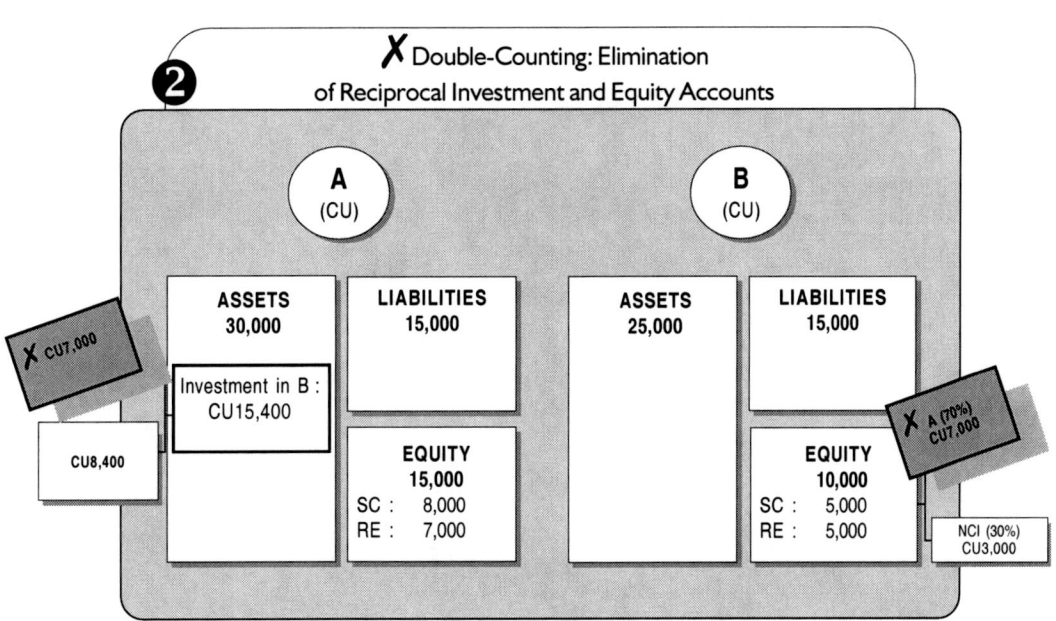

92 Part I Controlling Ownership

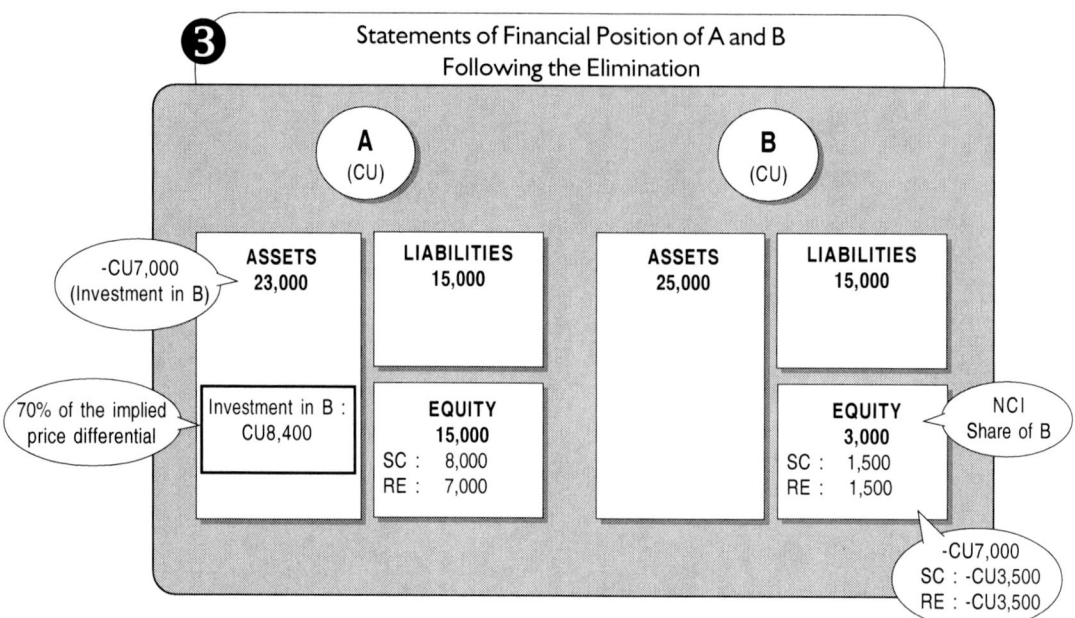

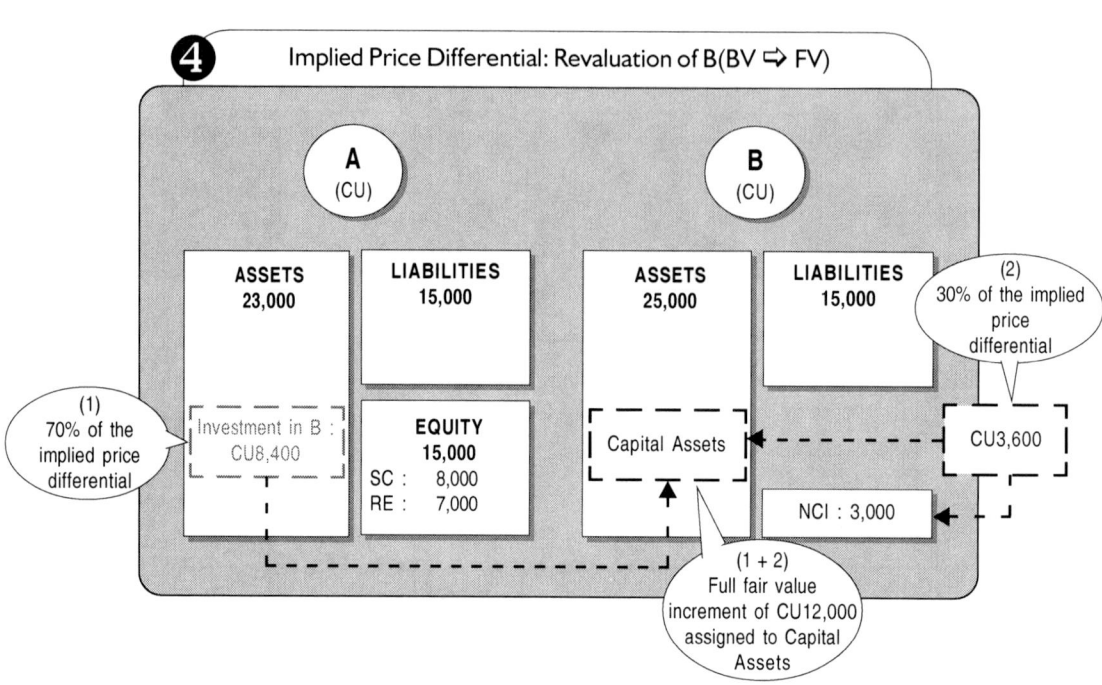

Chapter 3 Non-Wholly Owned Subsidiaries

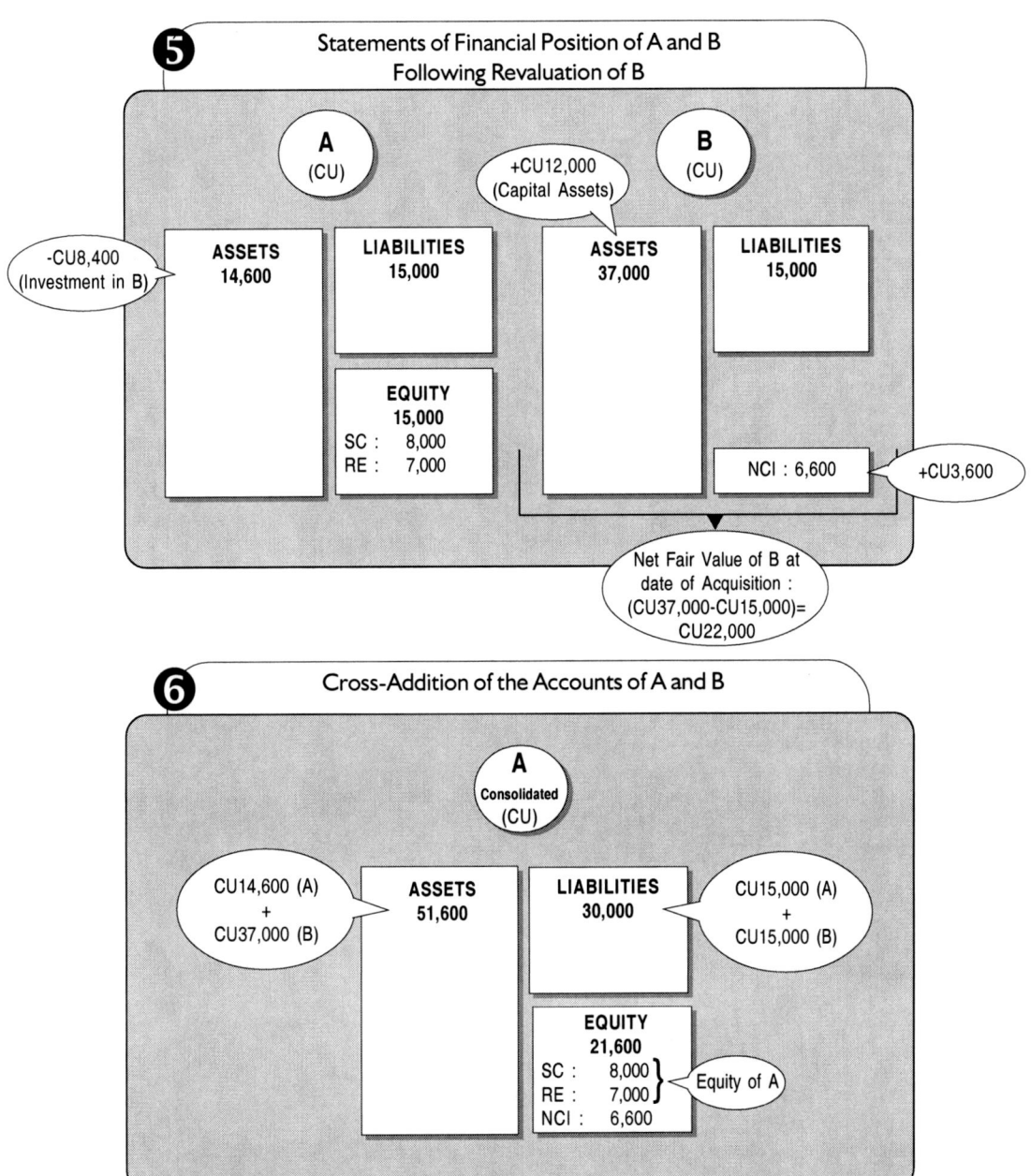

The subsidiary's assets and liabilities are consolidated at their fair values, and majority and minority interests in those net assets are valued consistently. Full fair value of Company B at the date of combination (CU22,000) has been assigned to the non-controlling interest (CU6,600) by allocating first, 30 percent of the net book value of Company B at the date of acquisition (CU10,000 X 30% = CU3,000; see figure #1), and second, 30 percent of the implied price differential (full fair value increment on Capital Assets of CU12,000 X 30% = CU3,600; see figure #4). Non-Controlling Interest must be displayed and labeled in the consolidated stockholders' equity.

Thirty percent of the full market value being allocated to non-controlling interest, the fair value of Company B as a whole can thus be added to the book value of Company A in the consolidation process. This approach is consistent with the economic entity model which results in the recognition of 100 percent of the acquisition-date fair value of the acquiree even though the acquirer holds less than 100 percent of the equity interest of the acquiree. Company A legally owns 70 percent of the voting stock of Company B, but in reality, exercises absolute control over Company B's resources. Conceptually, measuring and recognizing the fair value of Company B as a whole is consistent with reporting the substance rather than the form of business combinations.

② The Worksheet Approach

The consolidation entries required to combine Company A and Company B as of January 1, X1, are shown below along with the consolidation worksheet.

1a

Elimination of reciprocal investment and equity accounts (70 percent) so as to avoid double-counting

Common Shares (B)	3,500	
Retained Earnings (B)	3,500	
Investment in B (A)		7,000

1b

Allocation of the implied price differential (70 percent)

Capital Assets (B)	8,400	
Investment in B (A)		8,400

Chapter 3 Non-Wholly Owned Subsidiaries

2

Allocation of 30 percent of the implied purchase price to non-controlling interest

Common Shares (B)	1,500
Retained Earnings (B)	1,500
Capital Assets (B)	3,600
Non-Controlling Interest	6,600

30% [CU10,000 (B's NBV) + CU12,000 (implied price differential)] = CU6,600

Consolidation Worksheet

	A (CU)	B (CU)	Eliminations Adjustments (CU)	Consolidated (CU)
ASSETS				
Investment in B	15,400		(7,000) (1a) (8,400) (1b)	–
Other identifiable assets	14,600	25,000	8,400 (1b) 3,600 (2)	51,600
	30,000	25,000		51,600
LIABILITIES	15,000	15,000		30,000
EQUITY				
Common shares	8,000	5,000	(3,500) (1a) (1,500) (2)	8,000
Retained earnings	7,000	5,000	(3,500) (1a) (1,500) (2)	7,000
Non-controlling interest			6,600 (2)	6,600
	30,000	25,000		51,600

Consistent with the consolidation procedures introduced for a wholly owned subsidiary (see chapter 2), the investment account of A in B is eliminated via two entries. The first aims at avoiding double-counting (consolidation entry #1a), the second, at allocating 70 percent of the implied price differential (consolidation entry #1b). Additionally, since Company B is a non-wholly owned subsidiary, 30 percent of the fair value of Company B as a whole is assigned to the non-controlling interest (consolidation entry #2).

③ The Direct Approach

The following presents the independent computation of Company A's consolidated total assets, total liabilities and shareholders' equity balances as of the date of combination.

Assets	CU
• Parent (A) (excluding the investment in B)	14,600
• Subsidiary (B)	25,000
• Full fair value increment on Capital Assets at acquisition	12,000
Total	**51,600**

Liabilities	CU
• Parent (A)	15,000
• Subsidiary (B)	15,000
Total	**30,000**

Common Shares	CU
Parent (A) balance only as of January 1, X1	**8,000**

Retained Earnings	CU
Parent (A) balance only as of January 1, X1	**7,000**

Non-Controlling Interest — CU

- 30 percent of the implied purchase price or the full fair value of the subsidiary (B) as of January 1, X1

- Net book value at acquisition	10,000
- Implied price differential	12,000
	22,000

22,000 × 30% → **6,600**

> **Effect on Income Tax Allocation**
>
> Consideration of the full fair value increment on capital assets (CU12,000) gives rise to a temporary difference for consolidation purposes. Assuming a corporate tax rate of 30 percent, this temporary difference is equivalent to a Deferred Tax Liability of CU3,600 (CU12,000 X 30%). Increasing Company B's liabilities by CU3,600 at the date of acquisition forces the excess purchase price over Company B's net book value to go up, thereby increasing Goodwill by CU3,600.

3.2 Consolidation Following the Date of Acquisition

To analyze the full range of accounting complexities created by a non-wholly owned subsidiary, let's continue the development of Company A assuming that we are now five years subsequent to the date of combination. The condensed financial statements of the affiliated companies for the period ended December 31, X5, appear in Exhibit 3.3.

If we assume that Company A reports its investment in Company B on the cost basis, the balance of the investment account as of December 31, X5, will still be shown at CU15,400, that is, the initial price paid five years ago by Company A to acquire 70 percent of Company B's outstanding voting stock.

In addition, recall that a full fair value increment of CU12,000 has been assigned to capital assets at the date of combination. Therefore, depreciation expense on capital assets carried on Company B's records is undervalued for consolidation purposes. The remaining useful life of these assets from the date of acquisition being 12 years, and the depreciation expense being calculated on a straight-line basis, the annual understatement of depreciation expense amounts to CU1,000 (CU12,000 over 12 years). The details of this computation are provided in Chapter 2 (see Exhibit 2.5). The cumulative underdepreciation as of December 31, X5, is CU5,000 which consists of an annual underdepreciation of CU1,000 over 5 years (from X1 through X5, inclusive).

Exhibit 3.3 • Financial Statements of Company A and Company B for the Year Ended December 31, X5

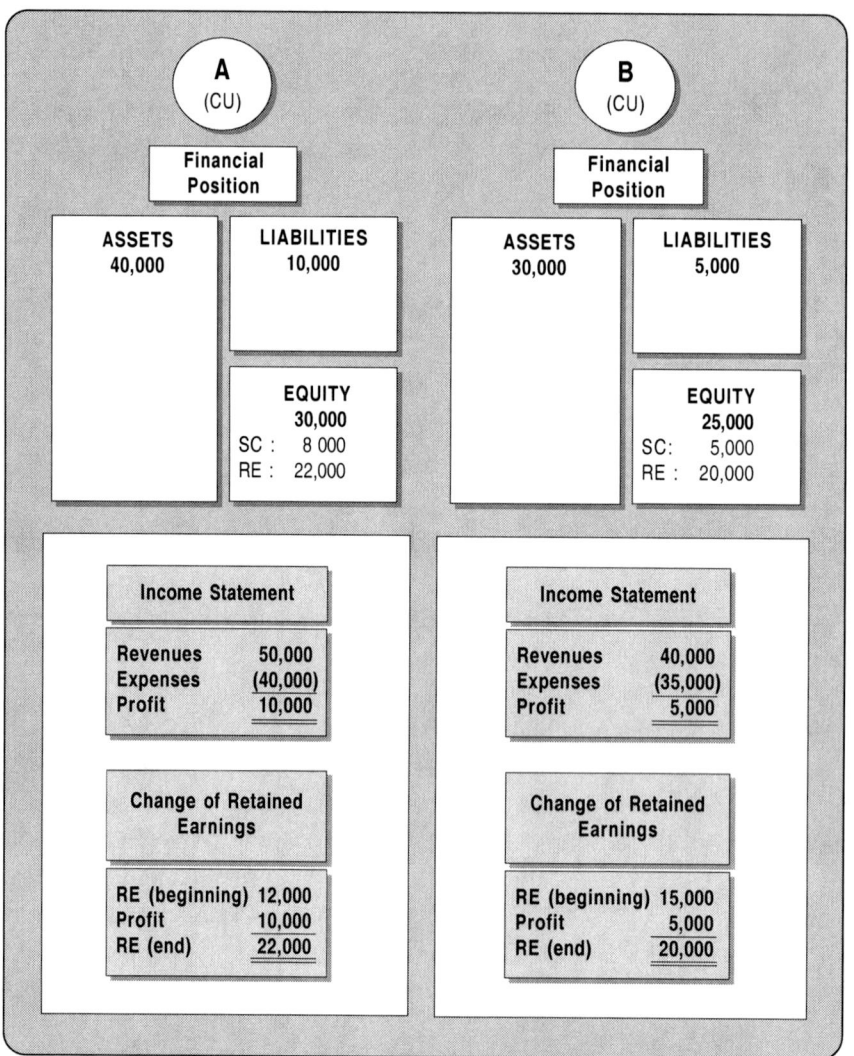

The net book value of Company B has increased by CU15,000 since acquisition as shown in Exhibit 3.4. This increase which consists of the change of Company B's Retained Earnings since the date of combination (CU20,000 - CU5,000 = CU15,000) must be allocated proportionally between Company A (CU15,000 X 70% = CU10,500) and the minority shareholders (CU15,000 X 30% = CU4,500).

Exhibit 3.4 • Net Book Value Increase of Company B Since Acquisition

Equity of B	Balance at Jan. 1, X1 (CU)	Change (CU)	Balance at Dec. 31, X5 (CU)
Common Shares	5,000	-	5,000
Retained Earnings	5,000	15,000	20,000
Total	10,000	15,000	25,000
Allocation of B's Equity			
Parent (A) (70 %)	7,000	10,500	17,500
Non-Controlling Interest (30 %)	3,000	4,500	7,500
Total	10,000	15,000	25,000

The consolidation process of the statement of financial position of Company A at December 31, X5, is presented using the following:

① The Visual Approach;

② The Worksheet Approach;

③ The Direct Approach.

The procedural steps involved in the consolidation of the income statement are introduced in a separate section.

3.2.1 Consolidation of the Statement of Financial Position

① The visual approach

The following figures illustrate the consolidation process of Company A at December 31, X5.

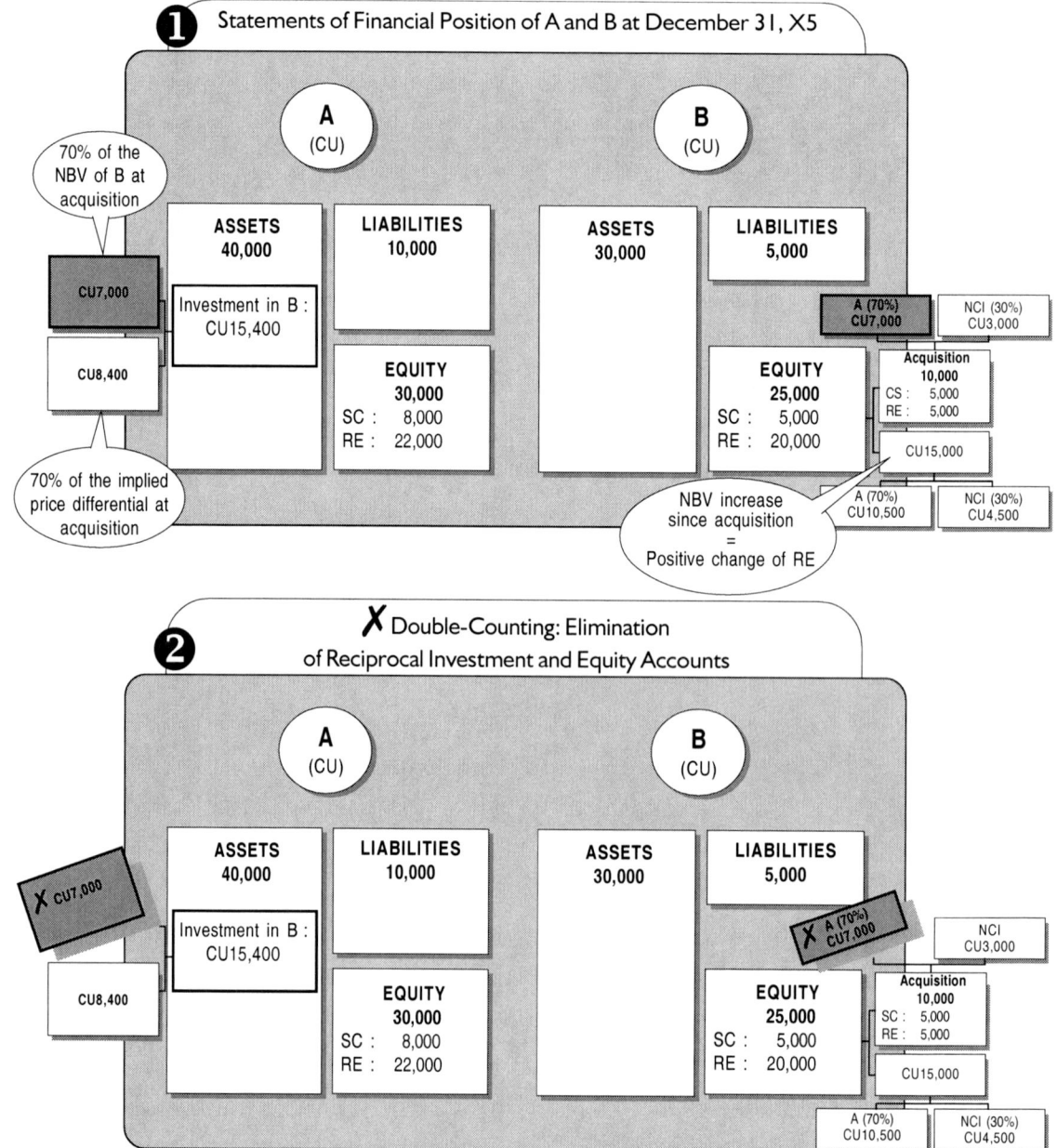

Chapter 3 Non-Wholly Owned Subsidiaries

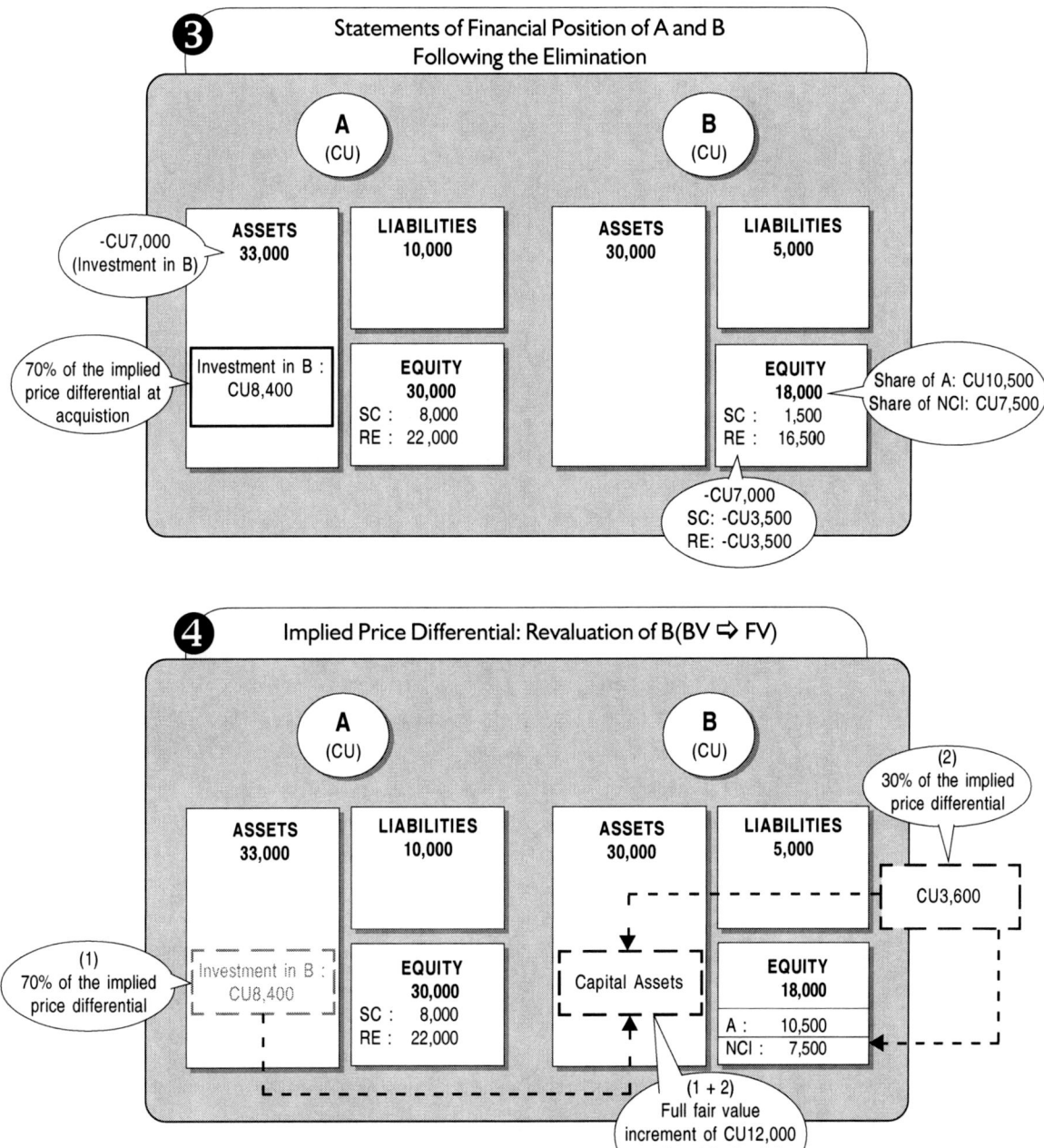

102 Part I Controlling Ownership

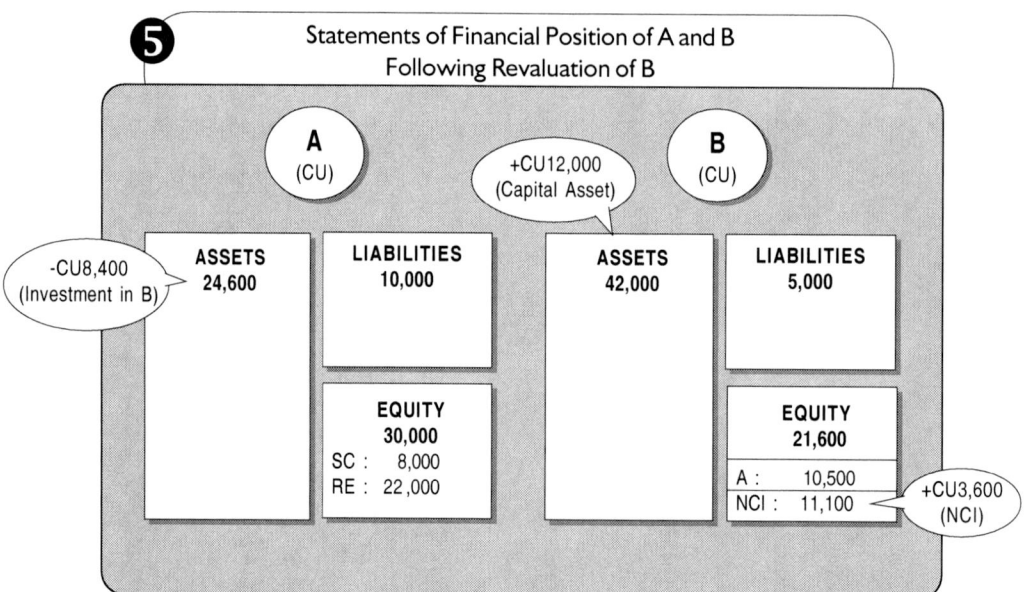

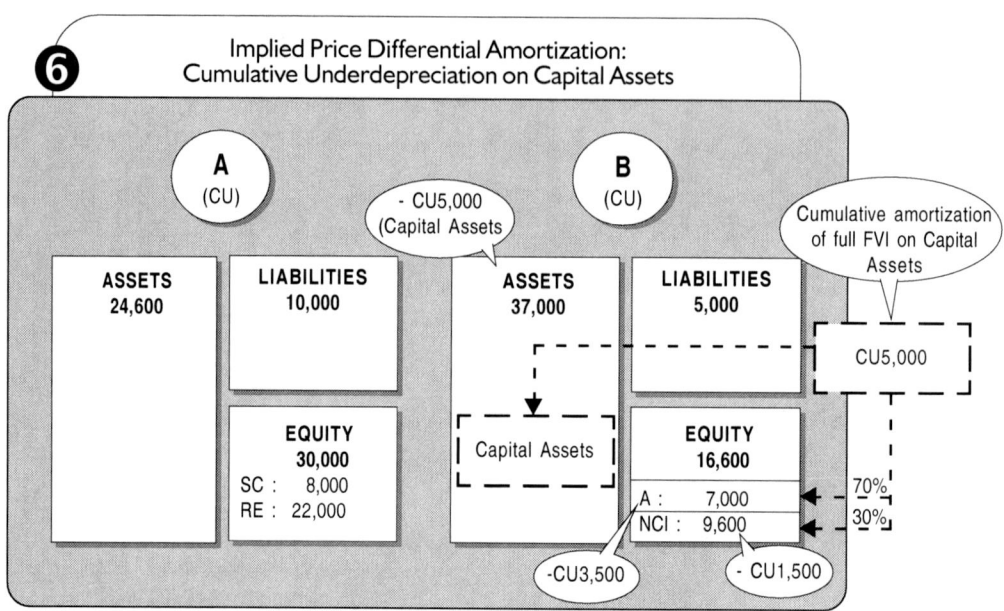

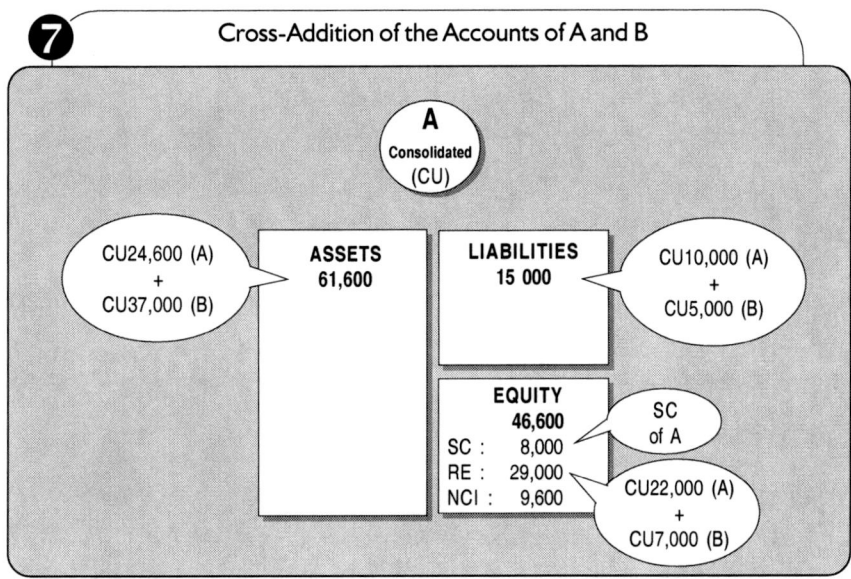

Figure 3.1 shows the different components of Company B's net adjusted value or consolidated value at the end of the consolidation process.

Company B's net adjusted value has been assigned consistently between Company A and the minority shareholders. More precisely, the balance of CU9,600 attributed to Non-Controlling Interest at the end of the consolidation process consists of 30 percent of Company B's net adjusted value as of December 31, X5 (CU32,000 X 30% = CU9,600) and includes the following four components:

1- 30 percent of the net book value of Company B at the date of acquisition
 (CU10,000 X 30% = CU3,000; see figure #1 from the visual approach),
2- Plus 30 percent of Company B's retained earnings increase since acquisition
 (CU15,000 X 30% = CU4,500; see figure #1),
3- Plus 30 percent of the implied purchase price differential
 (CU12,000 X 30% = CU3,600; see figure #4),
4- Less 30 percent of the implied price differential amortization since acquisition
 (CU5,000 X 30% = CU1,500; see figure #6).

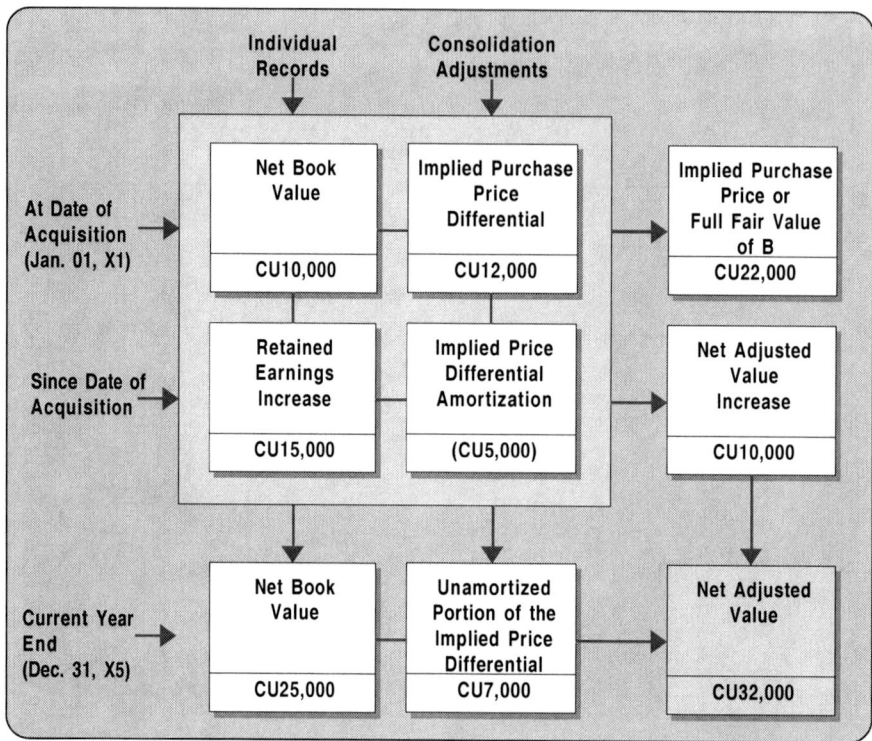

Figure 3.1 • Company B's Net Adjusted Value as of December 31, X5

The value of CU9,600 assigned to the non-controlling interest account is also equivalent to 30 percent of the implied purchase price (CU22,000 X 30% = CU6,600) plus 30 percent of Company B's net adjusted value since acquisition (CU10,000 X 30% = CU3,000). This value also consists of 30 percent of the net book value of Company B as of December 31, X5 (CU25,000 X 30% = CU7,500) plus 30 percent of the unamortized portion of the implied price differential at the end of the accounting period (CU7,000 X 30% = CU2,100).

② The Worksheet Approach

The consolidation worksheet of Company A for the year ending December 31, X5, is shown next along with the consolidation entries.

Chapter 3 Non-Wholly Owned Subsidiaries

Consolidation Worksheet

	A (CU)	B (CU)	Eliminations Adjustments (CU)	Consolidated (CU)
ASSETS				
Investment in B	15,400		(7,000) (1a) (8,400) (1b)	-
Other identifiable assets	24,600	30,000	8,400 (1b) (5,000) (2) 3,600 (3a)	61,600
	40,000	**30,000**		**61,600**
LIABILITIES	10,000	5,000		15,000
EQUITY				
Common shares	8,000	5,000	(3,500) (1a) (1,500) (3a)	8,000
Retained earnings	22,000	20,000	(3,500) (1a) (5,000) (2) (1,500) (3a) (3,000) (3b)	29,000
Non-controlling interest			6,600 (3a) 3,000 (3b)	9,600
	40,000	**30,000**		**61,600**

1a

Elimination of reciprocal investment and equity accounts (70 percent) at the date of acquisition so as to avoid double-counting

Common Shares (B)	3,500	
Retained Earnings (B)	3,500	
Investment inB (A)		7,000

1b

Allocation of the implied price differential (70 percent)

Capital Assets (B)	8 400	
Investment in B (A)		8 400

2

Implied price differential amortization since acquisition: Amortization of the full fair value increment on Capital Assets since acquisition

Retained Earnings (B)	5,000	
Accumulated Depreciation - Capital Assets (B)		5,000

(CU12,000 X 5/12) = CU5,000

3a

Allocation of 30 percent of the implied purchase price to non-controlling interest

Common Shares (B)	1,500	
Retained Earnings (B)	1,500	
Capital Assets (B)	3,600	
Non-Controlling Interest		6,600

30% [CU10,000 (B's net book value at acquisition) + CU12,000 (implied price differential)] = CU6,600

3b

Allocation of 30 percent of B's net adjusted value since acquisition to non-controlling interest

Retained Earnings (B)	3,000	
Non-Controlling Interest		3,000

30% [CU15,000 (B's retained earnings increase since acquisition) - CU5,000 (cumulative amortization of the full FVI on Capital Assets)] = CU3,000

Worksheet entries #1a, #1b and #3a are the same whether consolidated statement of financial position of Company A is prepared at the date of acquisition or for time periods subsequent to acquisition. However, in post-acquisition consolidations, adjustment #2 is added to account for the implied price differential amortization since acquisition (cumulative amortization of the full fair value increment on Capital Assets). Adjustment #3b is also required in order to assign to non-controlling shareholders their share of Company B's net adjusted value increase since acquisition.

Chapter 3 Non-Wholly Owned Subsidiaries

The presence of a non-controlling interest does not create a significant number of changes in the consolidation process since the acquisition-date full fair market value of the acquiree is first recognized regardless of whether the parent has full or partial control. Worksheet adjustment #2 is the same whether Company B is wholly owned or non-wholly owned. However, since Company B is partially owned by Company A, non-controlling interest must be recognized along the way. This is achieved by attributing to the minority interest its share of, first, the implied purchase price at the date of combination (adjustment #3a), and second, the net adjusted value of the subsidiary since the date of combination (adjustment #3b).

③ The Direct Approach

The following presents the independent computation of consolidated total assets, total liabilities and equity balances of Company A as of December 31, X5.

Assets	CU
• Parent (A)(excluding the investment in B)	24,600
• Subsidiary (B)	30,000
• Unamortized balance of the full fair value increment on Capital Assets (CU12,000 X 7/12)	7,000
Total	**61,600**

Liabilities	CU
• Parent (A)	10,000
• Subsidiary (B)	5,000
Total	**15,000**

Common Shares	CU
Parent (A) balance only as of December 31, X5	**8,000**

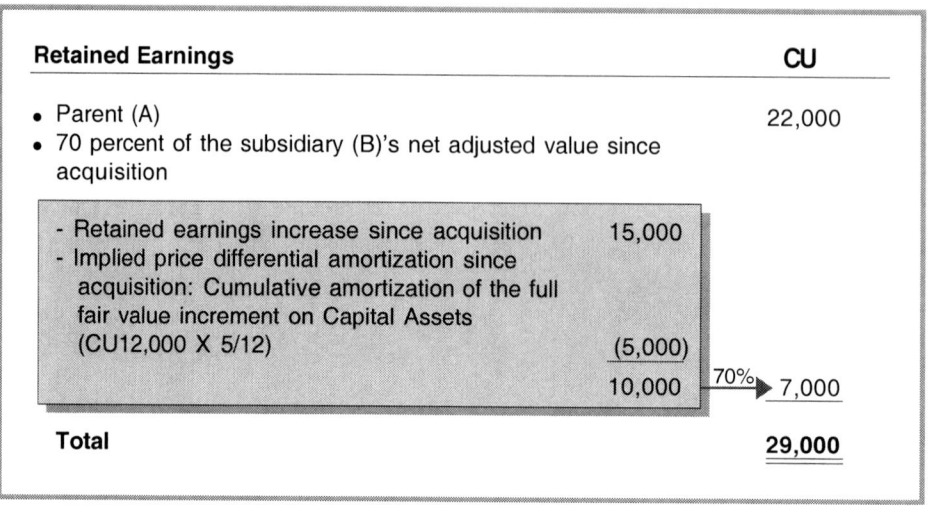

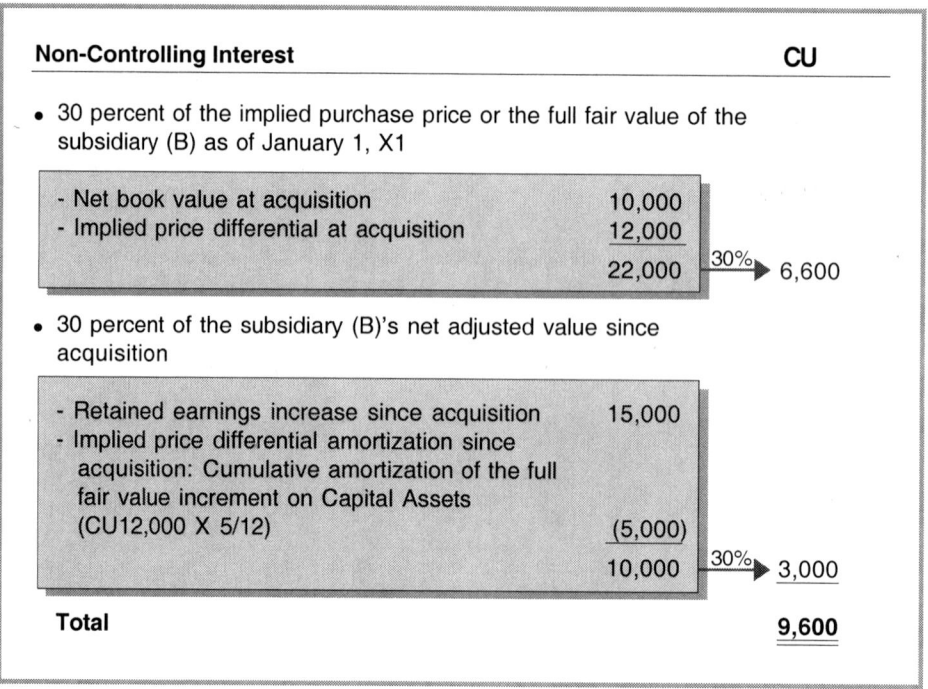

3.2.2 Consolidation of the Income Statement

The approach to consolidate the income statement is similar to the one illustrated in chapter 2. Recall that before combining all the revenue and expense balances of Company B and Company A, the acquisition-date full fair value increment of CU12,000 on Capital Assets must be amortized in order to correct the CU1,000 current-year underdepreciation. More

precisely, the overall underdepreciation on capital assets since acquisition (X1- X5) amounts to CU5,000 and must be allocated to:
- Prior years (X1-X4) while decreasing the opening balance of Retained Earnings by CU4,000 (CU1,000 X 4 years).
- Current year (X5) while increasing Depreciation Expense by CU1, 000.

Therefore, consolidation entry #2 previously introduced when preparing the consolidated statement of financial position of Company A must be broken down as the following:

Retained Earnings (beginning)	4,000
Depreciation Expense (current year)	1,000
Accumulated Depreciation - Capital Assets	5,000

Once this adjustment is entered into the consolidation process, cross-addition of the income statement accounts of Company A and Company B will provide the consolidated information. Thus, the consolidated profit for the year must be allocated to majority and minority interests as shown below.

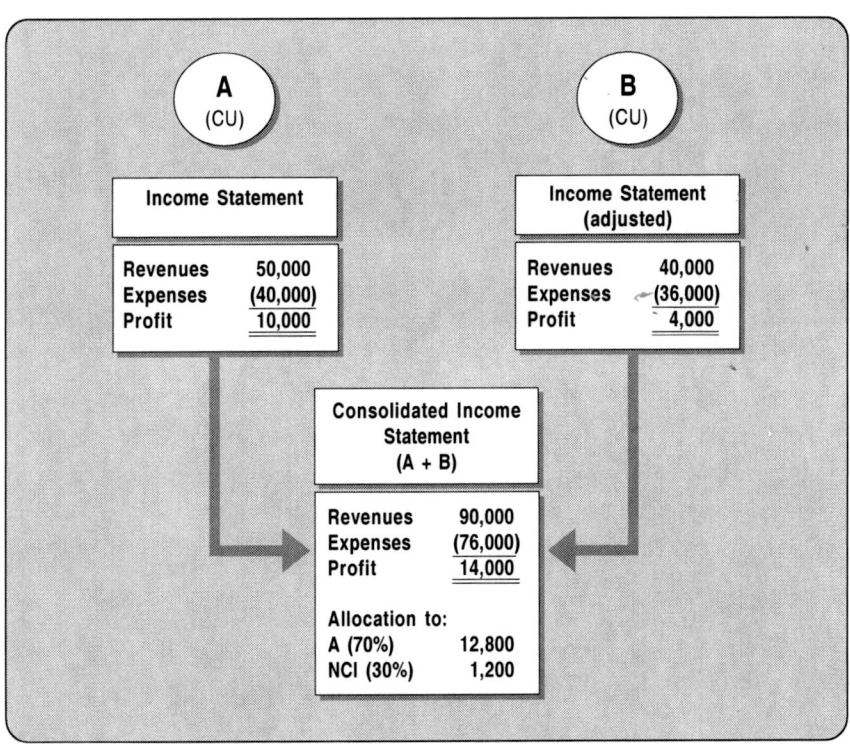

♦ Consolidated Profit for the Year		CU
• A's profit		10,000
• B's adjusted profit:		
- B's profit	5,000	
- Implied price differential amortization:		
Current-year underdepreciation on Capital		
Assets (CU12,000/12)	(1,000)	4,000
Total		14,000

Consolidated Profit Allocated to Non-Controlling Interest	CU
30 percent of B's adjusted profit (CU4,000 X 30%)	1,200

Consolidated Profit Allocated to A	CU
• A's profit	10,000
• 70 percent of B's adjusted profit (CU4,000 X 70%)	2,800
Total	12,800

Consolidated profit (CU14,000) is the same regardless of whether Company A owns 100 percent or 70 percent of Company B's voting stock (see chapter 2). In either case, since Company A controls all the resources of Company B, 100 percent of the financial activities and operations of the subsidiary is accounted for in the consolidation process. However, when partial control ownership exists, the consolidated profit of the subsidiary is allocated consistently between minority and majority interests. Reporting non-controlling interest's share of consolidated profit as an allocation rather than an expense is consistent with the entity approach which views majority and minority shareholders as two separate groups, each having an interest in the consolidated entity.

Effect on Income Tax Allocation

As the full fair value increment on Capital Assets (CU12,000) is being amortized, the temporary difference that must have been recognized at the date of acquisition (CU12,000 X 30% tax rate = CU3,600) is progressively consumed. More precisely, the annual amortization of the full fair value increment being CU1,000 (CU12,000/12 years), Deferred Tax Liability must be reduced by CU300 every year (CU1,000 X 30% tax rate or CU3,600/12 years) with an offsetting effect on Income Tax Expense. The cumulative impact of this tax allocation since acquisition is CU1,500 (CU300 X 5 years), that is, CU1,200 for prior-periods (X1 through X4, inclusive) and CU300 for the current period (X5). The following presents the additional consolidation entry that would have been required had the income tax allocation been considered.

Deferred Tax Liability	1,500	
Income Tax Expense		300
Retained Earnings		1,200

Comprehensive Illustration

Basic Information

Let's return to the acquisition of Rain Enterprise by Para Corporation (see Comprehensive Illustration in chapter 2), and assume that, on January 1, X6, Para Corporation acquired 60 percent (instead of 100 percent) of the outstanding voting stock of Rain Enterprise for CU60,000 (instead of CU100,000).

Basic information related to this acquisition remains the same. Recall that, on the date of acquisition, the identifiable assets and liabilities of Rain Enterprise had fair values that were equal to their carrying values except for land and buildings, which had a fair value of CU10,000 and CU15,000, respectively, greater than their carrying values. The net book value of Rain at the date of combination was CU65,000 and was made up of Share Capital of CU55,000 (Common Shares) and Retained Earnings of CU10,000. From the date of acquisition, buildings had a remaining useful life of 10 years. Both companies use the straight-line method to calculate all depreciation and amortization. You are asked to consolidate the financial statements of Para Corporation for the year ended December 31, X10, that is, five years subsequent to acquisition.

Exhibit 3.5 presents the financial statements of Para Corporation and Rain Enterprise for the year ended December 31, X10.

Exhibit 3.5 • Financial Statements of Para Corporation and Rain Enterprise for the Year Ended December 31, X10

Income Statements
Year Ended December 31, X10
(in CU)

	Para	Rain
Sales	500,000	230,000
Sales expenses	250,000	90,000
Administration expenses	200,000	130,000
Profit for the year	**50,000**	**10,000**

Chapter 3 Non-Wholly Owned Subsidiaries

Statements of Financial Position
December 31, X10
(in CU)

	Para	Rain
Assets		
Cash	80,000	15,000
Accounts receivable	12,000	50,000
Land		55,000
Buildings (net)	200,000	25,000
Investment in Rain	60,000	
Total assets	**352,000**	**145,000**
Liabilities and equities		
Bank loan	25,000	10,000
Accounts payable	10,000	15,000
Bonds payable	75,000	
Share capital	150,000	55,000
Retained earnings	92,000	65,000
Total liabilities and equities	**352,000**	**145,000**

Statements of Changes in Equity
Year Ended December 31, X10
(in CU)

	Para			Rain		
	Share Capital	Retained Earnings	Total	Share Capital	Retained Earnings	Total
Balance at January 1, X10	150,000	42,000	192,000	55,000	55,000	110,000
Profit for the year		50,000	50,000		10,000	10,000
Balance at December 31, X10	150,000	92,000	242,000	55,000	65,000	120,000

Since Para applies the cost method of accounting for its investment in Rain, the value of the investment account has not been revised since acquisition and, therefore, is still shown at CU60,000 (purchase price) at the end of the current period.

The net book value of Rain has increased by CU55,000 since acquisition. This amount is reflected in the change of Retained Earnings from January 1, X6 (CU10,000) to December 31,

X10 (CU65,000). Rain's value increase since acquisition will be allocated to Para (CU55,000 X 60% = CU33,000) and non-controlling interest (CU55,000 X 40% = CU22,000) in the consolidation process after proper adjustments are made.

1- Full Goodwill Approach

Under the economic unit-full goodwill concept, full fair market value must be allocated to both the parent company and the controlling interest. Thus, implied purchase price or imputed purchase price of 100 percent ownership should first be calculated. If we assume that Para paid no control premium to acquire Rain, the imputed total value can simply be obtained by dividing the actual purchase price (CU60,000) by the percentage ownership acquired (60 percent). Therefore, the implied purchase price is CU100,000 (CU60,000/0.60). The allocation of the implied purchase price is shown in Exhibit 3.6.

Exhibit 3.6 • Acquisition of 60 percent of the Outstanding Voting Stock of Rain by Para on January 1, X6 - Allocation of the Implied Purchase Price

	Implied (100%) CU	Para (60%) CU	Minority (40%) CU
Cost of investment in Rain	100,000	60,000	40,000
Shareholders' equity of Rain at the date of acquisition:			
Share capital 55,000			
Retained earnings 10,000	65,000	39,000	26,000
Price differential	35,000	21,000	14,000
Fair value increments:			
Land	(10,000)	(6,000)	(4,000)
Buildings	(15,000)	(9,000)	(6,000)
Goodwill	10,000	6,000	4,000

Goodwill has not been impaired since acquisition allowing its full value (CU10,000) to be recognized in the consolidated statement of financial position as of December 31, X10. Furthermore, the consolidated balance of land and buildings must be increased by CU10,000 and CU15,000, respectively, to account for their full estimated market value at the date of combination. Since the land has not been sold by Rain, no further adjustments are required. However, the full fair value increment on buildings must be amortized over the remaining useful life of the asset (10 years) so as to adjust for the annual underdepreciation of CU1,500 (CU15,000/10 = CU1,500).

The implied price differential amortization schedule is displayed in Exhibit 3.7.

Exhibit 3.7 • Consolidation of the Financial Statements of Para Corporation - Implied Price Differential Amortization Schedule

Items	Implied Price Differential Balance at Acquisition (CU)	Amortization Prior Years (X6-X9) (CU)	Amortization Current Year (X10) (CU)	Unamortized Excess at Dec. 31, X10 (CU)
Land	10,000	-	-	10,000
Buildings	15,000	6,000	1,500	7,500
Goodwill	10,000	-	-	10,000
Total	**35,000**	**6,000**	**1,500**	**27,500**
Allocation to:				
Para (60%)	21,000	3,600	900	16,500
Minority (40%)	14,000	2,400	600	11,000

The cumulative underdepreciation on buildings since acquisition is CU7,500 or CU6,000 from X6 through X9, inclusive (prior years) and CU1,500 for X10 (current year). The unamortized balance of the full fair value increment on buildings as of December 31, X10, is CU7,500. The full fair value increment on land (CU10,000) and the full amount assigned to goodwill at the date of acquisition (CU10,000) remain unchanged. Recognition and amortization of the implied price differential must be allocated in the consolidation process to Para (60 percent) and non-controlling interest (40 percent).

 Note...

The determination of the implied purchase price is obtained through the practice of imputing a total subsidiary valuation on the basis of the price paid by the parent company for its majority ownership. This treatment is appealing when the parent acquires essentially all the subsidiary's outstanding voting stock for cash. If only a slim majority is acquired, the approach is still acceptable if the price paid by the buyer for the controlling share is the same as the price that the buyer would have paid to the remaining minority shareholders. Such a condition generally applies to jurisdictions offering good protection to minority shareholders.

> **What If...**
>
> If the price paid for the controlling block is inflated, in other words, if a *control premium* is paid by the buyer, the amount of goodwill allocated to non-controlling interest can not be proportional to the goodwill included in the buyer's acquisition cost. For example, assume that the fair value of Rain as a whole is CU97,000 instead of CU100,000 because a control premium has been paid by Para to acquire the control of Rain. Hence, full goodwill will be CU7,000 rather than CU10,000. If goodwill assigned to Para is CU6,000 as previously determined (see Exhibit 3.6), this leaves CU1,000 as goodwill attributable to non-controlling interest (instead of CU4,000).

Consolidation of Financial Statements

The following illustrates the consolidation process of Para Corporation as of December 31, X10, using:

① The Worksheet Approach;

② The Direct Approach.

① The Worksheet Approach

The consolidation entries required for the preparation of the consolidated information of Para Corporation as of December 31, X10, are listed below.

1a

Elimination of reciprocal investment and equity accounts (60 percent) at the date of acquisition so as to avoid double-counting

Common Shares (Rain)	33,000	
Retained Earnings (Rain)	6,000	
Investment in Rain (Para)		39,000

1b

Allocation of the implied price differential (60 percent)

Land (Rain)	6,000	
Buildings (Rain)	9,000	
Goodwill (Rain)	6,000	
Investment in Rain (Para)		21,000

2

Implied price differential amortization since acquisition: Amortization of the full fair value increment on Buildings since acquisition

Retained Earnings (Rain)	6,000	
Depreciation Expense (Rain)	1,500	
Accumulated Depreciation - Buildings (Rain)		7,500

(CU15,000 X 5/10) = CU7,500

The overall underdepreciation of CU7,500 on buildings since acquisition (X6-X10) has been allocated as follows (see Exhibit 3.7):

▸ Prior years (X6-X9) while decreasing the opening balance of Retained Earnings by CU6,000 (CU1,500 X 4 years).

▸ Current year (X10) while increasing Depreciation Expense by CU1,500.

3a

Allocation of 40 percent of the implied purchase price to non-controlling interest

Common Shares (Rain)	22,000	
Retained Earnings (Rain)	4,000	
Land (Rain)	4,000	
Buildings (Rain)	6,000	
Goodwill (Rain)	4,000	
Non-Controlling Interest		40,000

40% [CU65,000 (Rain's net book value at acquisition) + CU35,000 (implied price differential)] = CU40,000

3b

Allocation of 40 percent of Rain's net adjusted value since acquisition to non-controlling interest

Retained Earnings (Rain)	19,000	
Non-Controlling Interest		19,000

40% [CU55,000 (Rain's retained earnings increase) - CU7,500 (cumulative amortization of the full FVI on Buildings)] = CU19,000

Consolidation Worksheet

	Para (CU)	Rain (CU)	Eliminations Adjustments (CU)	Consolidated (CU)
ASSETS				
Cash	80,000	15,000		95,000
Accounts receivable	12,000	50,000		62,000
Land	-	55,000	6,000 (1b)	65,000
			4,000 (3a)	
Buildings (net)	200,000	25,000	9,000 (1b)	232,500
			(7,500) (2)	
			6,000 (3a)	
Investment in Rain	60,000		(39,000) (1a)	-
			(21,000) (1b)	
Goodwill			6,000 (1b)	10,000
			4,000 (3a)	
	352,000	**145,000**		**464,500**
LIABILITIES				
Bank loan	25,000	10,000		35,000
Accounts payable	10,000	15,000		25,000
Bonds payable	75,000			75,000
EQUITY				
Common shares	150,000	55,000	(33,000) (1a)	150,000
			(22,000) (3a)	
Retained earnings	92,000	65,000	(36,500)	120,500
Non-controlling interest			40,000 (3a)	59,000
			19,000 (3b)	
	352,000	**145,000**		**464,500**
Revenues	500,000	230,000		730,000
Sales expenses	250,000	90,000	1,500 (2)	341,500
Administration expenses	200,000	130,000		330,000
Profit	**50,000**	**10,000**		**58,500**
Retained earnings (beginning)	42,000	55,000	(6,000) (1a)	62,000
			(6,000) (2)	
			(4,000) (3a)	
			(19,000) (3b)	
Retained earnings (end)	**92,000**	**65,000**	**(36,500)**	**120,500**

Net impact on the ending balance of RE

Effect on Income Tax Allocation

Assuming a corporate tax rate of 30 percent, temporary differences that consist of the full fair value increments on Land (CU10,000) and Buildings (CU15,000) should have been translated into a Deferred Tax Liability of CU7,500 (CU25,000 X 30%) at the date of acquisition. Consequently, the change of these temporary differences arising from post-acquisition price differential amortization must be recognized. Price differential amortization in prior-years (X6 through X9, inclusive) amounts to CU6,000 (see Exhibit 3.7) which reduces Deferred Tax Liability by CU1,800 (CU6,000 X 30%). Price differential amortization in the current year (X10) amounts to CU1,500 which reduces Income Tax Expense of CU450 (CU1,500 X 30%). Had a Deferred Tax Liability of CU7,500 been considered at the date of acquisition, the additional consolidation adjustments for X10 would be the following:

Deferred Tax Liability	2,250	
Income Tax Expense		450
Retained Earnings		1,800

② The Direct Approach

Exhibit 3.8 presents the consolidated financial statements of Para Corporation as of December 31, X10. The balance of the account taken from the books of the affiliated companies is reported in brackets. For more sophisticated computations, a note is added.

Exhibit 3.8 • Consolidated Financial Statements of Para Corporation for the Year Ended December 31, X10

Consolidated Income Statement of Para Corporation
Year Ended December 31, X10
(in CU)

Revenues (CU500,000 + CU230,000)	730,000
Sales expenses (1)	341,500
Administration expenses (CU200,000 + CU130,000)	330,000
Profit for the year (2)	**58,500**
Allocation to:	
Para (3)	55,100
Non-controlling interest (4)	3,400
	58,500

Consolidated Statement of Financial Position of Para Corporation
December 31, X10
(in CU)

Assets

Cash (CU80,000 + CU15,000)	95,000
Accounts receivable (CU12,000 + CU50,000)	62,000
Land **(5)**	65,000
Buildings (net) **(6)**	232,500
Goodwill (at acquisition)	10,000
Total assets	**464,500**

Liabilities and equities

Bank loan (CU25,000 + CU10,000)	35,000
Accounts payable (CU10,000 + CU15,000)	25,000
Bonds payable (Para)	75,000
Share capital (Para)	150,000
Retained earnings **(7)**	120,500
Non-controlling interest **(8)**	59,000
Total liabilities and equities	**464,500**

Consolidated Statement of Changes in Equity of Para Corporation
Year Ended December 31, X10
(in CU)

	Share Capital	Retained Earnings	NCI	Total
Balance at January 1, X10	150,000	65,400	55,600	271,000
Profit for the year		55,100	3,400	58,500
Balance at December 31, X10	**150,000**	**120,500**	**59,000**	**329,500**

(1) **Sales Expenses**	CU
• Parent (Para)	250,000
• Subsidiary (Rain)	90,000
• Current-year underdepreciation on Buildings (CU15,000/10)	1,500
Total	**341,500**

(2) **Consolidated Profit for the Year**		CU
• Para's profit		50,000
• Rain's adjusted profit:		
- Rain's profit	10,000	
- Implied price differential amortization:		
Current-year underdepreciation on Buildings		
(CU15,000/10)	(1,500)	8,500
Total		**58,500**

(3) **Consolidated Profit Allocated to Para**	CU
• Para's profit	50,000
• 60 percent of Rain's adjusted profit (CU8,500 X 60%)	5,100
Total	**55,100**

(4) **Consolidated Profit Allocated to Non-Controlling Interest**	CU
40 percent of Rain's adjusted Profit (CU8,500 X 40%)	**3,400**

(5) **Land**	CU
• Subsidiary (Rain)	55,000
• Full fair value increment at the date of acquisition	10,000
Total	**65,000**

(6) **Buildings** (net)	CU
• Parent (Para)	200,000
• Subsidiary (Rain)	25,000
• Unamortized balance of the full fair value increment (CU15,000 X 5/10)	7,500
Total	**232,500**

(7) **Retained Earnings** — CU

- Parent (Para) — 92,000
- 60 percent of the subsidiary (Rain)'s net adjusted value since acquisition

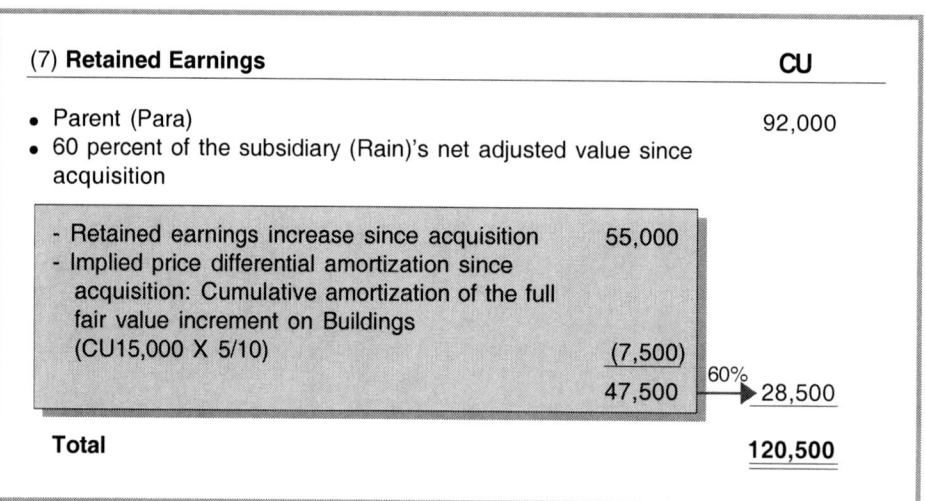

- Retained earnings increase since acquisition — 55,000
- Implied price differential amortization since acquisition: Cumulative amortization of the full fair value increment on Buildings (CU15,000 X 5/10) — (7,500)
- 47,500 × 60% → 28,500

Total — **120,500**

(8) **Non-Controlling Interest** — CU

- 40 percent of the implied purchase price or the full fair value of the subsidiary (Rain) as of January 1, X6

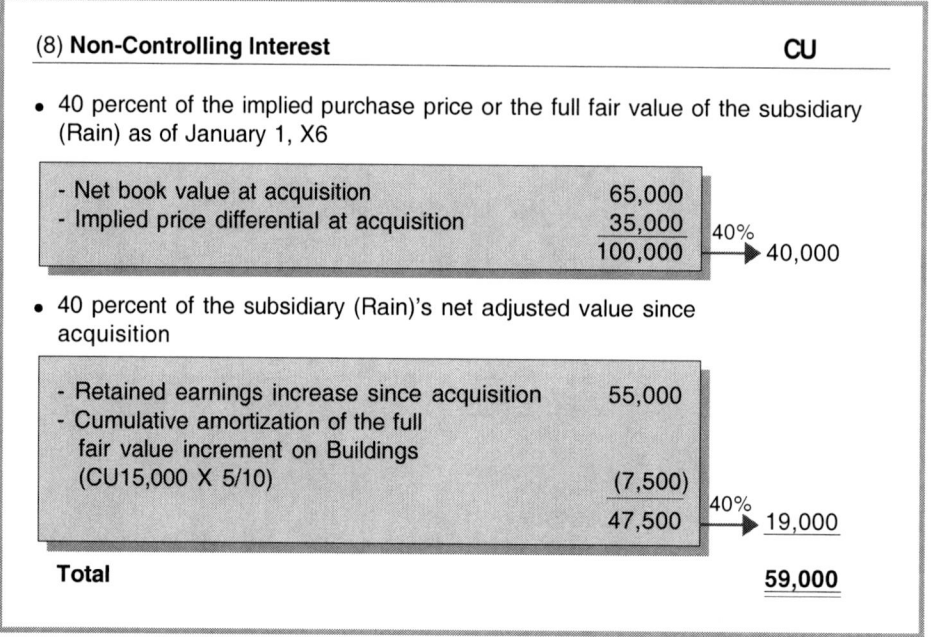

- Net book value at acquisition — 65,000
- Implied price differential at acquisition — 35,000
- 100,000 × 40% → 40,000

- 40 percent of the subsidiary (Rain)'s net adjusted value since acquisition

- Retained earnings increase since acquisition — 55,000
- Cumulative amortization of the full fair value increment on Buildings (CU15,000 X 5/10) — (7,500)
- 47,500 × 40% → 19,000

Total — **59,000**

To summarize, Figure 3.2 presents the net adjusted value of Rain as of December 31, X10.

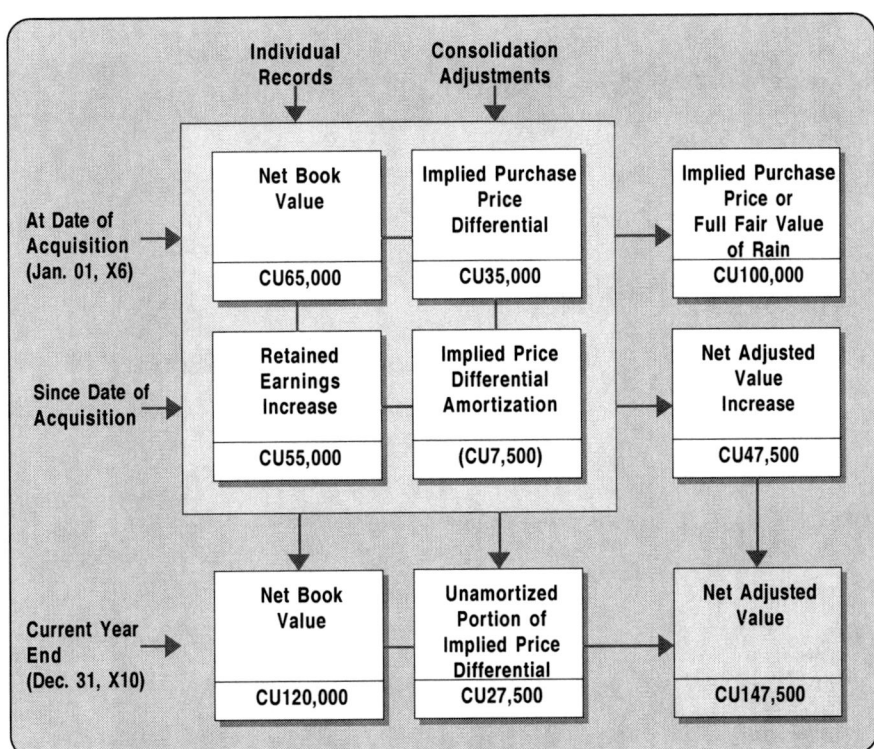

Figure 3.2 • Rain's Net Adjusted Value as of December 31, X10

2- Partial Goodwill Approach (IFRS #3)
2.1- Measurement Basis for NCI: Fair Value of Subsidiary's Net Assets

If non-controlling interest is measured based on the fair value of Rain's net assets at date of acquisition, goodwill will be recorded to the extent of Para's percentage of Rain (60%) and no goodwill will be assigned to Rain's minority shareholders. The purchase price allocation will be based on the price paid by Para, that is, CU60,000 (see Exhibit 3.6). Goodwill of CU6,000, instead of CU10,000, will be brought into the consolidation process. The value allocated to non-controlling interest will be CU36,000 instead of CU40,000, that is, 40% of Rain's full fair value of net identifiable assets at date of acquisition (CU90,000 X 40% = CU36,000). The fair value of net assets (CU90,000) is comprised of the book value (CU65,000) and full fair value increments on Land (CU10,000) and Buildings (CU15,000).

Compared to the full goodwill approach, consolidation entries required at the end of X10 are the same except for entry #3a that must be replaced with the following entry (the recording of goodwill is removed).

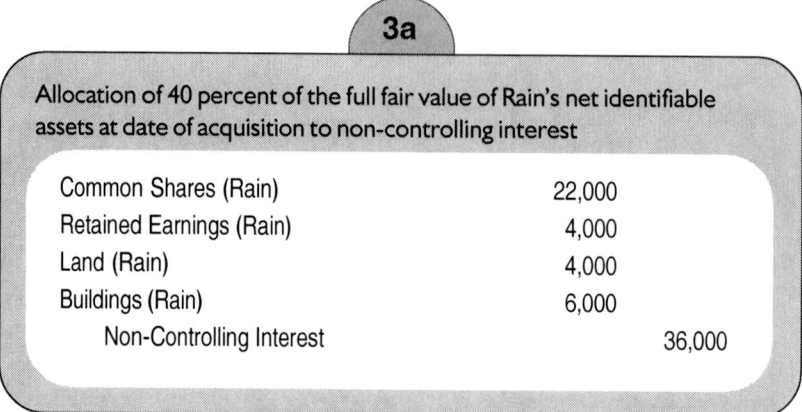

The direct approach to compute non-controlling interest is also changed accordingly as follows.

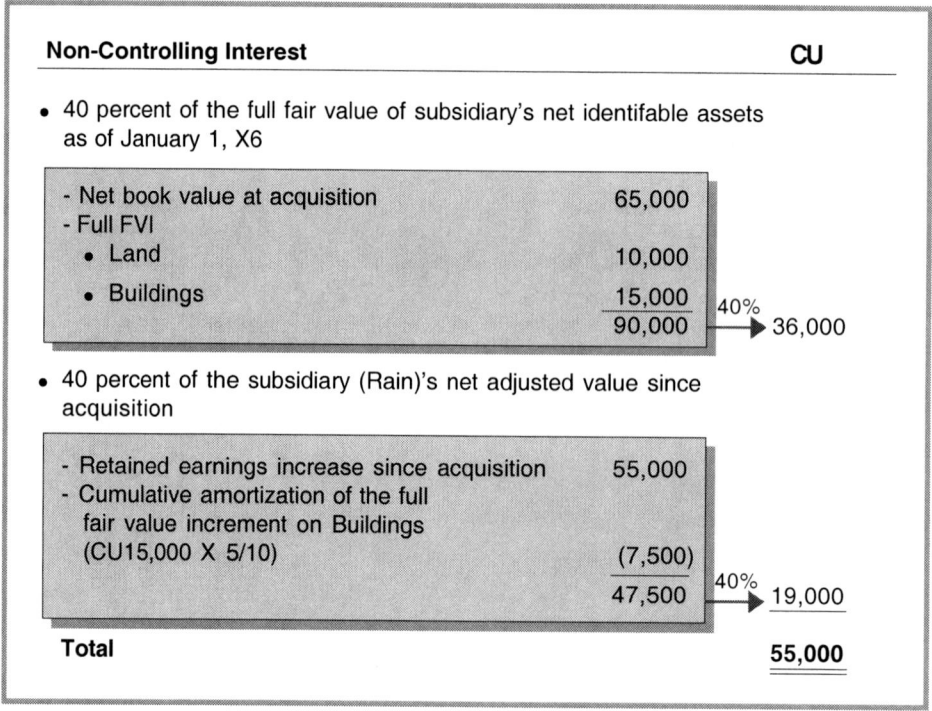

 What If...

If goodwill had been impaired, the full amount of impairment would have been assigned to the parent company since no goodwill is allocated to non-controlling interest.

2.2- Measurement Basis for NCI: Fair Value of NCI

Assume that the fair value of the non-controlling interest at the date of combination is CU38,000 based on the market price of the shares that the acquirer does not obtain. Exhibit 3.9 presents the allocation of the purchase price and the allocation of the fair value of the non-controlling interest.

Exhibit 3.9 • Acquisition of 60 percent of the Outstanding Voting Stock of Rain by Para on January 1, X6 - Allocation of the Purchase Price and the Fair Value of the Non-Controlling Interest

		(100%) CU	Para (60%) CU	Minority (40%) CU
Cost of investment in Rain			60,000	
Fair value of NCI				38,000
Shareholders' equity of Rain at the date of acquisition:				
Share capital	55,000			
Retained earnings	10,000	65,000	39,000	26,000
Price differential			21,000	12,000
Fair value increments:				
Land		(10,000)	(6,000)	(4,000)
Buildings		(15,000)	(9,000)	(6,000)
Goodwill			6,000	2,000

Goodwill allocated to the non-controlling interest amounts to CU2,000 which reflects the excess fair value of the non-controlling interest over the non-controlling interest's proportionate share of Rain's net fair value. The overall goodwill that will be brought into the consolidated statement of financial position amounts to CU8,000, that is, Para's share (CU6,000) and the non-controlling interest's share (CU2,000) combined. Compared to the full goodwill approach, only consolidation entry #3a must be modified (goodwill allocated to the non-controlling interest is CU2,000 instead of CU4,000).

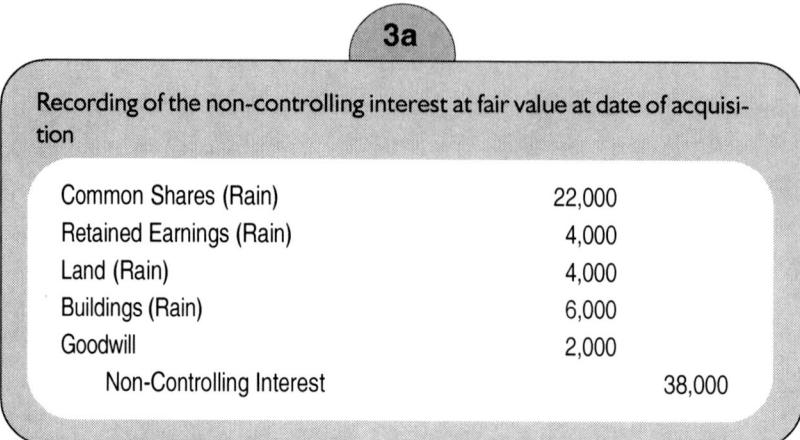

The direct approach to compute the balance of the non-controlling interest at the end of year X10 must reflect the new valuation of non-controlling interest at date of acquisition.

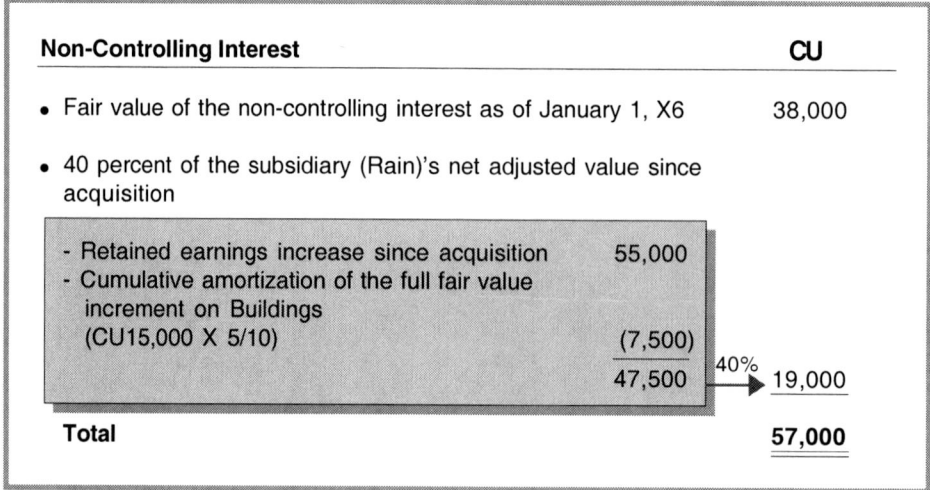

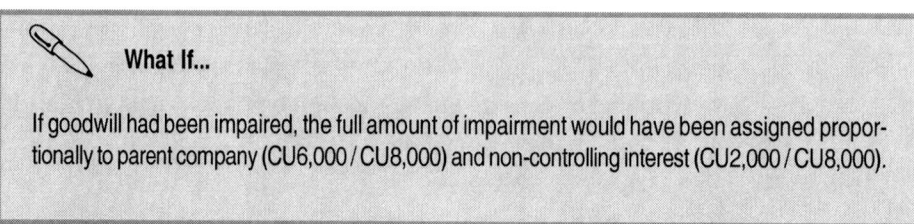

To summarize, Exhibit 3.10 presents on a comparative basis the consolidated statements of financial position of Para as of December 31, X10 under the full and partial goodwill approaches.

Exhibit 3.10 • Comparison of Consolidated Information under Full and Partial Goodwill Alternatives

Consolidated Statements of Financial Position of Para Corporation
December 31, X10
(in CU)

	Full goodwill	Partial goodwill	
		No goodwill to NCI	NCI at FV
Assets			
Cash	95,000	95,000	95,000
Accounts receivable	62,000	62,000	62,000
Land	65,000	65,000	65,000
Buildings (net)	232,500	232,500	232,500
Goodwill (at acquisition)	10,000	6,000	8,000
Total assets	**464,500**	**460,500**	**462,500**
Liabilities and equities			
Bank loan	35,000	35,000	35,000
Accounts payable	25,000	25,000	25,000
Bonds payable	75,000	75,000	75,000
Share capital	150,000	150,000	150,000
Retained earnings	120,500	120,500	120,500
Non-controlling interest	59,000	55,000	57,000
Total liabilities and equities	**464,500**	**460,500**	**462,500**

Differences in the valuation of goodwill are ultimately reflected in the balance of the non-controlling interest.

Summary of the Consolidation Adjustments in Journal Entry Form

At the Date of Acquisition

1. Elimination of the Investment Account in the Subsidiary

a)
Common Shares (B)	XX	
Retained Earnings (B)	XX	
Investment in B (A)		XX

To eliminate reciprocal investment and equity accounts.

b)
Asset-Related Full Fair Value Increments (B)	XX	
Liability-Related Full Fair Value Decrements (B)	XX	
Goodwill (B)	XX	
Other assets not recorded by B (B)	XX	
Liability-Related Full Fair Value Increments (B)		XX
Asset-Related Full Fair Value Decrements (B)		XX
Investment in B (A)		XX

To allocate Parent's proportionate share of subsidiary's full fair value.

2. Non-Controlling Interest

Common Shares (B)	XX	
Retained Earnings (B)	XX	
Asset-Related Full Fair Value Increments (B)	XX	
Liability-Related Full Fair Value Decrements (B)	XX	
Goodwill (B) (if NCI at FV)	XX	
Other assets not recorded by B (B)	XX	
Liability-Related Full Fair Value Increments (B)		XX
Asset-Related Full Fair Value Decrements (B)		XX
Non-Controlling Interest		XX

To allocate the fair value of subsidiary's identifiable net assets to non-controlling interest.

Effect on Income Tax Allocation

Future Income Tax related to full fair value increments and decrements must be accounted for at the date of acquisition. Adding this account in the implied purchase price allocation will have an offsetting effect on Goodwill.

Chapter 3 Non-Wholly Owned Subsidiaries 129

Following the Date of Acquisition		
1. Elimination of the Investment Account in the Subsidiary (Cost Basis)		
a) Common Shares (B)	XX	
Retained Earnings (B)	XX	
Investment in B (A)		XX
To eliminate reciprocal investment and equity accounts at acquisition.		
b) Asset-Related Full Fair Value Increments (B)	XX	
Liability-Related Full Fair Value Decrements (B)	XX	
Goodwill (B)	XX	
Other assets not recorded by B (B)	XX	
Liability-Related Full Fair Value Increments (B)		XX
Asset-Related Full Fair Value Decrements (B)		XX
Investment in B (A)		XX
To allocate Parent's proportionate share of subsidiary's full fair value at date of acquisition.		
2. Implied Price Differential Amortization/Realization Since Acquisition		
a) Retained Earnings (prior-period amortization)	XX	
Depreciation Expense (current-year amortization)	XX	
Accumulated Depreciation		XX
To amortize any full fair value increment (decrement) on depreciable asset (liability).		
Accumulated Depreciation	XX	
Depreciation Expense (current-year amortization)		XX
Retained Earnings (prior-period amortization)		XX
To amortize any full fair value decrement (increment) on depreciable asset (liability).		
b) Retained Earnings (if disposal in a prior year)	XX	
Gain or Loss (if disposal in the current year)	XX	
Asset (or liability)		XX
To recognize any unamortized portion of the full fair value increment (decrement) when related asset (liability) is disposed of.		
Asset (or liability)	XX	
Gain or Loss (if disposal in the current year)		XX
Retained Earnings (if disposal in a prior year)		XX
To recognize any unamortized portion of the full fair value decrement (increment) when related asset (liability) is disposed of.		
c) Retained Earnings (if impairment in prior years)	XX	
Impairment Loss (if impairment in the current year)	XX	
Goodwill		XX
To account for any goodwill impairment.		

Following the Date of Acquisition (continued...)		
3. Non-Controlling Interest		
a) Common Shares (B)	XX	
Retained Earnings (B)	XX	
Asset-Related Full Fair Value Increments (B)	XX	
Liability-Related Full Fair Value Decrements (B)	XX	
Goodwill (B) (if NCI at FV)	XX	
Other assets not recorded by B (B)	XX	
Liability-Related Full Fair Value Increments (B)		XX
Asset-Related Full Fair Value Decrements (B)		XX
Non-Controlling Interest		XX
To allocate the fair value of subsidiary's identifiable net assets at date of acquisition to non-controlling interest.		
b) Retained Earnings (B)	XX	
Non-Controlling Interest		XX
To allocate the subsidiary (B)'s net adjusted value since acquisition to non-controlling interest. <u>Subsidiary's net adjusted value</u>: Change in subsidiary's retained earnings since acquisition (-) Cumulative price differential amortization/realization since acquisition When non-controlling interest is valued based on the fair value of subsidiary's net assets, goodwill impairment, if any, must be assigned to parent company only.		

Effect on Consolidated Profit Allocation
 Consolidated profit must be allocated to majority and minority interests in the income statement as follows:
     Majority interest: Parent's profit (+) Parent's share of subsidiary's adjusted profit
     Minority interest: Minority's share of subsidiary's adjusted profit.
     <u>Subsidiary's adjusted profit</u>: Subsidiary's profit (-) Current-year price differential amortization/realization
     When non-controlling interest is valued based on the fair value of subsidiary's net assets, current-year goodwill impairment, if any, must be assigned to parent company only.		

Effect on Income Tax Allocation Deferred Tax related to full fair value increments and decrements must be accounted for at the date of acquisition. Following the date of acquisition, any change in temporary differences arising from implied price differential amortization or realization must be recognized for consolidation purposes. Assuming that a Deferred Tax Liability has been created at the date of acquisition, the adjustment required in post-acquisition periods to account for the change in temporary differences is journalized below.		
Deferred Tax Liability	XX	
Income Tax Expense (current-year)		XX
Retained Earnings (prior-years)		XX

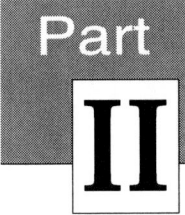

Intercompany Transactions

Structure and Content of Part II

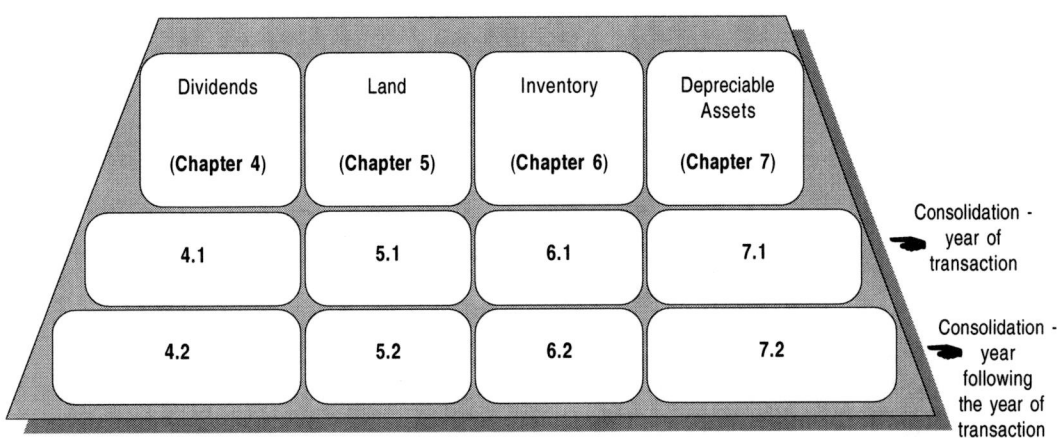

Chapter 4

Intercompany Dividends

Double-Counting of Subsidiary's Earnings

In this chapter

4.1 Consolidation in Period of Intercompany Dividends 134

4.2 Consolidation in Period Subsequent to the Year of Intercompany Dividends 138

✎ Summary of the Consolidation Adjustments in Journal Entry Form 139

Key Concepts: Intercompany Transactions; Intercompany Dividends; Double-Counting of Subsidiary's Earnings

An *intercompany transaction* is a transaction that occurs between two units of the same entity. Intercompany transactions are recognized in the financial records of the affiliated companies as if the transactions were conducted between unrelated parties. However, from the point of view of the economic entity, separate affiliates constitute a single entity for external reporting purposes. Therefore, any effect of internal transactions contained within the consolidated entity must be eliminated. The objective of consolidation adjustments is to report on the financial position and operating results of the consolidated group as it would have appeared if intercompany transactions had never taken place.

Affiliated companies can engage among themselves in different types of transactions. This chapter focuses exclusively on *intercompany dividends* whereas the next three chapters cover intercompany sales of assets. Intercompany dividends are one way for the parent company to transfer cash flows from its subsidiaries. This chapter provides guidance in consolidating financial statements, first, for the year of intercompany dividends, and second, for periods subsequent to the year of transfer.

4.1 Consolidation in Period of Intercompany Dividends

Assume that Company A owns 100 percent of the outstanding voting stock of Company B and employs the cost method to account for all its strategic investments. Recall that under the cost basis, dividends declared by the subsidiary are accounted for by the parent company as revenue in the income statement (Dividend Income). In this regard, assume that Company B declared and paid dividends of CU5,000 in the current year. The entries on the books of the affiliated companies to account for the intercompany transfer appear below.

Books of A

Cash	5,000	
Dividend Income		5,000

Books of B

Dividends Declared	5,000	
Cash		5,000

Condensed financial statements of Company A and Company B prior to the intercompany dividends are reproduced in Exhibit 4.1. The impact of the intercompany dividends on these financial statements is highlighted in Exhibit 4.2. Understanding how intercompany transactions impact the financial statements of the units involved will help determine how to adjust the consolidated financial information using worksheet consolidation entries.

Exhibit 4.1 • Financial Statements of Company A and Company B Prior to the Intercompany Dividends

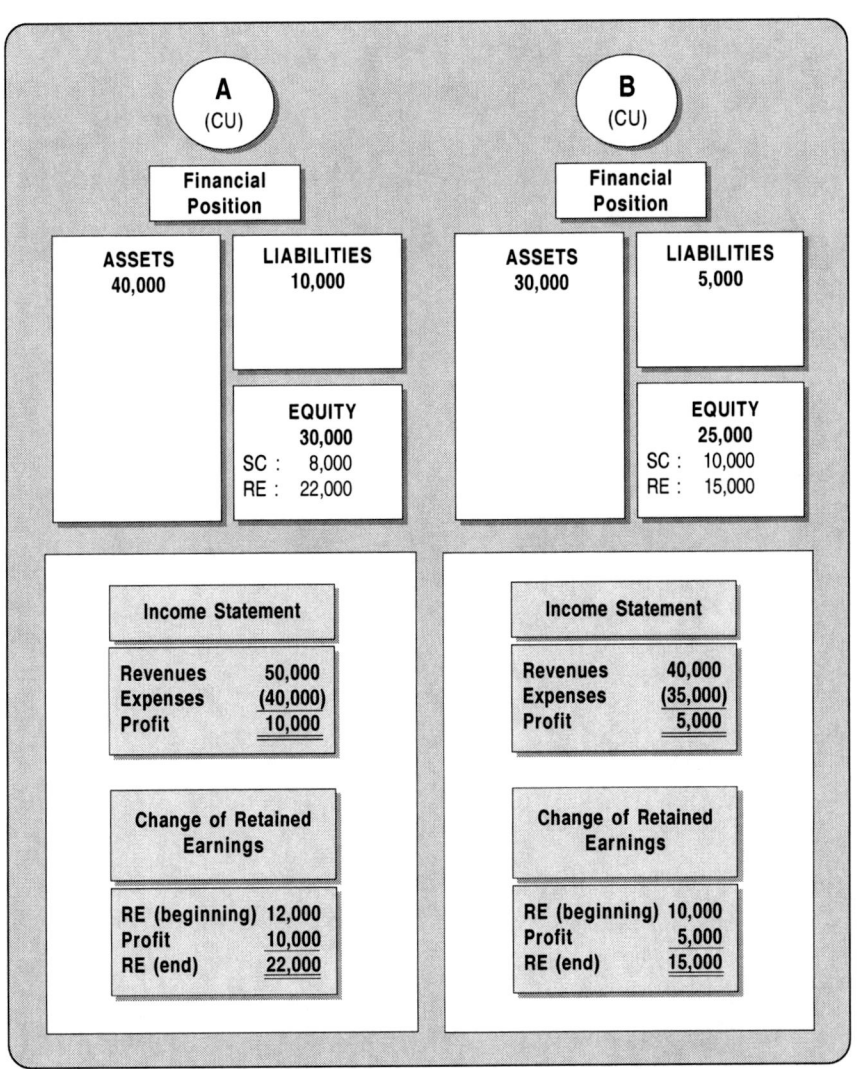

Exhibit 4.2 • Financial Statements of Company A and Company B Following the Intercompany Dividends

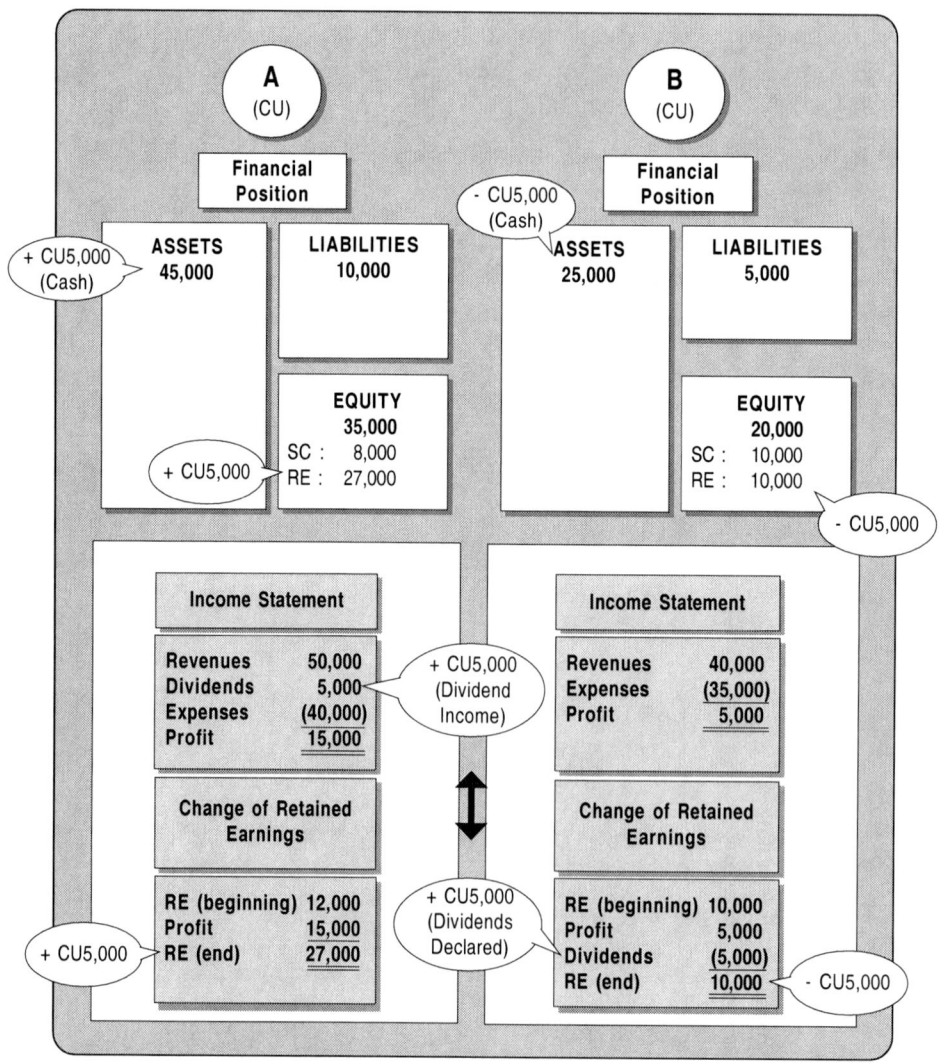

As evidenced from Exhibit 4.2, the ending balance of Company B's Retained Earnings decreased by CU5,000, that is, the amount of dividends declared during the year. Conversely, the full amount of intercompany dividends has been recognized by Company A as revenue and subsequently closed to retained earnings. Therefore, Company A's Retained Earnings increased by CU5,000, cancelling out any effect of intercompany dividends on the net consolidated value. Likewise, the balance of Company B's cash account decreased by CU5,000 following the payment of the dividends while the balance of Company A's cash account increased by the same amount. Since intercompany dividends, when fully paid by the subsidiary by the end of the accounting period, have no impact on the consolidated statement of financial position, no adjustment is required.

> **What If...**
>
> If consolidated financial statements are prepared between the time a subsidiary declares and the time it pays dividends, the parent's records will show a dividend receivable account and the subsidiary, a dividend payable account. To avoid overstating current assets and current liabilities in the consolidated statement of financial position, reciprocal intercompany balances must be eliminated.
>
> To illustrate, assume that the CU5,000 intercompany dividends declared by Company B are still unpaid at the end of the period. Entries on the books of the affiliated companies to account for the transfer are reported below.
>
> | Company A | | | Company B | | |
> |---|---|---|---|---|---|
> | **Dividends Receivable** | 5,000 | | Dividends Declared | 5,000 | |
> | Dividend Income | | 5,000 | **Dividends Payable** | | 5,000 |
>
> The following consolidation entry would have been required to eliminate reciprocal receivable and payable accounts.
>
> | | | |
> |---|---|---|
> | Dividends Payable (B) | 5,000 | |
> | Dividends Receivable (A) | | 5,000 |

In order to consolidate the income statement, Dividend Income recorded by Company A must be eliminated. This elimination is necessary in order to avoid *double-counting of subsidiary's earnings* of CU5,000. More precisely, dividends are generally declared when profit is realized and accumulated over time. Dividends could also be seen as deriving from the profit of the current period. In our illustration, one can see that the CU5,000 intercompany dividends is equivalent to Company B's profit for the period. Since consolidation of the income statement consists of cross-adding all the revenue and expense accounts of the affiliated companies, eliminating Company A's Dividend Income in the process is required to avoid counting Company B's earnings twice. The workpaper entry to eliminate double-counting of Company B's earnings is reproduced below.

Dividend Income (A)	5,000	
Dividends Declared (B)		5,000

The consolidated profit for the period of intercompany dividends can be computed directly as the following:

♦ Consolidated Profit for the Year		CU
• A's adjusted profit:		
- A's profit	15,000	
- Intercompany dividends	(5,000)	10,000
• B's profit		5,000
Total		15,000

Note that consolidated profit (CU15,000) consists of the profit of Company A (CU10,000) plus the profit of Company B (CU5,000) as stated in their respective records immediately prior to the intercompany dividends (see Exhibit 4.1).

> **What If...**
>
> Assume that Company A owns 70 percent of the voting stock of Company B rather than 100 percent. In that case, if Company B declares CU5,000 dividends, only CU3,500 (CU5,000 X 70%) will be paid to Company A. Dividend income thus recognized by Company A must be eliminated for consolidation purposes so as to avoid double-counting of CU3,500. Moreover, Non-Controlling Interest must be decreased by CU1,500 (CU5 000 X 30%) so as to assign to the minority shareholders their share of the dividends declared by Company B. Recall that this consideration has already been dealt with through adjustment #3b (see chapter 3) which consists of allocating to the minority shareholders their share of Company B's net adjusted value since acquisition. Therefore, to be consistent with adjustment #3b, the following combined consolidation entry will be required in order to eliminate the dividends declared by Company B.
>
> | | | |
> |---|---|---|
> | Dividend Income (A) | 3,500 | |
> | Retained Earnings (minority share) | 1,500 | |
> | Dividends Declared (B) | | 5,000 |

4.2 Consolidation in Period Subsequent to the Year of Intercompany Dividends

As previously illustrated, intercompany dividends have no impact on the net consolidated value and, as a result, require no consolidation adjustment in time periods subsequent to the year of transfer.

Summary of the Consolidation Adjustments in Journal Entry Form

Period of Intercompany Dividends			If non-wholly owned subsidiary
Dividend Income (A) Retained Earnings (minority share vs entry #3b, Chapter 3) Dividends Declared (B) To eliminate the intercompany dividends.	XX XX	XX	✓
Periods Subsequent to the Year of Intercompany Dividends			
No adjustment required			

Chapter 5

Intercompany Sales of Land

Intercompany Gains and Losses

In this chapter

5.1 Consolidation in Period of Intercompany Sale of Land 142
    5.1.1 The Land is Held by the Purchasing Affiliate 145
    5.1.2 The Land Has Been Resold to an Outsider 146

5.2 Consolidation in Period Subsequent to the Year of Intercompany Sale of Land 149
    5.2.1 The Land is Still Held by the Purchasing Affiliate 150
    5.2.2 The Land Has Been Resold to an Outsider 151

Summary of the Consolidation Adjustments in Journal Entry Form 156

Key Concepts: Unrealized Intercompany Gains and Losses; Upstream Transactions; Downstream Transactions

This chapter examines the impact of *intercompany sales of land*, a noncurrent, nondepreciable asset, on the consolidation process. Taking the land as an example of intercorporate transfer helps to illustrate the basic concepts and procedures involved with unrealized gains and losses. The next two chapters will introduce further complexities while dealing more specifically with intercorporate sales of inventory (chapter 6) and depreciable assets (chapter 7).

The sale of an asset between affiliated units at a price other than book value gives rise to profit or loss that will be considered as being unrealized from the viewpoint of the consolidated entity, for as long as the asset remains in the group at the end of the year. Since only transactions realized between the economic entity and external parties are accounted for in the consolidated financial statements, *unrealized intercompany gains or losses* on sales of assets must be eliminated. More precisely, consolidation adjustments required in the case of an intercompany sale depend on whether consolidated financial statements are prepared for the year of transaction or a period subsequent to the year of transaction, and whether or not the asset remains within the consolidated group at the end of the accounting period. These different scenarios are explored in this chapter.

When the sale flows from the parent to the subsidiary, the transaction is referred to as *downstream*. However, if the sale is initiated by the subsidiary, the transaction is referred to as *upstream*. The direction of intercompany transfers is important only for affiliation structures with non-wholly owned subsidiaries. More precisely, when a sale is downstream, intercompany gain or loss is charged against the parent company and consolidated profit. However, when a sale is upstream, any gain or loss on the transfer accrues to the shareholders of the subsidiary, that is, the parent company and the non-controlling shareholders. In this case, any unrealized intercompany gain or loss must be divided proportionally between the parent company and the minority shareholders. The effect of intercompany transfers on non-controlling interest valuation is examined in special notes throughout the chapter.

5.1 Consolidation in Period of Intercompany Sale of Land

Assume land is purchased from Company A by Company B, a wholly owned subsidiary, for CU10,000. The original cost of the land reported on the books of Company A before the sale is CU6,000. At the date of the intercompany sale of the land, the affiliated companies recorded the following journal entries:

Books of A

Cash	10,000	
Land		6,000
Gain on Sale of Land		4,000

Chapter 5 Intercompany Sale of Land 143

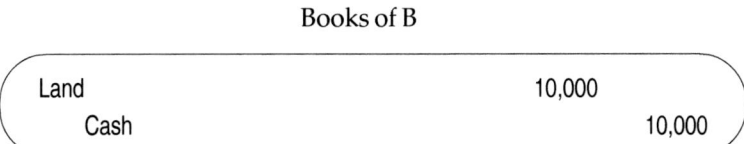

Books of B

Land 10,000
    Cash 10,000

The condensed financial statements of Company A and Company B immediately prior to the intercompany sale of land appear in Exhibit 5.1. The impact of the intercompany transaction on these financial statements is illustrated in Exhibit 5.2.

Exhibit 5.1 • Financial Statements of Company A and Company B Prior to the Intercompany Sale of Land

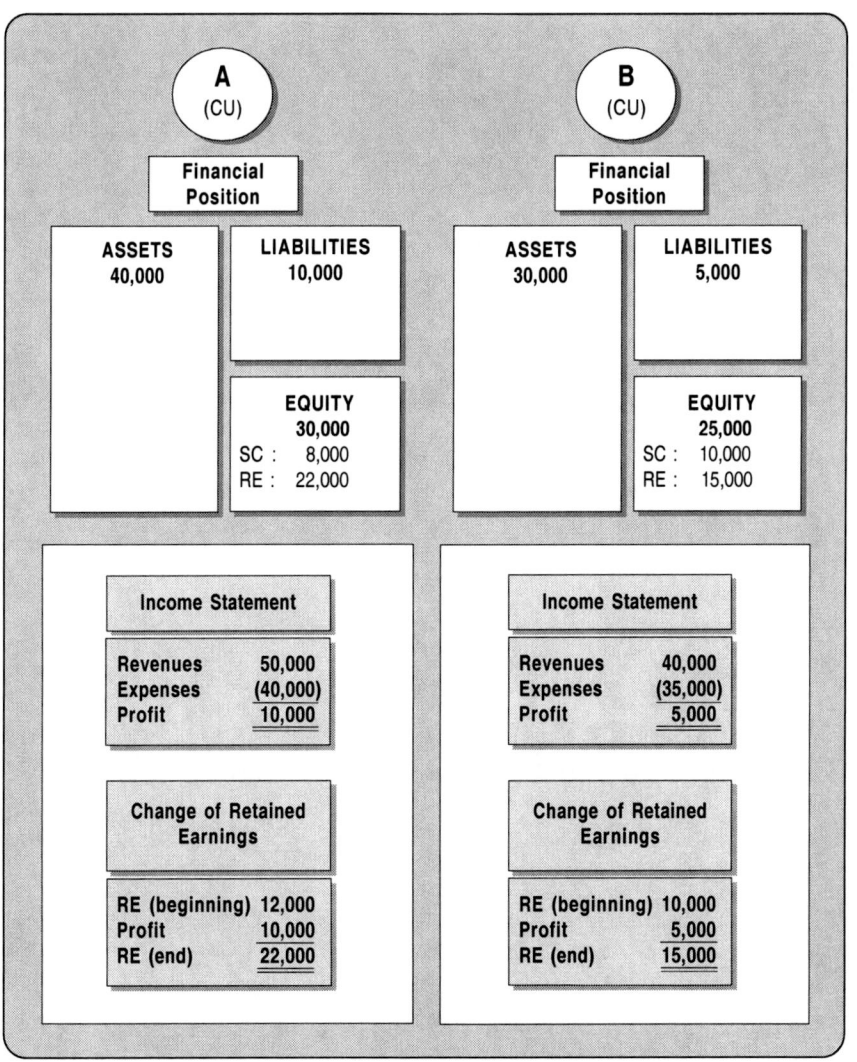

The historical cost of the land on Company A's financial records being CU6,000 and the selling or transfer price of that land to Company B being set at CU10,000, Company A recognized a gain on sale of CU4,000 (CU10,000 - CU6,000). As a result, Company A's profit for the year and retained earnings have both been increased by CU4,000 following the sale. The land is now carried on the books of Company B at a cost of CU10,000. This value reflects the transfer price and, as such, contains the intercompany gain on sale of CU4,000.

Exhibit 5.2 • Financial Statements of Company A and Company B Subsequent to the Intercompany Sale of Land

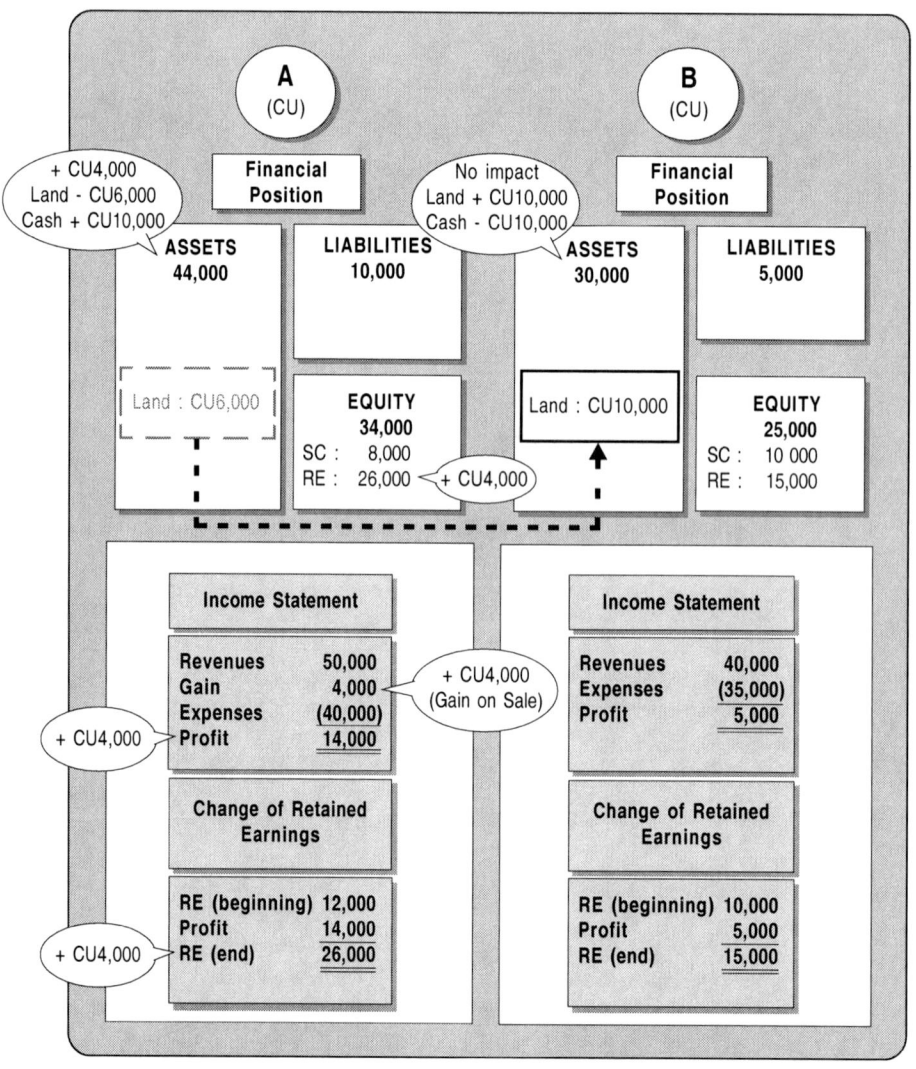

Consolidation adjustments in year of transaction will depend on whether or not the land has been resold by Company B to an unrelated party prior to the end of the current accounting period. These two scenarios are analyzed in the following sections.

5.1.1 The Land is Held by the Purchasing Affiliate

If the land has not been resold by the purchasing affiliate, the gain on sale of CU4,000 initially recognized by Company A must be considered to be unrealized. Consistent with the consolidated entity's perspective, the intercompany sale of land never occurred because it did not involve a party outside the consolidated group. Hence, the initial gain on sale of CU4,000 must be eliminated or deferred and the cost of land reported by Company B must return to its original historical cost of CU6,000. The consolidation entry necessary to accomplish these adjustments is shown below.

Gain on Sale of Land (A)	4,000	
Land (B)		4,000

> **What If...**
>
> Illustrations provided in this book involve intercompany gain transactions. However, if the intercompany sale of asset had resulted in a loss rather than a gain, the same reasoning would apply unless the loss indicates an impairment of the asset being sold. In this case, the decline in value of the transferred asset must be recognized in the consolidated income statement. The intercompany loss would be considered as fully realized and no elimination would be required.

The following presents the computation of the consolidated profit for the year for the period of transaction.

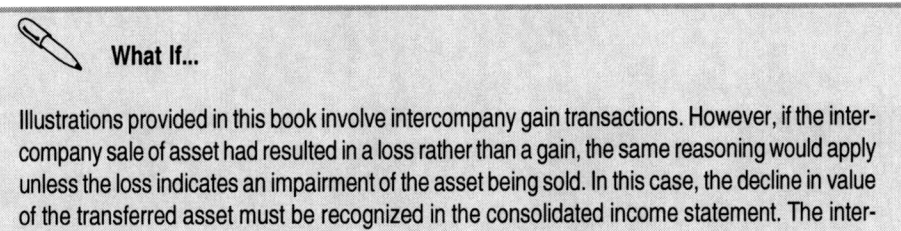

◆ Consolidated Profit for the Year		CU
• A's adjusted profit:		
- A's profit	14,000	
- Unrealized gain on downstream sale of land	(4,000)	10,000
• B's profit		5,000
Total		**15,000**

Consolidated profit (CU15,000) consists of the profit of Company A (CU10,000) plus the profit of Company B (CU5,000) as stated immediately prior to the intercompany sale of land (see Exhibit 5.1). In sum, the objective of the consolidation elimination is to show the financial position and operating results of the consolidated entity as it would have appeared if the intercompany sale of land had never taken place.

Assume that only Company A's consolidated statement of financial position is prepared. Since the current-year gain on downstream sale of land has been closed to Company

A's Retained Earnings, this account must be reduced by CU4,000 so as to remove the intercompany gain. Moreover, the cost of the transferred land on the books of Company B includes the intercorporate gain and, thus, must be reduced by CU4,000 as well. The workpaper entry required to remove the current-year intercompany gain from the affiliated companies' statements of financial position is shown below.

Retained Earnings (A)	4,000	
Land (B)		4,000

Effect on Income Tax Allocation

The gain on sale of land recognized by Company A will be taxed in the current period. However, for consolidation purposes, the gain is considered as being unrealized. This situation gives rise to a temporary difference until the land is ultimately sold to an outsider. Assuming a tax rate of 30 percent, the related tax to be removed from Company A's income statement amounts to CU1,200 (CU4,000 X 30%). Had the income tax allocation been considered in the consolidation of Company A, the following additional entry would have been required.

Deferred Tax	1,200	
Income Tax Expense		1,200

5.1.2 The Land Has Been Resold to an Outsider

Exhibit 5.3 depicts the impact of the resale of the land by Company B to an unrelated party, assuming a selling price of CU15,000. In this case, a gain on sale of CU5,000 is recognized by Company B as the difference between the proceeds from the sale (CU15,000) and the cost of the land as shown on Company B's records (CU10,000). The following presents the journal entry on the books of Company B to account for the resale of the land.

Cash	15,000	
Land		10,000
Gain on Sale of Land		5,000

The gain on sale, recognized first by Company A following the intercompany sale of land (CU4,000) and subsequently by Company B following the resale of the land the same year to an outsider (CU5,000), will be combined in the consolidation process. The consolidated gain on sale of CU9,000 (CU4,000 + CU5,000) that will be reported in the consolidated income statement will reflect the total gain realized by the consolidated entity.

Effect on Non-Controlling Interest Valuation

The consolidated adjustments illustrated so far are similar regardless of whether the transaction is downstream or upstream, for as long as the subsidiary B is wholly owned by Company A. If we assume that Company A had a 70 percent interest in Company B instead of 100 percent, the following additional considerations would have been needed.

If the transaction were downstream

If the intercompany sale of land were downstream, only Company A's profit should have been adjusted so as to eliminate the intercompany gain on sale of CU4,000. Therefore, the allocation of the CU15,000 consolidated profit to minority and majority shareholders would have been the following:

Consolidated Profit Allocated to A		CU
A's adjusted profit:		
- A's profit	14,000	
- Unrealized gain on sale of land	(4,000)	10,000
70 percent of B's profit (CU5,000 X 70%)		3,500
Total		13,500

Consolidated Profit Allocated to Minority Shareholders	
30 percent of B's profit (CU5,000 X 30%)	1,500

Notice that the CU4,000 unrealized gain is assigned entirely to Company A.

If the transaction were upstream

If the intercompany sale of land were upstream, Company B's profit should have been adjusted so as to eliminate the intercompany gain on sale of CU4,000. Therefore, the allocation of the CU15,000 consolidated profit to minority and majority shareholders would have been the following:

Consolidated Profit Allocated to A			CU
A's profit			10,000
70 percent of B's adjusted profit:			
- B's profit (which would include the intercompany gain)	9,000		
- Unrealized gain on sale of land	(4,000)		
	5,000	X 70%	3,500
Total			13,500

Consolidated Profit Allocated to Minority Shareholders	
30 percent of B's adjusted profit (CU5,000 X 30%)	1,500

The CU4,000 unrealized gain is assigned proportionally between the parent company and the non-controlling interest.

One can also view this gain as the gain that Company A would have recognized had Company A sold the land directly to an unrelated party for CU15,000. In such a scenario, the entry that Company A would have reported is shown next.

Cash	15,000	
Land		6,000
Gain on Sale of Land		9,000

No consolidation adjustment is required. Consolidated profit of CU24,000 is comprised of Company A's profit of CU14,000 (which includes a current-year gain of CU4,000 on intercompany sale of land) and Company B's profit of CU10,000 (which includes a current-year gain of CU5,000 on resale of land). Since the land is no longer held by the consolidated entity and the realization of the gain is complete, no further considerations need be given the intercompany sale of land in future periods.

Exhibit 5.3 • Financial Statements of Company A and Company B Following the Resale of the Land to an Outside Party for CU15,000

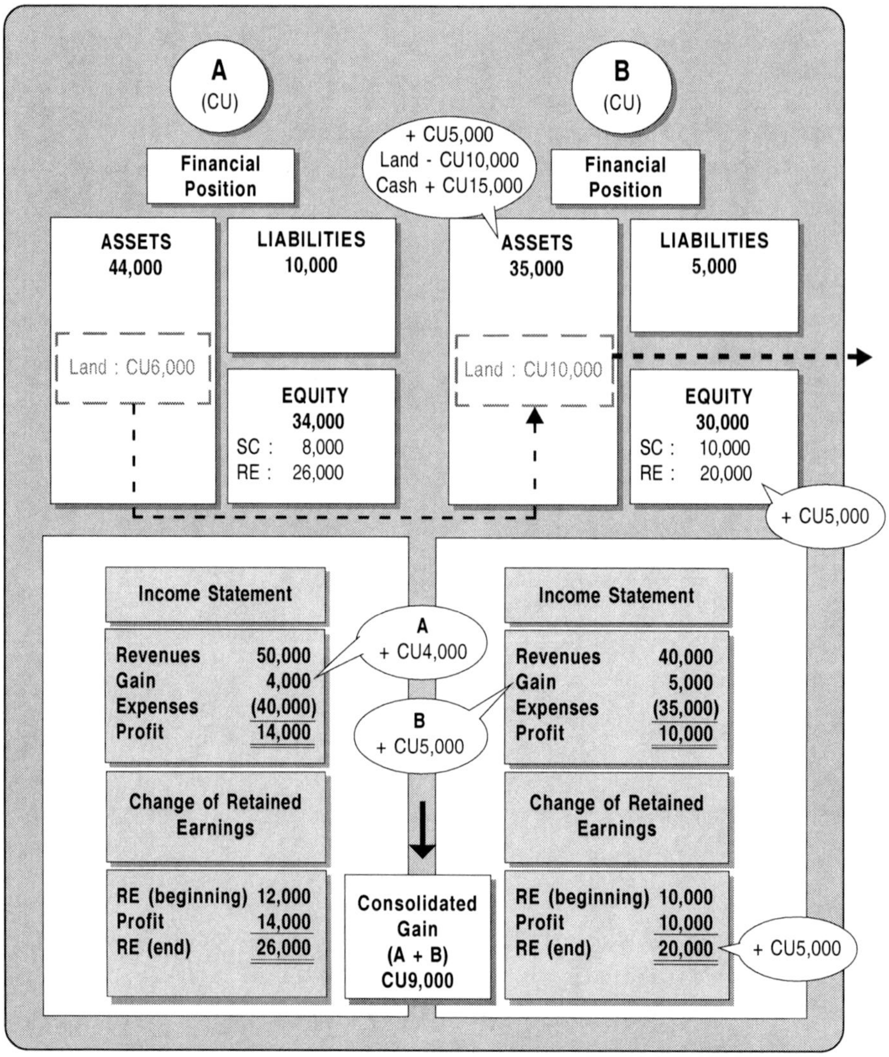

What If...

Assume that Company A loans CU10,000 to Company B at the beginning of the current period so that Company B can purchase the land. A note payable on demand is then signed by both parties with interest at 10 percent. The following presents the entries on the books of the affiliated companies to record the intercompany note payable as well as the intercompany payment of interest at the end of the current accounting period.

Company A			Company B		
Note Receivable	10,000		Cash	10,000	
Cash		10,000	**Note Payable**		10,000
Cash	1,000		Interest Expense	1,000	
Interest Revenue		1,000	Cash		1,000

From the viewpoint of the economic entity, reciprocal balances must be eliminated. Consolidation entries required in such a case are journalized below.

Note Payable (B)	10,000	
Note Receivable (A)		10,000

Interest Revenue (A)	1,000	
Interest Expense (B)		1,000

Notice that these elimination entries have no impact on the net consolidated value and aim only at eliminating reciprocal receivables and payables in the statement of financial position as well as reciprocal revenues and expenses in the income statement.

5.2 Consolidation in Period Subsequent to the Year of Intercompany Sale of Land

Let's continue the development of Company A by assuming that the land has not been resold by Company B during the year of intercompany sale. We are now in the period following transfer. Exhibit 5.4 presents the condensed financial statements of the affiliated companies for that period.

Recall that consolidation entries are made on a working paper and, as such, are never posted to the individual affiliates's books. Therefore, Company A's Retained Earnings and Company B's Land as of the beginning of the current accounting period contain the unrealized gain of CU4,000 from prior-year downstream sale of land.

Exhibit 5.4 • Financial Statements of Company A and Company B for the Year Following the Year of the Intercompany Sale of Land

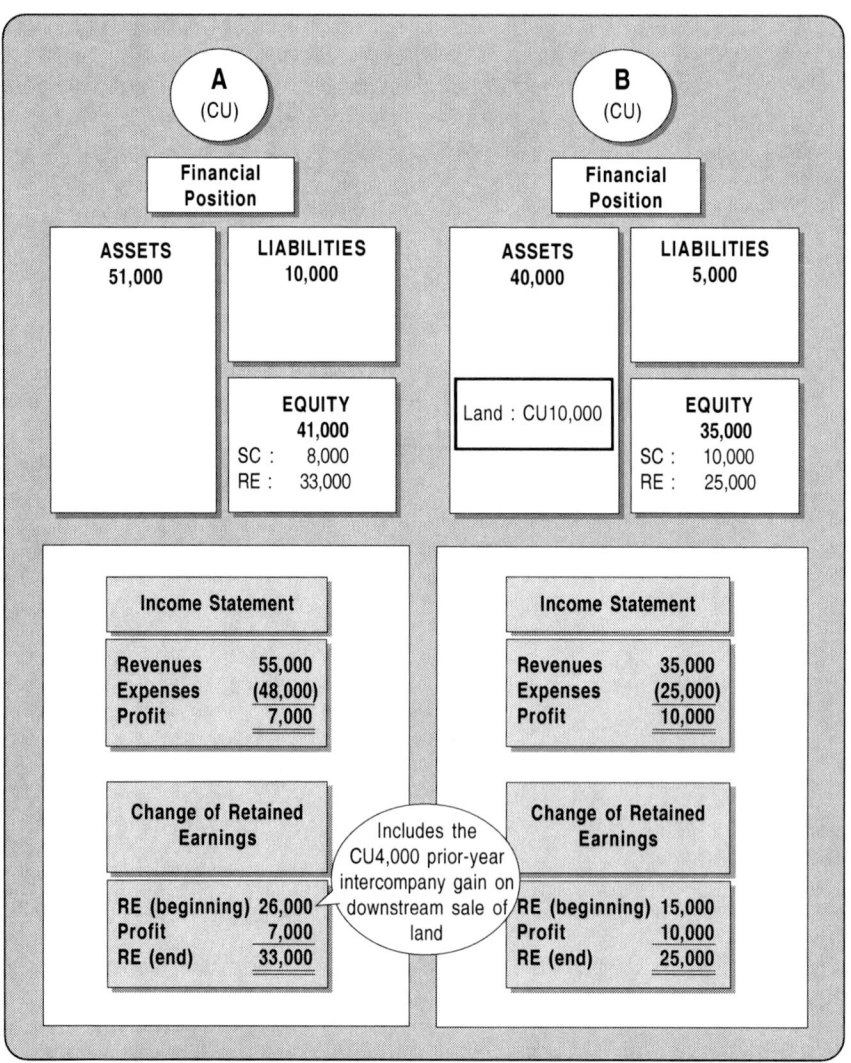

As for consolidation in the year of sale, adjustments for post-transaction consolidations will depend on whether or not the land has been resold by Company B during the year to an unrelated party. These two scenarios are analyzed once more in the following sections.

5.2.1 The Land is Still Held by the Purchasing Affiliate

If the land remains in the consolidated group at the end of the year, the initial gain of CU4,000 previously recognized by Company A is still considered to be unrealized from the viewpoint of the economic entity. Recall that the realization of the gain will be complete only if the land is ultimately sold to an unrelated party. Meanwhile, prior-year intercompany gain must be deferred. Since the gain on sale is included in Company A's Retained Earnings and

Company B's Land, the gain must be removed from these two accounts. The consolidation entry necessary to eliminate the CU4,000 prior-year intercorporate gain is presented below.

> Retained Earnings (A)   4,000
>   Land (B)   4,000

This elimination entry must be repeated in subsequent consolidation periods for as long as the land is not sold to an outside party.

Since the current-year consolidated income statement is not affected by the elimination of prior-year intercorporate gain on sale, the consolidated profit (CU17,000) is equivalent to the profit of Company A (CU7,000) plus the profit of Company B (CU10,000), as stated in their individual records (see Exhibit 5.4).

Effect on Income Tax Allocation

Because prior-year gain on sale of land is still unrealized at the end of the current period, the temporary difference recognized in the year of transfer remains untouched. Therefore, the following additional entry would have been necessary to restore the opening tax balances.

> Deferred Tax   1,200
>   Retained Earnings   1,200

(CU4,000 X 30%) = CU1,200

Effect on Non-Controlling Interest Valuation

Assume that Company A had a 70 percent interest in Company B instead of 100 percent. Since the elimination of prior-year downstream gain on sale of land has no impact on the consolidated income statement of the period, the allocation of the consolidated profit for the year to majority and minority shareholders is not affected. However, if the intercompany transfer were upstream, Company B's net value since acquisition should have been decreased so as to eliminate the CU4,000 prior-year gain that is still unrealized at the end of the current period. Following this correction, the net adjusted value of Company B since acquisition would be allocated proportionally between the minority and majority interests in the consolidation process (see chapter 3).

5.2.2 The Land Has Been Resold to an Outsider

Assume that Company B sold the transferred land to an unrelated party for CU15,000. Hence, Company B recognized a gain on sale to the outside party of CU5,000 which is equal to the difference between the selling price (CU15,000) and prior-year transfer price (CU10,000) (see Exhibit 5.5).

Exhibit 5.5 • Financial Statements of Company A and Company B Following the Year of the Intercompany Sale of Land - Company B Has Resold the Land to an Outside Party for CU15,000

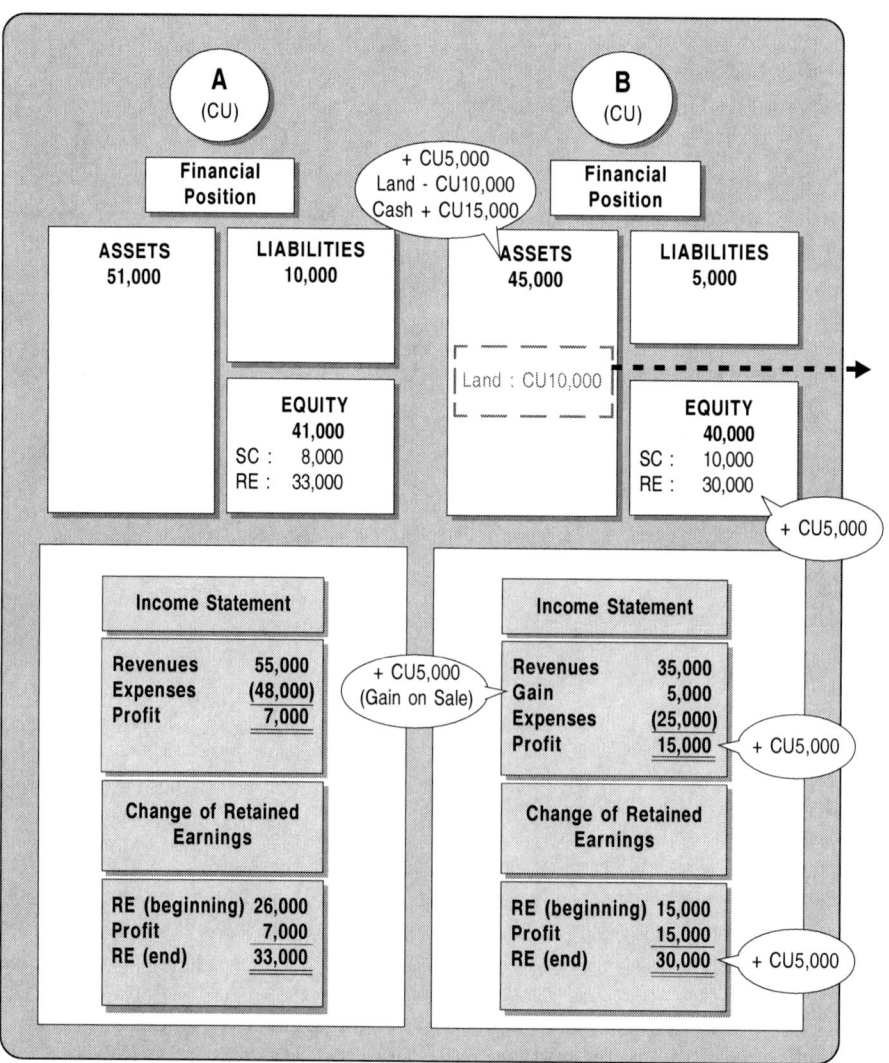

Since this transaction completes the realization of the gain from the consolidated entity's perspective, the CU4,000 prior-period deferred gain on downstream sale of land is now being fully realized and must be added back into the current consolidated profit. Recall that the gain on sale of land is included in the opening balance of Company A's Retained Earnings. Therefore, the transfer of the gain in the current year is achieved by reducing the opening balance of Company A's Retained Earnings by CU4,000. This amount is then reclassified as a realized gain in the current period. Exhibit 5.6 illustrates the process.

Chapter 5 Intercompany Sale of Land   153

Exhibit 5.6 • Financial Statements of Company A and Company B Following the Year of the Intercompany Sale of Land - Recognition of Prior-Year Deferred Intercompany Gain

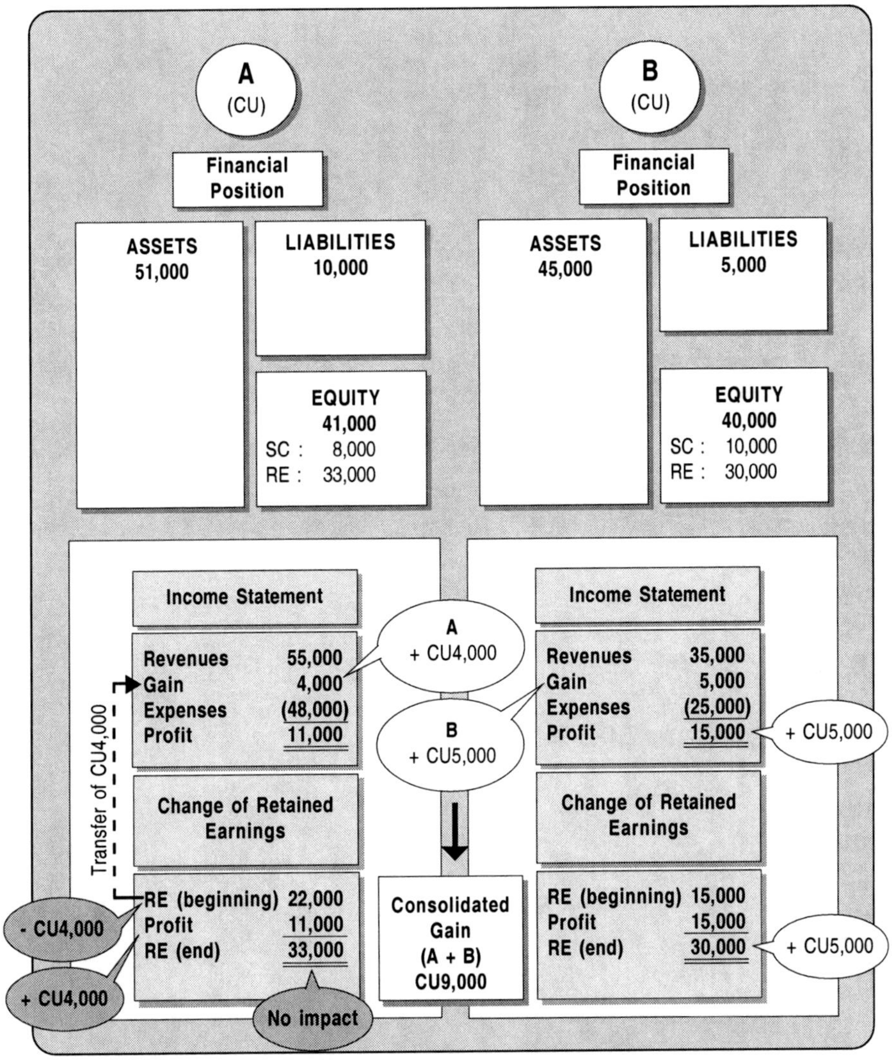

The following consolidation adjustment is required to recognize the CU4,000 prior-year deferred gain in the current accounting period.

Retained Earnings (A)	4,000	
Gain on Sale of Land (A)		4,000

With this entry, the timing of income recognition has been switched from the year of transaction into the year in which the land is sold to an external party. The total gain on sale of CU9,000 that will be reported in the consolidated income statement will reflect the gain that would have been accounted for by Company A if Company A had sold the land to an outsider in the current period for CU15,000. The computation of the consolidated profit for the year is reported below.

◆ Consolidated Profit for the Year		CU
• A's adjusted profit:		
- A's profit	7,000	
- Recognition of prior-period deferred gain on downstream sale of land	4,000	11,000
• B's profit (which includes a gain on resale of land of CU5,000)		15,000
Total		26,000

The realization of the gain has no impact on the net consolidated value at the end of the current period. In fact, consolidated Retained Earnings will consist of Company A's Retained Earnings, which already includes the CU4,000 prior-year gain on downstream sale of land, plus Company B's Retained Earnings, which includes the CU5,000 current-year gain on resale of land. Moreover, the land is no longer retained within the consolidated entity. Therefore, no adjustment is needed if only the consolidated statement of financial position of Company A is prepared. From a consolidated viewpoint, all aspects of the intercompany transaction are complete.

Effect on Income Tax Allocation

Prior-year gain on sale of land has been realized in the current period. Therefore, the temporary difference recognized in the year of transfer has now been consumed. The following additional entry would have been necessary in order to defer to the current period the income tax paid by Company A in the prior period.

Income Tax Expense	1,200	
Retained Earnings		1,200

(CU4,000 X 30%) = CU1,200

Effect on Non-Controlling Interest Valuation

If we assume that Company A had a 70 percent interest in Company B instead of 100 percent, the following additional considerations would have been needed.

If the transaction were downstream

If the intercompany sale of land were downstream, only Company A's profit should have been adjusted so as to account for the realization of the CU4,000 prior-year deferred gain. Therefore, the allocation of the CU26,000 consolidated profit to minority and majority shareholders would have been the following:

Consolidated Profit Allocated to A		CU
· A's adjusted profit:		
- A's profit	7,000	
- Recognition of prior-year deferred gain	4,000	11,000
· 70 percent of B's profit (CU15,000 X 70%)		10,500
Total		**21,500**

Consolidated Profit Allocated to Minority Shareholders	
30 percent of B's profit (CU15,000 X 30%)	**4,500**

Notice that the CU4,000 realized gain is assigned entirely to Company A.

If the transaction were upstream

If the intercompany sale of land were upstream, Company B's profit should have been adjusted so as to account for the realization of the CU4,000 prior-year deferred gain. Therefore, the allocation of the CU26,000 consolidated profit to minority and majority shareholders would have been the following:

Consolidated Profit Allocated to A		CU
· A's profit		7,000
· 70 percent of B's adjusted profit:		
- B's profit	15,000	
- Recognition of prior-year deferred gain	4,000	
	19,000 X 70%	13,300
Total		**20,300**

Consolidated Profit Allocated to Minority Shareholders	
30 percent of B's adjusted profit (CU19,000 X 30%)	**5,700**

The CU4,000 realized gain is assigned proportionally between the parent company and the non-controlling interest.

Summary of the Consolidation Adjustments in Journal Entry Form

Period of Intercompany Sale of Land

If the Land is Held by the Purchasing Affiliate

Consolidation Entry
Gain on Sale of Land	xx	
Land		xx

To eliminate current-year intercompany gain on sale of land and reduce land to its cost basis.

Effect on Non-Controlling Interest Valuation
If the transfer is upstream and initiated by a non-wholly owned subsidiary, subsidiary's net value since acquisition and subsidiary's profit for the period must be decreased by the amount of intercompany gain. Subsidiary's net adjusted value since acquisition and subsidiary's adjusted profit for the period are then assigned proportionally between the parent company and the non-controlling interest.

Effect on Income Tax Allocation
Unrealized gain at the end of the period gives rise to a temporary difference that must be accounted for as follows:

Deferred Tax	xx	
Income Tax Expense		xx

(Unrealized current-year intercompany gain × Tax rate)

If the Land is Resold to an Outsider

No adjustment required

NOTE: The same principles would apply to an intercompany loss for as long as the loss does not reflect a decline in the value of the transferred asset.

Period Subsequent to the Year of Intercompany Sale of Land

If the Land is Still Held by the Purchasing Affiliate

Consolidation Entry
Retained Earnings	xx	
Land		xx

To eliminate prior-year intercompany gain on sale of land that is still unrealized and reduce land to its cost basis.

Effect on Non-Controlling Interest Valuation
If the transfer is upstream and initiated by a non-wholly owned subsidiary, subsidiary's net value since acquisition must be decreased by the amount of prior-year intercompany gain. Subsidiary's net adjusted value since acquisition is then assigned proportionally between the parent company and the non-controlling interest.

Effect on Income Tax Allocation
Since prior-year intercompany gain is still unrealized at the end of the period, the temporary difference recognized in year of transfer must be restored as the following.

Deferred Tax	xx	
Retained Earnings		xx

(Prior-year intercompany gain still unrealized X Tax rate)

If the Land is Resold to an Outsider

Consolidation Entry
Retained Earnings	xx	
Gain on Sale of Land		xx

To recognize prior-year deferred gain on sale of land.

Effect on Non-Controlling Interest Valuation
If the transfer is upstream and initiated by a non-wholly owned subsidiary, subsidiary's profit for the period must be increased by the amount of prior-year intercompany gain. Subsidiary's adjusted profit for the period is then allocated proportionally between the parent company and the non-controlling interest in the consolidated income statement.

Effect on Income Tax Allocation
Since prior-year intercompany gain is realized, the temporary difference recognized in year of transfer is consumed. Therefore, the following entry is necessary in order to defer to the current period the income tax paid by the selling affiliate in the previous period.

Income Tax Expense	xx	
Retained Earnings		xx

(Prior-year intercompany gain now realized X Tax rate)

Chapter 6

Intercompany Sales of Inventory

Intercompany Profits/Losses and Reciprocal Sales-Cost of Goods Sold

In this chapter

6.1 Consolidation in Period of Intercompany Sale of Inventory 160
    6.1.1 All the Inventory is Held by the Purchasing Affiliate 163
    6.1.2 All the Inventory Has Been Resold to External Parties 166
    6.1.3 Only a Portion of the Inventory Has Been Resold to External
         Parties 168

6.2 Consolidation in Period Subsequent to the Year of Intercompany
    Sale of Inventory 172

✎ Summary of the Consolidation Adjustments in Journal Entry Form 175

Key Concepts: Unrealized Intercompany Profits and Losses; Reciprocal Sales and Cost of Goods Sold

This chapter deals with *intercompany sales of inventory*. Inventory transactions are the most common form of intercompany exchange. The acquired items are either used within the company's operations or resold to external parties. In addition, intercompany profits or losses are not considered to be realized from the viewpoint of the consolidated entity until the earnings process culminates in a sale to external parties. Transferred inventory is normally disposed of currently or in the year following transfer. Any amount of transferred inventory retained within the group at the end of the year gives rise to *unrealized intercompany profit or loss* whereas any resale of merchandise in the year of intercorporate transfer gives rise to *reciprocal Sales and Cost of Goods Sold*. Unrealized intercompany profits and losses as well as reciprocal Sales and Cost of Goods Sold balances must be eliminated in the consolidation process.

Building on the basic consolidation procedures introduced in the previous chapter, this chapter examines the impact of intercompany transfers of inventory on the consolidated financial statements, first, for the accounting period during which the sale occurred, and second, for the period subsequent to the year of transaction.

6.1 Consolidation in Period of Intercompany Sale of Inventory

Assume that units of inventory were purchased from Company A by Company B, a wholly owned subsidiary, for CU10,000. The original cost of the inventory reported on the books of Company A before the sale is CU6,000. Company A's markup on this sale is 40 percent (gross profit of CU4,000/transfer price of CU10,000). The following presents the journal entries reported respectively by Company A and Company B to account for the intercompany transfer of inventory.

Books of A

Cash	10,000	
Sales		10,000

Cost of Goods Sold	6,000	
Inventory		6,000

Books of B

Inventory	10,000	
Cash		10,000

Condensed financial statements of Company A and Company B immediately prior to and after the intercompany sale of inventory are shown respectively in Exhibits 6.1 and 6.2.

Exhibit 6.1 • Financial Statements of Company A and Company B Prior to the Intercompany Sale of Inventory

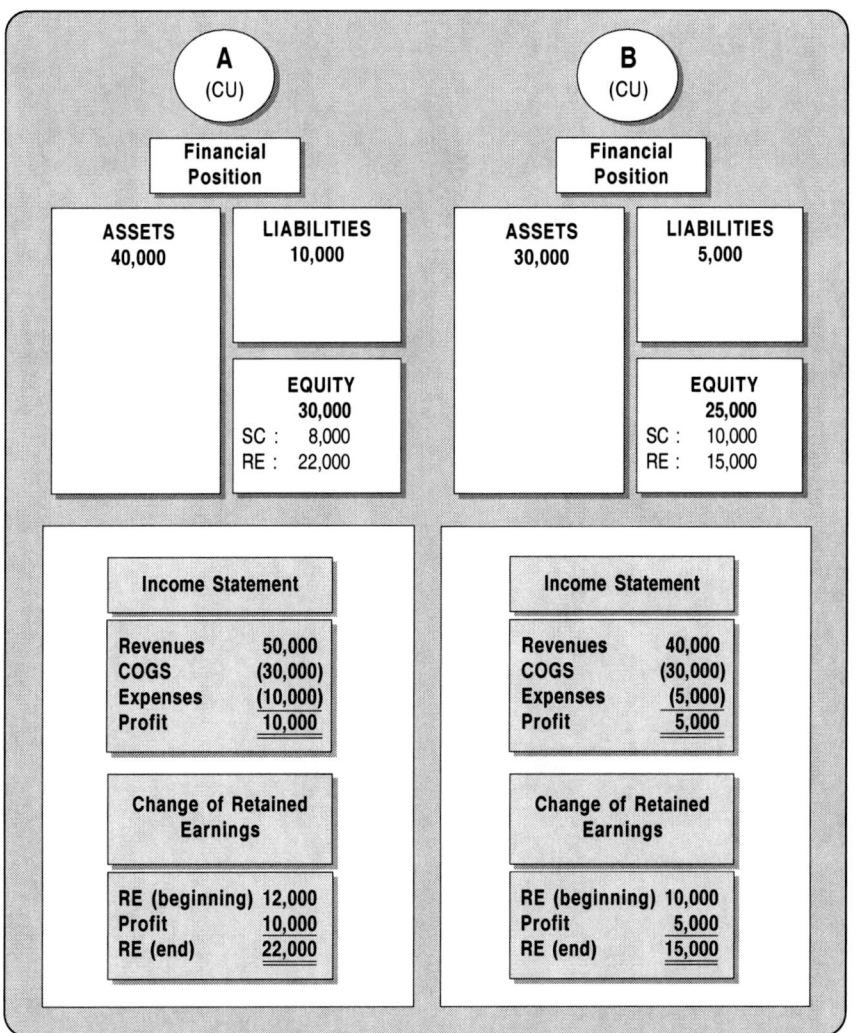

Following the intercompany transaction, Company A recognized a gross profit of CU4,000 which consists of the difference between the transfer price to Company B (CU10,000) and the original cost of the units being sold (CU6,000). As a result, Company A's profit for the year and retained earnings account at the end of the accounting period have both been increased by CU4,000, and the inventory is now carried on the books of Company B at a cost of CU10,000.

Exhibit 6.2 • Financial Statements of Company A and Company B Subsequent to the Intercompany Sale of Inventory

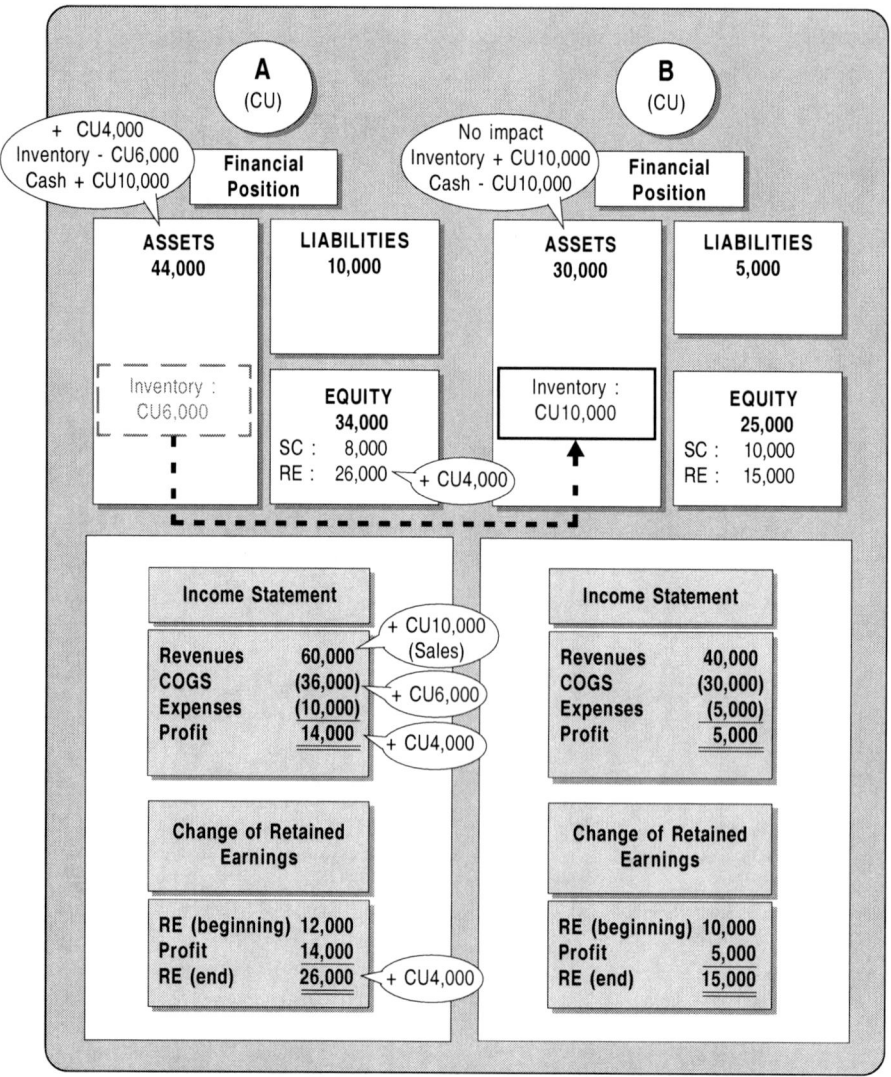

One of the three following scenarios must be taken into consideration in the preparation of the consolidated information for the period of inventory transfers:

1. All the inventory is held by the purchasing affiliate;
2. All the inventory has been resold to external parties;
3. Only a portion of the inventory has been resold to external parties.

Consolidation adjustments required under each of these three scenarios are reviewed next.

> **Note...**
>
> Illustrations are based on companies using a perpetual inventory system. The choice between periodic and perpetual inventory systems results in different entries on the books of the affiliated companies. However, at the end of the accounting period, when accounts are closed, the two systems should provide the same information regarding the value of the inventory to be reported in the statement of financial position and the cost of goods sold to be reported in the income statement. Consolidation entries introduced in this chapter aim at adjusting these two accounts and, as such, apply to companies that are using either a perpetual or a periodic inventory control system.

6.1.1 All the Inventory is Held by the Purchasing Affiliate

If all the units purchased by Company B from Company A are retained within the consolidated group at the end of the current period, the intercorporate gross profit of CU4,000 recognized initially by Company A must be considered as being unrealized from the viewpoint of the economic entity. The profit will be ultimately realized by subsequent reselling of the transferred goods to unrelated parties. In the meantime, the CU4,000 intercompany profit must be eliminated or deferred, and the cost of the retained units returned to their original cost, that is, CU6,000. Eliminating gross profit of CU4,000 is accomplished by reducing Company A's Sales and Cost of Goods Sold by CU10,000 and CU6,000, respectively. The consolidation entry to be entered in the consolidation worksheet is journalized below.

Sales (A)	10,000	
Cost of Goods Sold (A)		6,000
Inventory (B)		4,000

The internal movement of inventory is an event that creates no net change in the financial position of the economic entity. Therefore, the worksheet elimination previously introduced returns the Sales, Cost of Goods Sold and Inventory accounts to the amounts that would have existed had the intercompany transaction never occurred. As a result, consolidated profit (CU15,000) is comprised of the profit of Company A (CU 10,000) plus the profit of Company B (CU5,000) as reported by each affiliate prior to the intercompany sale of inventory (see Exhibit 6.1).

The following shows the computation of the current consolidated profit for the year.

◆ Consolidated Profit for the Year		CU
• A's adjusted profit:		
- A's profit	14,000	
- Unrealized profit on downstream sale of inventory	(4,000)	10,000
• B's profit		5,000
Total		<u>15,000</u>

If only Company A's consolidated statement of financial position is prepared, adjustments must be made to Retained Earnings and Inventory. More precisely, since the current-year gross profit on downstream sale of inventory has been closed to Company A's Retained Earnings, this account must be reduced by CU4,000 so as to remove the intercompany profit. Moreover, the cost of inventory held on hand by Company B includes the intercorporate profit and, thus, must be reduced by CU4,000 as well. The consolidation entry required to adjust the separate-entity statements of financial position appears below.

Retained Earnings (A)	4,000	
Inventory (B)		4,000

Effect on Income Tax Allocation

The gross profit on sale of inventory recognized by Company A will be taxed in the current period. However, for consolidation purposes, the profit is considered to be unrealized, thereby creating a temporary difference. This temporary difference will be consumed when the inventory will ultimately be sold to nonaffiliates, probably in the subsequent period. In the meantime, income tax paid by Company A on the intercompany profit must be deferred. Assuming a tax rate of 30 percent, the related tax to be removed from Company A's income statement amounts to CU1,200 (CU4,000 X 30%). The following additional entry would have been required.

Deferred Tax	1,200	
Income Tax Expense		1,200

Effect on Non-Controlling Interest Valuation

The consolidated adjustments illustrated so far are similar regardless of whether the transaction is downstream or upstream, for as long as the subsidiary B is wholly owned by Company A. If we assume that Company A had a 70 percent interest in Company B instead of 100 percent, the following additional considerations would have been needed.

If the transaction were downstream

If the intercompany sale of inventory were downstream, only Company A's profit should have been adjusted so as to eliminate the intercompany gross profit of CU4,000. Therefore, the allocation of the CU15,000 consolidated profit to minority and majority shareholders would have been the following:

Consolidated Profit Allocated to A		CU
A's adjusted profit:		
- A's profit	14,000	
- Unrealized profit on sale of inventory	(4,000)	10,000
70 percent of B's profit (CU5,000 X 70%)		3,500
Total		**13,500**

Consolidated Profit Allocated to Minority Shareholders	
30 percent of B's profit (CU5,000 X 30%)	**1,500**

Notice that the CU4,000 unrealized gross profit is assigned entirely to Company A.

If the transaction were upstream

If the intercompany sale of inventory were upstream, Company B's profit should have been adjusted so as to eliminate the intercompany gross profit of CU4,000. Therefore, the allocation of the CU15,000 consolidated profit to minority and majority shareholders would have been the following:

Consolidated Profit Allocated to A			CU
A's profit			10,000
70 percent of B's adjusted profit:			
- B's profit (which would include the intercompany profit)	9,000		
- Unrealized profit on sale of inventory	(4,000)		
	5,000	X 70%	3,500
Total			**13,500**

Consolidated Profit Allocated to Minority Shareholders	
30 percent of B's adjusted profit (CU5,000 X 30%)	**1,500**

The CU4,000 unrealized gross profit is assigned proportionally between the parent company and the non-controlling interest.

6.1.2 All the Inventory Has Been Resold to External Parties

Assume that during the year, Company B resold all the units of inventory to outsiders for CU15,000. Exhibit 6.3 depicts the impact of this transaction on the financial statements of the affiliated companies.

Exhibit 6.3 • Financial Statements of Company A and Company B Following the Resale of Inventory to Outside Parties for CU15,000

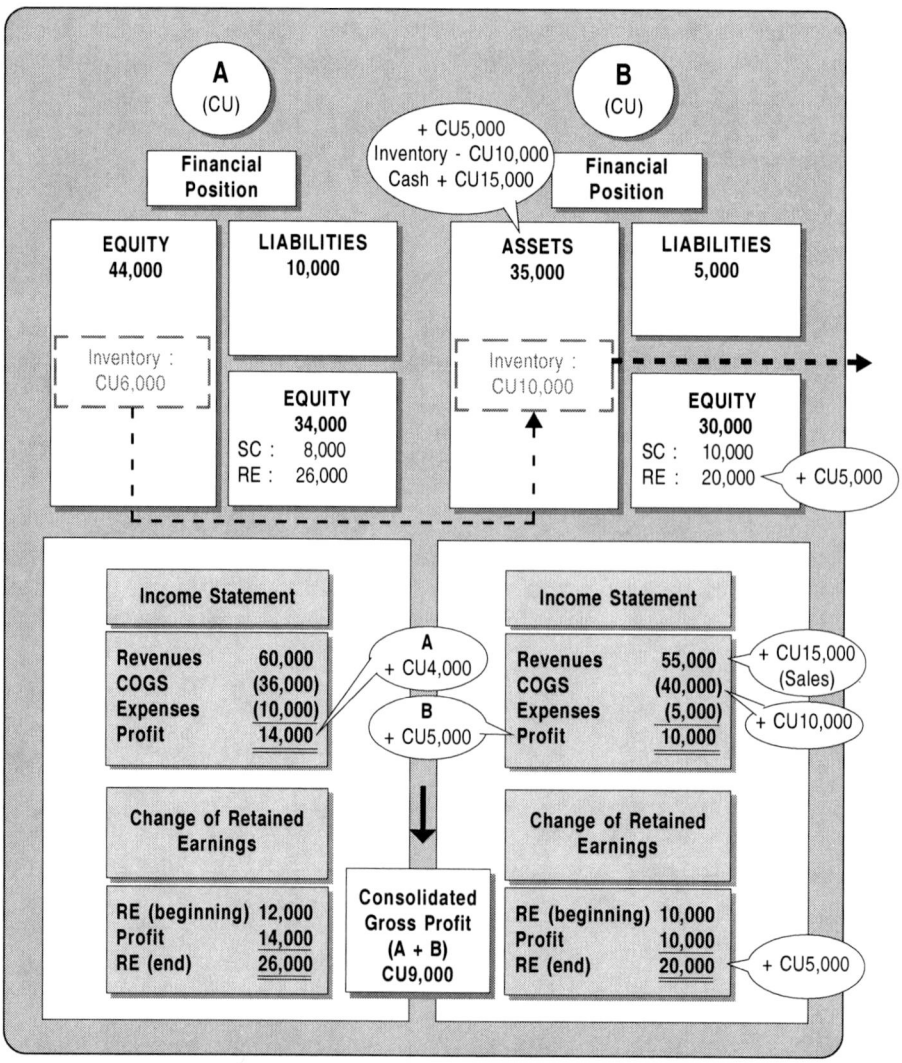

Company B recognized a gross profit of CU5,000, that is, the difference between the selling price (CU15,000) and the cost of the units being sold (CU10,000). Journal entries on the books of Company B following the resale are shown below.

Cash	15,000	
Sales		15,000

Cost of Goods Sold	10,000	
Inventory		10,000

The current-year gross profit on sales, recognized first by Company A following the intercompany sale of inventory (CU4,000) and subsequently by Company B following the resale of this inventory to outsiders (CU5,000), will be combined in the consolidation process. The consolidated gross profit of CU9,000 (CU4,000 + CU5,000) will then reflect the profit realized by the consolidated entity, which is also the profit that would have been realized by Company A if Company A had sold all the units directly to unrelated parties for CU15,000. In this scenario, the journal entries that Company A would have reported are shown below.

Cash	15,000	
Sales		15,000

Cost of Goods Sold	6,000	
Inventory		6,000

The consolidated profit of CU24,000 is made up of Company A's profit of CU 14,000 (which includes a current-year gross profit of CU4,000 on intercompany sale of inventory) and Company B's profit of CU10,000 (which includes a current-year gross profit of CU5,000 on resale of inventory). As the transferred inventory is no longer held by the consolidated entity and the intercompany gross profit of CU4,000 has now been earned, there is no need to consider this intercorporate transaction in subsequent consolidations.

Since the intercorporate profit is viewed as being realized, one could conclude that no adjustment is required for consolidation purposes. However, the resale of inventory to external parties in a period of intercorporate transfer leads to reciprocal Sales and Cost of Goods Sold balances in the income statement. As illustrated in Exhibit 6.4, both accounts are inflated by CU10,000. This amount reflects the price paid by Company B for the units being resold.

Exhibit 6.4 • Resale of Inventory in Period of Intercorporate Transfer - Impact on the Income Statement Balances of the Affiliated Companies

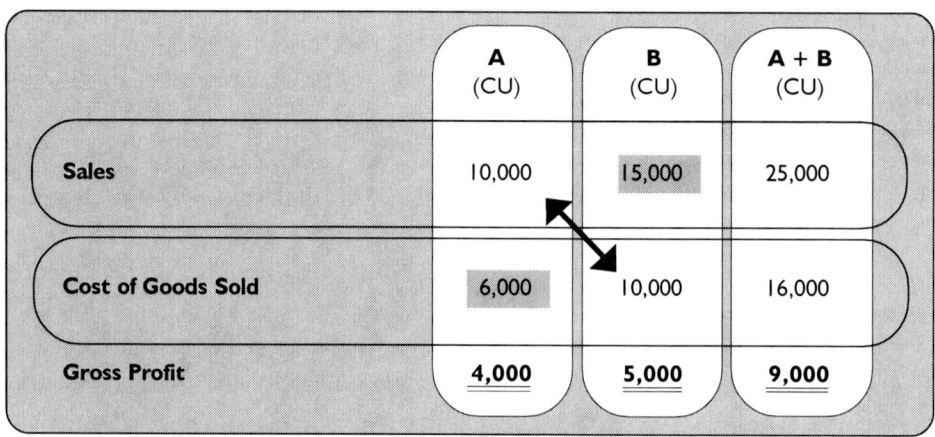

From the viewpoint of the consolidated entity, only the value of the inventory on the original owner's financial records (Company A) and the selling price of this inventory to unrelated parties must be reported in the consolidated income statement, that is, CU6,000 and CU15,000, respectively (shaded values in Exhibit 6.4). Therefore, reciprocal Sales and Cost of Goods Sold balances must be eliminated with the following consolidation entry.

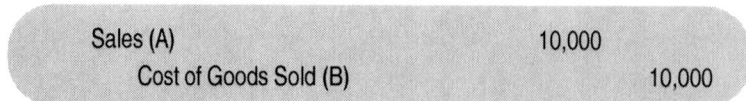

Overstatement of both sales and cost of goods sold has no impact on the consolidated statement of financial position. Therefore, if only the consolidated statement of financial position of Company A were prepared, no adjustment would have been required.

6.1.3 Only a Portion of the Inventory Has Been Resold to External Parties

If we assume that only a portion of the transferred inventory has been resold by Company B to unrelated parties (or if we assume that a portion of the transferred inventory is retained by Company B at the end of the period), two consolidation issues must be dealt with. The first relates to the units held by Company B in its ending inventory which will include an intercorporate gross profit. The second, relates to the units being resold by Company B to unrelated parties which will give rise to reciprocal Sales and Cost of Goods Sold. Recall that intercompany gross profits in ending inventories as well as reciprocal Sales and Cost of Goods Sold must be eliminated.

To illustrate, assume that Company B resold 60 percent of the transferred inventory to unrelated parties for CU7,500. Following the sale, Company B has recognized a gross profit of CU1,500, that is, the difference between the proceeds from the sale (CU7,500) and the cost of the units being sold (CU10,000 (transfer price) X 60% = CU6,000). Journal entries on the books of Company B to account for the resale are reproduced below.

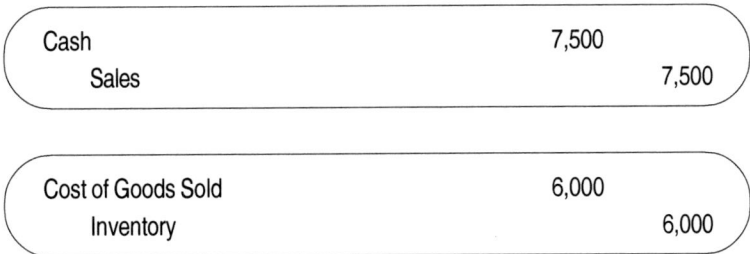

Exhibit 6.5 depicts the overall impact of the inventory transfer and subsequent resale on the separate-entity income statements of the affiliated companies.

Exhibit 6.5 • Resale of 60 Percent of Inventory in Period of Intercorporate Transfer - Impact on the Income Statement Balances of the Affiliated Companies

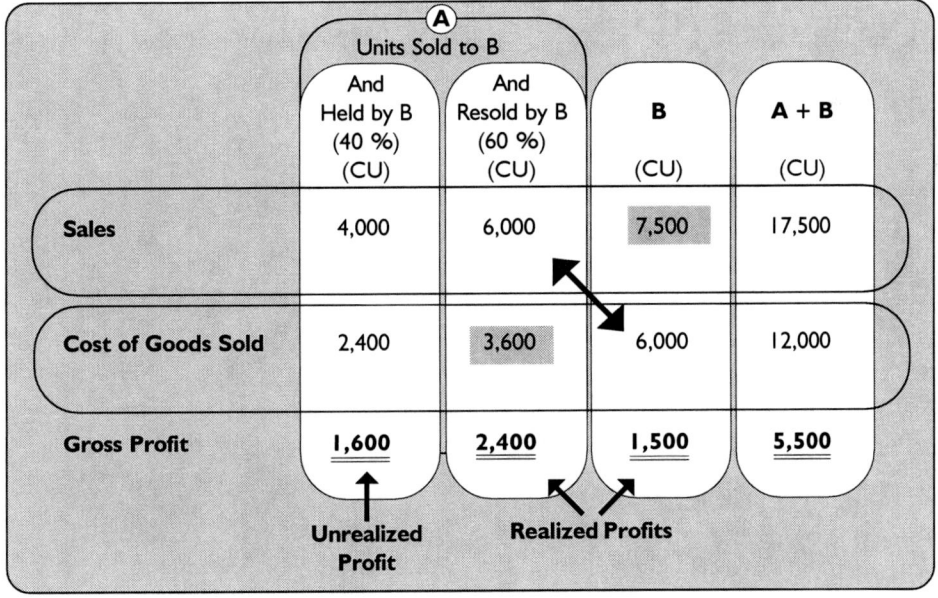

Elimination of Intercompany Profit on Sale of Inventory

40 percent of the transferred units are retained within the consolidated group at the end of the current period. The cost of these units for Company B equals CU4,000 (transfer price of CU10,000 X 40%). Recall that Company A's markup over sales is 40%. Therefore, an intercor-

porate profit of CU1,600 (CU4,000 X 40%) is included in Company B's ending inventory. This profit has been recognized by Company A but must be considered as being unrealized from the viewpoint of the economic entity and, as such, must be eliminated. Elimination of the CU1,600 unrealized profit is accomplished by reducing Company A's Sales and Cost of Goods Sold by CU4,000 and CU2,400 respectively (these figures are taken from the first column in Exhibit 6.5). In addition, the ending inventory carried on the books of Company B must be reduced by CU1,600 so as to return its value to its original cost (CU2,400). Consolidation adjustment required to remove the intercompany gross profit is shown below.

Sales (A)	4,000	
Cost of Goods Sold (A)		2,400
Inventory (B)		1,600

Elimination of Reciprocal Sales and Cost of Goods Sold

Since 60 percent of the transferred inventory has been resold to outsiders, 60 percent of the intercorporate gross profit, that is CU2,400 (total intercompany profit of CU4,000 X 60%), has been realized (see second column in Exhibit 6.5). However, the purchase and the subsequent resale of the transferred units give rise to CU6,000 overstatement of Sales and Cost of Goods Sold. The overstatement reflects the price paid by Company B for the units being resold. The consolidation entry necessary to eliminate reciprocal Sales and Cost of Goods Sold balances is reproduced below.

Sales (A)	6,000	
Cost of Goods Sold (B)		6,000

The two previous consolidation entries can easily be combined into a single adjusting entry as the following:

Sales (A)	10,000	
Cost of Goods Sold (A and B)		8,400
Inventory (B)		1,600

In sum, the amounts to be reported in the consolidated income statement are those that reflect the original cost of the units sold to external parties (CU3,600) and the price paid by the outsiders for these units (CU7,500) (see shaded values in Exhibit 6.5). All the remaining figures from Exhibit 6.5 are eliminated via the combined consolidation entry previously introduced. This includes Sales of CU10,000 (CU4,000 + CU6,000) and Cost of Goods Sold of CU8,400 (CU2,400 + CU6,000).

If only Company A's consolidated statement of financial postion is prepared, adjustment must remove the CU1,600 unrealized gross profit from Company A's ending retained earnings. The same amount must also be removed from Company B's ending inventory. The consolidation adjustment required to eliminate the current-year intercompany profit from the statement of financial position is journalized below.

Retained Earnings (A)	1,600	
Inventory (B)		1,600

 What If...

Intercompany transfers of inventory often give rise to reciprocal receivable and payable accounts. These offsetting balances at the end of the period must be canceled out in order to avoid overstating consolidated current assets and liabilities.

To illustrate, assume that, in the case of Company A and Company B, these reciprocal balances amount to CU5,000 at the end of the current period. Therefore, the following additional consolidation entry would be required.

Accounts Payable (B)	5,000	
Accounts Receivable (A)		5,000

Effect on Income Tax Allocation

Any taxes paid by the selling affiliate on unrealized intercompany profits must be deferred for consolidation purposes. In our illustration, an unrealized gross profit of CU1,600 has been recognized by Company A. Assuming a tax rate of 30 percent, the related tax to be removed from Company A's income statement amounts to CU480 (CU1,600 X 30%). Had the income tax been considered, the following additional consolidation entry would be required.

Deferred Tax	480	
Income Tax Expense		480

6.2 Consolidation in Period Subsequent to the Year of Intercompany Sale of Inventory

Companies rarely carry the cost of inventory purchased from an affiliate for more than one accounting period. Therefore, it is most likely that any remaining transferred inventory at the end of an accounting period will be resold in the subsequent year. In this case, the resale of the units to external parties will complete the realization of profit. As a result, the unrealized profit from the prior year will be viewed as being realized in the current period.

To illustrate, we continue the case where all the units transferred to Company B were held at the end of the year. Unless specified otherwise, we can assume that all the units are resold in the current period. Recall that consolidation entries to eliminate the intercompany profit in the year of transfer have not been posted to the affiliates' books. Therefore, the CU4,000 deferred profit is carried into the affiliates' beginning balances, that is, Company A's Retained Earnings and Company B's Inventory. Consequently, to recognize the profit in the current period, Company A's Retained Earnings must be reduced by CU4,000. This amount is then transferred back into the income statement of the period as shown below.

Because the CU4,000 unrealized intercompany profit from the prior year is included in Company B's beginning inventory, the full amount of intercorporate profit has been charged by Company B during the year to Cost of Goods Sold when the transferred inventory was resold. Therefore, to recognize prior-year deferred profit in the current period, Cost of Goods Sold of Company B must be decreased by CU4,000.

Note that recognition of the deferred profit has no impact on the net consolidated value at the end of the current period. Since the units of inventory have been disposed of and the intercompany profit is now fully realized, no adjustment is needed if only the consolidated statement of financial position of Company A is prepared. Moreover, no additional considerations need be given the intercompany sale of inventory in future consolidation periods.

Assume that the profits of Company A and Company B as stated in their individual records are CU7,000 and CU15,000, respectively. Computation of the consolidated profit for the year is shown next.

◆ Consolidated Profit for the Year		CU
• A's adjusted profit :		
- A's profit	7,000	
- Recognition of prior-period deferred profit on downstream sale of inventory	4,000	11,000
• B's profit (which includes the gross profit or loss on resale of inventory)		15,000
Total		<u>26,000</u>

Effect on Income Tax Allocation

Since the prior-year gross profit on sale of inventory has been realized in the current period, the temporary difference recognized in the year of transfer has now been consumed. Therefore, the following additional entry would have been necessary in order to defer to the current period the income tax paid by Company A in the prior period.

Income Tax Expense	1,200	
Retained Earnings		1,200

(CU4,000 X 30%) = CU1,200

Effect on Non-Controlling Interest Valuation

If we assume that Company A had a 70 percent interest in Company B instead of 100 percent, the following additional considerations would have been needed.

If the transaction were downstream
If the intercompany sale of inventory were downstream, only Company A's profit should have been adjusted so as to account for the realization of the CU4,000 prior-year deferred gross profit. Therefore, the allocation of the CU26,000 consolidated profit to minority and majority shareholders would have been the following:

Consolidated Profit Allocated to A		CU
· A's adjusted profit:		
- A's profit	7,000	
- Recognition of prior-year deferred profit	4,000	11,000
· 70 percent of B's profit (CU15,000 X 70%)		10,500
Total		**21,500**

Consolidated Profit Allocated to Minority Shareholders	
30 percent of B's profit (CU15,000 X 30%)	**4,500**

Notice that the CU4,000 realized profit is assigned entirely to Company A.

If the transaction were upstream
If the intercompany sale of inventory were upstream, Company B's profit should have been adjusted so as to account for the realization of the CU4,000 prior-year deferred gross profit. Therefore, the allocation of the CU26,000 consolidated profit to minority and majority shareholders would have been the following:

Consolidated Profit Allocated to A			CU
· A's profit			7,000
· 70 percent of B's adjusted profit:			
- B's profit	15,000		
- Recognition of prior-year deferred profit	4,000		
	19,000	X 70%	13,300
Total			**20,300**

Consolidated Profit Allocated to Minority Shareholders	
30 percent of B's adjusted profit (CU19,000 X 30%)	**5,700**

The CU4,000 realized gross profit is assigned proportionally between the parent company and the non-controlling interest.

Chapter 6 Intercompany Sale of Inventory

Summary of the Consolidation Adjustments in Journal Entry Form

Period of Intercompany Sale of Inventory

If the Inventory (or a Portion of it) is Held by the Purchasing Affiliate

Consolidation Entry
Sales	XX	
Cost of Goods Sold		XX
Inventory (unrealized profit)		XX

To eliminate current-year intercompany profit on sale of inventory, eliminate any reciprocal Sales and Cost of Goods Sold balances and reduce inventory to its cost basis.

Effect on Non-Controlling Interest Valuation
If the transfer is upstream and initiated by a non-wholly owned subsidiary, subsidiary's net value since acquisition and subsidiary's profit for the period must be decreased by the amount of intercompany gross profit. Subsidiary's net adjusted value since acquisition and subsidiary's adjusted profit for the period are then assigned proportionally between the parent company and the non-controlling interest.

Effect on Income Tax Allocation
Unrealized profit at the end of the period gives rise to a temporary difference that must be accounted for as the following:

Deferred Tax	XX	
Income Tax Expense		XX

(Unrealized current-year intercompany profit X Tax rate)

If the Inventory (or a Portion of it) is Resold to External Parties

Sales	XX	
Cost of Goods Sold		XX

To eliminate reciprocal Sales and Cost of Goods Sold balances.

Period Subsequent to the Year of Intercompany Sale of Inventory

If the Inventory is Resold to External Parties (Most Likely Scenario)

Consolidation Entry

Retained Earnings	XX	
Cost of Goods Sold		XX

To recognize prior-year deferred profit on sale of inventory.

Effect on Non-Controlling Interest Valuation

If the transfer is upstream and initiated by a non-wholly owned subsidiary, subsidiary's profit for the period must be increased by the amount of prior-year intercompany profit. Subsidiary's adjusted profit for the period is then allocated proportionally between the parent company and the non-controlling interest in the consolidated income statement.

Effect on Income Tax Allocation

Since prior-year intercompany profit is realized, the temporary difference recognized in year of transfer is consumed. Therefore, the following entry is necessary in order to defer to the current period the income tax paid by the selling affiliate in the previous period.

Income Tax Expense	XX	
Retained Earnings		XX

(Prior-year intercompany profit now realized $\times$ Tax rate)

NOTE: The same principles would apply to an intercompany loss for as long as the loss does not reflect a decline in the value of the transferred inventory.

Chapter 7

Intercompany Sales of Depreciable Assets

Realization of Intercompany Gains and Losses Over the Remaining Economic Life of the Transferred Asset

In this chapter

7.1 Consolidation in Period of Intercompany Sale of Asset 178
7.2 Consolidation in Periods Subsequent to the Year of Intercompany Sale of Asset 183

✎ Summary of the Consolidation Adjustments in Journal Entry Form 188

Key Concepts: Excess Depreciation.

This chapter introduces consolidation techniques dealing with *intercompany sales of depreciable assets*. Recall that on intercompany sales of land (chapter 5) or inventory (chapter 6), intercompany profits or losses are realized when the transferred asset is eventually sold to nonaffiliates. However, for depreciable assets, the ultimate realization of the intercorporate gain or loss normally occurs gradually over the remaining economic life of the asset as it is used by the purchasing affiliate in generating revenue. More precisely, if an intercompany gain on sale of a depreciable asset occurs, the buyer will compute depreciation expense on the inflated transfer cost. As a result, depreciation expense on the books of the purchasing affiliate will be overstated for consolidation purposes. One can view this *excess depreciation* as progressively offsetting or consuming the intercompany gain over the life of the transferred asset. Likewise, eliminating the excess depreciation in the consolidation process leads to considering a portion of the deferred intercompany gain as being realized.

This chapter illustrates the consolidation procedures required in the case of intercompany sale of depreciable assets, first, for the period of intercompany sale, and second, for time periods subsequent to the year of transaction.

7.1 Consolidation in Period of Intercompany Sale of Asset

Assume that a piece of equipment is purchased from Company A by Company B, a wholly owned subsidiary, for CU10,000. The equipment originally cost Company A CU6,000 when purchased a few days ago from a nonaffiliate company. Therefore, the net book value of the equipment immediately before the intercompany sale is CU6,000. The following presents the journal entries on the books of the affiliated companies to account for the transfer.

Books of A

Cash	10,000	
Equipment		6,000
Gain on Sale of Equipment		4,000

Books of B

Equipment	10,000	
Cash		10,000

Condensed financial statements of Company A and Company B prior to the intercompany sale of equipment are shown in Exhibit 7.1. The impact of the intercorporate transfer on the individual financial records of both affiliated companies is depicted in Exhibit 7.2.

Exhibit 7.1 • Financial Statements of Company A and Company B Prior to the Intercompany Sale of Equipment

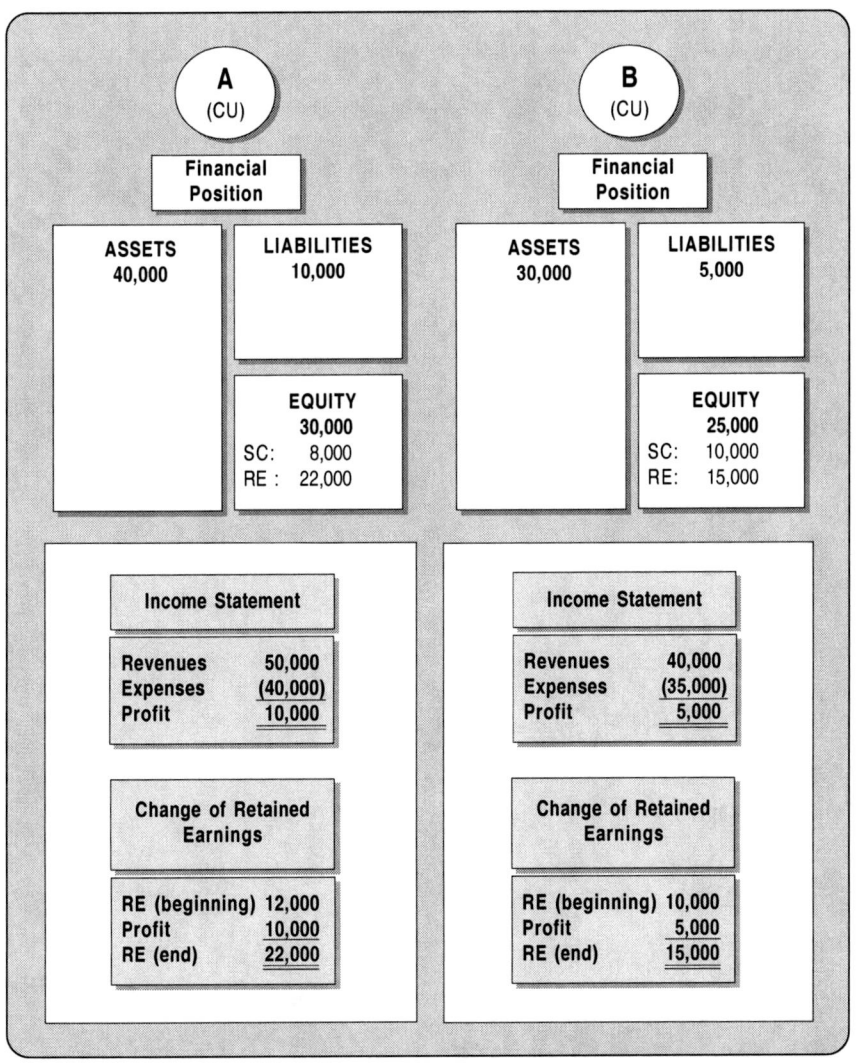

Company A recognized a gain on sale of CU4,000 which consists of the difference between the selling price (CU10,000) and the net book value of the equipment recorded at the time of the sale (CU6,000). Since the gain on sale of equipment is closed to Company A's retained earnings at the end of the period, the balance of that account has increased by CU4,000. Moreover, the value of the equipment now carried on the books of Company B (CU10,000) is based on the transfer price and, consequently, includes the intercompany gain on sale of CU4,000.

Exhibit 7.2 • Financial Statements of Company A and Company B Subsequent to the Intercompany Sale of Equipment

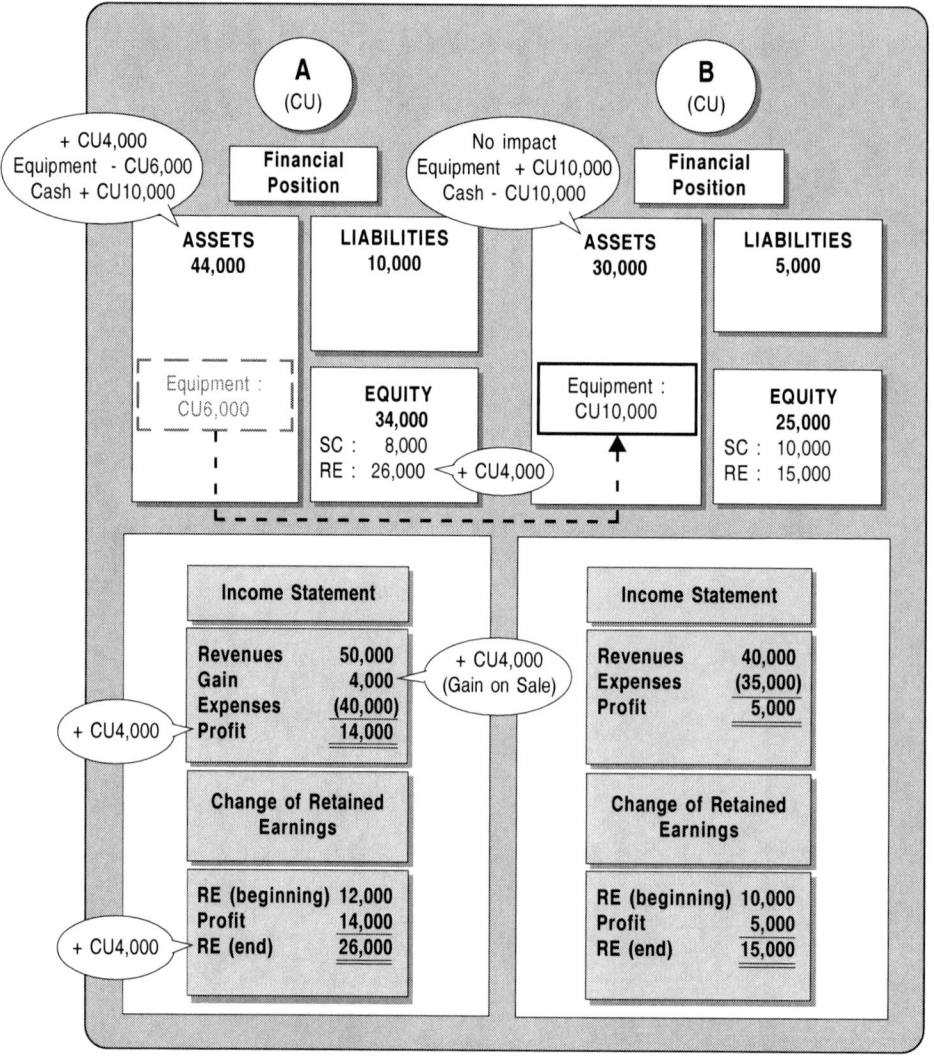

For consolidation purposes in the period of sale, two adjustments are needed, first, to eliminate the intercorporate gain on sale of equipment recognized by the selling affiliate (Company A), and second, to adjust the excess depreciation expensed by the purchasing affiliate (Company B). These two adjustments are analyzed in the following sections.

Elimination of Intercorporate Gain on Sale of Equipment

From the economic entity perspective, the intercompany gain on sale of equipment is considered to be unrealized as the transferred asset is retained in the consolidated group at the end of the year. Consistent with any other type of intercompany sale of assets, the intercorporate gain must be eliminated and the cost of the asset being sold returned to its original cost. The following workpaper entry is necessary to remove the intercompany gain.

Gain on Sale of Equipment (A)	4,000	
Equipment (B)		4,000

Adjustment of Excess Depreciation Expense on Equipment

Assume that the equipment is being used by the purchasing affiliate to generate revenue and, as such, is being depreciated using the straight-line method over a ten-year remaining useful life from the date of transfer. In addition, assume that there is no salvage value and that Company B is using a full year of depreciation for the year of acquisition. Therefore, the annual depreciation expense on equipment recorded by Company B amounts to CU1,000 (CU10,000/10 years) and is journalized as the following:

Depreciation Expense (B)	1,000	
Accumulated Depreciation (B)		1,000

Since depreciation expense on equipment reported by Company B is based on the transfer price (CU10,000), the expense includes a portion of the intercompany gain on sale of CU4,000. However, from a consolidated viewpoint, the intercompany gain is not recognized, thus, resulting in a depreciation expense being inflated. More precisely, had the asset not been sold to Company B, depreciation expense should have been CU600 (original cost of CU6,000 for the selling affiliate/10 years) rather than CU1,000. Therefore, the annual excess depreciation is CU400 (CU1,000 - CU600). This amount can also be obtained by dividing the intercompany gain over the remaining useful life of the equipment from the date of transfer (CU4,000/10 years). Details of this calculation are provided in Exhibit 7.3.

The adjusting entry required under the worksheet approach to correct the current-year excess depreciation is reported below.

This entry must be repeated for all ten years of the equipment's life.

Exhibit 7.3 • Consolidation of the Financial Statements of Company A - The Annual Excess Depreciation on Equipment

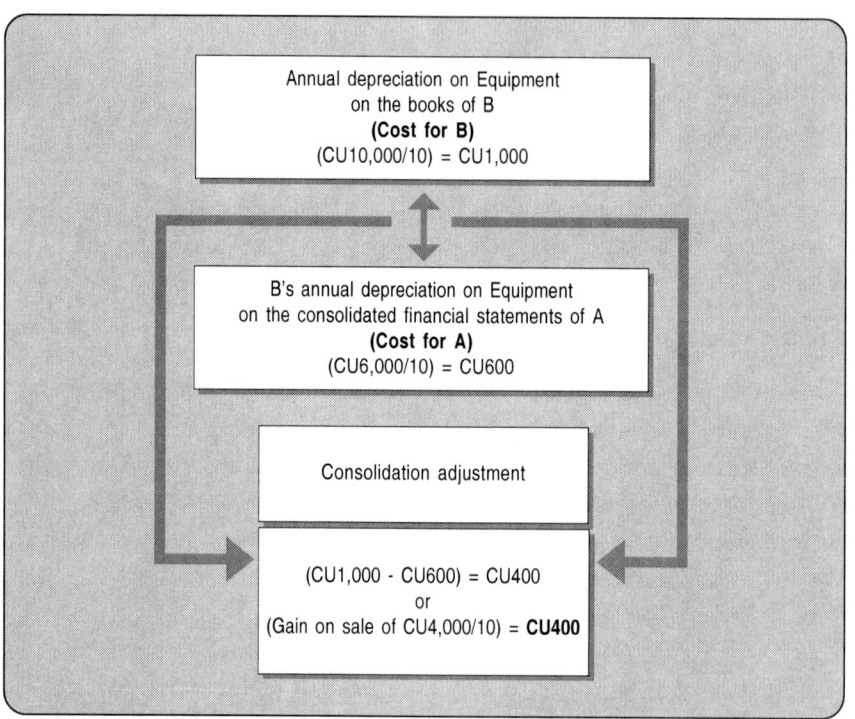

If only the consolidation of Company A's statement of financial position is prepared, adjustments must be made to Retained Earnings and Equipment. More precisely, as a result of eliminating the gain on downstream sale of equipment, consolidated Retained Earnings must be reduced by CU4,000. Conversely, consolidated Retained Earnings must be increased by CU400 following the adjustment of the current-year excess depreciation. In sum, a net amount of CU3,600 (CU4,000 - CU400) must be closed to Retained Earnings. This amount, which reflects the unamortized or unrealized portion of the intercompany gain at the end of the year, must be removed simultaneously from Retained Earnings and Equipment. The following presents the consolidation adjustment in journal entry form necessary to restate the statement of financial position accounts.

Effect on Income Tax Allocation

The gain on sale of equipment recognized by Company A (CU4,000) will be taxed in the current period. Conversely, the excess amortization expense (CU400) will reduce Company B's income tax for the same period. In sum, a net gain of CU3,600 will be taxed. Since this net gain is considered as being unrealized for consolidation purposes, a temporary difference is created. Assuming an average tax rate of 30 percent, the related tax to be removed from the consolidated income statement amounts to CU1,080 (CU3,600 X 30%) . Therefore, the following additional entry would have been required.

Deferred Tax	1,080	
Income Tax Expense		1,080

Effect on Non-Controlling Interest Valuation

The consolidated adjustments illustrated so far are similar regardless of whether the transaction is downstream or upstream for as long as the subsidiary B is wholly owned by Company A. If Company A had a 70 percent interest in Company B instead of 100 percent, the following additional considerations would have been needed.

If the transaction were downstream
If the intercompany sale of equipment were downstream, the unamortized portion of the gain at the end of the year (CU4,000 - CU400 = CU3,600) should be assigned entirely to Company A.

If the transaction were upstream
If the intercompany sale of equipment were upstream, the unamortized portion of the gain at the end of the year (CU4,000 - CU400 = CU3,600) should be assigned proportionally to majority and minority interests.

7.2 Consolidation in Periods Subsequent to the Year of Intercompany Sale of Asset

In subsequent years, the consolidation adjustments for the remaining or unamortized gain on sale of equipment will reflect the depreciation taken to date. The CU4,000 unrealized gain at the date of transaction will be realized over the following ten years (including the year of transfer) at a rate of CU400 per year while adjusting for the annual excess depreciation. After ten years, the intercompany gain will be fully realized and no further elimination will be needed. The following diagram illustrates the realization process of the gain.

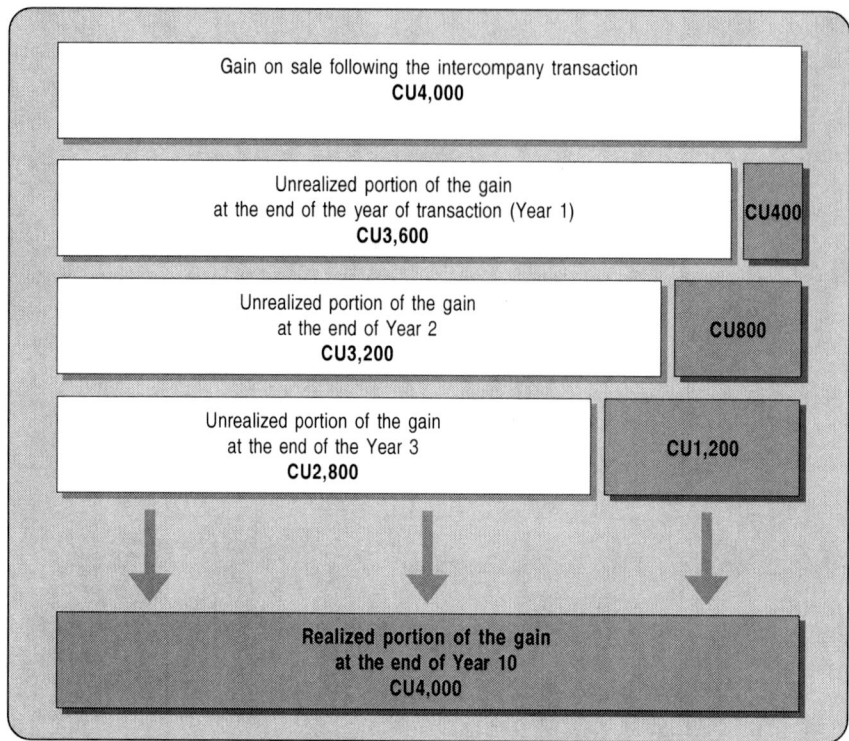

Consolidation Following the Year of Transaction (Year 2)

Consolidation adjustments made in the year of transfer do not remove the effect of the intercompany sale from the individual records of the affiliated companies. Therefore, if we proceed with the consolidation of Company A's financial statements for the period following the year of transaction (Year 2), the net gain or unrealized gain on sale of equipment at the beginning of the period (CU3,600) must be removed from the opening balance of Retained Earnings. This net gain is composed of the initial gain (CU4,000) less the portion of that gain being realized in year 1 (CU400). The first consolidation adjustment is to account for the unrealized portion of the gain at the beginning of the period. It is journalized as follows:

Retained Earnings (A and B)	3,600	
Accumulated Depreciation (B)	400	
Equipment (B)		4,000

In addition, the portion of the gain being realized in the current period (Year 2) must be accounted for by correcting the excess depreciation (CU400). The second adjustment necessary to achieve this objective is shown next.

Accumulated Depreciation (B)	400	
Depreciation Expense (B)		400

If only the consolidation of the statement of financial position is prepared, the net gain at the end of the second year should be removed from Retained Earnings and Equipment as follows:

Retained Earnings (A and B)	3,200	
Accumulated Depreciation (B)	800	
Equipment (B)		4,000

Effect on Non-Controlling Interest Valuation

If Company A had a 70 percent interest in Company B instead of 100 percent, the following additional considerations would have been needed.

If the transaction were downstream
If the intercompany sale of equipment were downstream, the unamortized portion of the gain at the end of the year (CU4,000 - CU800 = CU3,200) should be assigned entirely to Company A. In the income statement, the portion of the gain being realized (CU400) should also be assigned entirely to Company A.

If the transaction were upstream
If the intercompany sale of equipment were upstream, the unamortized portion of the gain at the end of the year (CU4,000 - CU800 = CU3,200) should be assigned proportionally to majority and minority interests. In the income statement, the portion of the gain being realized (CU400) should also be assigned proportionally to controlling and minority interests.

Consolidation for Year 7

Assume that we are now preparing the consolidated financial statements of Company A for Year 7. The first step would consist of computing the unrealized portion of the gain at the beginning of the period. For this, we have to recognize the fact that the equipment has already been amortized for six years, that is, Year 1 through Year 6, inclusive. Therefore, the portion of the gain being realized in prior years equals CU2,400 (CU400 X 6 years) and the unamortized portion of the gain at the beginning of the current year is CU1,600 (CU4,000 - CU2,400) as shown next.

Unrealized Gain at the Beginning of Year 7

- Initial gain on sale of equipment — 4,000
- Portion of the gain being realized from year 1 through year 6, inclusive, while adjusting the excess depreciation (CU400 X 6 years) — (2,400)

Total — **1,600**

The first adjustment aims at eliminating the net gain at the start of the period. It is journalized as follows:

```
Retained Earnings (A and B)        1,600
Accumulated Depreciation (B)       2,400
     Equipment (B)                            4,000
```

The second adjustment accounts for the realization of the gain in the current period (Year 7) while correcting the excess depreciation.

```
Accumulated Depreciation (B)         400
     Depreciation Expense (B)                  400
```

Effect on Income Tax Allocation

Since the initial unrealized gain on sale of equipment (CU4,000) is being realized at a rate of CU400 a year (CU4,000/10 years), the temporary difference of CU1,200 (CU4,000 X 30% tax rate) recognized at the date of transfer decreases at a rate of CU120 a year (CU400 X 30% tax rate). Deferred Tax at the end of Year 7 is equal to CU360 and reflects the tax related to the unrealized portion of the gain at the end of the period (CU400 X 3 remaining years X 30% tax rate). The following presents the additional consolidation entry that would have been required for Year 7 had the income tax allocation been considered.

```
Deferred Tax                         360
Income Tax Expense                   120
     Retained Earnings                         480
```

Consolidation after Year 10

At the end of Year 10, the equipment is completely depreciated and the gain on sale of equipment fully realized. The only consolidation adjustment required consists of removing the initial gain of CU4,000 simultaneously from Accumulated Depreciation and Equipment as shown below.

Accumulated Depreciation (B)	4,000	
Equipment (B)		4,000

This consolidation entry has no impact on the net consolidated value and will have to be repeated in subsequent periods until the equipment is either retired or written off.

 What If...

If the equipment is ever resold to an outside party prior to the end of its economic life, the remaining portion of the gain at the date of the sale would be realized and, as such, would have to be recognized on the consolidated income statement.

To illustrate, assume that the equipment is sold by Company B to an outsider at the beginning of year 7. Thus, the unrealized portion of the gain at that time (CU1,600) must be recognized in Year 7 as follows:

Retained Earnings	1,600	
Gain on Sale of Equipment		1,600

Summary of the Consolidation Adjustments in Journal Entry Form

Period of Intercompany Sale of Depreciable Asset

If the Asset is Used by the Purchasing Affiliate to Generate Revenue (Most Likely Scenario)

Consolidation Entries

Gain on Sale of Asset	XX	
Asset		XX

To eliminate current-year intercompany gain on sale of asset and reduce asset to its cost basis.

Accumulated Depreciation	XX	
Depreciation Expense		XX

To recognize a portion of the gain as being realized in the current period.

Effect on Non-Controlling Interest Valuation

If the transfer is upstream and initiated by a non-wholly owned subsidiary, subsidiary's net value since acquisition and subsidiary's profit for the period must be decreased by the unrealized portion of the intercompany gain at the end of the period. Subsidiary's net adjusted value since acquisition and subsidiary's adjusted profit for the period are then assigned proportionally between the parent company and the non-controlling interest.

Effect on Income Tax Allocation

Unrealized portion of the gain at the end of the period gives rise to a temporary difference that must be accounted for as the following:

Deferred Tax	XX	
Income Tax Expense		XX

(Unrealized portion of intercompany gain × Tax rate)

Periods Subsequent to the Year of Intercompany Sale of Equipment

If the Asset is Used by the Purchasing Affiliate to Generate Revenue (Most Likely Scenario)

Consolidation Entries

Retained Earnings	XX	
Accumulated Depreciation	XX	
Asset		XX

To eliminate the unrealized portion of the gain at the beginning of the period.

Accumulated Depreciation	XX	
Depreciation Expense		XX

To recognize a portion of the gain as being realized in the current period.

Effect on Non-Controlling Interest Valuation

If the transfer is upstream and initiated by a non-wholly owned subsidiary, subsidiary's net value since acquisition must be decreased by the unrealized portion of the intercompany gain at the end of the period. In addition, subsidiary's profit must be increased by the portion of the gain being realized in the current period. Subsidiary's net adjusted value since acquisition and subsidiary's adjusted profit for the period are then assigned proportionally between the parent company and the non-controlling interest.

Effect on Income Tax Allocation

Unrealized portion of the gain at the end of the period gives rise to a temporary difference that must be accounted for along with the realization of the gain in the current year.

Deferred Tax (unrealized portion at the end of the year)	XX	
Income Tax Expense (current-year realization)	XX	
Retained Earnings (unrealized portion at the beginning of the year)		XX
(Unrealized portion of intercompany gain X Tax rate)		

NOTE: The same principles would apply to an intercompany loss for as long as the loss does not reflect a decline in the value of the transferred asset.

Part III — Summary

In this part:

 Chapter 8 : Practical Guide

 Chapter 9 : Comprehensive Illustration

Chapter 8

Practical Guide

Summary of the Consolidation Adjustments

In this chapter

8.1 Worksheet Approach 194
    8.1.1 Summary of the Consolidation Adjustments at the Date of
           Creation or Acquisition 194
    8.1.2 Summary of the Consolidation Adjustments Following
           the Date of Creation or Acquisition 197

8.2 Direct Approach 207

194 Part III Summary

This chapter presents a user-friendly guide for the preparation of consolidated financial statements. The practical guide is built around the various scenarios introduced throughout the book and, as such, should apply to most consolidation cases. Adjustments required for the consolidation of a particular company can easily be selected from the guide, thus providing a customized walk-through solution format. The first part of the chapter summarizes the consolidation entries under the worksheet method. The second part presents the approach to computing consolidated balances under the direct method.

8.1 Worksheet Approach

Consistent with the structure and the content of the book, Figure 8.1 portrays all the most common consolidation scenarios. The number assigned to each scenario is taken from the corresponding section of the book for quick reference. Figure 8.1 represents a useful first step in the preparation of consolidated financial statements. The procedure involved is straightforward and consists of identifying from the figure all the scenarios that apply to the case under investigation. Once this selection is made, the underlying consolidation entries can quickly be sorted out and organized so as to provide a customized solution framework.

8.1.1 Summary of the Consolidation Adjustments at the Date of Creation or Acquisition

1.1	If the Subsidiary (B) is Founded by the Parent (A)		
	Common Shares (B)	XX	
	Investment in B (A)		XX
	To eliminate reciprocal investment and equity accounts.		

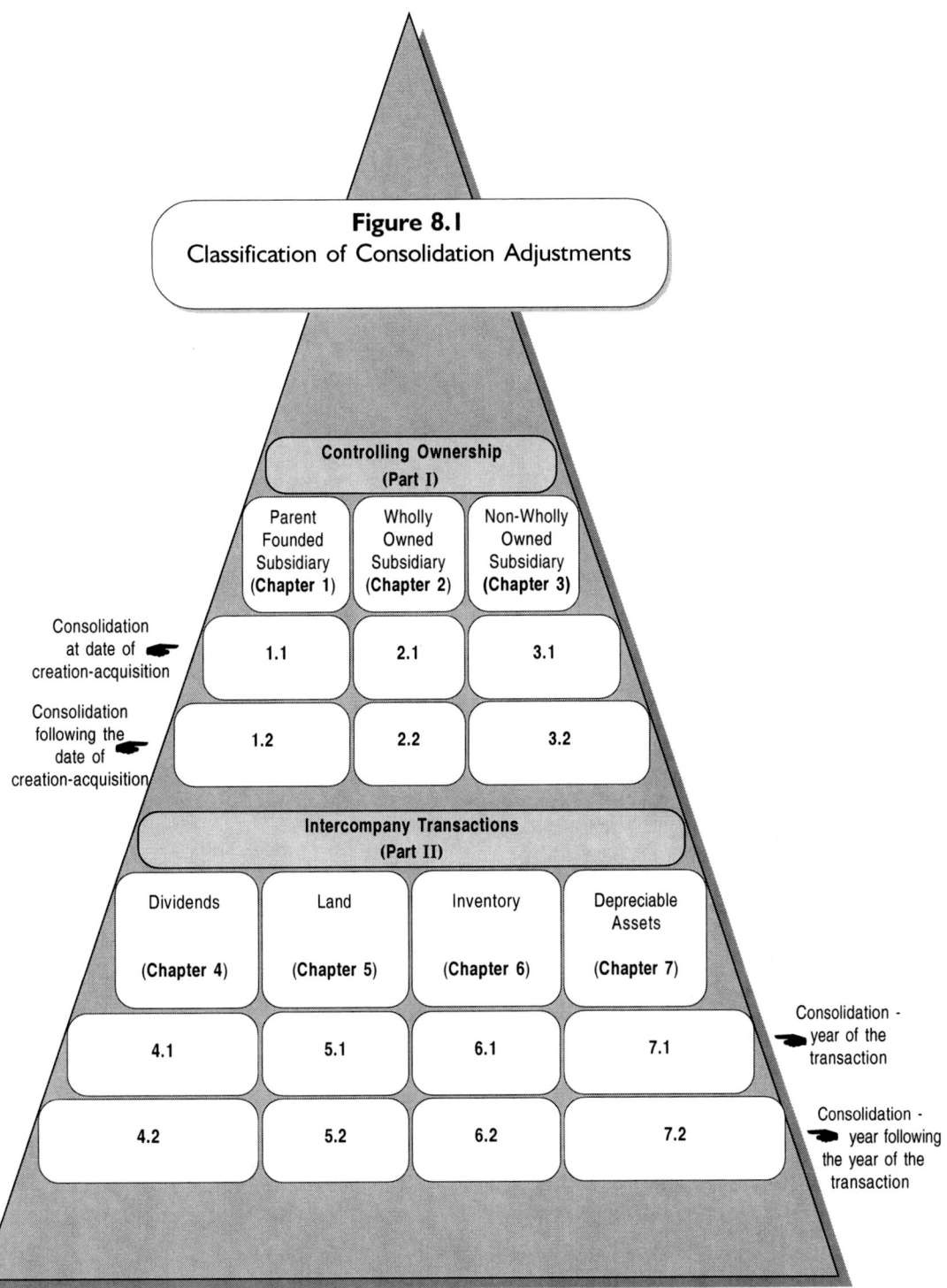

Figure 8.1
Classification of Consolidation Adjustments

2.1	**If the Subsidiary (B) is Wholly Owned**		
	Elimination of the Investment Account in the Subsidiary		
	a) Common Shares (B)	XX	
	Retained Earnings (B)	XX	
	Investment in B (A)		XX
	To eliminate reciprocal investment and equity accounts.		
	b) Asset-Related Fair Value Increments (B)	XX	
	Liability-Related Fair Value Decrements (B)	XX	
	Goodwill (B)	XX	
	Other assets not recorded by B (B)	XX	
	Liability-Related Fair Value Increments (B)		XX
	Asset-Related Fair Value Decrements (B)		XX
	Investment in B (A)		XX
	To allocate the price differential so as to account for the subsidiary's fair value at the date of acquisition.		

3.1	**If the Subsidiary (B) is Non-Wholly Owned**		
	1. Elimination of the Investment Account in the Subsidiary		
	a) Common Shares (B)	XX	
	Retained Earnings (B)	XX	
	Investment in B (A)		XX
	To eliminate reciprocal investment and equity accounts.		
	b) Asset-Related Full Fair Value Increments (B)	XX	
	Liability-Related Full Fair Value Decrements (B)	XX	
	Goodwill (B)	XX	
	Other assets not recorded by B (B)	XX	
	Liability-Related Full Fair Value Increments (B)		XX
	Asset-Related Full Fair Value Decrements (B)		XX
	Investment in B (A)		XX
	To allocate Parent's proportionate share of subsidiary's full fair value.		

3.1	If the Subsidiary (B) is Non-Wholly Owned (continued)		
	2. Non-Controlling Interest		
	Common Shares (B)	XX	
	Retained Earnings (B)	XX	
	Asset-Related Full Fair Value Increments (B)	XX	
	Liability-Related Full Fair Value Decrements (B)	XX	
	Goodwill (B) (If NCI at FV)	XX	
	Other assets not recorded by B (B)	XX	
	Liability-Related Full Fair Value Increments (B)		XX
	Asset-Related Full Fair Value Decrements (B)		XX
	Non-Controlling Interest		XX
	To allocate the fair value of subsidiary's identifiable net assets to non-controlling interest.		

8.1.2 Summary of the Consolidation Adjustments Following the Date of Creation or Acquisition

The following summarizes the consolidation adjustments required in preparing consolidated financial statements for post-acquisition or creation periods. These adjustments are classified into two categories depending on whether they relate to controlling ownership or to intercompany transactions. For this latter category, adjustments are provided assuming an intercompany gain has occurred. Note that the same principles would apply had the transfer resulted in an intercompany loss for as long as the loss does not reflect a decline in the value of the transferred asset. Otherwise, the loss should be considered as being realized for consolidation purposes and no adjustment would be required.

The proposed format is purely a matter of preference. In fact, the consolidation entries listed below can be either decomposed, combined or restructured. The end result will obviously be the same.

Adjustments Related To Controlling Ownership

1.2	If the Subsidiary (B) is Founded by the Parent (A)		
	Common Shares (B)	XX	
	Investment in B (A)		XX
	To eliminate reciprocal investment and equity accounts at the date of creation.		

2.2	If the Subsidiary (B) is Wholly Owned		
1.	**Elimination of the Investment Account in the Subsidiary (Cost Basis)**		
a)	Common Shares (B) Retained Earnings (B) Investment in B (A) To eliminate reciprocal investment and equity accounts at the date of acquisition.	XX XX	 XX

b)	Asset-Related Fair Value Increments (B)
	 Liability-Related Fair Value Decrements (B)
	 Goodwill (B)
	 Other assets not recorded by B (B)
	     Liability-Related Fair Value Increments (B)
	     Asset-Related Fair Value Decrements (B)
	     Investment in B (A)
	 To allocate the price differential so as to account for the subsidiary's fair value at the date of acquisition.
		XX
		 XX
		 XX
		 XX
			
			 XX
			 XX
			 XX

2.	**Price Differential Amortization/Realization Since Acquisition**		
a)	Retained Earnings (prior-period amortization) Depreciation Expense (current-year amortization) Accumulated Depreciation To amortize any fair value increment (decrement) on depreciable asset (liability).	XX XX	 XX

	Accumulated Depreciation
	     Depreciation Expense (current-year amortization)
	     Retained Earnings (prior-period amortization)
	 To amortize any fair value decrement (increment) on depreciable asset (liability).
		XX	
			 XX
			 XX

b)	Retained Earnings (if disposal in a prior year) Gain or Loss (if disposal in the current year) Asset (or liability) To recognize any unamortized portion of fair value increment (decrement) when related asset (liability) is disposed of.	XX XX	 XX

	Asset (or liability)
	     Gain or Loss (if disposal in the current year)
	     Retained Earnings (if disposal in a prior year)
	 To recognize any unamortized portion of fair value decrement (increment) when related asset (liability) is disposed of.
		XX	
			 XX
			 XX

c)	Retained Earnings (if impairment in prior years) Impairment Loss (if impairment in the current year) Goodwill To account for any goodwill impairment.	XX XX	 XX

Chapter 8 Practical Guide

3.2 If the Subsidiary (B) is Non-Wholly Owned

1. Elimination of the Investment Account in the Subsidiary (Cost Basis)

a)
Common Shares (B)	XX	
Retained Earnings (B)	XX	
Investment in B (A)		XX

To eliminate reciprocal investment and equity accounts at acquisition.

b)
Asset-Related Full Fair Value Increments (B)	XX	
Liability-Related Full Fair Value Decrements (B)	XX	
Goodwill (B)	XX	
Other assets not recorded by B (B)	XX	
Liability-Related Full Fair Value Increments (B)		XX
Asset-Related Full Fair Value Decrements (B)		XX
Investment in B (A)		XX

To allocate Parent's proportionate share of subsidiary's full fair value at date of acquisition.

2. Implied Price Differential Amortization/Realization Since Acquisition

a)
Retained Earnings (prior-period amortization)	XX	
Depreciation Expense (current-year amortization)	XX	
Accumulated Depreciation		XX

To amortize any full fair value increment (decrement) on depreciable asset (liability).

Accumulated Depreciation	XX	
Depreciation Expense (current-year amortization)		XX
Retained Earnings (prior-period amortization)		XX

To amortize any full fair value decrement (increment) on depreciable asset (liability).

b)
Retained Earnings (if disposal in a prior year)	XX	
Gain or Loss (if disposal in the current year)	XX	
Asset (or liability)		XX

To recognize any unamortized portion of the full fair value increment (decrement) when related asset (liability) is disposed of.

Asset (or liability)	XX	
Gain or Loss (if disposal in the current year)		XX
Retained Earnings (if disposal in a prior year)		XX

To recognize any unamortized portion of the full fair value decrement (increment) when related asset (liability) is disposed of.

c)
Retained Earnings (if impairment in prior years)	XX	
Impairment Loss (if impairment in the current year)	XX	
Goodwill		XX

To account for any goodwill impairment.

3.2	If the Subsidiary (B) is Non-Wholly Owned (continued...)

3. Non-Controlling Interest

a)
Common Shares (B)	XX	
Retained Earnings (B)	XX	
Asset-Related Full Fair Value Increments (B)	XX	
Liability-Related Full Fair Value Decrements (B)	XX	
Goodwill (B) (If NCI at FV)	XX	
Other assets not recorded by B (B)	XX	
Liability-Related Full Fair Value Increments (B)		XX
Asset-Related Full Fair Value Decrements (B)		XX
Non-Controlling Interest		XX

To allocate the fair value of subsidiary's identifiable net assets at date of acquisition to non-controlling interest.

b)
Retained Earnings (B)	XX	
Non-Controlling Interest		XX

To allocate the subsidiary (B)'s net adjusted value since acquisition to non-controlling interest.

<u>Subsidiary's net adjusted value</u> (if no upstream transaction):
Change in subsidiary's retained earnings since acquisition (-) Cumulative price differential amortization/realization since acquisition
When non-controlling interest is valued based on the fair value of subsidiary's net assets, goodwill impairment, if any, must be assigned to parent company only.

Consolidated Profit Allocation
Consolidated profit must be allocated to majority and minority interests in the income statement as follows:
    Majority interest: Parent's profit (+) Parent's share of subsidiary's adjusted profit
    Minority interest: Minority's share of subsidiary's adjusted profit.
    <u>Subsidiary's adjusted profit</u> (if no upstream transaction):
    Subsidiary's profit (-) Current-year price differential amortization/realization
    When non-controlling interest is valued based on the fair value of subsidiary's net assets, current-year goodwill impairment, if any, must be assigned to parent company only.

Chapter 8 Practical Guide

Adjustments Related to Intercompany Transactions

4.1	**Intercompany Dividends** **Year of Transfer**			If non-wholly owned subsidiary
	Dividend Income (A)	XX		✓
	Retained Earnings (minority share vs entry #3b, scenario 3.2)	XX		
	Dividends Declared (B)		XX	
	To eliminate the intercompany dividends.			

4.2	**Intercompany Dividends** **Year Subsequent to Year of Transfer**	If non-wholly owned subsidiary
	No adjustment required	

5.1	**Intercompany Sale of Non-Depreciable Asset (Land)** **Year of Transfer**		
	If the Land is Held by the Purchasing Affiliate		
	Gain on Sale of Land	XX	
	Land		XX
	To eliminate current-year intercompany gain on sale of land and reduce land to its cost basis.		
	If the Land is Resold to an Outsider		
	No adjustment required		

5.2 Intercompany Sale of Non-Depreciable Asset (Land) Year Subsequent to Year of Transfer

If the Land is Still Held by the Purchasing Affiliate

Retained Earnings	XX	
Land		XX
To eliminate prior-year intercompany gain on sale of land that is still unrealized and reduce land to its cost basis.		

If the Land is Resold to an Outsider

Retained Earnings	XX	
Gain on Sale of Land		XX
To recognize prior-year deferred gain on sale of land.		

6.1 Intercompany Sale of Inventory Year of Transfer

If the Inventory (or a Portion of it) is Held by the Purchasing Affiliate

Sales	XX	
Cost of Goods Sold		XX
Inventory (unrealized profit)		XX
To eliminate current-year intercompany profit on sale of inventory, eliminate any reciprocal Sales and Cost of Goods Sold balances and reduce inventory to its cost basis.		

If the Inventory (or a Portion of it) is Resold to External Parties

Sales	XX	
Cost of Goods Sold		XX
To eliminate reciprocal Sales and Cost of Goods Sold balances.		

6.2 Intercompany Sale of Inventory Year Subsequent to Year of Transfer

If the Inventory is Resold to External Parties (Most Likely Scenario)

Retained Earnings	XX	
Cost of Goods Sold		XX
To recognize prior-year deferred profit on sale of inventory.		

7.1 Intercompany Sale of Depreciable Asset
Year of Transfer

If the Asset is Used by the Purchasing Affiliate to Generate Revenue (Most Likely Scenario)

Gain on Sale of Asset	XX	
Asset		XX
To eliminate current-year intercompany gain on sale of asset and reduce asset to its cost basis.		
Accumulated Depreciation	XX	
Depreciation Expense		XX
To recognize a portion of the gain as being realized in the current period.		

7.2 Intercompany Sale of Depreciable Asset
Year Subsequent to Year of Transfer

If the Asset is Used by the Purchasing Affiliate to Generate Revenue (Most Likely Scenario)

Retained Earnings	XX	
Accumulated Depreciation	XX	
Asset		XX
To eliminate the unrealized portion of the gain at the beginning of the period.		
Accumulated Depreciation	XX	
Depreciation Expense		XX
To recognize a portion of the gain as being realized in the current period.		

Non-Controlling Interest Valuation

The following summarizes the effect on the non-controlling interest valuation when the transfer is upstream and initiated by a non-wholly owned subsidiary.

**NCI — Non-Controlling Interest Valuation
Year of Transfer**

If the Asset is Held by the Parent Company

Subsidiary's net value since acquisition and subsidiary's profit for the period must be decreased by the amount of intercompany gain. Subsidiary's net adjusted value since acquisition and subsidiary's adjusted profit for the period are then assigned proportionally between the parent company and the non-controlling interest in the consolidation process.

If the Asset is Resold to an Outsider

No adjustment required

**NCI — Non-Controlling Interest Valuation
Year Subsequent to Year of Transfer**

If the Asset is Still Held by the Parent Company

Subsidiary's net value since acquisition must be decreased by the amount of prior-year intercompany gain. Subsidiary's net adjusted value since acquisition is then assigned proportionally between the parent company and the non-controlling interest.

If the Asset is Resold to an Outsider

Subsidiary's profit for the period must be increased by the amount of prior-year intercompany gain. Subsidiary's adjusted profit for the period is then allocated proportionally between the parent company and the non-controlling interest in the consolidated income statement.

Income Tax Allocation

TAX — **Income Tax Allocation Related to Business Combinations Date of Acquisition**

Deferred Tax related to (full) fair value increments and decrements must be accounted for at the date of acquisition. Adding this account in the purchase price allocation will have an offsetting effect on Goodwill.

TAX — **Income Tax Allocation Related to Business Combinations Year Subsequent to Acquisition**

Following the date of acquisition, any change in temporary differences arising from price differential amortization or realization must be recognized for consolidation purposes as shown below.

Deferred Tax Liability	XX	
Income Tax Expense (current-year)		XX
Retained Earnings (prior-years)		XX

TAX — **Income Tax Allocation Related to Intercompany Transfers Year of Transfer**

If the Asset is Held by the Purchasing Affiliate

Unrealized gain at the end of the period gives rise to a temporary difference that must be accounted for as the following:

Deferred Tax	XX	
Income Tax Expense		XX
(Unrealized current-year intercompany gain X Tax rate)		

If the Asset is Resold to an Outsider

No adjustment required

TAX	**Income Tax Allocation Related to Intercompany Transfers Year Subsequent to Year of Transfer**		
	If the Asset is Still Held by the Purchasing Affiliate		

	Since prior-year intercompany gain is still unrealized at the end of the period, the temporary difference recognized in year of transfer must be restored as the following:
	    Deferred Tax
	        Retained Earnings
	    (Prior-year intercompany gain still unrealized X Tax rate)
		XX	XX

	If the Asset is Resold to an Outsider		

	Since prior-year intercompany gain is realized, the temporary difference recognized in year of transfer is consumed. Therefore, the following entry is necessary in order to defer to the current period the income tax paid by the selling affiliate in the previous period.
	    Income Tax Expense
	        Retained Earnings
	    (Prior-year intercompany gain now realized X Tax rate)
		XX	XX

8.2 Direct Approach

The following presents the approach to computing the consolidated balances directly.

♦ Assets

	Balance on the books of the parent
(+)	Balance on the books of the subsidiary
+ (-)	Unamortized portion of any asset-related fair value increment (decrement)
- (+)	Unamortized portion of any unrealized intercompany gain (loss)
(-)	Any reciprocal balances

♦ Liabilities

	Balance on the books of the parent
(+)	Balance on the books of the subsidiary
+ (-)	Unamortized portion of any liability-related fair value increment (decrement)
(-)	Any reciprocal balances

♦ Deferred Tax

Related to Business Combinations:

Unamortized portion of any fair value increments (decrements) at the end of the current period X Tax rate

Related to Intercompany Transactions:

Any unrealized gain (loss) at the end of the current period X Tax rate

♦ Common Shares

Balance on the books of the parent

♦ Retained Earnings

	Balance on the books of the parent
- (+)	Any unrealized gain (loss) from **downstream** transactions (net of tax)
(+)	Parent share of subsidiary's net adjusted value since acquisition

♦ Non-Controlling Interest

	Minority share of the fair value of subsidiary's net assets at the date of acquisition or quoted value of the shares held by minority shareholders at date of acquisition
(+)	Minority share of subsidiary's net adjusted value since acquisition

♦ Subsidiary's Net Adjusted Value Since Acquisition

	Subsidiary's retained earnings since acquisition
(-)	Price differential amortization since acquisition (net of tax)
- (+)	Any unrealized gain (loss) from **upstream** transactions (net of tax)

♦ Sales

	Balance on the books of the parent
(+)	Balance on the books of the subsidiary
(−)	Any amount of intercompany sales

♦ Cost of Goods Sold

	Balance on the books of the parent
(+)	Balance on the books of the subsidiary
(−)	Any amount of intercompany sales
− (+)	Any prior-year deferred profit (loss) on sale of inventory being realized in the current period
+ (−)	Any unrealized current-year profit (loss) on sale of inventory

♦ Expenses

	Balance on the books of the parent
(+)	Balance on the books of the subsidiary
(−)	Any reciprocal revenue and expense
+ (−)	Current-year amortization of fair value increment on asset (liability)
− (+)	Current-year amortization of fair value decrement on asset (liability)
(+)	Any current-year goodwill impairment

◆ Consolidated Profit for the Year

Adjusted profit of the parent:

	Profit of the parent
− (+)	Any unrealized current-year gain (loss) from **downstream** transactions (net of tax)
+ (−)	Any prior-year deferred gain (loss) from **downstream** transactions being realized in the current period (net of tax)
(−)	Intercompany dividends (if investment accounted for on a cost basis)

Adjusted profit of the subsidiary:

	Profit of the subsidiary
(−)	Current-period price differential amortization (net of tax)
− (+)	Any unrealized current-year gain (loss) from **upstream** transactions (net of tax)
+ (−)	Any prior-year deferred gain (loss) from **upstream** transactions being realized in the current period (net of tax)

↓

Allocation

↙ ↘

Majority Shareholder

Adjusted profit of the parent
(+)
Parent's share of the subsidiary's adjusted profit

Minority Shareholders

Minority's share of the subsidiary's adjusted profit

Chapter 9

Comprehensive Illustration

Plus Inc

In this chapter

- 9.1 Basic Information 212
- 9.2 Preliminary Analysis 214
    - 9.2.1 Controlling Ownership 216
    - 9.2.2 Intercompany Transactions 218
- 9.3 Consolidation of Financial Statements 219
    - 9.3.1 Worksheet Approach 220
    - 9.3.2 Direct Approach 227
- 9.4 Investment Account on Equity Basis 233

This chapter presents a comprehensive case that covers many consolidation scenarios introduced in this book. The practical guide from Chapter 8 is used to provide the solution format for this case. The consolidated financial statements are prepared successively under the worksheet approach and the direct approach. Income tax allocation related to business combination and intercompany gains and losses is discussed in special notes throughout the chapter. The last part of the chapter presents the additional consolidation adjustments required had the parent company used the equity method rather than the cost method to account for its controlling ownership.

9.1 Basic Information

On January 1, X3, Plus Inc purchased 80 percent of Lortis's outstanding common stock for cash of CU 7.8 million. Exhibit 9.1 shows the statement of financial position of Lortis at the date of acquisition along with the appraised value of its identifiable assets and liabilities assumed.

Exhibit 9.1 • Statement of Financial Position of Lortis as of January 1, X3

	Carrying Values (CU)	Fair Values (CU)
Assets		
Cash	500,000	500,000
Accounts receivable	1,500,000	1,500,000
Inventory	3,000,000	4,000,000
Land	1,500,000	1,000,000
Buildings (net)	6,000,000	8,000,000
Patents	-	500,000
Total assets	12,500,000	
Liabilities and equities		
Current liabilities	1,000,000	1,000,000
Long-term liabilities	4,500,000	6,000,000
Share capital	3,000,000	
Retained earnings	4,000,000	
Total liabilities and equities	12,500,000	

You are asked to prepare the consolidated financial statements of Plus Inc for the year ended December 31, X7, that is, five years from the date of acquisition. Separate financial statements of the affiliated companies for that period are shown in Exhibit 9.2.

Exhibit 9.2 • Financial Statements of Plus and Lortis for the Year Ended December 31, X7

Statements of Financial Position
December 31, X7
(in CU)

	Plus	Lortis
Assets		
Cash	3,000,000	700,000
Accounts receivable	7,500,000	2,100,000
Inventory	14,300,000	5,600,000
Land	9,000,000	2,500,000
Buildings (net)	15,800,000	5,500,000
Patents	1,400,000	
Investment in Lortis	7,800,000	
Total assets	**58,800,000**	**16,400,000**
Liabilities and equities		
Current liabilities	8,500,000	1,200,000
Long-term liabilities	15,000,000	4,500,000
Share capital	20,000,000	3,000,000
Retained earnings	15,300,000	7,700,000
Total liabilities and equities	**58,800,000**	**16,400,000**

Income Statements
Year Ended December 31, X7
(in CU)

	Plus	Lortis
Revenues	16,500,000	7,000,000
Cost of goods sold	6,400,000	3,400,000
Other expenses	3,800,000	1,600,000
Profit for the year	**6,300,000**	**2,000,000**

Statements of Changes in Equity
Year Ended December 31, X7
(in CU)

	Plus			Lortis		
	Share Capital	Retained Earnings	Total	Share Capital	Retained Earnings	Total
Balance at January 1, X7	20,000,000	11,000,000	31,000,000	3,000,000	6,700,000	9,700,000
Dividends		(2,000,000)	(2,000,000)		(1,000,000)	(1,000,000)
Profit for the year		6,300,000	6,300,000		2,000,000	2,000,000
Balance at December 31, X7	20,000,000	15,300,000	35,300,000	3,000,000	7,700,000	10,700,000

Additional Information

1) On January 1, X3, Lortis had buildings with a remaining useful life of 20 years.
2) All the inventory retained by Lortis at January 1, X3, had been sold to external parties in X3.
3) On January 1, X3, Lortis had software that had not yet been patented. However, a market study conducted during X4 revealed that the sofware had no value.
4) No capital asset has been disposed of by Lortis since acquisition.
5) Goodwill has not been impaired since acquisition.
6) Maturity date of all long-term liabilities is ten years from the date of acquisition.
7) During X7, Lortis purchased land from Plus for CU1,000,000. The original cost of the land for the selling affiliate was CU500,000.
8) During X7, Lortis sold merchandise to Plus for CU2,000,000. On December 31, X7, CU500,000 of this merchandise remained in Plus's inventory.
9) During X6, Lortis sold merchandise to Plus. At the end of the year, CU800,000 of this merchandise remained in Plus's inventory.
10) Lortis sells its merchandise at a markup of 30 percent over sales.
11) Both affiliated companies use the straight-line method to calculate all depreciation and amortization.
12) The market price of the shares held by minority shareholders at the date of acquisition is CU1,900,000.

9.2 Preliminary Analysis

Figure 9.1 lists the consolidation scenarios that apply to Plus.

Chapter 9 Comprehensive Illustration 215

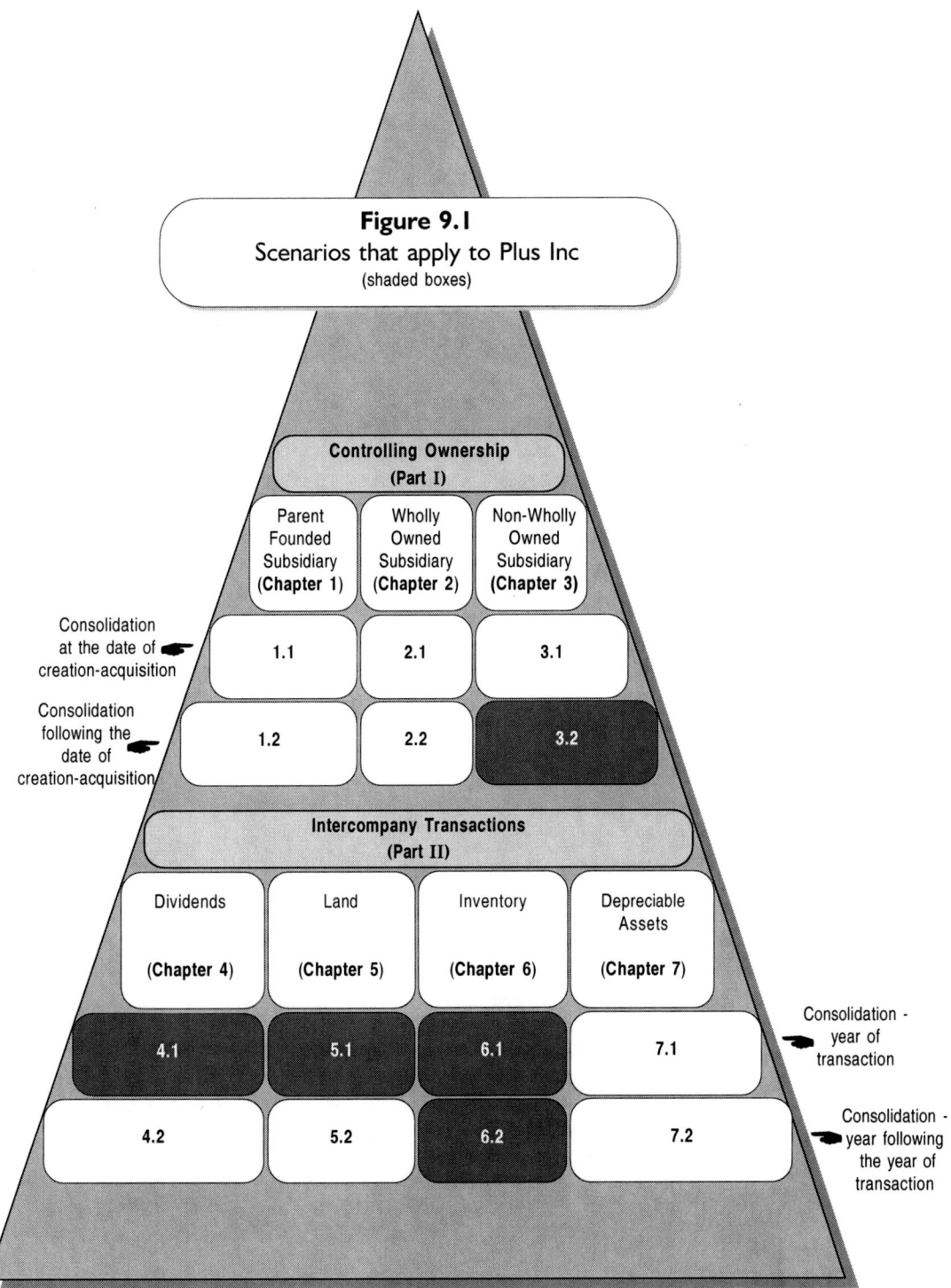

Figure 9.1
Scenarios that apply to Plus Inc
(shaded boxes)

9.2.1 Controlling Ownership

Exhibit 9.3 presents the allocation of purchase price as well as the allocation of the fair value of the non-controlling interest. The fair value is based on the market price of the shares held by the minority shareholders at date of acquisition, that is, CU1,900,000 (Additional Information #12)

Exhibit 9.3 • Acquisition of 80 percent of the Outstanding Voting Stock of Lortis by Plus on January 1, X3 - Allocation of the Purchase Price and the Fair Value of the Non-Controlling Interest

		(100%) CU	Plus (80%) CU	Minority (20%) CU
Cost of investment in Lortis			7,800,000	
Fair Value of NCI				1,900,000
Shareholders' equity of Lortis at the date of acquisition:				
- Share capital	3,000,000			
- Retained earnings	4,000,000	7,000,000	5,600,000	1,400,000
Price differential			2,200,000	500,000
Fair value increments (+) and decrements (-):				
- Inventory (+)		(1,000,000)	(800,000)	(200,000)
- Land (-)		500,000	400,000	100,000
- Buildings (+)		(2,000,000)	(1,600,000)	(400,000)
- Software (+)		(500,000)	(400,000)	(100,000)
- Long-term liabilities (+)		1,500,000	1,200,000	300,000
Goodwill			1,000,000	200,000

The full fair value of Lortis's identifiable net assets at date of acquisition will be brought into the consolidation process. Overall, goodwill of CU1,200,000 will also be considered. In post-acquisition periods, special attention should be devoted to price differential amortization and/or realization as discussed next.

Full Fair Value Increment on Inventory

A full fair value increment of CU1,000,000 must be assigned to the inventory at the date of acquisition. However, since all the inventory units have been sold to external parties in the year following acquisition (X3), the acquisition-date full fair value increment has been fully realized in X3 (Additional Information #2).

Full Fair Value Decrement on Land

A full fair value decrement of CU500,000 must be assigned to the land at the date of acquisition. Since the land is still held by Lortis at the end of the current year (X7) (Additional Information #4), the value of the land carried on Lortis's records must be reduced by CU500,000 so as to reflect the acquisition-date full market value.

Full Fair Value Increment on Buildings

A full fair value increment of CU2,000,000 must be assigned to the buildings at the date of combination. Since buildings are amortized by Lortis on a straight-line basis over a remaining useful life of 20 years from the date of acquisition (Additional Information #1 and #11), the annual depreciation expense is undervalued by CU100,000 (CU2,000,000/20 years) for consolidation purposes. The cumulative underdepreciation on buildings since acquisition amounts to CU500,000 (CU100,000 X 5 years, that is, X3 through X7, inclusive).

Full Fair Value Increment on Software

No software was recorded by Lortis at the date of acquisition. Therefore, the full fair value increment of CU500,000 assigned to software at the date of combination reflects the observable full market value of the asset at that date. However, since the software appears to have no value in X4 (Additional Information #3), the full fair value increment of CU500,000 can be considered as being fully realized in X4.

Full Fair Value Increment on Long-Term Liabilities

An acquisition-date full fair value increment of CU1,500,000 must be allocated to long-term liabilities. This fair value increment must be amortized on a straight-line basis over a ten year period from the date of acquisition or until the maturity date of the relevant liabilities (Additional Information #6 and #11).

For consolidation purposes, a fair value increment on liabilities can be treated like a premium on bonds payable. The amortization of the bond premium causes interest expense to be lower than the cash interest payment. Likewise, the amortization of the fair value increment on long-term liabilities will decrease the interest expense recorded by Lortis. More precisely, the annual correction amounts to CU150,000 (CU1,500,000/10 years). The cumulative impact of the amortization since acquisition amounts to CU750,000 (CU150,000 X 5 years, that is, X3 through X7, inclusive).

Goodwill

Goodwill has not been impaired since acquisition (Additional Information #5). Therefore, goodwill of CU1,200,000 computed at the date of acquisition remains unchanged as of December 31, X7.

To summarize, Exhibit 9.4 presents the implied price differential amortization schedule.

Exhibit 9.4 • Consolidation of the Financial Statements of Plus - Price Differential Amortization Schedule

Items	Price Differential Balance at Acquisition (CU)	Amortization Current Year (X7) (CU)	Amortization Prior Years (X3-X6) (CU)	Unamortized Excess at 31-12-X7 (CU)
Full Fair Value Increments and Decrements				
• Inventory	1,000,000	-	1,000,000	-
• Land	(500,000)	-	-	(500,000)
• Buildings	2,000,000	100,000	400,000	1,500,000
• Software	500,000	-	500,000	-
• LT Liabilities	(1,500,000)	(150,000)	(600,000)	(750,000)
Goodwill	1,200,000	-	-	1,200,000
Total	2,700,000	(50,000)	1,300,000	1,450,000

Note that the value of the investment of Plus in Lortis has not been revised since acquisition. In fact, the balance of the investment account as of December 31, X7, reflects the purchase price of CU7,800,000. This signals the use by Plus of the cost method to account for its strategic investments.

9.2.2 Intercompany Transactions

Transactions conducted between the affiliated companies are analyzed below.

Intercompany Dividends

During X7, Lortis declared dividends for CU1,000,000 (see Exhibit 9.2). Since there is no indication of reciprocal receivable and payable balances at the end of the year, one can assume that dividends declared by Lortis were fully paid in the current accounting period.

Furthermore, since the investment of Plus in Lortis is accounted for using the cost method, dividends received by Plus (CU1,000,000 X 80% = CU800,000) must have been recorded as revenue in the income statement. To avoid double-counting of Lortis's earnings, intercompany dividends must be eliminated.

Downstream Sale of Land (Additional Information #7)

Land has been transferred from Plus to Lortis in the current period. A gain of CU500,000 has been recognized by the selling affiliate which consists of the difference between the selling price (CU1,000,000) and the historical cost of the land (CU500,000). Since the land remains in the consolidated group at the end of the current period (Additional Information #4), the intercompany gain must be considered as being unrealized from the viewpoint of the economic entity and, as such, must be eliminated. Similarly, since the land now carried on the books of Lortis contains the intercompany gain, this account must be reduced by CU500,000 so as to return its value back to the price originally paid by the selling affiliate.

Upstream Sale of Inventory (Additional Information #8, #9 and #10)

During X6, Lortis sold merchandise to Plus. CU800,000 of this merchandise remained in Plus's inventory at the end of the year. Considering a markup of 30 percent over sales, an unrealized profit of CU240,000 (CU800,000 X 30%) has been deferred in X6. Since the transferred inventory has been resold by Plus to external parties in the current period, prior-year intercompany profit of CU240,000 has now been fully realized and, as such, must be recognized in X7.

During X7, Lortis sold merchandise to Plus for CU2,000,000. On December 31, X7, CU500,000 of this merchandise remains in Plus's inventory. Consequently, three adjustments are required for the consolidation of Plus. First, the unrealized intercompany profit of CU150,000 (CU500,000 X 30%) must be removed. Second, reciprocal Sales and Cost of Goods Sold of CU 1,500,000 must be eliminated. This amount corresponds to the transfer price of the units being resold by Plus in the current year, that is, CU2,000,000 (transfer price of the units sold to Plus) less CU500,000 (unsold units at the end of the period). Third, since the transaction is upstream and Lortis is a non-wholly owned subsidiary, non-controlling interest must be adjusted so as to account for their share (20 percent) of the unrealized profit at the end of the period (CU150,000 X 20% = CU30,000).

9.3 Consolidation of Financial Statements

The following illustrates the consolidation of the financial statements of Plus Inc as of December 31, X7, under, first, the worksheet approach, and second, the direct approach.

9.3.1 Worksheet Approach

Entries that will be entered into the consolidation worksheet of Plus are listed below (see the practical guide in chapter 8).

Adjustments Related To Controlling Ownership

1- Elimination of the Investment Account in the Subsidiary (see purchase price allocation in Exhibit 9.3)

(1a) To eliminate reciprocal investment and equity accounts at the date of acquisition.

Common Shares (Lortis)	2,400,000	
Retained Earnings (Lortis)	3,200,000	
Investment in Lortis (Plus)		5,600,000

(1b) To allocate Plus's proportionate share of Lortis's full fair value at the date of acquisition.

Inventory (Lortis)	800,000	
Buildings (Lortis)	1,600,000	
Patents (Lortis)	400,000	
Goodwill	1,000,000	
Land (Lortis)		400,000
Long-Term Liabilities (Lortis)		1,200,000
Investment in Lortis (Plus)		2,200,000

2- Price Differential Amortization Since Acquisition (see amortization schedule in Exhibit 9.4)

(2a) To recognize the prior-year realization of the full fair value increment on inventory.

Retained Earnings (Lortis)	1,000,000	
Inventory (Lortis)		1,000,000

(2b) To amortize the full fair value increment on buildings.

Retained Earnings (Lortis)	400,000	
Other Expenses (Lortis)	100,000	
Buildings (Lortis)		500,000

(2c) To recognize the prior-year realization of the full fair value increment on software.

Retained Earnings (Lortis)	500,000	
Patents (Lortis)		500,000

(2d) To amortize the full fair value increment on long-term liabilities.

Long-Term Liabilities (Lortis)	750,000	
Retained Earnings (Lortis)		600,000
Other Expenses (Lortis)		150,000

3- Non-Controlling Interest

(3a) To record the fair value of the non-controlling interest at the date of acquisition (see Exhibit 9.3).

Common Shares (Lortis)	600,000	
Retained Earnings (Lortis)	800,000	
Inventory (Lortis)	200,000	
Buildings (Lortis)	400,000	
Patents (Lortis)	100,000	
Goodwill	200,000	
Land (Lortis)		100,000
Long-Term Liabilities (Lortis)		300,000
Non-Controlling Interest		1,900,000

(3b) To allocate the subsidiary's net adjusted value since acquisition to non-controlling interest.

Retained Earnings	460,000	
Non-Controlling Interest		460,000

Lortis's net adjusted value increase since acquisition amounts to CU2,300,000 as shown below.

Subsidiary's Net Adjusted Value Since Acquisition	CU
• Subsidiary's retained earnings since acquisition (CU7,700,000 - CU4,000,000)	3,700,000
• Price differential amortization since acquisition (see amortization schedule in Exhibit 9.4)	(1,250,000)
• Unrealized profit from upstream sale of inventory	(150,000)
Total	**2,300,000**

Non-controlling interest's share of Lortis's net adjusted value increase:
(CU2,300,000 X 20%) = CU460,000

What If...

If Plus elects to recognize the non-controlling interest based on the fair value of Lortis's identifiable assets and liabilities instead of the fair value of the non-controlling interest at date of acquisition, consolidation entry 3a must be changed to the following entry (the recording of goodwill is removed).

Common Shares (Lortis)	600,000	
Retained Earnings (Lortis)	800,000	
Inventory (Lortis)	200,000	
Buildings (Lortis)	400,000	
Patents (Lortis)	100,000	
Land (Lortis)		100,000
Long-Term Liabilities (Lortis)		300,000
Non-Controlling Interest (Lortis)		1,700,000

Goodwill will be recorded to the extent of Plus's percentage of Lortis (80%). Since goodwill has not been impaired, the rest of the consolidation entries are the same. Had goodwill been impaired, the full amount of impairment would have been allocated to Plus.

Effect on Income Tax Allocation

Assuming a corporate tax rate of 20 percent, additional entries would have been required to account for the income tax related to Lortis's acquisition. More precisely, temporary differences created by fair value increments and decrements amount to CU1,500,000 at the date of acquisition and include (see Exhibit 9.4): CU1,000,000 (Inventory) - CU500,000 (Land) + CU2,000,000 (Buildings) + CU500,000 (Software) - CU1,500,000 (Long-Term Liabilities). The net temporary differences can be translated into a CU300,000 Future Income Tax Liability (CU1,500,000 X 20% tax rate) at the date of combination.

Following the date of acquisition, the change in temporary differences arising from price differential amortization or realization must be recognized. The change of temporary differences in prior-years amounts to CU1,300,000 (see Exhibit 9.4) which is equivalent to a reduction of Deferred Tax Liability of CU260,000 (CU1,300,000 X 20%). The change of temporary differences in the current year is equal to an increase of Income Tax Expense of CU10,000 (CU50,000 X 20%). Had a Deferred Tax Liability of CU300,000 been recognized at the date of acquisition, the additional consolidation adjustments required for the current period (X7) would have been the following:

Deferred Tax Liability	250,000	
Income Tax Expense	10,000	
Retained Earnings		260,000

Adjustments Related to Intercompany Transactions

(4) Intercompany Dividends

Revenues (Dividends) (Plus)	800,000	
Retained Earnings (Lortis)	200,000	
Dividends Declared (Lortis)		1,000,000

To eliminate current-year intercompany dividends. Dividends assigned to non-controlling shareholders (CU200,000) reduce Retained Earnings so as to be consistent with adjustment #3b.

(5) Downstream Sale of Land

Revenues (Gain) (Plus)	500,000	
Land (Lortis)		500,000

To eliminate current-year intercompany gain on sale of land and reduce land to its cost basis.

(6) Upstream Sale of Inventory During X6

Retained Earnings (Lortis)	240,000	
Cost of Goods Sold (Lortis)		240,000

To recognize prior-year deferred profit on sale of inventory.

(7) Upstream Sale of Inventory During X7

Revenues (Sales) (Lortis)	2,000,000	
Cost of Goods Sold (Plus and Lortis)		1,850,000
Inventory (Plus)		150,000

To eliminate current-year unrealized profit on sale of inventory, eliminate reciprocal Sales and Cost of Goods Sold balances and reduce inventory to its cost basis.

Exhibit 9.5 summarizes the information for this adjustment. Note that the amounts reported in the consolidated income statement are those that reflect the original cost of the units sold to external parties and the price paid by the outsiders for these units (shaded boxes in Exhibit 9.5). All the remaining figures from Exhibit 9.5 are eliminated via the consolidation entry #7. This includes Sales of CU2,000,000 (CU500,000 + CU1,500,000) and Cost of Goods Sold of CU1,850,000 (CU350,000 + CU1,500,000).

Exhibit 9.5 • Intercompany Sale of Inventory by Lortis - Impact on the Income Statement Balances of the Affiliated Companies

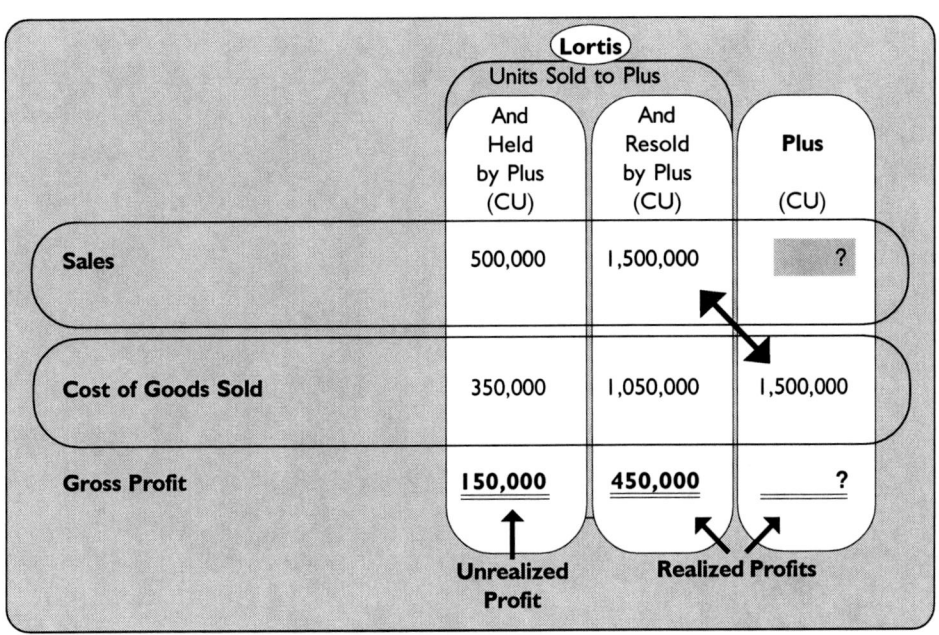

Effect on Income Tax Allocation

Assuming a corporate tax rate of 20 percent, the following additional entries would have been required to account for the income tax related to intercompany profits.

▸ Realization in the current period of the deferred gross profit on upstream sale of inventory:
(CU240,000 X 20%) = CU48,000

Income Tax Expense	48,000	
Retained Earnings		48,000

▸ Unrealized current-year profit on upstream sale of inventory: (CU150,000 X 20%) = CU30,000

Deferred Tax	30,000	
Income Tax Expense		30,000

▸ Unrealized current-year gain on downstream sale of land: (CU500,000 X 20%) = CU100,000

Deferred Tax	100,000	
Income Tax Expense		100,000

Part III Summary

The following presents the consolidation worksheet of Plus Inc for the period ended December 31, X7.

Consolidation Worksheet

	Plus (CU)	Lortis (CU)	Eliminations Adjustments (CU)		Plus Consolidated (CU)
ASSETS					
Cash	3,000,000	700,000			3,700,000
Accounts receivable	7,500,000	2,100,000			9,600,000
Inventory	14,300,000	5,600,000	800,000	(1b)	19,750,000
			(1,000,000)	(2a)	
			200,000	(3a)	
			(150,000)	(7)	
Land	9,000,000	2,500,000	(400,000)	(1b)	10,500,000
			(100,000)	(3a)	
			(500,000)	(5)	
Buildings (net)	15,800,000	5,500,000	1,600,000	(1b)	22,800,000
			(500,000)	(2b)	
			400,000	(3a)	
Investment in Lortis	7,800,000		(5,600,000)	(1a)	–
			(2,200,000)	(1b)	
Patents	1,400,000		400,000	(1b)	1,400,000
			(500,000)	(2c)	
			100,000	(3a)	
Goodwill			1,000,000	(1b)	1,200,000
			200,000	(3a)	
	58,800,000	**16,400,000**			**68,950,000**
LIABILITIES					
Current liabilities	8,500,000	1,200,000			9,700,000
Long-term liabilities	15,000,000	4,500,000	1,200,000	(1b)	20,250,000
			(750,000)	(2d)	
			300,000	(3a)	
EQUITY					
Common shares	20,000,000	3,000,000	(2,400,000)	(1a)	20,000,000
			(600,000)	(3a)	
Retained earnings	15,300,000	7,700,000	(6,360,000)		16,640,000
Non-controlling interest			1,900,000	(3a)	2,360,000
			460,000	(3b)	
	58,800,000	**16,400,000**			**68,950,000**

Net impact of the adjustments on the ending balance of RE

Consolidation Worksheet (continued)

	Plus (CU)	Lortis (CU)	Eliminations Adjustments (CU)	Plus Consolidated (CU)
Revenues	16,500,000	7,000,000	(800,000) (4) (500,000) (5) (2,000,000) (7)	20,200,000
Cost of goods sold	6,400,000	3,400,000	(240,000) (6) (1,850,000) (7)	7,710,000
Other expenses	3,800,000	1,600,000	100,000 (2b) (150,000) (2d)	5,350,000
Profit	**6,300,000**	**2,000,000**		**7,140,000**
Retained earnings	11,000,000	6,700,000	(3,200,000) (1a) (1,000,000) (2a) (400,000) (2b) (500,000) (2c) 600,000 (2d) (800,000) (3a) (460,000) (3b) (200,000) (4) (240,000) (6)	
Dividends	2,000,000	1,000,000	(1,000,000) (4)	
Retained earnings (end)	**15,300,000**	**7,700,000**	**(6,360,000)**	**16,640,000**

Net impact of the adjustments on the ending balance of RE

9.3.2 Direct Approach

Consolidated financial statements of Plus Inc for the year ended December 31, X7, are presented in Exhibit 9.6. The balance of the account from the books of the affiliated companies is shown in brackets. More sophisticated computations are portrayed in a separate note.

Exhibit 9.6 • Consolidated Financial Statements of Plus Inc for the Year Ended December 31, X7

Consolidated Statement of Financial Position of Plus Inc
December 31, X7
(in CU)

Assets
Cash (CU3,000,000 + CU700,000)	3,700,000
Accounts receivable (CU7,500,000 + CU2,100,000)	9,600,000
Inventory (1)	19,750,000
Land (2)	10,500,000
Buildings (net) (3)	22,800,000
Patents (Plus)	1,400,000
Goodwill (4)	1,200,000
Total assets	**68,950,000**

Liabilities and equities
Current liabilities (CU8,500,000 + CU1,200,000)	9,700,000
Long-term liabilities (5)	20,250,000
Share capital (Plus)	20,000,000
Retained earnings (6)	16,640,000
Non-controlling interest (7)	2,360,000
Total liabilities and equities	**68,950,000**

Consolidated Income Statement of Plus Inc
Year Ended December 31, X7
(in CU)

Revenues (8)	20,200,000
Cost of goods sold (9)	7,710,000
Other expenses (10)	5,350,000
Profit for the year (11)	**7,140,000**
Allocation to:	
Plus (12)	6,712,000
Non-controlling interest (13)	428,000
	7,140,000

Consolidated Statement of Changes in Equity of Plus Inc
Year Ended December 31, X10
(in CU)

	Share Capital	Retained Earnings	NCI	Total
Balance at January 1, X10	20,000,000	11,928,000	2,132,000	34,060,000
Dividends		(2,000,000)		(2,000,000)
Dividends to NCI			(200,000)	(200,000)
Profit for the year		6,712,000	428,000	7,140,000
Balance at December 31, X10	20,000,000	16,640,000	2,360,000	39,000,000

(1) **Inventory**	CU
• Parent (Plus)	14,300,000
• Subsidiary (Lortis)	5,600,000
• Unrealized profit on upstream sale	(150,000)
Total	**19,750,000**

(2) **Land**	CU
• Parent (Plus)	9,000,000
• Subsidiary (Lortis)	2,500,000
• Full fair value decrement	(500,000)
• Unrealized gain on downstream sale	(500,000)
Total	**10,500,000**

(3) **Buildings** (net)	CU
• Parent (Plus)	15,800,000
• Subsidiary (Lortis)	5,500,000
• Unamortized balance of the full fair value increment (CU2,000,000 X 15/20)	1,500,000
Total	**22,800,000**

(4) **Goodwill**	CU
Goodwill at the date of acquisition	
• Parent (Plus)	1,000,000
• Non-controlling interest	200,000
Total	**1,200,000**

(5) **Long-Term Liabilities**	CU
• Parent (Plus)	15,000,000
• Subsidiary (Lortis)	4,500,000
• Unamortized balance of the full fair value increment (CU1,500,000 × 5/10)	750,000
Total	**20,250,000**

(6) **Retained Earnings**	CU
• Parent (Plus)	15,300,000
• 80 percent of the subsidiary (Lortis)'s net adjusted value since acquisition	

- Retained earnings increase since acquisition (CU7,700,000 - CU4,000,000)	3,700,000	
- Price differential amortization since acquisition (see amortization schedule in Exhibit 9.4: CU2,700,000 - CU1,450,000)	(1,250,000)	
- Unrealized profit on upstream sale of inventory	(150,000)	
	2,300,000	
	80% →	1,840,000

• Unrealized gain on downstream sale of land	(500,000)
Total	**16,640,000**

(7) Non-Controlling Interest — CU

- Fair value of the non-controlling interest at the date of acquisition 1,900,000
- 20 percent of the subsidiary (Lortis)'s net adjusted value since acquisition

- Retained earnings increase since acquisition (CU7,700,000 - CU4,000,000)	3,700,000
- Price differential amortization since acquisition (see amortization schedule in Exhibit 9.4: CU2,700,000 - CU1,450,000)	(1,250,000)
- Unrealized profit on upstream sale of inventory	(150,000)
	2,300,000

  × 20% → 460,000

Total   **2,360,000**

---

(8) Revenues (including dividends and gains on sale) — CU

- Parent (Plus)   16,500,000
- Subsidiary (Lortis)   7,000,000
- Intercompany sales   (2,000,000)
- Intercompany dividends   (800,000)
- Unrealized gain on downstream sale of land   (500,000)

Total   **20,200,000**

---

(9) Cost of Goods Sold — CU

- Parent (Plus)   6,400,000
- Subsidiary (Lortis)   3,400,000
- Intercompany sales   (2,000,000)
- Prior-year deferred profit that has been realized in the current period   (240,000)
- Unrealized current-year profit   150,000

Total   **7,710,000**

(10) **Other Expenses** (including depreciation expense)	CU
• Parent (Plus)	3,800,000
• Subsidiary (Lortis)	1,600,000
• Current-year price differential amortizations (see amortization schedule in Exhibit 9.4). Includes full fair value increments on:	
- Long-term liabilities (CU1,500,000/10)	(150,000)
- Buildings (CU2,000,000/20)	100,000
Total	**5,350,000**

(11) **Consolidated Profit for the Year**		CU
• Plus's adjusted profit:		
- Plus's profit	6,300,000	
- Current-year gain on downstream sale of land	(500,000)	
- Intercompany dividends	(800,000)	5,000,000
• Lortis's adjusted profit:		
- Lortis's profit	2,000,000	
- Current-year implied price differential amortization (see amortization schedule in Exhibit 9.4). Full fair value increments on:		
- Long-term liabilities (CU1,500,000/10)	150,000	
- Buildings (CU2,000,000/20)	(100,000)	
- Profits on upstream sales of inventory:		
- Prior-year deferred profit now being realized	240,000	
- Current-year unrealized profit	(150,000)	2,140,000
Total		**7,140,000**

(12) **Consolidated Profit Allocated to Plus**	CU
• Plus's adjusted profit	5,000,000
• 80 percent of Lortis's adjusted profit (CU2,140,000 X 80%)	1,712,000
Total	**6,712,000**

(13) **Consolidated Profit Allocated to Non-Controlling Interest**	CU
20 percent of Lortis's adjusted profit (CU2,140,000 X 20%)	428,000

9.4 Investment Account on Equity Basis

The *equity method* of accounting for strategic investments in common stocks aims at reflecting the investor's changing interest in the investee. More precisely, the investment is recorded at the initial purchase price and adjusted each period for the investor's proportionate share of the investee's earnings and dividends (when declared by the investee).

Assume that this method is employed by Plus to account for its investment in Lortis instead of the cost method. The individual financial statements of Plus as of December 31, X7, are shown in Exhibit 9.7. Consolidated information is also reported on a comparative basis.

Note that Share Capital and Retained Earnings are the same under the equity method and full consolidation. The balances of these accounts are CU20,000,000 and CU16,640,000, respectively. Moreover, the profit of Plus under the equity method is equal to the consolidated profit allocated to Plus in the consolidation process, that is, CU6,712,000. Because of these similarities, the equity method is often referred to as one-line consolidation: one line in the statement of financial position, the investment account, that shows the net value or consolidated value of the subsidiary, and one line in the income statement, the equity in earnings account, that shows the net earnings from the subsidiary.

The main difference between the two methods lies in the detail presented. More precisely, under the equity method, only the accounts carried on the books of Plus are shown. Conversely, under full consolidation, accounts of the affiliated companies are combined. Consolidated information does not show the investment in Lortis nor the Equity in Earnings of Lortis. One could see the process of consolidation as disaggregating, first, the investment account into the subsidiary's detailed assets and liabilities, and second, the equity in earnings account into the subsidiary's detailed revenues and expenses.

Exhibit 9.7 • Financial Statements of Plus Inc for the Year Ended December 31, X7 - The Investment in Lortis is Accounted for Using the Equity Method.

Statements of Financial Position of Plus Inc
December 31, X7
(in CU)

	Equity Method	Consolidated
Assets		
Cash	3,000,000	3,700,000
Accounts receivable	7,500,000	9,600,000
Inventory	14,300,000	19,750,000
Land	9,000,000	10,500,000
Buildings (net)	15,800,000	22,800,000
Patents	1,400,000	1,400,000
Investment in Lortis	9,140,000	
Goodwill		1,200,000
Total assets	60,140,000	68,950,000
Liabilities and equities		
Current liabilities	8,500,000	9,700,000
Long-term liabilities	15,000,000	20,250,000
Share capital	**20,000,000**	**20,000,000**
Retained earnings	**16,640,000**	**16,640,000**
Non-controlling interest		**2,360,000**
Total liabilities and equities	60,140,000	68,950,000

Statements of Changes in Equity
Year Ended December 31, X7
(in CU)

	Equity Method			Consolidated			
	Share Capital	Retained Earnings	Total	Share Capital	Retained Earnings	NCI	Total
Balance at January 1, X7	20,000,000	11,928,000	31,928,000	20,000,000	11,928,000	2,132,000	34,060,000
Dividends		(2,000,000)	(2,000,000)		(2,000,000)		(2,000,000)
Dividends to NCI						(200,000)	(200,000)
Profit for the year		6,712,000	6,712,000		6,712,000	428,000	7,140,000
Balance at December 31, X7	20,000,000	16,640,000	36,640,000	20,000,000	16,640,000	2,360,000	39,000,000

Income Statements of Plus Inc
Year Ended December 31, X7
(in CU)

	Equity Method	Consolidated
Revenues	15,700,000	20,200,000
Equity in earnings of Lortis	1,212,000	
Cost of goods sold	6,400,000	7,710,000
Other expenses	3,800,000	5,350,000
Profit for the year	6,712,000	7,140,000
Allocated to:		
Plus	6,712,000	6,712,000
Non-controlling interest		428,000
	6,712,000	7,140,000

Under the equity method, changes in the investee's shareholders' equity is accounted for by recognizing the income realized and the dividends declared by the investee as the following:

1- Recognition of Income

| Investment in Subsidiary | XX | |
| Equity in Earnings of Subsidiary | | XX |

2- Recognition of Dividends (When Declared)

| Cash | XX | |
| Investment in Subsidiary | | XX |

The approach to computing equity in earnings and investment accounts is shown in Exhibits 9.8 and 9.9, respectively.

Exhibit 9.8 • The Equity Method - Computation of Equity in Earnings of Subsidiary

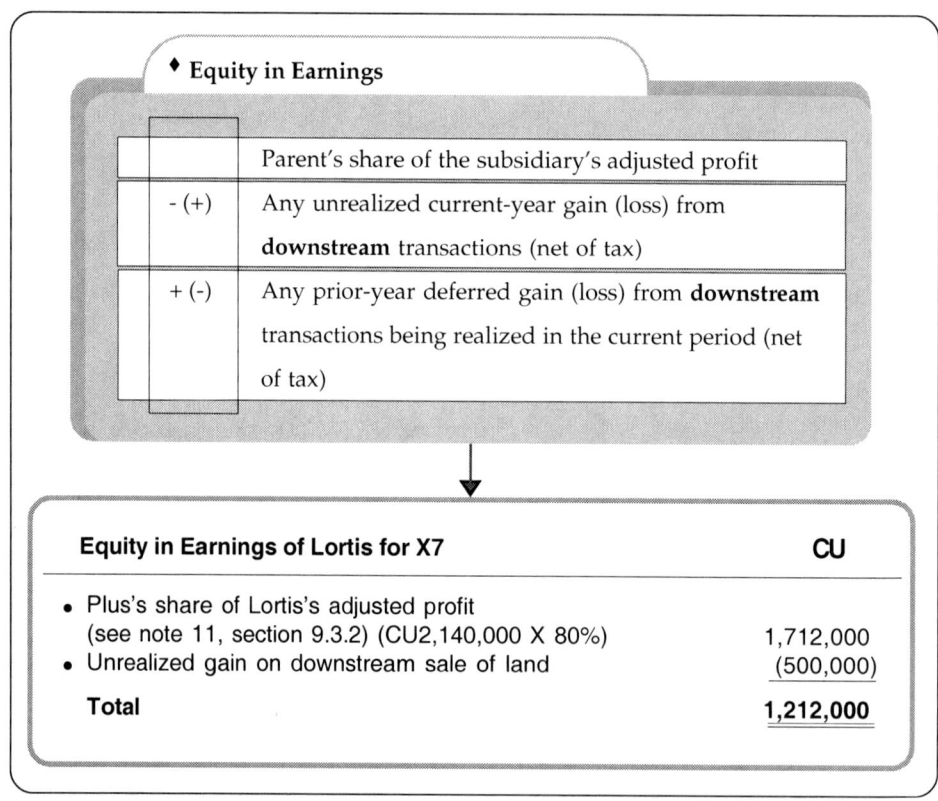

The following presents the journal entries that Plus must have recorded in X7 to account for its investment in Lortis under the equity method.

1- Equity in Earnings of Lortis

Investment in Lortis	1,212,000	
Equity in Earnings of Lortis		1,212,000

2- Dividends Declared by Lortis

(CU1,000,000 X 80%) = CU800,000

Exhibit 9.9 • The Equity Method - Computation of the Balance of the Investment Account

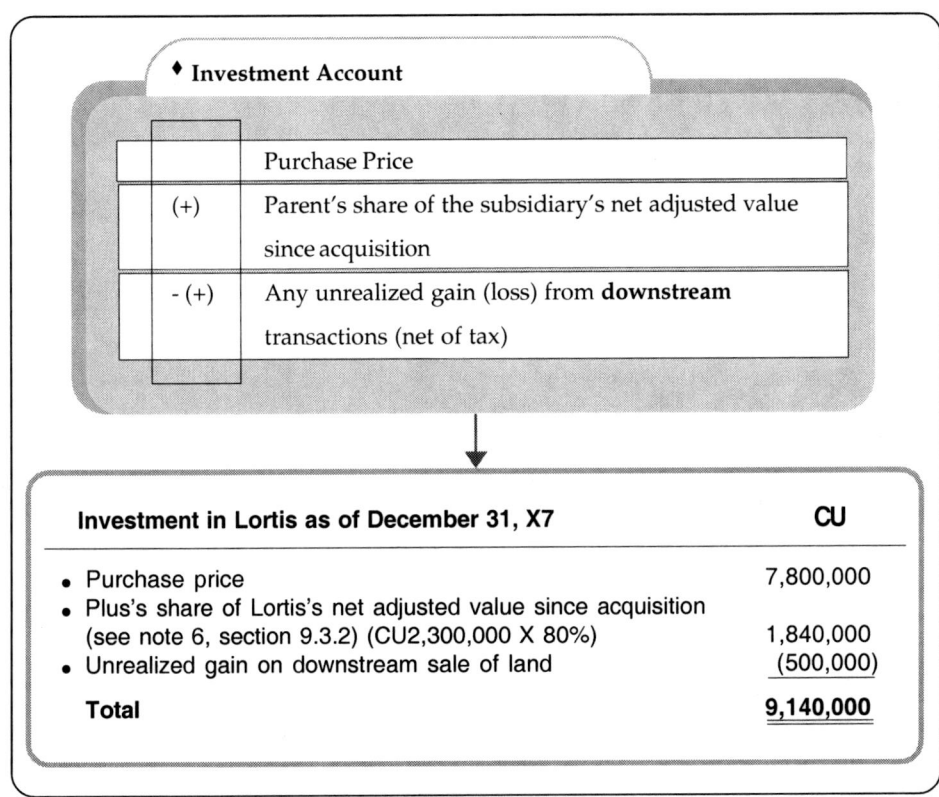

Had Plus been using the equity method to account for its investment in Lortis instead of the cost method, these two journal entries should have been eliminated via the following additional consolidation entries.

Additional Consolidation Entry #1

Equity in Earnings of Lortis (Plus)	1,212,000	
Investment in Lortis (Plus)		1,212,000

To eliminate equity in earnings of Lortis.

Additional Consolidation Entry #2 (replacing entry #4)

Investment in Lortis (Plus)	800,000	
Dividends Declared (Lortis)		800,000

To eliminate intercompany dividends.

After these two entries are entered into the consolidation worksheet, the remaining balance of the investment in Lortis amounts to CU 928,000 as shown below.

	CU
Balance of the investment in Lortis as of December 31, X7, under the equity method (see Exhibit 9.6)	9,140,000
• Purchase price (already eliminated via entries #1a and #1b)	(7,800,000)
• Equity in earnings of X7 (additional consolidation entry #1)	(1,212,000)
• Dividends declared in X7 (additional consolidation entry #2)	800,000
Remaining balance of the investment in Lortis	**928,000**

The remaining balance of CU928,000 reflects the increase of the investment account from the date of acquisition to the beginning of the current year and must be eliminated with the following final consolidation entry.

Additional Consolidation Entry #3

Retained Earnings (Plus)	928,000	
Investment in Lortis (Plus)		928,000

To eliminate the remaining balance of the investment account.

Part IV

Cases and Solutions

In this part:

- Case 1 : Fast Inc
- Case 2 : Prime Inc
- Case 3 : Global Inc
- Case 4 : Mother Inc
- Case 5 : Parent Inc
- Case 6 : Big Inc
- Case 7 : Plus Inc
- Case 8 : Large Inc
- Case 9 : Total Inc
- Case 10 : Giant Inc

Case 1

Fast Inc

What this Case is About

- ☑ Consolidation of a Parent Founded Subsidiary
- ☑ In a Period Subsequent to Establishment
- ☑ With Intercompany Transactions Involving Dividends and Note Payable.
- ☑ Illustration Under the Cost and Equity Methods

Contents

1	Basic Information	242
2	Preliminary Analysis	245
3	Consolidation of Financial Statements	245
	3.1 Worksheet Approach	245
	3.2 Direct Approach	248
4	Investment Account on Equity Basis	251

Fast Inc

1 Basic Information

During X3, Fast Inc established a new subsidiary named Slow Corporation in order to facilitate the conduct of a new line of business. The initial cash investment of Fast in Slow amounted to CU700,000. Since the creation, Fast is maintaining full control over Slow.

You are asked to prepare the consolidated financial statements of Fast Inc for the year ended December 31, X7. Separate financial statements of the affiliated companies for that period are presented in the accompanying Exhibit.

Exhibit 1 • Financial Statements of Fast and Slow for the Year Ended December 31, X7

Statements of Financial Position
December 31, X7
(in CU)

	Fast	Slow
Assets		
Cash	75,000	15,000
Current receivables	410,000	120,000
Inventory	920,000	670,000
Plant and equipment (net)	1,500,000	400,000
Investment in Slow	700,000	
Total assets	**3,605,000**	**1,205,000**
Liabilities and equities		
Current liabilities	140,000	305,000
Share capital	500,000	700,000
Retained earnings	2,965,000	200,000
Total liabilities and equities	**3,605,000**	**1,205,000**

Case 1 Fast Inc

Income Statements
Year Ended December 31, X7
(in CU)

	Fast	Slow
Revenues	400,000	250,000
Dividend income	1,000	
Cost of goods sold	300,000	100,000
Operating expenses	50,000	35,000
Other expenses	10,000	50,000
Profit for the year	**41,000**	**65,000**

Statements of Changes in Equity
Year Ended December 31, X7
(in CU)

	Fast			Slow		
	Share Capital	Retained Earnings	Total	Share Capital	Retained Earnings	Total
Balance at January 1, X7	500,000	2,924,000	3,424,000	700,000	136,000	836,000
Dividends	-	-	-		(1,000)	(1,000)
Profit for the year		41,000	41,000		65,000	65,000
Balance at December 31, X7	**500,000**	**2,965,000**	**3,465,000**	**700,000**	**200,000**	**900,000**

Additional Information

1) Slow declared a CU1,000 cash dividend in December 31, X7, payable in January X8.
2) Slow borrowed CU100,000 from Fast on June 30, X7, with the note maturing on June 30, X8, at 10 percent interest. Correct accruals have been recorded by both companies.

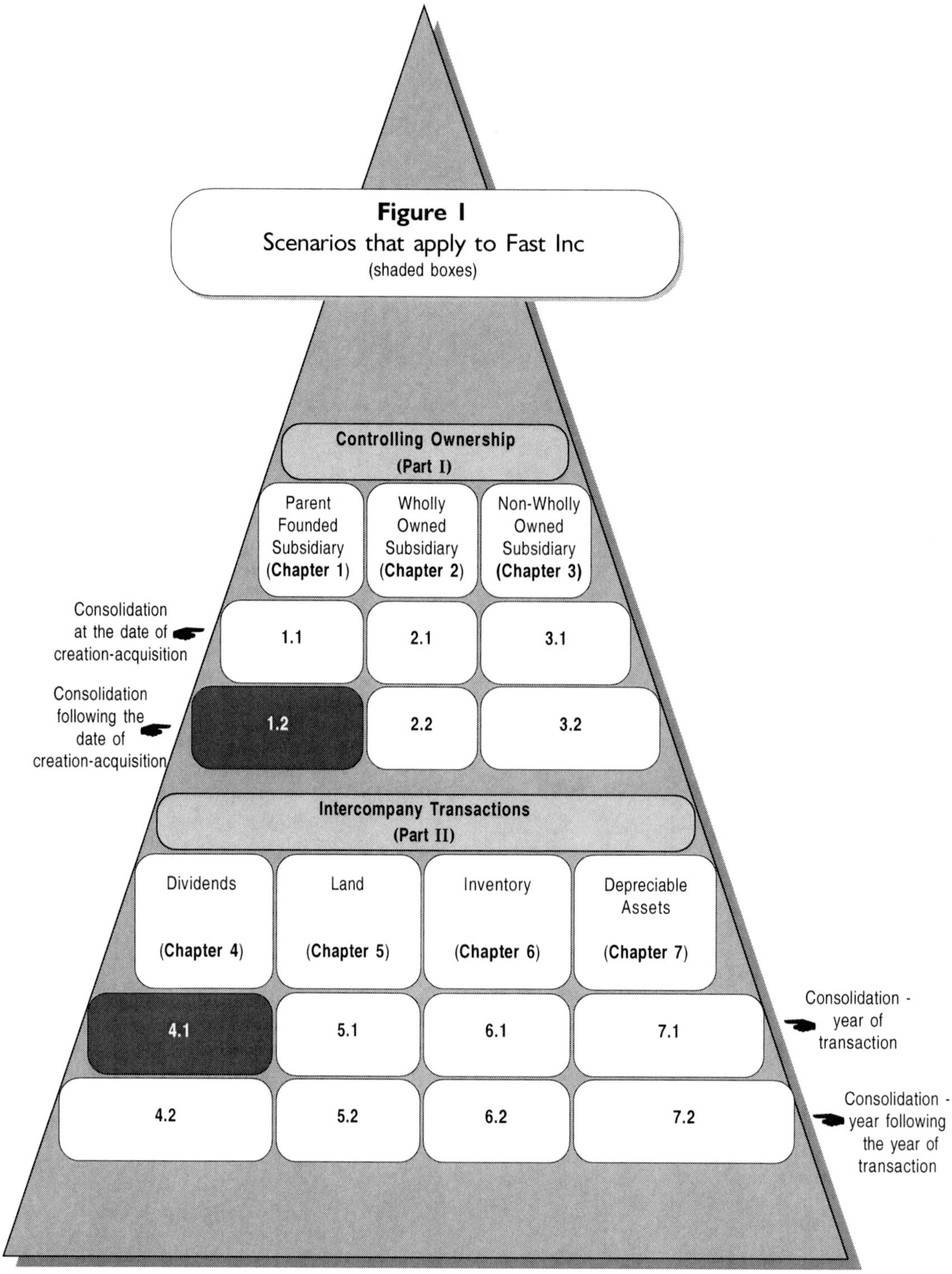

244 Part IV Cases and Solutions

Figure 1
Scenarios that apply to Fast Inc
(shaded boxes)

Controlling Ownership (Part I)

	Parent Founded Subsidiary (Chapter 1)	Wholly Owned Subsidiary (Chapter 2)	Non-Wholly Owned Subsidiary (Chapter 3)
Consolidation at the date of creation-acquisition	1.1	2.1	3.1
Consolidation following the date of creation-acquisition	**1.2**	2.2	3.2

Intercompany Transactions (Part II)

	Dividends (Chapter 4)	Land (Chapter 5)	Inventory (Chapter 6)	Depreciable Assets (Chapter 7)
Consolidation - year of transaction	**4.1**	5.1	6.1	7.1
Consolidation - year following the year of transaction	4.2	5.2	6.2	7.2

2 Preliminary Analysis

Figure 1 lists the consolidation scenarios that apply to Fast. The intercompany note payable is not included in the figure but should be considered as well in the consolidation of Fast's financial statements.

Note that the balance of the investment of Fast in Slow as of December 31, X7, amounts to CU700,000, which consists of the initial cash investment made by Fast at the establishment of Slow. This signals the use by Fast of the cost method to account for its strategic investments. In non-consolidated statements, Fast could have elected to report its subsidiary on the equity basis. This scenario is explored in Section 4.

Transactions conducted between the affiliated companies are analyzed next.

Intercompany Dividends

In December 31, X7, Slow declared dividends of CU1,000. The dividends are payable in January X8, therefore, resulting in reciprocal receivables and payables of CU1,000 at the end of the accounting period. These reciprocal balances must be eliminated. Furthermore, since the investment of Fast in Slow is accounted for using the cost method, dividends received by Fast (CU1,000) have been recorded as Dividend Income in the income statement. To avoid double-counting of Slow's earnings, intercompany dividends must be eliminated.

Intercompany Note Payable

On June 30, X7, Slow borrowed CU100,000 from Fast. The note is maturing on June 30, X8, and bears interest at 10% per annum. Therefore, the year-end reciprocal note receivable and note payable of CU100,000 must be eliminated. In addition, reciprocal interest expense and interest revenue and reciprocal interest payable and interest receivable for the current year must be removed. These reciprocal balances amount to CU5,000, respectively (CU100,000 X 10% X 1/2 = CU5,000).

3 Consolidation of Financial Statements

The following illustrates the consolidation of the financial statements of Fast Inc as of December 31, X7, under, first, the worksheet approach, and second, the direct approach.

3.1 Worksheet Approach

Entries that will be entered into the consolidation worksheet of Fast are listed next.

Adjustments Related To Controlling Ownership

1- Elimination of the Investment Account in the Subsidiary

Common Shares (Slow)	700,000	
Investment in Slow (Fast)		700,000

To eliminate reciprocal investment and equity accounts at the date of creation so as to avoid double-counting.

Adjustments Related to Intercompany Transactions

(2) Intercompany Dividends

Dividend Income (Fast)	1,000	
Dividends Declared (Slow)		1,000

To eliminate current-year intercompany dividends.

(3) Reciprocal Balances

(3a) From Intercompany Dividends

Current Liabilities (Slow)	1,000	
Current Receivables (Fast)		1,000

(3b) From Intercompany Loan

Current Liabilities (Slow)	105,000	
Current Receivables (Fast)		105,000

Revenues (Fast)	5,000	
Other Expenses (Slow)		5,000

The following presents the consolidation worksheet of Fast Inc for the period ended December 31, X7.

Consolidation Worksheet

	Fast (CU)	Slow (CU)	Eliminations Adjustments (CU)	Fast Consolidated (CU)
ASSETS				
Cash	75,000	15,000		90,000
Current receivables	410,000	120,000	(1,000) (3a) (105,000) (3b)	424,000
Inventory	920,000	670,000		1,590,000
Plant and equipment	1,500,000	400,000		1,900,000
Investment in Slow	700,000		(700,000) (1)	–
	3,605,000	1,205,000		4,004,000
LIABILITIES				
Current liabilities	140,000	305,000	(1,000) (3a) (105,000) (3b)	339,000
EQUITY				
Common shares	500,000	700,000	(700,000) (1)	500,000
Retained earnings	2,965,000	200,000		3,165,000
	3,605,000	1,205,000		4,004,000

Consolidation Worksheet (continued)

	Fast (CU)	Slow (CU)	Eliminations Adjustments (CU)	Fast Consolidated (CU)
Revenues	400,000	250,000	(5,000) (3b)	645,000
Dividend income	1,000		(1,000) (2)	-
Cost of goods sold	300,000	100,000		400,000
Operating Exp.	50,000	35,000		85,000
Other expenses	10,000	50,000	(5,000) (3b)	55,000
Profit	41,000	65,000	(1,000)	105,000
Retained earnings	2,924,000	136,000		3,060,000
Dividends		1,000	(1,000) (2)	-
Retained earnings (end)	2,965,000	200,000	-	3,165,000

3.2 Direct Approach

Consolidated financial statements of Fast Inc for the year ended December 31, X7, are shown in Exhibit 2. The balances from the books of the affiliated companies are shown in brackets. More sophisticated computations are shown in a separate note.

Exhibit 2 • Consolidated Financial Statements of Fast Inc for the Year Ended December 31, X7

Consolidated Statement of Financial Position of Fast Inc
December 31, X7
(in CU)

Assets	
Cash (CU75,000 + CU15,000)	90,000
Current receivables (1)	424,000
Inventory (CU920,000 + CU670,000)	1,590,000
Plant and equipment (net) (CU1,500,000 + CU400,000)	1,900,000
Total assets	**4,004,000**
Liabilities and equities	
Current liabilities (2)	339,000
Share capital (Fast)	500,000
Retained earnings (CU2,965,000 + CU200,000)	3,165,000
Total liabilities and equities	**4,004,000**

Consolidated Income Statement of Fast Inc
Year Ended December 31, X7
(in CU)

Revenues (3)	645,000
Cost of goods sold (CU300,00 + CU100,000)	400,000
Operating expenses (CU50,000 + CU35,000)	85,000
Other expenses (4)	55,000
Profit for the year (5)	**105,000**

Consolidated Statement of Changes in Equity of Fast Inc
Year Ended December 31, X7
(in CU)

	Share Capital	Retained Earnings	Total
Balance at January 1, X7	500,000	3,060,000	3,560,000
Profit for the year		105,000	105,000
Balance at December 31, X7	**500,000**	**3,165,000**	**3,665,000**

(1) **Current Receivables**	CU
• Parent (Fast)	410,000
• Subsidiary (Slow)	120,000
• Intercompany receivables (CU1,000 + CU105,000)	(106,000)
Total	**424,000**

(2) **Current Liabilities**	CU
• Parent (Fast)	140,000
• Subsidiary (Slow)	305,000
• Intercompany payables (CU1,000 + CU105,000)	(106,000)
Total	**339,000**

(3) **Revenues** (including interest revenue)	CU
• Parent (Fast)	400,000
• Subsidiary (Slow)	250,000
• Intercompany interest	(5,000)
Total	**645,000**

(4) **Other Expenses** (including interest expense)	CU
• Parent (Fast)	10,000
• Subsidiary (Slow)	50,000
• Intercompany interest	(5,000)
Total	**55,000**

(5) **Consolidated Profit for the Year**		CU
• Fast's adjusted profit:		
- Fast's profit	41,000	
- Intercompany dividends	(1,000)	40,000
• Slow's profit		65,000
Total		**105,000**

4 Investment Account on Equity Basis

Assume that the equity method is employed by Fast to account for its investment in Slow instead of the cost method. The individual financial statements of Fast as of December 31, X7, are shown in Exhibit 3. Consolidated information is also reported on a comparative basis.

Exhibit 3 • Financial Statements of Fast Inc for the Year Ended December 31, X7 - The Investment in Slow is Accounted for Using the Equity Method.

Statements of Financial Position of Fast Inc.
December 31, X7
(in CU)

	Equity Method	Consolidated
Assets		
Cash	75,000	90,000
Current receivables	410,000	424,000
Inventory	920,000	1,590,000
Plant and equipment	1,500,000	1,900,000
Investment in Slow	900,000	
Total assets	3,805,000	4,004,000
Liabilities and equities		
Current liabilities	140,000	339,000
Share capital	**500,000**	**500,000**
Retained earnings	**3,165,000**	**3,165,000**
Total liabilities and equities	3,805,000	4,004,000

Income Statements of Fast Inc
Year Ended December 31, X7
(in CU)

	Equity Method	Consolidated
Revenues	400,000	645,000
Equity in earnings of Slow	**65,000**	
Cost of goods sold	300,000	400,000
Operating expenses	50,000	85,000
Other expenses	10,000	55,000
Profit for the year	105,000	105,000

Statements of Changes in Equity of Fast Inc.
Year Ended December 31, X7
(in CU)

	Equity Method			Consolidated		
	Share Capital	Retained Earnings	Total	Share Capital	Retained Earnings	Total
Balance at January 1, X7	500,000	3,060,000	3,560,000	500,000	3,060,000	3,560,000
Profit for the year		105,000	105,000		105,000	105,000
Balance at December 31, X7	500,000	3,165,000	3,665,000	500,000	3,165,000	3,665,000

Consolidation and equity method are closely related. As one can see, the net consolidated value (Share Capital and Retained Earnings) is the same as the net value of Fast under the equity method. Moreover, the profit of Fast under the equity method is equal to the consolidated profit, that is, CU105,000.

The approach to computing the balance of the investment account is shown below.

Investment in Slow as of December 31, X7	CU
• Initial investment at the creation of Slow	700,000
• Fast's share of Slow's retained earnings (CU200,000 X 100%)	200,000
Total	**900,000**

The following presents the journal entries that Fast must have recorded in X7 to account for its investment in Slow using the equity method.

1- Equity in Earnings of Slow

| Investment in Slow | 65,000 | |
| Equity in Earnings of Slow | | 65,000 |

Fast's share of Slow's net income (CU65,000 X 100%) = CU65,000

2- Dividends Declared by Slow

Current Receivables	1,000	
Investment in Slow		1,000

Had Fast been using the equity method to account for its investment in Slow instead of the cost method, these two journal entries should have been eliminated via the following additional consolidation entries.

Additional Consolidation Entry #1

Equity in Earnings of Slow (Fast)	65,000	
Investment in Slow (Fast)		65,000

To eliminate equity in earnings of Slow.

Additional Consolidation Entry #2 (replacing entry #2)

Investment in Slow (Fast)	1,000	
Dividends Declared (Slow)		1,000

To eliminate intercompany dividends.

After these two entries are entered into the consolidation worksheet, the remaining balance of the investment in Slow amounts to CU136,000 as shown below.

	CU
Balance of the investment in Slow as of December 31, X7, under the equity method	900,000
• Initial investment (already eliminated via entry #1)	(700,000)
• Equity in earnings of X7 (additional consolidation entry #1)	(65,000)
• Dividends declared in X7 (additional consolidation entry #2)	1,000
Remaining balance of the investment in Slow	**136,000**

The remaining balance of CU136,000 consists of Slow's retained earnings at the beginning of the period. It reflects the increase of the investment account from the date of creation to the beginning of the current year and must be eliminated with the following final consolidation entry.

Additional Consolidation Entry #3

Retained Earnings (Fast)	136,000	
Investment in Slow (Fast)		136,000

To eliminate the remaining balance of the investment account.

Prime Inc

Case 2

What this Case is About

- ☑ Consolidation of a Parent Founded Subsidiary
- ☑ In a Period Subsequent to Establishment
- ☑ With Intercompany Transactions Involving Inventory, Dividends and Loan.
- ☑ Illustration Under the Cost and Equity Methods

Contents

1	Basic Information	256
2	Preliminary Analysis	259
3	Consolidation of Financial Statements	260
	3.1 Worksheet Approach	260
	3.2 Direct Approach	262
4	Investment Account on Equity Basis	265

Prime Inc

1 Basic Information

During X4, Prime Inc established a new subsidiary named Little Inc in order to serve a specific market segment. The initial cash investment of Prime in Little amounted to CU200,000. Since Prime has full control over Little, you must prepare the consolidated financial statements of Prime Inc for the year ended December 31, X7. Separate financial statements of the affiliated companies for that period are shown in Exhibit 1.

Exhibit 1 • Financial Statements of Prime and Little for the Year Ended December 31, X7

Statements of Financial Position
December 31, X7
(in CU)

	Prime	Little
Assets		
Cash	26,800	35,000
Accounts receivable	33,000	40,000
Inventory	120,000	190,000
Land	70,000	20,000
Buildings (net)	125,000	115,000
Long-term note receivable	50,000	
Investment in Little	200,000	
Total assets	**624,800**	**400,000**
Liabilities and equities		
Current liabilities	100,000	15,000
Long-term note payable		50,000
Share capital	300,000	200,000
Retained earnings	224,800	135,000
Total liabilities and equities	**624,800**	**400,000**

Income Statements
Year Ended December 31, X7
(in CU)

	Prime	Little
Revenues	400,000	200,000
Cost of goods sold	280,000	120,000
Operating expenses	50,000	25,000
Other expenses	10,000	20,000
Profit for the year	**60,000**	**35,000**

Statements of Changes in Equity
Year Ended December 31, X7
(in CU)

	Prime			Little		
	Share Capital	Retained Earnings	Total	Share Capital	Retained Earnings	Total
Balance at January 1, X7	300,000	164,800	464,800	200,000	110,000	310,000
Dividends		-	-		(10,000)	(10,000)
Profit for the year		60,000	60,000		35,000	35,000
Balance at December 31, X7	300,000	224,800	524,800	200,000	135,000	335,000

Additional Information

1) Little sells some of its output to Prime Inc. For the current year, intercompany sales amount to CU100,000. However, no transferred units were retained within the consolidated group at the end of the period. Prime has accounts payable to Little for CU25,000 as a result of intercompany sales.
2) The long-term note payable on Little's books represents a three-year loan from Prime. The note bears interest at 10% per annum, payable once a year on June 30. The loan has been issued on July 01, X6 and is due on June 30, X9.

258 Part IV Cases and Solutions

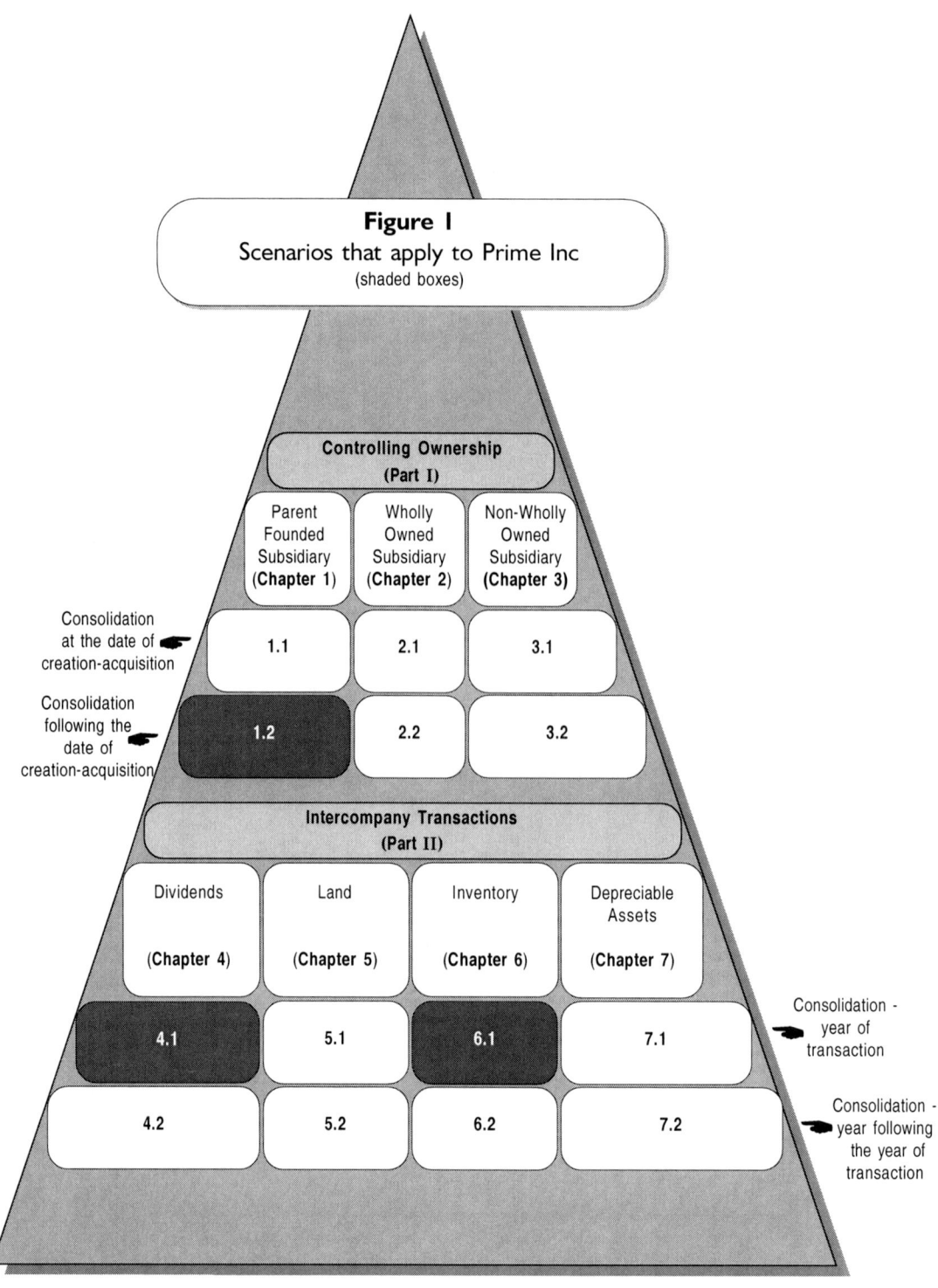

2 Preliminary Analysis

Figure 1 lists the consolidation scenarios that apply to Prime. The intercompany loan is not included in the figure but should be considered as well in the preparation of Prime's consolidated financial statements.

Note that the value of the investment of Prime in Little has not been revised since creation. In fact, the balance of the investment account as of December 31, X7, reflects the initial cash investment of CU200,000 made by Prime at the establishment of Little. Therefore, the investment in the subsidiary is reported on the cost basis.

Transactions conducted between the affiliated companies are analyzed below.

Intercompany Dividends

During X7, Little declared dividends for CU10,000 (see Exhibit 1). Since there is no indication of dividends payable at the end of the year, one can assume that dividends declared by Little were fully paid in the current accounting period. Furthermore, since the investment of Prime in Little is accounted for using the cost method, dividends received by Prime (CU10,000) must have been recorded as revenue in the income statement. To avoid double-counting of Little's earnings, intercompany dividends must be eliminated.

Intercompany Sales of Inventory

During X7, Little sold merchandise to Prime for CU100,000. Since no transferred units remained in Prime's inventory at the end of the year, Sales and Cost of Goods Sold for the period are both overstated by CU100,000. Reciprocal Sales and Cost of Goods Sold must be eliminated. Moreover, as a result of intercompany sales of inventory, Prime has accounts payable to Little for CU25,000. Reciprocal Payable and Receivable must also be eliminated.

Intercompany Loan

On July 01, X6, Little had a long-term loan of CU50,000 from Prime. Therefore, year-end reciprocal long-term note payable and long-term note receivable of CU50,000 must be eliminated. In addition, since the loan bears interest at 10% per annum, reciprocal interest expense and interest revenue for the year must be eliminated as well. These reciprocal balances amount to CU5,000 (CU50,000 X 10% = CU5,000). Finally, since the interest is due on June 30, outstanding reciprocal interest payable and interest receivable at the end of the current accounting period must be removed. These reciprocal balances amount to CU2,500 (CU50,000 X 10% X 6/12 = CU2,500).

3 Consolidation of Financial Statements

The following illustrates the consolidation of the financial statements of Prime Inc as of December 31, X7, under, first, the worksheet approach, and second, the direct approach.

3.1 Worksheet Approach

Entries that will be entered into the consolidation worksheet of Prime are listed below.

Adjustments Related To Controlling Ownership

1- Elimination of the Investment Account in the Subsidiary

Common Shares (Little)	200,000	
Investment in Little (Prime)		200,000

To eliminate reciprocal investment and equity accounts at the date of creation so as to avoid double-counting.

Adjustments Related to Intercompany Transactions

(2) Intercompany Dividends

Revenues (Dividends) (Prime)	10,000	
Dividends Declared (Little)		10,000

To eliminate current-year intercompany dividends.

(3) Reciprocal Balances

(3a) From Intercompany Sales of Inventory

Revenues (Little)	100,000	
Cost of Goods Sold (Prime)		100,000

Current Liabilities (Prime)	25,000	
Accounts Receivable (Little)		25,000

(3b) From Intercompany Loan

Long-Term Note Payable (Little)	50,000	
Long-Term Note Receivable (Prime)		50,000

Current Liabilities (Little)	2,500	
Accounts Receivable (Prime)		2,500

Revenues (Prime)	5,000	
Other Expenses (Little)		5,000

The following presents the consolidation worksheet of Prime Inc for the period ended December 31, X7.

Consolidation Worksheet

	Prime (CU)	Little (CU)	Eliminations Adjustments (CU)	Prime Consolidated (CU)
Revenues	400,000	200,000	(10,000) (2) (100,000) (3a) (5,000) (3b)	485,000
Cost of goods sold	280,000	120,000	(100,000) (3a)	300,000
Operating Exp.	50,000	25,000		75,000
Other expenses	10,000	20,000	(5,000) (3b)	25,000
Profit	60,000	35,000	(10,000)	85,000
Retained earnings	164,800	110,000		274,800
Dividends		10,000	(10,000) (2)	–
Retained earnings (end)	224,800	135,000	–	359,800

Consolidation Worksheet (continued)

	Prime (CU)	Little (CU)	Eliminations Adjustments (CU)	Prime Consolidated (CU)
ASSETS				
Cash	26,800	35,000		61,800
Accounts receivable	33,000	40,000	(25,000) (3a) (2,500) (3b)	45,500
Inventory	120,000	190,000		310,000
Land	70,000	20,000		90,000
Buildings (net)	125,000	115,000		240,000
Investment in Little	200,000		(200,000) (1)	–
Long-term note rec.	50,000		(50,000) (3b)	–
	624,800	**400,000**		**747,300**
LIABILITIES				
Current liabilities	100,000	15,000	(25,000) (3a) (2,500) (3b)	87,500
Long-term note pay.		50,000	(50,000) (3b)	–
EQUITY				
Common shares	300,000	200,000	(200,000) (1)	300,000
Retained earnings	224,800	135,000		359,800
	624,800	**400,000**		**747,300**

3.2 Direct Approach

Consolidated financial statements of Prime Inc for the year ended December 31, X7, are shown in Exhibit 2. Figures reported in brackets come from the books of Prime and Little. When the balance needs consolidation adjustments, a note is introduced to show the details of the calculation.

Exhibit 2 • Consolidated Financial Statements of Prime Inc for the Year Ended December 31, X7

Consolidated Statement of Financial Position of Prime Inc
December 31, X7
(in CU)

Assets	
Cash (CU26,800 + CU35,000)	61,800
Accounts receivable **(1)**	45,500
Inventory (CU120,000 + CU190,000)	310,000
Land (CU70,000 + CU20,000)	90,000
Buildings (net) (CU125,000 + CU115,000)	240,000
Total assets	**747,300**
Liabilities and equities	
Current liabilities **(2)**	87,500
Share capital (Prime)	300,000
Retained earnings (CU224,800 + CU135,000)	359,800
Total liabilities and equities	**747,300**

Consolidated Income Statement of Prime Inc
Year Ended December 31, X7
(in CU)

Revenues **(3)**	485,000
Cost of goods sold **(4)**	300,000
Operating expenses (CU50,000 + CU25,000)	75,000
Other expenses **(5)**	25,000
Profit for the year (6)	**85,000**

Consolidated Statement of Changes in Equity of Prime Inc
Year Ended December 31, X7
(in CU)

	Share Capital	Retained Earnings	Total
Balance at January 1, X7	300,000	274,800	574,800
Profit for the year		85,000	85,000
Balance at December 31, X7	**300,000**	**359,800**	**659,800**

(1) **Accounts Receivable**	CU
• Parent (Prime)	33,000
• Subsidiary (Little)	40,000
• Intercompany receivables (CU2,500 +CU25,000)	(27,500)
Total	**45,500**

(2) **Current Liabilities**	CU
• Parent (Prime)	100,000
• Subsidiary (Little)	15,000
• Intercompany payables (CU2,500 + CU25,000)	(27,500)
Total	**87,500**

(3) **Revenues** (including dividends and interest)	CU
• Parent (Prime)	400,000
• Subsidiary (Little)	200,000
• Intercompany sales	(100,000)
• Intercompany dividends	(10,000)
• Intercompany interest	(5,000)
Total	**485,000**

(4) **Cost of Goods Sold**	CU
• Parent (Prime)	280,000
• Subsidiary (Little)	120,000
• Intercompany sales	(100,000)
Total	**300,000**

(5) **Other Expenses** (including interest expense)	CU
• Parent (Prime)	10,000
• Subsidiary (Little)	20,000
• Intercompany Interest	(5,000)
Total	**25,000**

(6) Consolidated Profit for the Year		CU
• Prime's adjusted profit:		
- Prime's profit	60,000	
- Intercompany dividends	(10,000)	50,000
• Little's profit		35,000
Total		85,000

4 Investment Account on Equity Basis

Assume that the equity method is employed by Prime to account for its investment in Little instead of the cost method. The individual financial statements of Prime as of December 31, X7, are shown in Exhibit 3. Consolidated information is also reported on a comparative basis.

Exhibit 3 • Financial Statements of Prime Inc for the Year Ended December 31, X7 - The Investment in Little is Accounted for Using the Equity Method.

Statements of Financial Position of Prime Inc
December 31, X7
(in CU)

	Equity Method	Consolidated
Assets		
Cash	26,800	61,800
Accounts receivable	33,000	45,500
Inventory	120,000	310,000
Land	70,000	90,000
Buildings (net)	125,000	240,000
Long-term note receivable	50,000	
Investment in Little	335,000	
Total assets	759,800	747,300
Liabilities and equities		
Current liabilities	100,000	87,500
Share capital	300,000	300,000
Retained earnings	359,800	359,800
Total liabilities and equities	759,800	747,300

Income Statements of Prime Inc
Year Ended December 31, X7
(in CU)

	Equity Method	Consolidated
Revenues	390,000	485,000
Equity in earnings of Little	35,000	
Cost of goods sold	280,000	300,000
Operating expenses	50,000	75,000
Other expenses	10,000	25,000
Profit for the year	**85,000**	**85,000**

Statements of Changes in Equity of Prime Inc
Year Ended December 31, X7
(in CU)

	Equity Method			Consolidated		
	Share Capital	Retained Earnings	Total	Share Capital	Retained Earnings	Total
Balance at January 1, X7	300,000	274,800	574,800	300,000	274,800	574,800
Profit for the year		85,000	85,000		85,000	85,000
Balance at December 31, X7	300,000	359,800	659,800	300,000	359,800	659,800

Note that consolidated Share Capital, Retained Earnings and profit for the year are equal to Prime's separate-entity Share Capital, Retained Earnings and profit for the year under the equity method.

The approach to computing the balance of the investment account is shown below.

Investment in Little as of December 31, X7	CU
• Initial investment at the creation of Little	200,000
• Prime's share of Little's retained earnings (CU135,000 X 100%)	135,000
Total	**335,000**

The following presents the journal entries that Prime must have recorded in X7 to account for its investment in Little using the equity method.

1- Equity in Earnings of Little

Investment in Little	35,000	
Equity in Earnings of Little		35,000

Prime's share of Little's net income (CU35,000 X 100%) = CU35,000

2- Dividends Declared by Little

Cash	10,000	
Investment in Little		10,000

Had Prime been using the equity method to account for its investment in Little instead of the cost method, these two journal entries should have been eliminated via the following additional consolidation entries.

Additional Consolidation Entry #1

Equity in Earnings of Little (Prime)	35,000	
Investment in Little (Prime)		35,000

To eliminate equity in earnings of Little.

Additional Consolidation Entry #2 (replacing entry #2)

Investment in Little (Prime)	10,000	
Dividends Declared (Little)		10,000

To eliminate intercompany dividends.

After these two entries are entered into the consolidation worksheet, the remaining balance of the investment in Little amounts to CU110,000 as shown next.

	CU
Balance of the investment in Little as of December 31, X7, under the equity method	335,000
• Initial investment (already eliminated via entry #1)	(200,000)
• Equity in earnings of X7 (additional consolidation entry #1)	(35,000)
• Dividends declared in X7 (additional consolidation entry #2)	10,000
Remaining balance of the investment in Little	110,000

The remaining balance of CU110,000 is equal to the balance of Little's retained earnings at the beginning of the current period. This amount reflects the increase of the investment account from the date of creation to the beginning of the current year and must be eliminated with the following final consolidation entry.

Additional Consolidation Entry #3

Retained Earnings (Prime)	110,000	
Investment in Little (Prime)		110,000

To eliminate the remaining balance of the investment account.

Global Inc

Case 3

What this Case is About

☑ Consolidation of a Wholly Owned Subsidiary
☑ At the Date of Acquisition

Contents

1	Basic Information	270
2	Preliminary Analysis	271
3	Consolidation of Financial Statements	271
	3.1 Worksheet Approach	271
	3.2 Direct Approach	273

Global Inc

1 Basic Information

On January 1, X8, Global Inc purchased on the open market 100 percent of Local's outstanding common stock for cash of CU485,000. You are asked to prepare the consolidated statement of financial position of Global at the date of combination. Exhibit 1 shows the summarized statements of financial position of the two companies at the date of combination.

Exhibit 1 • Statements of Financial Position of Global and Local as of January 1, X8

	Global (CU)	Local (CU)
Assets		
Cash	50,000	70,000
Accounts receivable	40,000	21,000
Inventory	60,000	5,600
Land	30,000	25,000
Buildings and equipment (net)	1,000,000	500,000
Patents	30,000	
Investment in Local	485,000	
Total assets	1,695,000	621,600
Liabilities and equities		
Current liabilities	60,000	20,000
Long-term liabilities	1,130,000	250,000
Share capital	200,000	100,000
Retained earnings	305,000	251,600
Total liabilities and equities	1,695,000	621,600

Additional Information

At the time of acquisition, Local's land had an estimated value of CU40,000, its buildings and equipment had a value of CU550,000, and its long-term notes payable a fair value of CU300,000. Book values and fair values were approximately equal for all other assets and liabilities.

2 Preliminary Analysis

The allocation of the purchase price is shown in the following Exhibit.

Exhibit 2 • Acquisition of 100 percent of the Outstanding Voting Stock of Local by Global on January 1, X8 - Allocation of the Purchase Price

		CU
Cost of investment in Local		485,000
Shareholders' equity of Local at the date of acquisition:		
- Share capital	100,000	
- Retained earnings	251,600	351,600
Price differential		133,400
Fair value increments:		
- Land		(15,000)
- Buildings		(50,000)
- Long-term liabilities		50,000
Goodwill		118,400

For consolidation purposes, the price differential of CU133,400 at the date of acquisition will be used to change Local's value from carrying value to full market value.

3 Consolidation of Financial Statements

The following illustrates the consolidation of the statement of financial position of Global Inc at the date of acquisition, under, first, the worksheet approach, and second, the direct approach.

3.1 Worksheet Approach

The following presents the consolidation worksheet of Global Inc at the date of acquisition.

Consolidation Worksheet

	Global (CU)	Local (CU)	Eliminations Adjustments (CU)	Global Consolidated (CU)
ASSETS				
Cash	50,000	70,000		120,000
Accounts receivable	40,000	21,000		61,000
Inventory	60,000	5,600		65,600
Land	30,000	25,000	15,000 (1b)	70,000
Buildings and equip.	1,000,000	500,000	50,000 (1b)	1,550,000
Investment in Local	485,000		(351,600) (1a) (133,400) (1b)	–
Patents	30,000			30,000
Goodwill			118,400 (1b)	118,400
	1,695,000	621,600		2,015,000
LIABILITIES				
Current liabilities	60,000	20,000		80,000
Long-term liabilities	1,130,000	250,000	50,000 (1b)	1,430,000
EQUITY				
Common shares	200,000	100,000	(100,000) (1a)	200,000
Retained earnings	305,000	251,600	(251,600) (1a)	305,000
	1,695,000	621,600		2,015,000

Entries that are entered into the consolidation worksheet of Global are listed below.

1- Elimination of the Investment Account in the Subsidiary

(1a) To eliminate reciprocal investment and equity accounts at the date of acquisition so as to avoid double-counting.

Common Shares (Local)	100,000	
Retained Earnings (Local)	251,600	
Investment in Local (Global)		351,600

(1b) To allocate the price differential so as to consider the fair value of Local at the date of acquisition.

Land (Local)	15,000	
Buildings and equipment (Local)	50,000	
Goodwill	118,400	
Long-Term Liabilities (Local)		50,000
Investment in Local (Global)		133,400

3.2 Direct Approach

The consolidated statement of financial position of Global Inc at the date of acquisition is shown in Exhibit 3. The balance of the account from the books of the affiliated companies is shown in brackets. More sophisticated computations are shown in a separate note.

(1) **Land**	CU
• Parent (Global)	30,000
• Subsidiary (Local)	25,000
• Fair value increment	15,000
Total	**70,000**

(2) **Buildings and Equipment** (net)	CU
• Parent (Global)	1,000,000
• Subsidiary (Local)	500,000
• Fair value increment	50,000
Total	**1,550,000**

Exhibit 3 • Consolidated Statement of Financial Position of Global Inc as of January 1, X8

	CU
Assets	
Cash (CU50,000 + CU70,000)	120,000
Accounts receivable (CU40,000 + CU21,000)	61,000
Inventory (CU60,000 + CU5,600)	65,600
Land **(1)**	70,000
Buildings and equipment (net) **(2)**	1,550,000
Patents (Global)	30,000
Goodwill	118,400
Total assets	**2,015,000**
Liabilities and equities	
Current liabilities (CU60,000 + CU20,000)	80,000
Long-term liabilities **(3)**	1,430,000
Share capital (Global)	200,000
Retained earnings (Global)	305,000
Total liabilities and equities	**2,015,000**

(3) Long-Term Liabilities	CU
• Parent (Global)	1,130,000
• Subsidiary (Local)	250,000
• Fair value increment	50,000
Total	**1,430,000**

Case 4

Mother Inc

What this Case is About

- ☑ Consolidation of a Wholly Owned Subsidiary
- ☑ One Year Subsequent to Acquisition
- ☑ With no Intercompany Transactions
- ☑ Illustration Under the Cost and Equity Methods

Contents

1	Basic Information	276
2	Preliminary Analysis	278
3	Consolidation of Financial Statements	279
	3.1 Worksheet Approach	279
	3.2 Direct Approach	282
4	Investment Account on Equity Basis	285

Mother Inc

1 Basic Information

Mother Inc acquired all outstanding CU10 par value voting common stock of Son Corporation on January 1, X7, in exchange for 35,000 shares. On December 31, X6, Mother's common stock had a closing market price of CU30 per share on a national stock exchange. Both companies continued to operate as separate business entities maintaining separate accounting records.

Prepare the consolidated financial statements of Mother Inc for the year ended December 31, X7, that is, one year subsequent to the date of acquisition. Separate financial statements of the affiliated companies for that period are shown in Exhibit 1.

Exhibit 1 • Financial Statements of Mother and Son for the Year Ended December 31, X7

Statements of Financial Position
December 31, X7
(in CU)

	Mother	Son
Assets		
Cash	570,000	150,000
Accounts receivable	860,000	350,000
Inventory	760,000	410,000
Land	200,000	100,000
Plant and equipment (net)	750,000	570,000
Investment in Son	1,050,000	
Total assets	4,190,000	1,580,000
Liabilities and equities		
Current liabilities	1,340,000	554,000
Share capital	1,700,000	600,000
Retained earnings	1,150,000	426,000
Total liabilities and equities	4,190,000	1,580,000

Income Statements
Year Ended December 31, X7
(in CU)

	Mother	Son
Net sales	3,840,000	1,500,000
Cost of goods sold	2,360,000	870,000
Operating expenses	1,100,000	440,000
Profit for the year	380,000	190,000

Statements of Changes in Equity
Year Ended December 31, X7
(in CU)

	Mother			Son		
	Share Capital	Retained Earnings	Total	Share Capital	Retained Earnings	Total
Balance at January 1, X7	1,700,000	770,000	2,470,000	600,000	236,000	836,000
Profit for the year		380,000	380,000		190,000	190,000
Balance at December 31, X7	1,700,000	1,150,000	2,850,000	600,000	426,000	1,026,000

Additional Information

1) At the date of acquisition, the fair value of Son's equipment exceeded its book value by CU54,000. The excess cost will be amortized over the estimated average remaining life of six years. In addition, the inventory had a fair value CU20,000 greater than its carrying value. The fair values of all of Son's other assets and liabilities were equal to their book values.
2) At December 31, X7, Mother management reviewed the amount attributed to goodwill as a result of its purchase of Son's common stock and concluded that an impairment loss of CU35,000 should be recognized in X7.
3) Mother and Son never engaged in transactions between themselves during X7.

Additional Information (continued)

4) Both affiliated companies use the straight-line method to calculate all depreciation and amortization. Inventory units are usually sold within six months.
5) At the date of acquisition, Son's equity consisted of Common Shares of CU600,000 and Retained Earnings of CU236,000.

2 Preliminary Analysis

The cost of the investment in Son amounts to CU1,050,000, that is, 35,000 shares of Mother at a market price of CU30 per share (35,000 X CU30 = CU1,050,000). The allocation of the purchase price is shown in the following Exhibit.

Exhibit 2 • Acquisition of 100 percent of the Outstanding Voting Stock of Son by Mother on January 1,X7 - Allocation of the Purchase Price

		CU
Cost of investment in Son		1,050,000
Shareholders' equity of Son at the date of acquisition:		
- Share capital	600,000	
- Retained earnings	236,000	836,000
Price differential		214,000
Fair value increments:		
- Inventory		20,000
- Equipment		54,000
Goodwill		140,000

For consolidation purposes, the price differential of CU214,000 at the date of acquisition will be used to change Son's value from carrying value to full market value. In post-acquisition consolidations, adjustments are required so as to account for price differential amortization and/or realization. This information is summarized in the following Exhibit.

Exhibit 3 • Consolidation of the Financial Statements of Mother - Price Differential Amortization Schedule

Items	Price Differential Balance at Acquisition (CU)	Amortization Current Year (X7) (CU)	Unamortized Excess at 31-12-X7 (CU)
Fair Value Increments			
• Inventory	20,000	20,000	-
• Equipment	54,000	9,000	45,000
Goodwill	140,000	35,000	105,000
Total	**214,000**	**(64,000)**	**150,000**

Note that the value of the investment of Mother in Son has not changed since acquisition (CU1,050,000) indicating the use by Mother of the cost method.

3 Consolidation of Financial Statements

The following illustrates the consolidation of the financial statements of Mother Inc as of December 31, X7, under, first, the worksheet approach, and second, the direct approach.

3.1 Worksheet Approach

Entries that will be entered into the consolidation worksheet of Mother are listed below.

1- Elimination of the Investment Account in the Subsidiary (see purchase price allocation in Exhibit 2)

(1a) To eliminate reciprocal investment and equity accounts at the date of acquisition so as to avoid double-counting.

Common Shares (Son)	600,000	
Retained Earnings (Son)	236,000	
Investment in Son (Mother)		836,000

(1b) To allocate the price differential so as to consider the fair value of Son at the date of acquisition.

Inventory (Son)	20,000	
Plant and Equipment (Son)	54,000	
Goodwill	140,000	
Investment in Son (Mother)		214,000

2- Price Differential Amortization Since Acquisition (see amortization schedule in Exhibit 3)

(2a) To recognize current-year realization of the fair value increment on inventory.

Cost of Goods Sold (Son)	20,000	
Inventory (Son)		20,000

(2b) To amortize the fair value increment on equipment.

Operating Expenses (Son)	9,000	
Plant and Equipment (Son)		9,000

(2c) To recognize current-year goodwill impairment.

Operating Expenses	35,000	
Goodwill		35,000

Case 4 Mother Inc

The following presents the consolidation worksheet of Mother Inc for the period ended December 31, X7.

Consolidation Worksheet

	Mother (CU)	Son (CU)	Eliminations Adjustments (CU)	Mother Consolidated (CU)
ASSETS				
Cash	570,000	150,000		720,000
Accounts receivable	860,000	350,000		1,210,000
Inventory	760,000	410,000	20,000 (1b) (20,000) (2a)	1,170,000
Land	200,000	100,000		300,000
Plant and equip. (net)	750,000	570,000	54,000 (1b) (9,000) (2b)	1,365,000
Investment in Son	1,050,000		(836,000) (1a) (214,000) (1b)	–
Goodwill			140,000 (1b) (35,000) (2c)	105,000
	4,190,000	1,580,000		4,870,000
LIABILITIES				
Current liabilities	1,340,000	554,000		1,894,000
EQUITY				
Common shares	1,700,000	600,000	(600,000) (1a)	1,700,000
Retained earnings	1,150,000	426,000	(300,000)	1,276,000
	4,190,000	1,580,000		4,870,000

Net impact of the adjustments on the ending balance of RE

Consolidation Worksheet (continued)

	Mother (CU)	Son (CU)	Eliminations Adjustments (CU)	Mother Consolidated (CU)
Net sales	3,840,000	1,500,000		5,340,000
Cost of goods sold	2,360,000	870,000	20,000 (2a)	3,250,000
Operating exp.	1,100,000	440,000	9,000 (2b) 35,000 (2c)	1,584,000
Profit	380,000	190,000	(64,000)	506,000
Retained earnings	770,000	236,000	(236,000) (1a)	770,000
Retained earnings (end)	1,150,000	426,000	(300,000)	1,276,000

Net impact of the adjustments on the ending balance of RE

3.2 Direct Approach

Consolidated financial statements of Mother Inc for the year ended December 31, X7, are portrayed in Exhibit 4. The balance of the account from the books of the affiliated companies is shown in brackets. More complex calculations are shown in a separate note.

(1) **Plant and Equipment** (net)	CU
• Parent (Mother)	750,000
• Subsidiary (Son)	570,000
• Unamortized balance of the fair value increment (CU54,000 X 5/6)	45,000
Total	1,365,000

(2) **Goodwill**	CU
• At the date of acquisition	140,000
• Portion impaired during the current period	(35,000)
Total	105,000

Exhibit 4 • Consolidated Financial Statements of Mother Inc for the Year Ended December 31, X7

Consolidated Statement of Financial Position of Mother Inc
December 31, X7
(in CU)

Assets
Cash (CU570,000 + CU150,000)	720,000
Accounts receivable (CU860,000 + CU350,000)	1,210,000
Inventory (CU760,000 + CU410,000)	1,170,000
Land (CU200,000 + CU100,000)	300,000
Plant and equipment (net) **(1)**	1,365,000
Goodwill **(2)**	105,000
Total assets	**4,870,000**

Liabilities and equities
Current liabilities (CU1,340,000 + CU554,000)	1,894,000
Share capital (Mother)	1,700,000
Retained earnings **(3)**	1,276,000
Total liabilities and equities	**4,870,000**

Consolidated Income Statement of Mother Inc
Year Ended December 31, X7
(in CU)

Net sales (CU3,840,000 + CU1,500,000)	5,340,000
Cost of goods sold **(4)**	3,250,000
Operating expenses **(5)**	1,584,000
Profit for the year (6)	**506,000**

Consolidated Statement of Changes in Equity of Mother Inc
Year Ended December 31, X7
(in CU)

	Share Capital	Retained Earnings	Total
Balance at January 1, X7	1,700,000	770,000	2,470,000
Profit for the year		506,000	506,000
Balance at December 31, X7	**1,700,000**	**1,276,000**	**2,976,000**

(3) **Retained Earnings**	CU
• Parent (Mother)	1,150,000
• 100 percent of the subsidiary (Son)'s net adjusted value since acquisition	

- Retained earnings increase since acquisition (CU426,000 - CU236,000)	190,000
- Price differential amortization since acquisition (see amortization schedule in Exhibit 3)	(64,000)
	126,000

100% → 126,000

Total	**1,276,000**

(4) **Cost of Goods Sold**	CU
• Parent (Mother)	2,360,000
• Subsidiary (Son)	870,000
• Current-year realization of fair value increment	20,000
Total	**3,250,000**

(5) **Operating Expenses** (including depreciation expense)	CU
• Parent (Mother)	1,100,000
• Subsidiary (Son)	440,000
• Current-year price differential amortization (see amortization schedule in Exhibit 3). Includes:	
- Fair value increment on equipment (CU54,000/6)	9,000
- Goodwill impairment	35,000
Total	**1,584,000**

(6) Consolidated Profit for the Year		CU
• Mother's profit		380,000
• Son's adjusted profit:		
- Son's profit	190,000	
- Current-year price differential amortization (see amortization schedule in Exhibit 3)	(64,000)	126,000
Total		**506,000**

4 Investment Account on Equity Basis

Assume that the equity method is employed by Mother to account for its investment in Son instead of the cost method. The individual financial statements of Mother as of December 31, X7, are shown in Exhibit 5. Consolidated information is also reported on a comparative basis.

Exhibit 5 • Financial Statements of Mother Inc for the Year Ended December 31, X7 - The Investment in Son is Accounted for Using the Equity Method.

Income Statements of Mother Inc
Year Ended December 31, X7
(in CU)

	Equity Method	Consolidated
Net sales	3,840,000	5,340,000
Equity in earnings of Son	**126,000**	
Cost of goods sold	2,360,000	3,250,000
Operating expenses	1,100,000	1,584,000
Profit for the year	**506,000**	**506,000**

Statements of Financial Position of Mother Inc
December 31, X7
(in CU)

	Equity Method	Consolidated
Assets		
Cash	570,000	720,000
Accounts receivable	860,000	1,210,000
Inventory	760,000	1,170,000
Land	200,000	300,000
Plant and equipment (net)	750,000	1,365,000
Investment in Son	1,176,000	
Goodwill		105,000
Total assets	4,316,000	4,870,000
Liabilities and equities		
Current liabilities	1,340,000	1,894,000
Share capital	**1,700,000**	**1,700,000**
Retained earnings	**1,276,000**	**1,276,000**
Total liabilities and equities	4,316,000	4,870,000

Statements of Changes in Equity of Mother Inc
Year Ended December 31, X7
(in CU)

	Equity Method			Consolidated		
	Share Capital	Retained Earnings	Total	Share Capital	Retained Earnings	Total
Balance at January 1, X7	1,700,000	770,000	2,470,000	1,700,000	770,000	2,470,000
Profit for the year		506,000	506,000		506,000	506,000
Balance at December 31, X7	1,700,000	1,276,000	2,976,000	1,700,000	1,276,000	2,976,000

Since the equity method takes into account the net effect of consolidation adjustments, Mother's Retained Earnings (CU1,276,000) and profit for the year (CU506,000) under the equity method are equal to consolidated Retained Earnings and consolidated profit for the year.

The approach to computing equity in earnings and investment accounts is shown in Exhibits 6 and 7, respectively.

Exhibit 6 • The Equity Method - Computation of Equity in Earnings of Son

Equity in Earnings of Son for X7	CU
Mother's share of Son's adjusted profit (see note 6, section 3.2) (CU126,000 X 100%)	__126,000__

Exhibit 7 • The Equity Method - Computation of the Balance of the Investment in Son

Investment in Son as of December 31, X7	CU
• Purchase price	1,050,000
• Mother's share of Son's net adjusted value since acquisition (see note 3, section 3.2) (CU126,000 X 100%)	126,000
Total	__1,176,000__

The following presents the journal entry that Mother must have recorded in X7 to account for its investment in Son using the equity method.

1- Equity in Earnings of Son

Investment in Son	126,000	
Equity in Earnings of Son		126,000

2- No dividends have been declared by Son during X7

Had Mother been using the equity method to account for its investment in Son instead of the cost method, this journal entry should have been eliminated via the following additional consolidation entry.

Additional Consolidation Entry

Equity in Earnings of Son (Mother)	126,000	
Investment in Son (Mother)		126,000

To eliminate equity in earnings of Son.

After this entry is entered into the consolidation worksheet, there is no remaining balance of the investment in Son as shown below.

	CU
Balance of the investment in Son as of December 31, X7, under the equity method (see Exhibit 7)	1,176,000
• Purchase price (already eliminated via entries #1a and #1b)	(1,050,000)
• Equity in earnings of X7 (additional consolidation entry)	(126,000)
Remaining balance of the investment in Son	-

Parent Inc

Case 5

What this Case is About

- ☑ Consolidation of a Wholly Owned Subsidiary
- ☑ In a Period Subsequent to Acquisition
- ☑ With Intercompany Transactions Involving Inventory
- ☑ Illustration Under the Cost and Equity Methods

Contents

1	Basic Information	290
2	Preliminary Analysis	292
	2.1 Controlling Ownership	294
	2.2 Intercompany Transactions	295
3	Consolidation of Financial Statements	296
	3.1 Worksheet Approach	296
	3.2 Direct Approach	300
4	Investment Account on Equity Basis	304

Parent Inc

1 Basic Information

On January 1, X6, Parent Inc acquired 100 percent of Subco's outstanding common stock for cash of CU1,255,000. A statement of financial position and market value information for Subco at the date of acquisition are presented in Exhibit 1.

Exhibit 1 • Statement of Financial Position of Subco as of January 1, X6

	Carrying Values (CU)	Fair Values (CU)
Assets		
Cash	40,000	40,000
Accounts receivable	110,000	130,000
Inventory	280,000	320,000
Land	310,000	400,000
Capital assets (net)	460,000	495,000
Total assets	**1,200,000**	
Liabilities and equities		
Current liabilities	250,000	250,000
Share capital	400,000	
Retained earnings	550,000	
Total liabilities and equities	**1,200,000**	

Prepare the consolidated financial statements of Parent Inc for the year ended December 31, X7, that is, two years subsequent to the date of acquisition. Separate financial statements of the affiliated companies for that period are shown in Exhibit 2.

Exhibit 2 • Financial Statements of Parent and Subco for the Year Ended December 31, X7

Statements of Financial Position
December 31, X7
(in CU)

	Parent	Subco
Assets		
Cash	55,000	40,000
Accounts receivable	140,000	110,000
Inventory	400,000	320,000
Land	670,000	385,000
Capital assets (net)	864,000	520,000
Investment in Subco	1,255,000	
Total assets	**3,384,000**	**1,375,000**
Liabilities and equities		
Current liabilities	248,000	180,000
Share capital	1,136,000	400,000
Retained earnings	2,000,000	795,000
Total liabilities and equities	**3,384,000**	**1,375,000**

Income Statements
Year Ended December 31, X7
(in CU)

	Parent	Subco
Sales	900,000	845,000
Cost of goods sold	542,000	479,000
Depreciation	120,000	110,000
Other expenses	128,000	126,000
Profit for the year	**110,000**	**130,000**

Statements of Changes in Equity
Year Ended December 31, X7
(in CU)

	Parent			Subco		
	Share Capital	Retained Earnings	Total	Share Capital	Retained Earnings	Total
Balance at January 1, X7	1,136,000	1,890,000	3,026,000	400,000	665,000	1,065,000
Profit for the year		110,000	110,000		130,000	130,000
Balance at December 31, X7	1,136,000	2,000,000	3,136,000	400,000	795,000	1,195,000

Additional Information

1) Subco's inventory is usually sold within seven months and the accounts receivable collected within six months.
2) Subco's capital assets will be depreciated over 10 years, straight-line, with no salvage value, from the date of acquisition.
3) During X6, Subco sold inventory to Parent for CU150,000 with a 20% markup on retail. At the end of X6, CU30,000 (at retail) of these goods were still in the inventory. Also during X6, Parent sold CU200,000 of goods to Subco with a 25% markup on retail, and CU40,000 (at retail) of these were still in inventory at the end of X6.
4) During X7, Parent sold inventory to Subco for CU180,000 with a 25% markup on retail. At the end of X7, CU50,000 (at retail) of these goods were still in the inventory. Also during X7, Subco sold CU220,000 of goods to Parent with a 20% markup on retail, and CU60,000 (at retail) of these were still in inventory at the end of X7.
5) Goodwill has not been impaired since acquisition.
6) Neither company paid any dividends during X6 and X7.

2 Preliminary Analysis

Figure 1 lists the consolidation scenarios that apply to Parent.

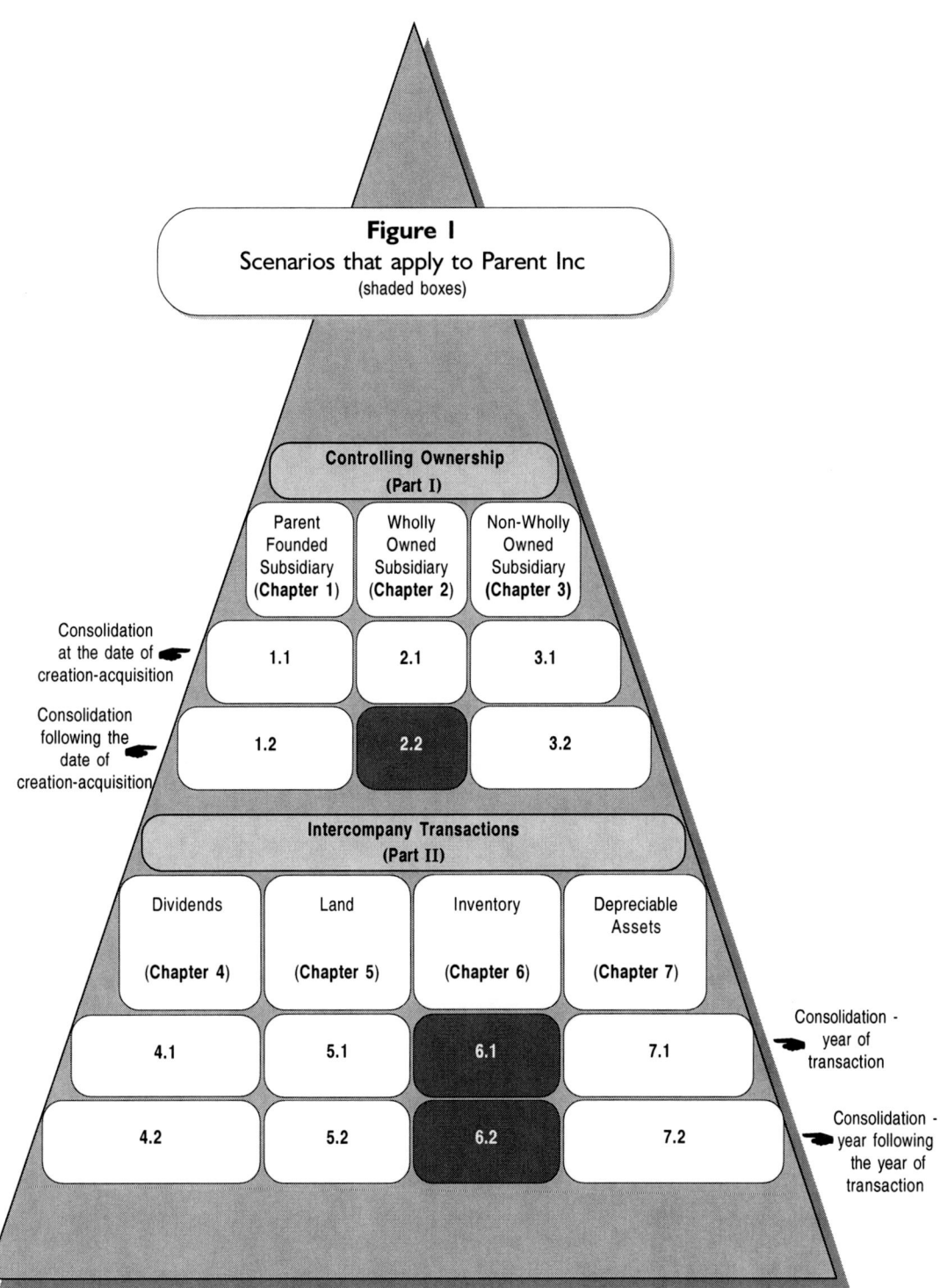

2.1 Controlling Ownership

The allocation of the purchase price is shown in the following Exhibit.

Exhibit 3 • Acquisition of 100 percent of the Outstanding Voting Stock of Subco by Parent on January 1, X6 - Allocation of the Purchase Price

		CU
Cost of investment in Subco		1,255,000
Shareholders' equity of Subco at the date of acquisition:		
- Share capital	400,000	
- Retained earnings	550,000	950,000
Price differential		305,000
Fair value increments :		
- Inventory		(40,000)
- Accounts receivable		(20,000)
- Land		(90,000)
- Capital assets		(35,000)
Goodwill		120,000

The price differential of CU305,000 at the date of acquisition will be used to change Subco's value from carrying value to full market value. Price differential must be adjusted so as to account for any fair value increment amortization and/or realization from the date of acquisition to the end of the current period. This information is summarized in Exhibit 4.

Note that the value of the investment of Parent in Subco has not been revised since acquisition. In fact, the balance of the investment account as of December 31, X7, reflects the purchase price of CU1,255,000. This signals the use by Parent of the cost method to account for its strategic investments.

Exhibit 4 • Consolidation of the Financial Statements of Parent - Price Differential Amortization Schedule

Items	Price Differential Balance at Acquisition (CU)	Amortization Current Year (X7) (CU)	Amortization Prior Year (X6) (CU)	Unamortized Excess at 31-12-X7 (CU)
Fair Value Increments				
• Inventory	40,000	-	40,000	-
• Accounts receiv.	20,000		20,000	-
• Land	90,000	-	-	90,000
• Capital assets	35,000	3,500	3,500	28,000
Goodwill	120,000	-	-	120,000
Total	305,000	(3,500)	(63,500)	238,000

2.2 Intercompany Transactions

Transactions conducted between the affiliated companies are analyzed below.

Intercompany Sales of Inventory during X6 (Additional Information #3)

During X6, Subco sold merchandise to Parent for CU150,000. CU30,000 of the transferred units remained in Parent's inventory at the end of X6. Taking into consideration a markup on retail of 20%, an unrealized profit of CU6,000 (CU30,000 X 20%) has been deferred in X6. However, this intercompany profit has been fully realized in X7.

Likewise, Parent sold merchandise to Subco during X6 for CU200,000. CU40,000 of the transferred units remained in Subco's inventory at the end of X6. Allowing for a markup on retail of 25%, an unrealized profit of CU10,000 (CU40,000 X 25%) has been deferred in X6. This intercompany profit has been fully realized in X7.

Intercompany Sales of Inventory during X7 (Additional Information #4)

During X7, Parent sold merchandise to Subco for CU180,000 with a 25% markup on retail. On December 31, X7, CU50,000 of this merchandise remains in Subco's inventory. Consequently, two adjustments are required for the consolidation of Parent. First, the unrealized intercompany profit of CU12,500 (CU50,000 X 25%) must be removed. Second, reciprocal Sales and Cost of Goods Sold of CU130,000 must be eliminated. This amount corresponds to the transfer price of the units being resold by Subco in the current year, that is, CU180,000 (transfer price of the units sold to Subco) less CU50,000 (unsold units at the end of the period).

Likewise, Subco sold merchandise to Parent during X7 for CU220,000 with a 20% markup on retail. On December 31, X7, CU60,000 of this merchandise remains in Parent's inventory. Consequently, two adjustments are required for the consolidation of Parent. First, the unrealized intercompany profit of CU12,000 (CU60,000 X 20%) must be removed. Second, reciprocal Sales and Cost of Goods Sold of CU160,000 must be eliminated. This amount corresponds to the transfer price of the units being resold by Parent in the current year, that is, CU220,000 (transfer price of the units sold to Parent) less CU60,000 (unsold units at the end of the period).

3 Consolidation of Financial Statements

The following illustrates the consolidation of the financial statements of Parent Inc as of December 31, X7, under, first, the worksheet approach, and second, the direct approach.

3.1 Worksheet Approach

Entries that will be entered into the consolidation worksheet of Parent are listed below.

Adjustments Related To Controlling Ownership

1- Elimination of the Investment Account in the Subsidiary (see purchase price allocation in Exhibit 3)

(1a) To eliminate reciprocal investment and equity accounts at the date of acquisition so as to avoid double-counting.

Common Shares (Subco)	400,000	
Retained Earnings (Subco)	550,000	
Investment in Subco (Parent)		950,000

(1b) To allocate the price differential so as to consider the fair value of Subco at the date of acquisition.

Inventory (Subco)	40,000	
Accounts Receivable (Subco)	20,000	
Land (Subco)	90,000	
Capital Assets (Subco)	35,000	
Goodwill	120,000	
Investment in Subco (Parent)		305,000

2- Price Differential Amortization Since Acquisition (see amortization schedule in Exhibit 4)

(2a) To recognize the prior-year realization of the fair value increment on inventory.

Retained Earnings (Subco)	40,000	
Inventory (Subco)		40,000

(2b) To recognize the prior-year realization of the fair value increment on accounts receivable.

Retained Earnings (Subco)	20,000	
Accounts Receivable (Subco)		20,000

(2c) To amortize the fair value increment on capital assets.

Retained Earnings (Subco)	3,500	
Depreciation (Subco)	3,500	
Capital Assets (Subco)		7,000

Adjustments Related to Intercompany Transactions

(3a) Intercompany Sales of Inventory During X6

Retained Earnings	16,000	
Cost of Goods Sold		16,000

To recognize prior-year deferred profit on sale of inventory (CU10,000 from downstream sales and CU6,000 from upstream sales).

(3b) Intercompany Sales of Inventory During X7

Downstream

Sales (Parent)	180,000	
Cost of Goods Sold (Parent & Subco)		167,500
Inventory (Subco)		12,500

Combined entry to eliminate current-year unrealized profit of CU12,500 on downstream sale of inventory, eliminate reciprocal Sales and Cost of Goods Sold balances and reduce inventory to its cost basis.

Upstream

Sales (Subco)	220,000	
Cost of Goods Sold (Parent & Subco)		208,000
Inventory (Parent)		12,000

Combined entry to eliminate current-year unrealized profit of CU12,000 on upstream sale of inventory, eliminate reciprocal Sales and Cost of Goods Sold balances and reduce inventory to its cost basis.

Combined Entry (Downstream and Upstream Sales)

Sales (CU180,000 + CU220,000)	400,000	
Cost of Goods Sold (CU167,500 + CU208,000)		375,500
Inventory (CU12,500 + CU12,000)		24,500

The following presents the consolidation worksheet of Parent Inc for the period ended December 31, X7.

Consolidation Worksheet

	Parent (CU)	Subco (CU)	Eliminations Adjustments (CU)	Parent Consolidated (CU)
ASSETS				
Cash	55,000	40,000		95,000
Accounts receivable	140,000	110,000	20,000 (1b) (20,000) (2b)	250,000
Inventory	400,000	320,000	40,000 (1b) (40,000) (2a) (24,500) (3b)	695,500
Land	670,000	385,000	90,000 (1b)	1,145,000
Capital assets (net)	864,000	520,000	35,000 (1b) (7,000) (2c)	1,412,000
Investment in Subco	1,255,000		(950,000) (1a) (305,000) (1b)	—
Goodwill			120,000 (1b)	120,000
	3,384,000	1,375,000		3,717,500
LIABILITIES				
Current liabilities	248,000	180,000		428,000
EQUITY				
Common shares	1,136,000	400,000	(400,000) (1a)	1,136,000
Retained earnings	2,000,000	795,000	(641,500)	2,153,500
	3,384,000	1,375,000		3,717,500

Net impact of the adjustments on the ending balance of RE

Consolidation Worksheet (continued)

	Parent (CU)	Subco (CU)	Eliminations Adjustments (CU)	Parent Consolidated (CU)
Sales	900,000	845,000	(400,000) (3b)	1,345,000
Cost of goods sold	542,000	479,000	(16,000) (3a) (375,500) (3b)	629,500
Depreciation	120,000	110,000	3,500 (2c)	233,500
Other expenses	128,000	126,000		254,000
Profit	**110,000**	**130,000**	**(12,000)**	**228,000**
Retained earnings	1,890,000	665,000	(550,000) (1a) (40,000) (2a) (20,000) (2b) (3,500) (2c) (16,000) (3a)	1,925,500
Retained earnings (end)	2,000,000	795,000	(641,500)	2,153,500

Net impact of the adjustments on the ending balance of RE

3.2 Direct Approach

Consolidated financial statements of Parent Inc for the year ended December 31, X7, are shown in Exhibit 5. When the consolidated balance is more than the sum of the two companies' balances, a note is introduced to present the calculations.

Exhibit 5 • Consolidated Financial Statements of Parent Inc for the Year Ended December 31, X7

Consolidated Statement of Financial Position of Parent Inc
December 31, X7
(in CU)

Assets

Cash (CU55,000 + CU40,000)	95,000
Accounts receivable (CU140,000 + CU110,000)	250,000
Inventory **(1)**	695,500
Land **(2)**	1,145,000
Capital assets (net) **(3)**	1,412,000
Goodwill **(4)**	120,000
Total assets	**3,717,500**

Liabilities and equities

Current liabilities (CU248,000 + CU180,000)	428,000
Share capital (Parent)	1,136,000
Retained earnings **(5)**	2,153,500
Total liabilities and equities	**3,717,500**

Consolidated Income Statement of Parent Inc
Year Ended December 31, X7
(in CU)

Sales **(6)**	1,345,000
Cost of goods sold **(7)**	629,500
Depreciation **(8)**	233,500
Other expenses (CU128,000 + CU126,000)	254,000
Profit for the year (9)	**228,000**

Consolidated Statement of Changes in Equity of Parent Inc
Year Ended December 31, X7
(in CU)

	Share Capital	Retained Earnings	Total
Balance at January 1, X7	1,136,000	1,925,500	3,061,500
Profit for the year		228,000	228,000
Balance at December 31, X7	**1,136,000**	**2,153,500**	**3,289,500**

(1) **Inventory**	CU
• Parent (Parent)	400,000
• Subsidiary (Subco)	320,000
• Unrealized profits on intercompany sales of inventory:	
- Upstream	(12,000)
- Downstream	(12,500)
Total	**695,500**

(2) **Land**	CU
• Parent (Parent)	670,000
• Subsidiary (Subco)	385,000
• Fair value increment	90,000
Total	**1,145,000**

(3) **Capital Assets** (net)	CU
• Parent (Parent)	864,000
• Subsidiary (Subco)	520,000
• Unamortized balance of the fair value increment (CU35,000 X 8/10)	28,000
Total	**1,412,000**

(4) **Goodwill**	CU
Goodwill at the date of acquisition	**120,000**

(5) **Retained Earnings**		CU
• Parent (Parent)		2,000,000
• 100 percent of the subsidiary (Subco)'s net adjusted value since acquisition		
- Retained earnings increase since acquisition (CU795,000 - CU550,000)	245,000	
- Price differential amortization since acquisition (see amortization schedule in Exhibit 4): (CU305,000 - CU238,000)	(67,000)	
- Unrealized profit on upstream sale of inventory	(12,000)	
	166,000	
	100% →	166,000
• Unrealized profit on downstream sale of inventory		(12,500)
Total		**2,153,500**

(6) **Sales**	CU
• Parent (Parent)	900,000
• Subsidiary (Subco)	845,000
• Intercompany sales	(400,000)
Total	**1,345,000**

(7) **Cost of Goods Sold**	CU
• Parent (Parent)	542,000
• Subsidiary (Subco)	479,000
• Intercompany sales	(400,000)
• Unrealized profits on sales of inventory:	
- Upstream	12,000
- Downstream	12,500
• Prior-year deferred profits on sales of inventory now realized:	
- Upstream	(6,000)
- Downstream	(10,000)
Total	**629,500**

(8) **Depreciation**	CU
• Parent (Parent)	120,000
• Subsidiary (Subco)	110,000
• Current-year price differential amortization (see amortization schedule in Exhibit 4).	
Fair value increment on capital assets (CU35,000/10)	3,500
Total	**233,500**

(9) **Consolidated Profit for the Year**		CU
• Parent's adjusted profit:		
- Parent's profit	110,000	
- Profits on downstream sales of inventory:		
- Prior-year deferred profit now realized	10,000	
- Current-year unrealized profit	(12,500)	107,500
• Subco's adjusted profit		
- Subco's profit	130,000	
- Current-year price differential amortization (see amortization schedule in Exhibit 4). Fair value increment on capital assets (CU35,000/10)	(3,500)	
- Profits on upstream sales of inventory:		
- Prior-year deferred profit now realized	6,000	
- Current-year unrealized profit	(12,000)	120,500
Total		**228,000**

4 Investment Account on Equity Basis

Assume that the equity method is employed by Parent to account for its investment in Subco instead of the cost method. The individual financial statements of Parent as of December 31, X7, are shown in Exhibit 6. Consolidated information is also reported on a comparative basis.

Exhibit 6 • Financial Statements of Parent Inc for the Year Ended December 31, X7 - The Investment in Subco is Accounted for Using the Equity Method.

Statements of Financial Position of Parent Inc
December 31, X7
(in CU)

	Equity Method	Consolidated
Assets		
Cash	55,000	95,000
Accounts receivable	140,000	250,000
Inventory	400,000	695,500
Land	670,000	1,145,000
Capital assets (net)	864,000	1,412,000
Investment in Subco	1,408,500	
Goodwill		120,000
Total assets	3,537,500	3,717,500
Liabilities and equities		
Current liabilities	248,000	428,000
Share capital	1,136,000	1,136,000
Retained earnings	2,153,500	2,153,500
Total liabilities and equities	3,537,500	3,717,500

Income Statements of Parent Inc
Year Ended December 31, X7
(in CU)

	Equity Method	Consolidated
Sales	900,000	1,345,000
Equity in earnings of Subco	118,000	
Cost of goods sold	542,000	629,500
Depreciation	120,000	233,500
Other expenses	128,000	254,000
Profit for the year	228,000	228,000

Statements of Changes in Equity of Parent Inc
Year Ended December 31, X7
(in CU)

	Equity Method			Consolidated		
	Share Capital	Retained Earnings	Total	Share Capital	Retained Earnings	Total
Balance at January 1, X7	1,136,000	1,925,500	3,061,500	1,136,000	1,925,500	3,061,500
Profit for the year		228,000	228,000		228,000	228,000
Balance at December 31, X7	1,136,000	2,153,500	3,289,500	1,136,000	2,153,500	3,289,500

The equity method captures the net effect of any consolidation adjustments. As a result, Retained Earnings and proft for the year are the same under the equity method and full consolidation.

The approach to computing equity in earnings and investment accounts is shown in Exhibits 7 and 8, respectively.

The following presents the journal entry that Parent must have recorded in X7 to account for its investment in Subco using the equity method.

1- Equity in Earnings of Subco

Investment in Subco	118,000	
Equity in Earnings of Subco		118,000

2- No dividends have been declared by Subco in X7

Had Parent been using the equity method to account for its investment in Subco instead of the cost method, this journal entry should have been eliminated via the following additional consolidation entry.

Exhibit 7 • The Equity Method - Computation of Equity in Earnings of Subco

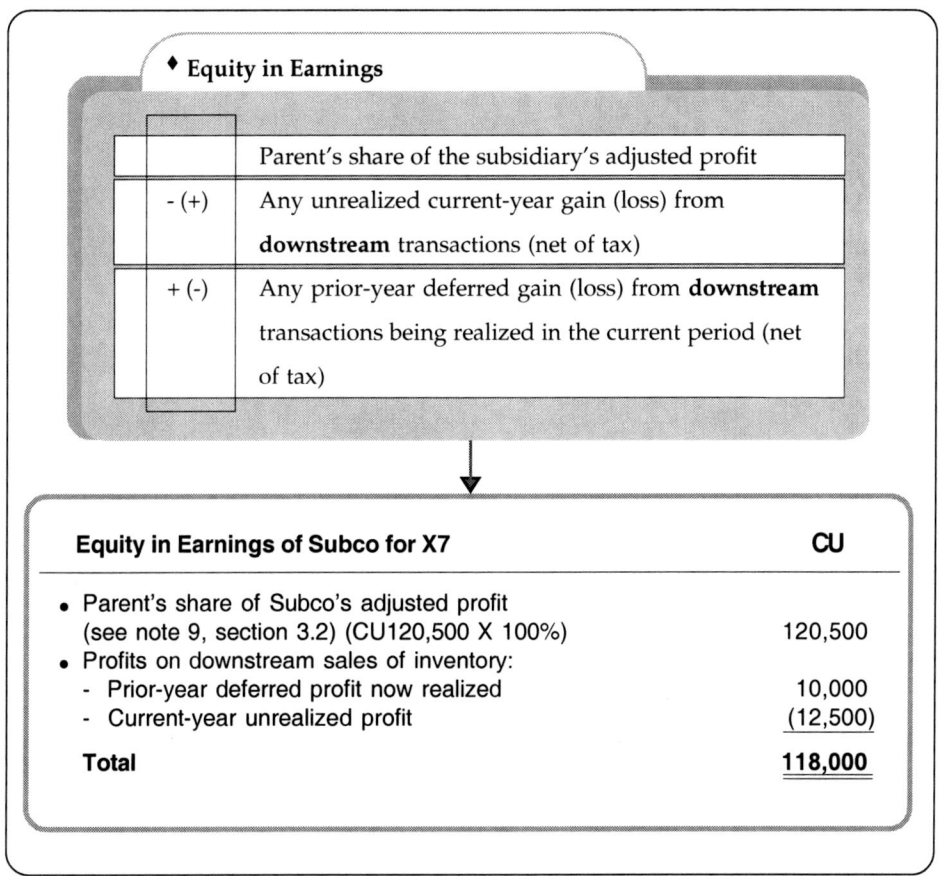

Additional Consolidation Entry #1

Equity in Earnings of Subco (Parent)	118,000	
Investment in Subco (Parent)		118,000

To eliminate equity in earnings of Subco.

Exhibit 8 • The Equity Method - Computation of the Balance of the Investment in Subco

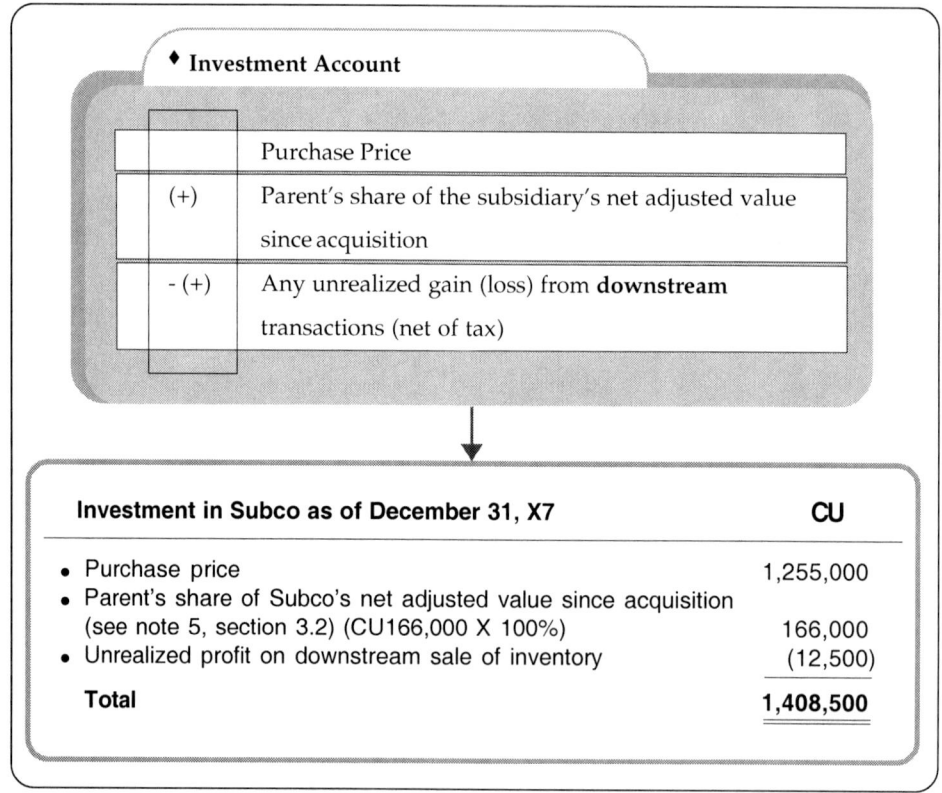

After this entry is entered into the consolidation worksheet, the remaining balance of the investment in Subco amounts to CU35,500 as shown below.

	CU
Balance of the investment in Subco as of December 31, X7, under the equity method (see Exhibit 8)	1,408,500
• Purchase price (already eliminated via entries #1a and #1b)	(1,255,000)
• Equity in earnings of X7 (additional consolidation entry #1)	(118,000)
Remaining balance of the investment in Subco	35,500

The remaining balance of CU35,500 reflects the increase of the investment account from the date of acquisition to the beginning of the current year (that is, for X6) and must be eliminated with the following final consolidation entry.

Additional Consolidation Entry #2

Retained Earnings (Parent)	35,500	
Investment in Subco (Parent)		35,500

To eliminate the remaining balance of the investment account.

Case 6

Big Inc

What this Case is About

- ☑ Consolidation of a Wholly Owned Subsidiary
- ☑ In a Period Subsequent to Acquisition
- ☑ With Intercompany Transactions Involving Equipment, Inventory and Dividends
- ☑ Illustration Under the Cost and Equity Methods

Contents

1	Basic Information	312
2	Preliminary Analysis	314
	2.1 Controlling Ownership	316
	2.2 Intercompany Transactions	317
3	Consolidation of Financial Statements	318
	3.1 Worksheet Approach	318
	3.2 Direct Approach	322
4	Investment Account on Equity Basis	326

Big Inc

1 Basic Information

On January 1, X5, Big Inc purchased a 100 percent interest in Small for cash of CU59,384,000. A statement of financial position including market value information at the date of acquisition is presented in Exhibit 1.

Exhibit 1 • Statement of Financial Position of Small as of January 1, X5

	Carrying Values (CU)	Fair Values (CU)
Assets		
Cash	8,285,000	8,285,000
Accounts receivable	5,450,000	5,450,000
Inventory	9,260,000	11,600,000
Land	6,275,000	6,350,000
Buildings (net)	16,900,000	19,300,000
Equipment (net)	8,125,000	10,375,000
Patents	-	3,264,000
Total assets	**54,295,000**	
Liabilities and equities		
Current liabilities	11,000,000	11,000,000
Share capital	36,850,000	
Retained earnings	6,445,000	
Total liabilities and equities	**54,295,000**	

You are asked to prepare the consolidated financial statements of Big Inc for the year ended December 31, X7, that is, three years from the date of acquisition. Separate financial statements of the affiliated companies for that period are shown in Exhibit 2.

Exhibit 2 • Financial Statements of Big and Small for the Year Ended December 31, X7

Statements of Financial Position
December 31, X7
(in CU)

	Big	Small
Assets		
Cash	22,750,000	5,700,000
Accounts receivable	73,500,000	7,100,000
Inventory	151,600,000	6,600,000
Land	46,300,000	6,350,000
Buildings (net)	123,600,000	25,500,000
Equipment (net)	42,900,000	15,350,000
Patents	10,400,000	
Investment in Small	59,384,000	
Total assets	**530,434,000**	**66,600,000**
Liabilities and equities		
Current liabilities	140,500,000	13,200,000
Bonds payable	200,000,000	
Share capital	11,500,000	36,850,000
Retained earnings	178,434,000	16,550,000
Total liabilities and equities	**530,434,000**	**66,600,000**

Statements of Income
Year Ended December 31, X7
(in CU)

	Big	Small
Revenues	280,000,000	38,000,000
Cost of goods sold	161,950,000	26,700,000
Other expenses	86,550,000	8,300,000
Profit for the year	**31,500,000**	**3,000,000**

Statements of Changes in Equity
Year Ended December 31, X7
(in CU)

	Big			Small		
	Share Capital	Retained Earnings	Total	Share Capital	Retained Earnings	Total
Balance at January 1, X7	11,500,000	155,184,000	166,684,000	36,850,000	14,150,000	51,000,000
Dividends		(8,250,000)	(8,250,000)		(600,000)	(600,000)
Profit for the year		31,500,000	31,500,000		3,000,000	3,000,000
Balance at December 31, X7	11,500,000	178,434,000	189,934,000	36,850,000	16,550,000	53,400,000

Additional Information

1) On January 1, X5, Small had buildings with a remaining useful life of 10 years and equipments with a remaining useful life of five years.
2) All the inventory retained by Small at January 1, X5, had been sold to external parties in X5.
3) All Small's patents have been sold to an external party in X6.
4) No capital asset has been disposed of by Small since acquisition.
5) Goodwill has not been impaired since acquisition.
6) During X5, Small purchased equipment from Big for CU1,500,000. The equipment had a book value of CU900,000 on Big's records. The remaining useful life of the equipment at the date of transfer is five years. Small is using the equipment to generate revenue.
7) During X7, Big sold merchandise to Small for CU5,500,000 all of which was sold by Small to external parties for CU7,000,000 prior to the end of the current accounting period.
8) Big sells its merchandise at a markup of 25 percent over sales.
9) Both affiliated companies use the straight-line method to calculate all depreciation and amortization. Full year of depreciation is also used by the affiliated companies for the year of any capital asset acquisitions.

2 Preliminary Analysis

Figure 1 lists the consolidation scenarios that apply to Big.

Case 6 Big Inc   315

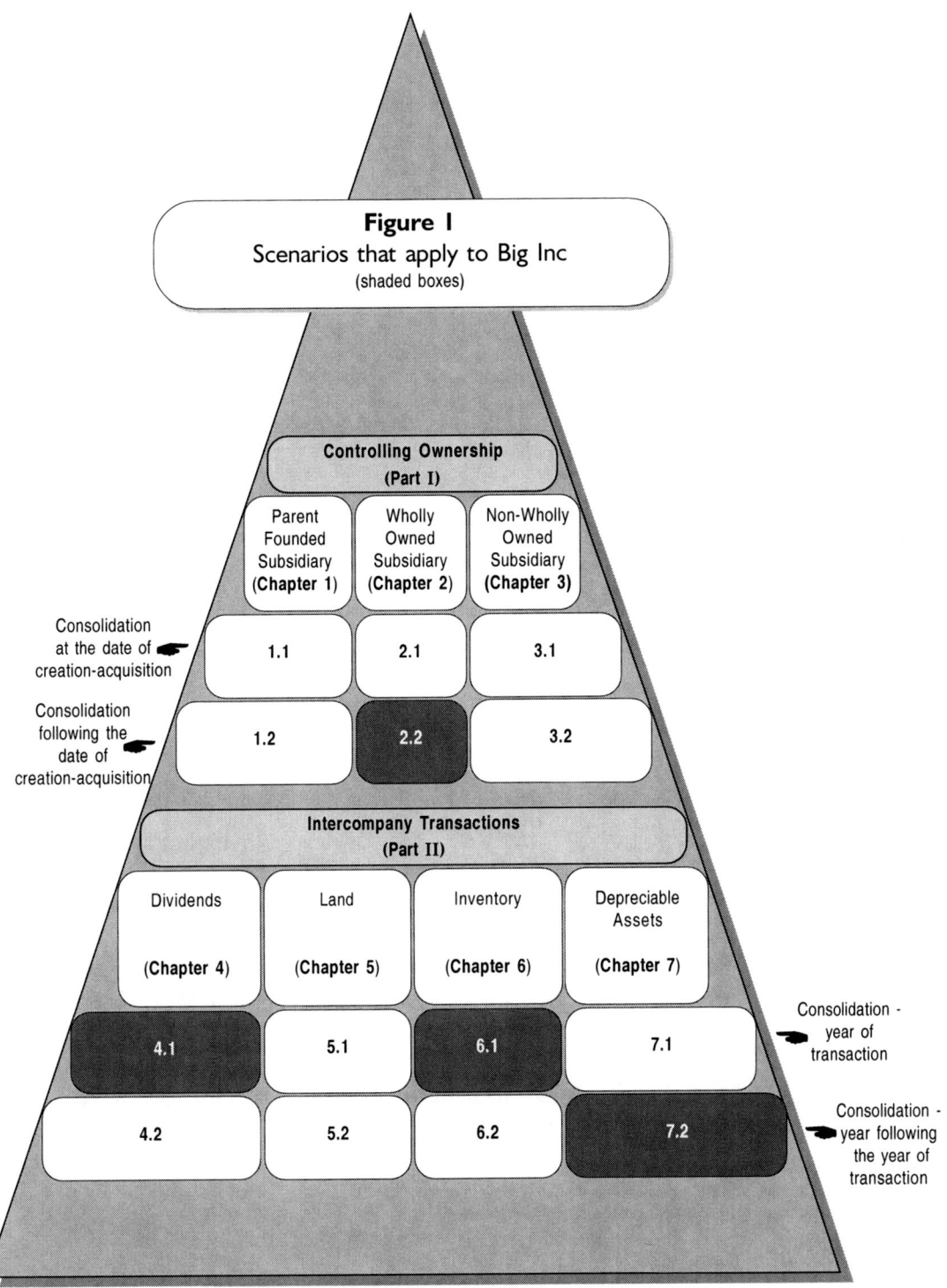

2.1 Controlling Ownership

The allocation of the purchase price is shown in the following Exhibit.

Exhibit 3 • Acquisition of 100 percent of the Outstanding Voting Stock of Small by Big on January 1, X5 - Allocation of the Purchase Price

		CU
Cost of investment in Small		59,384,000
Shareholders' equity of Small at the date of acquisition:		
- Share capital	36,850,000	
- Retained earnings	6,445,000	43,295,000
Price differential		16,089,000
Fair value increments :		
- Inventory		(2,340,000)
- Land		(75,000)
- Buildings		(2,400,000)
- Equipment		(2,250,000)
- Patents		(3,264,000)
Goodwill		5,760,000

Price differential of CU16,089,000 is used in the consolidation process to revalue Small so as to consider its full market value at the date of acquisition. Price differential must also be adjusted over time to account for fair value increment amortization and/or realization as well as goodwill imprairment, if any. A price differential amortization schedule is presented in Exhibit 4.

Note that the investment of Big in Small remains at the original cost in Big's separate-entity statement of financial position as of December 31, X7.

Exhibit 4 • Consolidation of the Financial Statements of Big - Price Differential Amortization Schedule

Items	Price Differential Balance at Acquisition (CU)	Amortization Current Year (X7) (CU)	Amortization Prior Years (X5-X6) (CU)	Unamortized Excess at 31-12-X7 (CU)
Fair Value Increments				
• Inventory	2,340,000	-	2,340,000	-
• Land	75,000	-	-	75,000
• Buildings	2,400,000	240,000	480,000	1,680,000
• Equipment	2,250,000	450,000	900,000	900,000
• Patents	3,264,000	-	3,264,000	-
Goodwill	5,760,000	-	-	5,760,000
Total	**16,089,000**	**(690,000)**	**(6,984,000)**	**8,415,000**

2.2 Intercompany Transactions

Transactions conducted between the affiliated companies are analyzed below.

Intercompany Dividends

During X7, Small declared dividends for CU600,000. Since there is no indication of reciprocal receivable and payable balances at the end of the year, one can assume that dividends declared by Small were fully paid in the current accounting period. Furthermore, since the investment of Big in Small is accounted for using the cost method, dividends received by Big (CU600,000) must have been recorded as revenue in the income statement. To avoid double-counting of Small's earnings, intercompany dividends must be eliminated.

Downstream Sale of Equipment (Additional Information #6 and #9)

During X5, equipment has been transferred from Big to Small. A gain of CU600,000 has been recognized by the selling affiliate which consists of the difference between the selling price (CU1,500,000) and the net book value of the equipment at the time of the sale (CU900,000). This gain, which must be considered as unrealized for consolidation purposes, will be consumed over the remaining useful life of the equipment at a rate of CU120,000 a year (initial gain of CU600,000/5 years). At the beginning of the current accounting period, the unrealized portion of the gain amounts to CU360,000 (CU600,000 X 3/5).

Downstream Sales of Inventory (Additional Information #7)

During X7, Big sold merchandise to Small for CU5,500,000. Since all the transferred inventory units have been sold to external parties by Small during the current year, the only issue concerns the overstatement of Sales and Cost of Goods Sold of CU5,500,000.

3 Consolidation of Financial Statements

The following illustrates the consolidation of the financial statements of Big Inc as of December 31, X7, under, first, the worksheet approach, and second, the direct approach.

3.1 Worksheet Approach

Entries that will be entered into the consolidation worksheet of Big are listed below.

Adjustments Related To Controlling Ownership

1- Elimination of the Investment Account in the Subsidiary (see purchase price allocation in Exhibit 3)

(1a) To eliminate reciprocal investment and equity accounts at the date of acquisition so as to avoid double-counting.

Common Shares (Small)	36,850,000	
Retained Earnings (Small)	6,445,000	
Investment in Small (Big)		43,295,000

(1b) To allocate the price differential so as to consider the fair value of Small at the date of acquisition.

Inventory (Small)	2,340,000	
Land (Small)	75,000	
Buildings (Small)	2,400,000	
Equipment (Small)	2,250,000	
Patents (Small)	3,264,000	
Goodwill	5,760,000	
Investment in Small (Big)		16,089,000

2- Price Differential Amortization Since Acquisition (see amortization schedule in Exhibit 4)

(2a) To recognize the prior-year realization of the fair value increment on inventory.

Retained Earnings (Small)	2,340,000	
Inventory (Small)		2,340,000

(2b) To amortize the fair value increment on buildings.

Retained Earnings (Small)	480,000	
Other Expenses (Small)	240,000	
Buildings (Small)		720,000

(2c) To amortize the fair value increment on equipment.

Retained Earnings (Small)	900,000	
Other Expenses (Small)	450,000	
Equipment (Small)		1,350,000

(2d) To recognize the prior-year realization of the fair value increment on patents.

Retained Earnings (Small)	3,264,000	
Patents (Small)		3,264,000

Adjustments Related to Intercompany Transactions

(3) Intercompany Dividends

Revenues (Dividends) (Big)	600,000	
Dividends Declared (Small)		600,000

To eliminate current-year intercompany dividends.

(4) Downstream Sale of Equipment

(4a) To eliminate the unrealized portion of the intercompany gain on sale of equipment at the beginning of X7.

Retained Earnings (Big & Small)	360,000	
Equipment (Small)		360,000

(4b) To recognize in the current year a portion of the intercompany gain on sale of equipment.

Equipment (Small)	120,000	
Other Expenses (Small)		120,000

(5) Downstream Sale of Inventory During X7

Revenues (Sales) (Big)	5,500,000	
Cost of Goods Sold (Small)		5,500,000

To eliminate reciprocal Sales and Cost of Goods Sold balances.

The following presents the consolidation worksheet of Big Inc for the period ended December 31, X7.

Consolidation Worksheet

	Big (CU)	Small (CU)	Eliminations Adjustments (CU)	Big Consolidated (CU)
ASSETS				
Cash	22,750,000	5,700,000		28,450,000
Accounts receivable	73,500,000	7,100,000		80,600,000
Inventory	151,600,000	6,600,000	2,340,000 (1b)	158,200,000
			(2,340,000) (2a)	
Land	46,300,000	6,350,000	75,000 (1b)	52,725,000
Buildings (net)	123,600,000	25,500,000	2,400,000 (1b)	150,780,000
			(720,000) (2b)	
Equipment (net)	42,900,000	15,350,000	2,250,000 (1b)	58,910,000
			(1,350,000) (2c)	
			(360,000) (4a)	
			120,000 (4b)	
Investment in Small	59,384,000		(43,295,000) (1a)	—
			(16,089,000) (1b)	
Patents	10,400,000		3,264,000 (1b)	10,400,000
			(3,264,000) (2d)	
Goodwill			5,760,000 (1b)	5,760,000
	530,434,000	66,600,000		545,825,000
LIABILITIES				
Current liabilities	140,500,000	13,200,000		153,700,000
Bonds payable	200,000,000			200,000,000
EQUITY				
Common shares	11,500,000	36,850,000	(36,850,000) (1a)	11,500,000
Retained earnings	178,434,000	16,550,000	(14,359,000)	180,625,000
	530,434,000	66,600,000		545,825,000

Net impact of the adjustments on the ending balance of RE

Consolidation Worksheet (continued)

	Big (CU)	Small (CU)	Eliminations Adjustments (CU)	Big Consolidated (CU)
Revenues	280,000,000	38,000,000	(600,000) (3) (5,500,000) (5)	311,900,000
Cost of goods sold	161,950,000	26,700,000	(5,500,000) (5)	183,150,000
Other expenses	86,550,000	8,300,000	240,000 (2b) 450,000 (2c) (120,000) (4b)	95,420,000
Profit	**31,500,000**	**3,000,000**	**(1,170,000)**	**33,330,000**
Retained earnings	155,184,000	14,150,000	(6,445,000) (1a) (2,340,000) (2a) (480,000) (2b) (900,000) (2c) (3,264,000) (2d) (360,000) (4a)	155,545,000
Dividends	8,250,000	600,000	(600,000) (3)	8,250,000
Retained earnings (end)	**178,434,000**	**16,550,000**	**(14,359,000)**	**180,625,000**

Net impact of the adjustments on the ending balance of RE

3.2 Direct Approach

Consolidated financial statements of Big Inc for the year ended December 31, X7, are reported in Exhibit 5. Amounts shown in brackets come from the financial statements of Big and Small. A note is added when the calculation of the consolidated figure requires consolidation adjustments.

Exhibit 5 • Consolidated Financial Statements of Big Inc for the Year Ended December 31, X7

Consolidated Statement of Financial Position of Big Inc
December 31, X7
(in CU)

Assets
Cash (CU22,750,000 + CU5,700,000)	28,450,000
Accounts receivable (CU73,500,000 + CU7,100,000)	80,600,000
Inventory (CU151,600 + CU6,600,000)	158,200,000
Land **(1)**	52,725,000
Buildings (net) **(2)**	150,780,000
Equipment (net) **(3)**	58,910,00
Patents (Big)	10,400,000
Goodwill **(4)**	5,760,000
Total assets	**545,825,000**

Liabilities and equities
Current liabilities (CU140,500,000 + CU13,200,000)	153,700,000
Bonds payable (Big)	200,000,000
Share capital (Big)	11,500,000
Retained earnings **(5)**	180,625,000
Total liabilities and equities	**545,825,000**

Consolidated Income Statement of Big Inc
Year Ended December 31, X7
(in CU)

Revenues **(6)**	311,900,000
Cost of goods sold **(7)**	183,150,000
Other expenses **(8)**	95,420,000
Profit for the year (9)	**33,330,000**

Consolidated Statement of Changes in Equity of Big Inc
Year Ended December 31, X7
(in CU)

	Share Capital	Retained Earnings	Total
Balance at January 1, X7	11,500,000	155,545,000	167,045,000
Dividends		(8,250,000)	(8,250,000)
Profit for the year		33,330,000	33,330,000
Balance at December 31, X7	**11,500,000**	**180,625,000**	**192,125,000**

---

(1) Land — CU

- Parent (Big) — 46,300,000
- Subsidiary (Small) — 6,350,000
- Fair value increment — 75,000

Total — 52,725,000

---

(2) Buildings (net) — CU

- Parent (Big) — 123,600,000
- Subsidiary (Small) — 25,500,000
- Unamortized balance of the fair value increment (CU2,400,000 X 7/10) — 1,680,000

Total — 150,780,000

---

(3) Equipment (net) — CU

- Parent (Big) — 42,900,000
- Subsidiary (Small) — 15,350,000
- Unamortized balance of the fair value increment (CU2,250,000 X 2/5) — 900,000
- Unamortized portion of intercompany gain (CU600,000 X 2/5) — (240,000)

Total — 58,910,000

(4) **Goodwill**	CU
Goodwill at the date of acquisition	**5,760,000**

(5) **Retained Earnings**		CU
• Parent (Big)		178,434,000
• 100 percent of the subsidiary (Small)'s net adjusted value since acquisition		
- Retained earnings increase since acquisition (CU16,550,000 - CU6,445,000)	10,105,000	
- Price differential amortization since acquisition (see amortization schedule in Exhibit 4) (CU16,089,000 - CU8,415,000)	(7,674,000)	
	2,431,000	
100% →		2,431,000
• Unrealized portion of intercompany gain on sale of equipment (CU600,000 X 2/5)		(240,000)
Total		**180,625,000**

(6) **Revenues** (including dividends)	CU
• Parent (Big)	280,000,000
• Subsidiary (Small)	38,000,000
• Intercompany sales	(5,500,000)
• Intercompany dividends	(600,000)
Total	**311,900,000**

(7) **Cost of Goods Sold**	CU
• Parent (Big)	161,950,000
• Subsidiary (Small)	26,700,000
• Intercompany sales	(5,500,000)
Total	**183,150,000**

(8) Other Expenses (including depreciation expense)	CU
• Parent (Big)	86,550,000
• Subsidiary (Small)	8,300,000
• Current-year price differential amortization (see amortization schedule in Exhibit 4). Includes fair value increments on:	
- Buildings (CU2,400,000/10)	240,000
- Equipment (CU2,250,000/5)	450,000
• Current-year portion of the intercompany gain on sale of equipment (CU600,000/5)	(120,000)
Total	**95,420,000**

(9) Consolidated Profit for the Year		CU
• Big's adjusted profit:		
- Big's profit	31,500,000	
- Current-year portion of the intercompany gain on sale of equipment (CU600,000/5)	120,000	
- Intercompany dividends	(600,000)	31,020,000
• Small's adjusted profit:		
- Small's profit	3,000,000	
- Current-year price differential amortization (see amortization schedule in Exhibit 4). Includes fair value increments on:		
- Buildings (CU2,400,000/10)	(240,000)	
- Equipment (CU2,250,000/5)	(450,000)	2,310,000
Total		**33,330,000**

4 Investment Account on Equity Basis

Assume that the equity method is employed by Big to account for its investment in Small instead of the cost method. The individual financial statements of Big as of December 31, X7, are shown in Exhibit 6. Consolidated information is also reported on a comparative basis.

Note that consolidated Share Capital, Retained Earnings and profit for the year equal Big's Share Capital, Retained Earnings and Profit for the Year under the equity method.

Exhibit 6 • Financial Statements of Big Inc for the Year Ended December 31, X7 - The Investment in Small is Accounted for Using the Equity Method.

Statements of Financial Position of Big Inc
December 31, X7
(in CU)

	Equity Method	Consolidated
Assets		
Cash	22,750,000	28,450,000
Accounts receivable	73,500,000	80,600,000
Inventory	151,600,000	158,200,000
Land	46,300,000	52,725,000
Buildings (net)	123,600,000	150,780,00
Equipment (net)	42,900,000	58,910,000
Patents	10,400,000	10,400,000
Investment in Small	61,575,000	
Goodwill		5,760,000
Total assets	532,625,000	545,825,000
Liabilities and equities		
Current liabilities	140,500,000	153,700,000
Bonds payable	200,000,000	200,000,000
Share capital	11,500,000	
Retained earnings	180,625,000	180,625,000
Total liabilities and equities	532,625,000	545,825,000

Income Statements of Big Inc
Year Ended December 31, X7
(in CU)

	Equity Method	Consolidated
Revenues	279,400,000	311,900,000
Equity in earnings of Small	2,430,000	
Cost of goods sold	161,950,000	183,150,000
Other expenses	86,550,000	95,420,000
Profit for the year	33,330,000	33,330,000

Statements of Changes in Equity of Big Inc
Year Ended December 31, X7
(in CU)

	Equity Method			Consolidated		
	Share Capital	Retained Earnings	Total	Share Capital	Retained Earnings	Total
Balance at January 1, X7	11,500,000	155,545,000	167,045,000	11,500,000	155,545,000	167,045,000
Dividends		(8,250,000)	(8,250,000)		(8,250,000)	(8,250,000)
Profit for the year		33,330,000	33,330,000		33,330,000	33,330,000
Balance at December 31, X7	11,500,000	180,625,000	192,125,000	11,500,000	180,625,000	192,125,000

The approach to computing equity in earnings and investment accounts is shown in Exhibits 7 and 8, respectively.

Exhibit 7 • The Equity Method - Computation of Equity in Earnings of Small

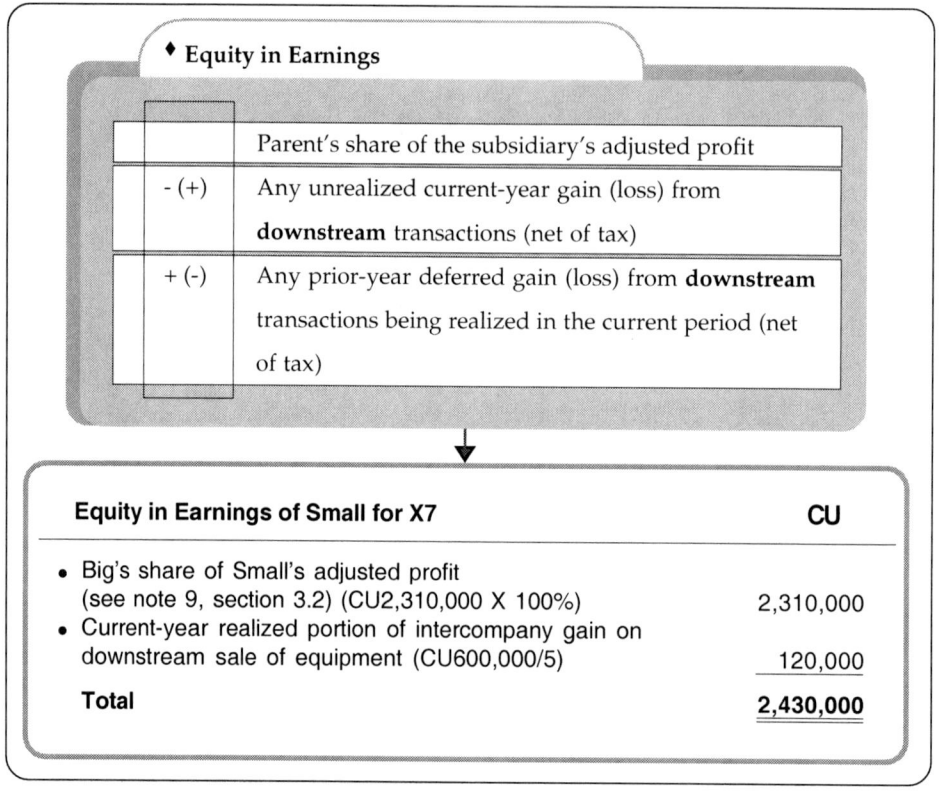

		Parent's share of the subsidiary's adjusted profit
	- (+)	Any unrealized current-year gain (loss) from **downstream** transactions (net of tax)
	+ (-)	Any prior-year deferred gain (loss) from **downstream** transactions being realized in the current period (net of tax)

Equity in Earnings of Small for X7	CU
• Big's share of Small's adjusted profit (see note 9, section 3.2) (CU2,310,000 X 100%)	2,310,000
• Current-year realized portion of intercompany gain on downstream sale of equipment (CU600,000/5)	120,000
Total	**2,430,000**

Exhibit 8 • The Equity Method - Computation of the Balance of the Investment in Small

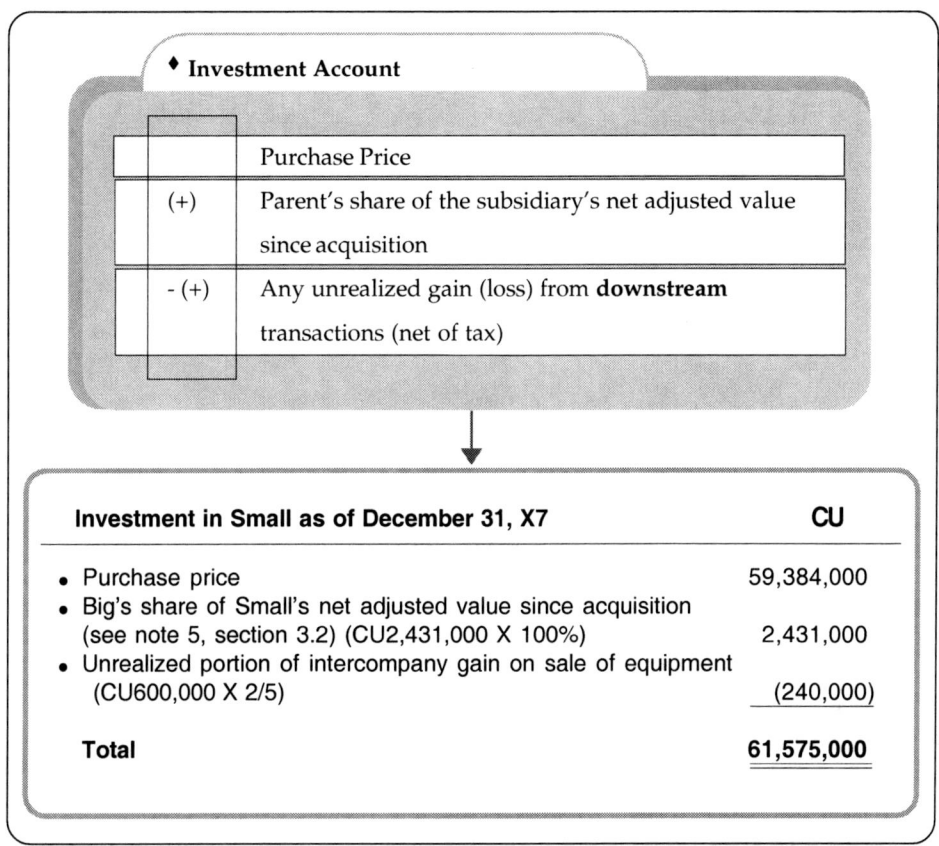

The following presents the journal entries that Big must have recorded in X7 to account for its investment in Small using the equity method.

1- Equity in Earnings of Small

Investment in Small	2,430,000	
Equity in Earnings of Small		2,430,000

2- Dividends Declared by Small

Cash	600,000	
Investment in Small		600,000

Had Big been using the equity method to account for its investment in Small instead of the cost method, these two journal entries should have been eliminated via the following additional consolidation entries.

Additional Consolidation Entry #1

Equity in Earnings of Small (Big)	2,430,000	
Investment in Small (Big)		2,430,000

To eliminate equity in earnings of Small.

Additional Consolidation Entry #2 (replacing entry #3)

Investment in Small (Big)	600,000	
Dividends Declared (Small)		600,000

To eliminate intercompany dividends.

After these two entries are entered into the consolidation worksheet, the remaining balance of the investment in Small amounts to CU361,000 as shown below.

	CU
Balance of the investment in Small as of December 31, X7, under the equity method (see Exhibit 8)	61,575,000
• Purchase price (already eliminated via entries #1a and #1b)	(59,384,000)
• Equity in earnings of X7 (additional consolidation entry #1)	(2,430,000)
• Dividends declared in X7 (additional consolidation entry #2)	600,000
Remaining balance of the investment in Small	361,000

The remaining balance of CU361,000 reflects the increase of the investment account from the date of acquisition to the beginning of the current year and must be eliminated with the following final consolidation entry.

Additional Consolidation Entry #3

Retained Earnings (Big)	361,000	
Investment in Small (Big)		361,000

To eliminate the remaining balance of the investment account.

Case 7

Plus Inc

What this Case is About

- ☑ Consolidation of a Wholly Owned Subsidiary
- ☑ In a Period Subsequent to Acquisition
- ☑ With Intercompany Transactions Involving Land, Inventory and Dividends
- ☑ Illustration Under the Cost and Equity Methods

Contents

1	Basic Information	334
2	Preliminary Analysis	336
	2.1 Controlling Ownership	338
	2.2 Intercompany Transactions	339
3	Consolidation of Financial Statements	339
	3.1 Worksheet Approach	339
	3.2 Direct Approach	343
4	Investment Account on Equity Basis	347

Plus Inc

1 Basic Information

On January 1, X3, Plus Inc purchased 100 percent of Lortis's outstanding common stock for cash of CU9,750,000. Exhibit 1 shows the statement of financial position of Lortis at the date of acquisition along with the appraised value of its identifiable assets and liabilities assumed.

Exhibit 1 • Statement of Financial Position of Lortis as of January 1, X3

	Carrying Values (CU)	Fair Values (CU)
Assets		
Cash	500,000	500,000
Accounts receivable	1,500,000	1,500,000
Inventory	3,000,000	4,000,000
Land	1,500,000	1,000,000
Buildings (net)	6,000,000	8,000,000
Patents	-	500,000
Total assets	**12,500,000**	
Liabilities and equities		
Current liabilities	1,000,000	1,000,000
Long-term liabilities	4,500,000	6,000,000
Share capital	3,000,000	
Retained earnings	4,000,000	
Total liabilities and equities	**12,500,000**	

You are asked to prepare the consolidated financial statements of Plus Inc for the year ended December 31, X7, that is, five years from the date of acquisition. Separate financial statements of the affiliated companies for that period are shown in Exhibit 2.

Exhibit 2 • Financial Statements of Plus and Lortis for the Year Ended December 31, X7

Statements of Financial Position
December 31, X7
(in CU)

	Plus	Lortis
Assets		
Cash	1,050,000	700,000
Accounts receivable	7,500,000	2,100,000
Inventory	14,300,000	5,600,000
Land	9,000,000	2,500,000
Buildings (net)	15,800,000	5,500,000
Patents	1,400,000	
Investment in Lortis	9,750,000	
Total assets	**58,800,000**	**16,400,000**
Liabilities and equities		
Current liabilities	8,500,000	1,200,000
Long-term liabilities	15,000,000	4,500,000
Share capital	20,000,000	3,000,000
Retained earnings	15,300,000	7,700,000
Total liabilities and equities	**58,800,000**	**16,400,000**

Statements of Income
Year Ended December 31, X7
(in CU)

	Plus	Lortis
Revenues	16,500,000	7,000,000
Cost of goods sold	6,400,000	3,400,000
Other expenses	3,800,000	1,600,000
Profit for the year	**6,300,000**	**2,000,000**

Statements of Changes in Equity
Year Ended December 31, X7
(in CU)

	Plus			Lortis		
	Share Capital	Retained Earnings	Total	Share Capital	Retained Earnings	Total
Balance at January 1, X7	20,000,000	11,000,000	31,000,000	3,000,000	6,700,000	9,700,000
Dividends		(2,000,000)	(2,000,000)		(1,000,000)	(1,000,000)
Profit for the year		6,300,000	6,300,000		2,000,000	2,000,000
Balance at December 31, X7	20,000,000	15,300,000	35,300,000	3,000,000	7,700,000	10,700,000

Additional Information

1) On January 1, X3, Lortis had buildings with a remaining useful life of 20 years.
2) All the inventory retained by Lortis at January 1, X3, had been sold to external parties in X3.
3) On January 1, X3, Lortis had software that had not yet been patented. However, a market study conducted during X4 revealed that the sofware had no value.
4) No capital asset has been disposed of by Lortis since acquisition.
5) Goodwill has not been impaired since acquisition.
6) Maturity date of all long-term liabilities is ten years from the date of acquisition.
7) During X7, Lortis purchased land from Plus for CU1,000,000. The original cost of the land for the selling affiliate was CU500,000.
8) During X7, Lortis sold merchandise to Plus for CU2,000,000. On December 31, X7, CU500,000 of this merchandise remained in Plus's inventory.
9) During X6, Lortis sold merchandise to Plus. At the end of the year, CU800,000 of this merchandise remained in Plus's inventory.
10) Lortis sells its merchandise at a markup of 30 percent over sales.
11) Both affiliated companies use the straight-line method to calculate all depreciation and amortization.

2 Preliminary Analysis

Figure 1 lists the consolidation scenarios that apply to Plus. Basic information is taken from the case illustrated in Chapter 9 with data updated to consider full control of Plus over Lortis (scenario 2.2) instead of partial control (scenario 3.2).

Case 7 Plus Inc 337

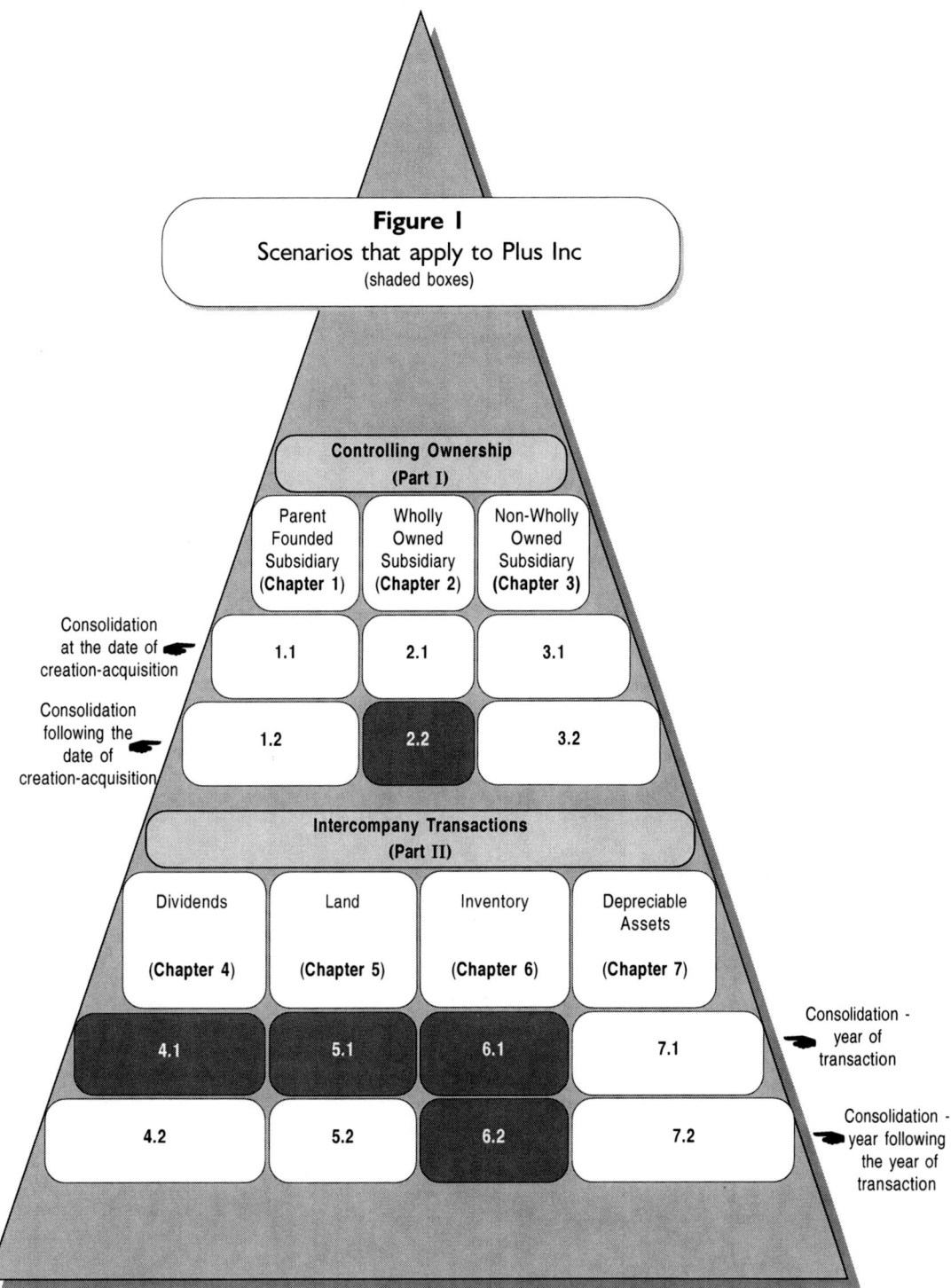

2.1 Controlling Ownership

The allocation of the purchase price is shown in Exhibit 3.

Exhibit 3 • Acquisition of 100 percent of the Outstanding Voting Stock of Lortis by Plus on January 1, X3 - Allocation of the Purchase Price

		CU
Cost of investment in Lortis		9,750,000
Shareholders' equity of Lortis at the date of acquisition:		
- Share capital	3,000,000	
- Retained earnings	4,000,000	7,000,000
Price differential		2,750,000
Fair value increments (+) and decrements (-):		
- Inventory (+)		(1,000,000)
- Land (-)		500,000
- Buildings (+)		(2,000,000)
- Software (+)		(500,000)
- Long-term liabilities (+)		1,500,000
Goodwill		1,250,000

For consolidation purposes, the price differential of CU2,750,000 at the date of acquisition will be used to change Lortis's value from carrying value to full market value. In post-acquisition consolidations, price differential must be adjusted so as to account for any fair value increment-decrement amortization and/or realization. In the case of Plus Inc, this information is summarized in the following Exhibit.

Exhibit 4 • Consolidation of the Financial Statements of Plus - Price Differential Amortization Schedule

Items	Price Differential Balance at Acquisition (CU)	Amortization Current Year (X7) (CU)	Amortization Prior Years (X3-X6) (CU)	Unamortized Excess at 31-12-X7 (CU)
Fair Value Increments and Decrements				
• Inventory	1,000,000	-	1,000,000	-
• Land	(500,000)	-	-	(500,000)
• Buildings	2,000,000	100,000	400,000	1,500,000
• Software	500,000	-	500,000	-
• LT Liabilities	(1,500,000)	(150,000)	(600,000)	(750,000)
Goodwill	1,250,000	-	-	1,250,000
Total	2,750,000	(50,000)	1,300,000	1,500,000

Note that the value of the investment of Plus in Lortis remains at the original cost (CU9,750,000). Therefore, in non-consolidated statements, the subsidiary is reported on the cost basis.

2.2 Intercompany Transactions

Transactions conducted between the affiliated companies are taken from the case in Chapter 9. Except for dividends, consolidation entries relating to intercompany transactions are the same regardless of whether Plus has full or partial control over Lortis. Under full control, Plus received the full amount of dividends declared by Lortis during the year (CU1,000,000 instead of CU800,000). Consistent with the use of the cost method, dividends have been recorded by Plus in its revenues. Intercompany dividends must be eliminated in order to avoid double-counting of Lortis's earnings.

3 Consolidation of Financial Statements

The following illustrates the consolidation of the financial statements of Plus Inc as of December 31, X7, under, first, the worksheet approach, and second, the direct approach.

3.1 Worksheet Approach

Entries that will be entered into the consolidation worksheet of Plus are listed next.

Adjustments Related To Controlling Ownership

1- Elimination of the Investment Account in the Subsidiary (see purchase price allocation in Exhibit 3)

(1a) To eliminate reciprocal investment and equity accounts at the date of acquisition so as to avoid double-counting.

Common Shares (Lortis)	3,000,000	
Retained Earnings (Lortis)	4,000,000	
Investment in Lortis (Plus)		7,000,000

(1b) To allocate the price differential so as to consider the fair value of Lortis at the date of acquisition.

Inventory (Lortis)	1,000,000	
Buildings (Lortis)	2,000,000	
Patents (Lortis)	500,000	
Goodwill	1,250,000	
Land (Lortis)		500,000
Long-Term Liabilities (Lortis)		1,500,000
Investment in Lortis (Plus)		2,750,000

2- Price Differential Amortization Since Acquisition (see amortization schedule in Exhibit 4)

(2a) To recognize the prior-year realization of the fair value increment on inventory.

Retained Earnings (Lortis)	1,000,000	
Inventory (Lortis)		1,000,000

(2b) To amortize the fair value increment on buildings.

Retained Earnings (Lortis)	400,000	
Other Expenses (Lortis)	100,000	
Buildings (Lortis)		500,000

(2c) To recognize the prior-year realization of the fair value increment on software.

Retained Earnings (Lortis)	500,000	
Patents (Lortis)		500,000

(2d) To amortize the fair value increment on long-term liabilities.

Long-Term Liabilities (Lortis)	750,000	
Retained Earnings (Lortis)		600,000
Other Expenses (Lortis)		150,000

Adjustments Related to Intercompany Transactions

(3) Intercompany Dividends

Revenues (Dividends) (Plus)	1,000,000	
Dividends Declared (Lortis)		1,000,000

To eliminate current-year intercompany dividends.

(4) Downstream Sale of Land

Revenues (Gain) (Plus)	500,000	
Land (Lortis)		500,000

To eliminate current-year intercompany gain on sale of land and reduce land to its cost basis.

(5) Upstream Sale of Inventory During X6

Retained Earnings (Lortis)	240,000	
Cost of Goods Sold (Lortis)		240,000

To recognize prior-year deferred profit on sale of inventory.

(6) Upstream Sale of Inventory During X7

Revenues (Sales) (Lortis)	2,000,000
Cost of Goods Sold (Plus and Lortis)	1,850,000
Inventory (Plus)	150,000

To eliminate current-year unrealized profit on sale of inventory, eliminate reciprocal Sales and Cost of Goods Sold balances and reduce inventory to its cost basis.

The following presents the consolidation worksheet of Plus Inc for the period ended December 31, X7.

Consolidation Worksheet

	Plus (CU)	Lortis (CU)	Eliminations Adjustments (CU)	Plus Consolidated (CU)
Revenues	16,500,000	7,000,000	(1,000,000) (3) (500,000) (4) (2,000,000) (6)	20,000,000
Cost of goods sold	6,400,000	3,400,000	(240,000) (5) (1,850,000) (6)	7,710,000
Other expenses	3,800,000	1,600,000	100,000 (2b) (150,000) (2d)	5,350,000
Profit	**6,300,000**	**2,000,000**	**(1,360,000)**	**6,940,000**
Retained earnings	11,000,000	6,700,000	(4,000,000) (1a) (1,000,000) (2a) (400,000) (2b) (500,000) (2c) 600,000 (2d) (240,000) (5)	12,160,000
Dividends	2,000,000	1,000,000	(1,000,000) (3)	2,000,000
Retained earnings (end)	15,300,000	7,700,000	(5,900,000)	17,100,000

Net impact of the adjustments on the ending balance of RE

Consolidation Worksheet (continued)

	Plus (CU)	Lortis (CU)	Eliminations Adjustments (CU)	Plus Consolidated (CU)
ASSETS				
Cash	1,050,000	700,000		1,750,000
Accounts receivable	7,500,000	2,100,000		9,600,000
Inventory	14,300,000	5,600,000	1,000,000 (1b) (1,000,000) (2a) (150,000) (6)	19,750,000
Land	9,000,000	2,500,000	(500,000) (1b) (500,000) (4)	10,500,000
Buildings (net)	15,800,000	5,500,000	2,000,000 (1b) (500,000) (2b)	22,800,000
Investment in Lortis	9,750,000		(7,000,000) (1a) (2,750,000) (1b)	–
Patents	1,400,000		500,000 (1b) (500,000) (2c)	1,400,000
Goodwill			1,250,000 (1b)	1,250,000
	58,800,000	**16,400,000**		**67,050,000**
LIABILITIES				
Current liabilities	8,500,000	1,200,000		9,700,000
Long-term liabilities	15,000,000	4,500,000	1,500,000 (1b) (750,000) (2d)	20,250,000
EQUITY				
Common shares	20,000,000	3,000,000	(3,000,000) (1a)	20,000,000
Retained earnings	15,300,000	7,700,000	(5,900,000)	17,100,000
	58,800,000	**16,400,000**		**67,050,000**

Net impact of the adjustments on the ending balance of RE

3.2 Direct Approach

Consolidated financial statements of Plus Inc for the year ended December 31, X7, are shown in Exhibit 6. Figures in brackets come from the books of the affiliated companies. More complex calculations are shown in a separate note.

Exhibit 6 • Consolidated Financial Statements of Plus Inc - Year Ended X7

Consolidated Statement of Financial Position of Plus Inc
December 31, X7
(in CU)

Assets
Cash (CU1,050,000 + CU700,000)	1,750,000
Accounts receivable (CU7,500,000 + CU2,100,000)	9,600,000
Inventory **(1)**	19,750,000
Land **(2)**	10,500,000
Buildings (net) **(3)**	22,800,000
Patents (Plus)	1,400,000
Goodwill **(4)**	1,250,000
Total assets	**67,050,000**

Liabilities and equities
Current liabilities (CU8,500,000 + CU1,200,000)	9,700,000
Long-term liabilities **(5)**	20,250,000
Share capital (Plus)	20,000,000
Retained earnings **(6)**	17,100,000
Total liabilities and equities	**67,050,000**

Consolidated Income Statement of Plus Inc
Year Ended December 31, X7
(in CU)

Revenues **(7)**	20,000,000
Cost of goods sold **(8)**	7,710,000
Other expenses **(9)**	5,350,000
Profit for the year (10)	**6,940,000**

Consolidated Statement of Changes in Equity of Plus Inc
Year Ended December 31, X7
(in CU)

	Share Capital	Retained Earnings	Total
Balance at January 1, X7	20,000,000	12,160,000	32,160,000
Dividends		(2,000,000)	(2,000,000)
Profit for the year		6,940,000	6,940,000
Balance at December 31, X7	**20,000,000**	**17,100,000**	**37,100,000**

(1) **Inventory**	CU
• Parent (Plus)	14,300,000
• Subsidiary (Lortis)	5,600,000
• Unrealized profit on upstream sale	(150,000)
Total	**19,750,000**

(2) **Land**	CU
• Parent (Plus)	9,000,000
• Subsidiary (Lortis)	2,500,000
• Fair value decrement	(500,000)
• Unrealized gain on downstream sale	(500,000)
Total	**10,500,000**

(3) **Buildings** (net)	CU
• Parent (Plus)	15,800,000
• Subsidiary (Lortis)	5,500,000
• Unamortized balance of the fair value increment (CU2,000,000 X 15/20)	1,500,000
Total	**22,800,000**

(4) **Goodwill**	CU
Goodwill at the date of acquisition	**1,250,000**

(5) **Long-Term Liabilities**	CU
• Parent (Plus)	15,000,000
• Subsidiary (Lortis)	4,500,000
• Unamortized balance of the fair value increment (CU1,500,000 X 5/10)	750,000
Total	**20,250,000**

(6) **Retained Earnings**	CU
• Parent (Plus)	15,300,000
• 100 percent of the subsidiary (Lortis)'s net adjusted value since acquisition	

> - Retained earnings increase since acquisition
>   (CU7,700,000 - CU4,000,000)   3,700,000
> - Price differential amortization since acquisition
>   (see amortization schedule in Exhibit 4):
>   (CU2,750,000 - CU1,500,000)   (1,250,000)
> - Unrealized profit on upstream sale of inventory (150,000)
>   2,300,000

(100%)	2,300,000
• Unrealized gain on downstream sale of land	(500,000)
Total	**17,100,000**

(7) **Revenues** (including dividends and gains on sale)	CU
• Parent (Plus)	16,500,000
• Subsidiary (Lortis)	7,000,000
• Intercompany sales	(2,000,000)
• Intercompany dividends	(1,000,000)
• Unrealized gain on downstream sale of land	(500,000)
Total	**20,000,000**

(8) **Cost of Goods Sold**	CU
• Parent (Plus)	6,400,000
• Subsidiary (Lortis)	3,400,000
• Intercompany sales	(2,000,000)
• Prior-year deferred profit that has been realized in the current period	(240,000)
• Unrealized current-year profit	150,000
Total	**7,710,000**

(9) **Other Expenses** (including depreciation expense)	CU
• Parent (Plus)	3,800,000
• Subsidiary (Lortis)	1,600,000
• Current-year price differential amortizations (see amortization schedule in Exhibit 4). Includes fair value increments on:	
- Long-term liabilities (CU1,500,000/10)	(150,000)
- Buildings (CU2,000,000/20)	100,000
Total	**5,350,000**

(10) **Consolidated Profit for the Year**		CU
• Plus's adjusted profit:		
- Plus's profit	6,300,000	
- Current-year gain on downstream sale of land	(500,000)	
- Intercompany dividends	(1,000,000)	4,800,000
• Lortis's adjusted profit:		
- Lortis's profit	2,000,000	
- Current-year price differential amortization (see amortization schedule in Exhibit 4). Fair value increments on:		
- Long-term liabilities (CU1,500,000/10)	150,000	
- Buildings (CU2,000,000/20)	(100,000)	
- Profits on upstream sales of inventory:		
- Prior-year deferred profit now being realized	240,000	
- Current-year unrealized profit	(150,000)	2,140,000
Total		**6,940,000**

4 Investment Account on Equity Basis

Assume that the equity method is employed by Plus to account for its investment in Lortis instead of the cost method. The individual financial statements of Plus as of December 31, X7, are shown in Exhibit 7. Consolidated information is also reported on a comparative basis.

Exhibit 7 • Financial Statements of Plus Inc for the Year Ended December 31, X7 - The Investment in Lortis is Accounted for Using the Equity Method

Statements of Financial Position of Plus Inc
December 31, X7
(in CU)

	Equity Method	Consolidated
Assets		
Cash	1,050,000	1,750,000
Accounts receivable	7,500,000	9,600,000
Inventory	14,300,000	19,750,000
Land	9,000,000	10,500,000
Buildings (net)	15,800,000	22,800,000
Patents	1,400,000	1,400,000
Investment in Lortis	11,550,000	
Goodwill		1,250,000
Total assets	60,600,000	67,050,000
Liabilities and equities		
Current liabilities	8,500,000	9,700,000
Long-term liabilities	15,000,000	20,250,000
Share capital	**20,000,000**	**20,000,000**
Retained earnings	**17,100,000**	**17,100,000**
Total liabilities and equities	60,600,000	67,050,000

Income Statements of Plus Inc
Year Ended December 31, X7
(in CU)

	Equity Method	Consolidated
Revenues	15,500,000	20,000,000
Equity in earnings of Lortis	1,640,000	
Cost of goods sold	6,400,000	7,710,000
Other expenses	3,800,000	5,350,000
Profit for the year	6,940,000	6,940,000

Statements of Changes in Equity of Plus Inc
Year Ended December 31, X7
(in CU)

	Equity Method			Consolidated		
	Share Capital	Retained Earnings	Total	Share Capital	Retained Earnings	Total
Balance at January 1, X7	20,000,000	12,160,000	32,160,000	20,000,000	12,160,000	32,160,000
Dividends		(2,000,000)	(2,000,000)		(2,000,000)	(2,000,000)
Profit for the year		6,940,000	6,940,000		6,940,000	6,940,000
Balance at December 31, X7	20,000,000	17,100,000	37,100,000	20,000,000	17,100,000	37,100,000

Recall that the net consolidated value comprised of Share Capital and Retained Earnings equals the net value of Plus under the equity method. Consolidated profit for the year is also the same as Plus's profit for the year under the equity method.

The approach to computing equity in earnings and investment accounts is shown in Exhibits 8 and 9, respectively.

The following presents the journal entries that Plus must have recorded in X7 to account for its investment in Lortis using the equity method.

1- Equity in Earnings of Lortis

Investment in Lortis	1,640,000	
Equity in Earnings of Lortis		1,640,000

2- Dividends Declared by Lortis

Cash	1,000,000	
Investment in Lortis		1,000,000

Had Plus been using the equity method to account for its investment in Lortis instead of the cost method, these two journal entries should have been eliminated via the following additional consolidation entries.

Exhibit 8 • The Equity Method - Computation of Equity in Earnings of Lortis

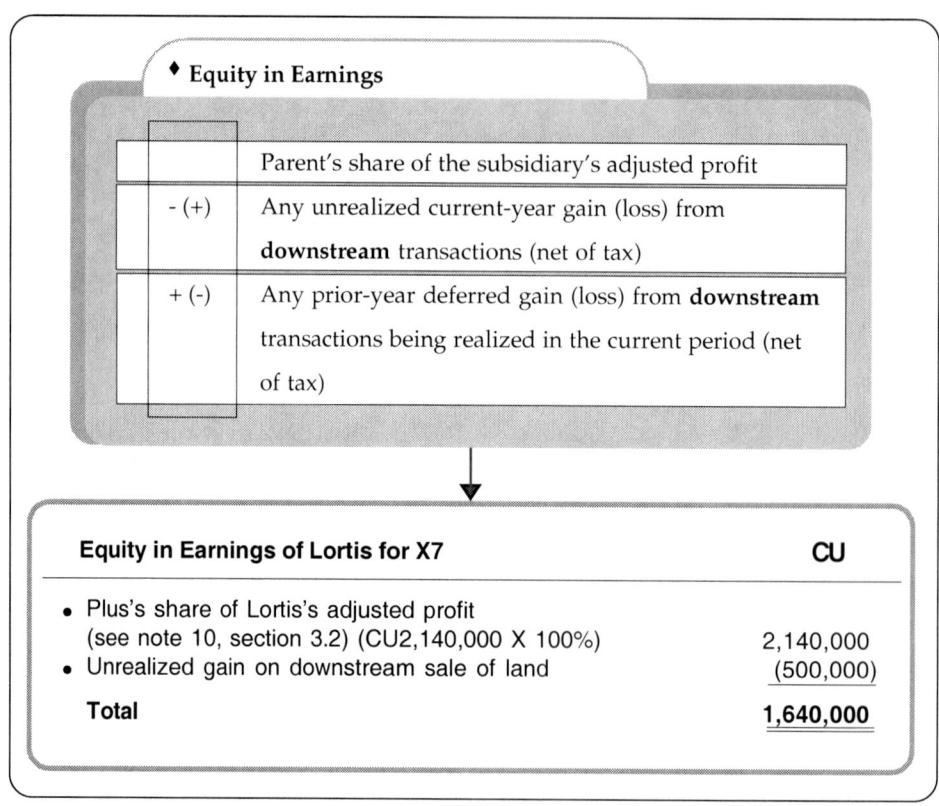

Additional Consolidation Entry #1

Equity in Earnings of Lortis (Plus)	1,640,000	
Investment in Lortis (Plus)		1,640,000

To eliminate equity in earnings of Lortis.

Additional Consolidation Entry #2 (replacing entry #3)

Investment in Lortis (Plus)	1,000,000	
Dividends Declared (Lortis)		1,000,000

To eliminate intercompany dividends.

Exhibit 9 • The Equity Method - Computation of the Balance of the Investment in Lortis

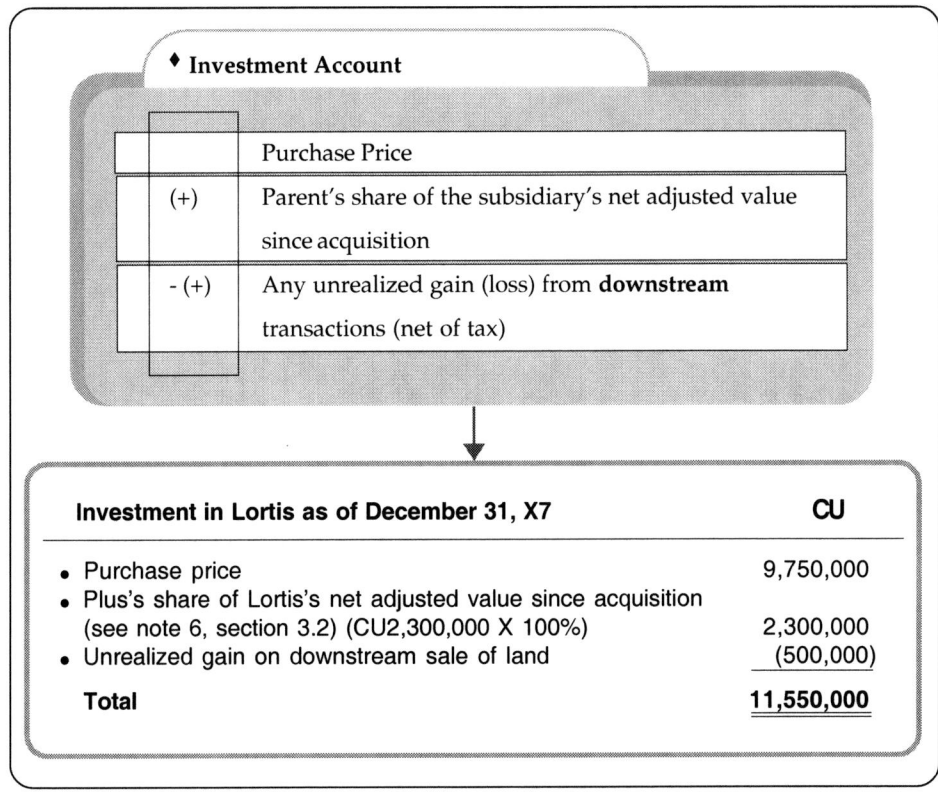

Investment in Lortis as of December 31, X7	CU
• Purchase price	9,750,000
• Plus's share of Lortis's net adjusted value since acquisition (see note 6, section 3.2) (CU2,300,000 X 100%)	2,300,000
• Unrealized gain on downstream sale of land	(500,000)
Total	**11,550,000**

After these two entries are entered into the consolidation worksheet, the remaining balance of the investment in Lortis amounts to CU1,160,000 as shown below.

	CU
Balance of the investment in Lortis as of December 31, X7, under the equity method (see Exhibit 9)	11,550,000
• Purchase price (already eliminated via entries #1a and #1b)	(9,750,000)
• Equity in earnings of X7 (additional consolidation entry #1)	(1,640,000)
• Dividends declared in X7 (additional consolidation entry #2)	1,000,000
Remaining balance of the investment in Lortis	1,160,000

The remaining balance of CU1,160,000 reflects the increase of the investment account from the date of acquisition to the beginning of the current year and must be eliminated with the following final consolidation entry.

Additional Consolidation Entry #3

Retained Earnings (Plus)	1,160,000	
Investment in Lortis (Plus)		1,160,000

To eliminate the remaining balance of the investment account.

Case 8

Large Inc

What this Case is About

- ☑ Consolidation of a Non-Wholly Owned Subsidiary
- ☑ At the Date of Acquisition
- ☑ Measurement Basis for Non-Controlling Interest: Fair Value of NCI

Contents

1 Basic Information 354

2 Preliminary Analysis 355

3 Consolidation of Financial Statements 356
   3.1 Worksheet Approach 356
   3.2 Direct Approach 359

Large Inc

1 Basic Information

On January 2, X7, Large Inc purchased 75 percent of Silk Corporation's outstanding common stock. In exchange for Silk's stock, Large issued bonds payable with a par and fair value of CU500,000 directly to the selling stockholders of Silk. The market price of the shares held by minority shareholders at the date of acquisition is CU200,000. Immediately prior to the combination, the book values and fair values of Silk's assets and liabilities were as portrayed in Exhibit 1.

Exhibit 1 • Statement of Financial Position of Silk as of January 2, X7

	Carrying Values (CU)	Fair Values (CU)
Assets		
Cash	9,000	9,000
Accounts receivable	30,000	30,000
Inventory	68,000	72,000
Land	50,000	70,000
Buildings (net)	450,000	500,000
Patents	-	40,000
Total assets	607,000	
Liabilities and equities		
Current liabilities	29,000	29,000
Bonds payable	100,000	90,000
Share capital	200,000	
Retained earnings	278,000	
Total liabilities and equities	607,000	

You are asked to prepare the consolidated statement of financial position of Large Inc at the date of acquisition. The summarized statement of financial position of Large Inc at the date of acquisition is shown in Exhibit 2.

Exhibit 2 • Statement of Financial Position of Large Inc as of January 2, X7

	CU
Assets	
Cash	12,000
Accounts receivable	39,000
Inventory	86,000
Land	55,000
Buildings (net)	549,000
Investment in Silk	500,000
Total assets	**1,241,000**
Liabilities and equities	
Current liabilities	38,000
Bonds payable	700,000
Share capital	300,000
Retained earnings	203,000
Total liabilities and equities	**1,241,000**

2 Preliminary Analysis

Exhibit 3 presents the allocation of purchase price (CU500,000) as well as the allocation of the non-controlling interest's fair value at date of acquisition (CU200,000).

Exhibit 3 • Acquisition of 75 percent of the Outstanding Voting Stock of Silk by Large on January 2, X7 - Allocation of the Purchase Price and the Fair Value of the Non-Controlling Interest

		(100%) CU	Large (75%) CU	Minority (25%) CU
Cost of investment in Silk			500,000	
Fair value of NCI				200,000
Shareholders' equity of Silk at the date of acquisition:				
- Share capital	200,000			
- Retained earnings	278,000	478,000	358,500	119,500
Price differential			141,500	80,500
Fair value increments (+) and decrements (-):				
- Inventory (+)		(4,000)	(3,000)	(1,000)
- Land (+)		(20,000)	(15,000)	(5,000)
- Buildings (+)		(50,000)	(37,500)	(12,500)
- Patents (+)		(40,000)	(30,000)	(10,000)
- Long-term liabilities (-)		(10,000)	(7,500)	(2,500)
Goodwill			48,500	49,500

3 Consolidation of Financial Statements

The following illustrates the consolidation of the statement of financial position of Large Inc as of the date of acquisition, under, first, the worksheet approach, and second, the direct approach.

3.1 Worksheet Approach

Entries that will be entered into the consolidation worksheet of Large are listed next.

1- Elimination of the Investment Account in the Subsidiary

(1a) To eliminate reciprocal investment and equity accounts at the date of acquisition.

Common Shares (Silk)	150,000	
Retained Earnings (Silk)	208,500	
Investment in Silk (Large)		358,500

(1b) To allocate Large's proportionate share of Silk's full fair value at the date of acquisition.

Inventory (Silk)	3,000	
Buildings (Silk)	37,500	
Land (Silk)	15,000	
Patents (Silk)	30,000	
Goodwill	48,500	
Bonds Payable (Silk)	7,500	
Investment in Silk (Large)		141,500

2- Non-Controlling Interest

Common Shares (Silk)	50,000	
Retained Earnings (Silk)	69,500	
Inventory (Silk)	1,000	
Buildings (Silk)	12,500	
Land (Silk)	5,000	
Patents (Silk)	10,000	
Goodwill	49,500	
Bonds Payable (Silk)	2,500	
Non-Controlling Interest		200,000

To record the fair value of the non-controlling interest at the date of acquisition.

Part IV Cases and Solutions

The following presents the consolidation worksheet of Large Inc as of January 2, X7.

Consolidation Worksheet

	Large (CU)	Silk (CU)	Eliminations Adjustments (CU)	Large Consolidated (CU)
ASSETS				
Cash	12,000	9,000		21,000
Accounts receivable	39,000	30,000		69,000
Inventory	86,000	68,000	3,000 (1b) 1,000 (2)	158,000
Land	55,000	50,000	15,000 (1b) 5,000 (2)	125,000
Buildings (net)	549,000	450,000	37,500 (1b) 12,500 (2)	1,049,000
Investment in Silk	500,000		(358,500) (1a) (141,500) (1b)	–
Patents			30,000 (1b) 10,000 (2)	40,000
Goodwill			48,500 (1b) 49,500 (2)	98,000
	1,241,000	607,000		1,560,000
LIABILITIES				
Current liabilities	38,000	29,000		67,000
Bonds payable	700,000	100,000	(7,500) (1b) (2,500) (2)	790,000
EQUITY				
Common shares	300,000	200,000	(150,000) (1a) (50,000) (2)	300,000
Retained earnings	203,000	278,000	(208,500) (1a) (69,500) (2)	203,000
Non-controlling int.			200,000 (2)	200,000
	1,241,000	607,000		1,560,000

3.2 Direct Approach

The consolidated statement of financial position of Large Inc at the date of combination is shown in Exhibit 4. The balance of the account from the books of the affiliated companies is shown in brackets. Balances that require adjustments are shown in a separate note.

Exhibit 4 • Consolidated Statement of Financial Position of Large Inc as of January 2, X7

	CU
Assets	
Cash (CU12,000 + CU9,000)	21,000
Accounts receivable (CU39,000 + CU30,000)	69,000
Inventory **(1)**	158,000
Land **(2)**	125,000
Buildings (net) **(3)**	1,049,000
Patents (Full fair value at acquisition)	40,000
Goodwill	98,000
Total assets	**1,560,000**
Liabilities and equities	
Current liabilities (CU38,000 + CU29,000)	67,000
Bonds payable **(4)**	790,000
Share capital (Large)	300,000
Retained earnings (Large)	203,000
Non-controlling interest **(5)**	200,000
Total liabilities and equities	**1,560,000**

(1) Inventory	CU
• Parent (Large)	86,000
• Subsidiary (Silk)	68,000
• Full fair value increment at acquisition	4,000
Total	**158,000**

(2) **Land**	CU
• Parent (Large)	55,000
• Subsidiary (Silk)	50,000
• Full fair value increment at acquisition	20,000
Total	**125,000**

(3) **Buildings** (net)	CU
• Parent (Large)	549,000
• Subsidiary (Silk)	450,000
• Full fair value increment at acquisition	50,000
Total	**1,049,000**

(4) **Bonds Payable**	CU
• Parent (Large)	700,000
• Subsidiary (Silk)	100,000
• Full fair value decrement at acquisition	(10,000)
Total	**790,000**

(5) **Non-Controlling Interest**	CU
• Fair value of the non-controlling interest at the date of acquisition	**200,000**

Case 9

Total Inc

What this Case is About

- ☑ Consolidation of a Non-Wholly Owned Subsidiary
- ☑ In a Period Subsequent to Acquisition
- ☑ With No Intercompany Transactions
- ☑ Illustration Under the Cost and Equity Methods
- ☑ Measurement Basis for Non-Controlling Interest: Fair Value of Subsidiary's Net Assets

Contents

1	Basic Information	362
2	Preliminary Analysis	364
3	Consolidation of Financial Statements	365
	3.1 Worksheet Approach	365
	3.2 Direct Approach	369
4	Investment Account on Equity Basis	374

Total Inc

1 Basic Information

On January 1, X5, Total Inc purchased 80 percent of Part's outstanding common stock by issuing common shares worth CU800,000. You are asked to prepare the consolidated financial statements of Total Inc for the year ended December 31, X7, that is, three years from the date of acquisition. Separate financial statements of the affiliated companies for that period are presented in Exhibit 1.

Exhibit 1 • Financial Statements of Total and Part for the Year Ended December 31, X7

Statements of Financial Position
December 31, X7
(in CU)

	Total	Part
Assets		
Cash	45,000	80,000
Accounts receivable	700,000	475,000
Inventory	430,000	300,000
Land	90,000	500,000
Buildings (net)	1,300,000	900,000
Equipment (net)	1,200,000	
Investment in Part	800,000	
Total assets	4,565,000	2,255,000
Liabilities and equities		
Current liabilities	575,000	350,000
Bonds payable		400,000
Share capital	3,000,000	250,000
Retained earnings	990,000	1,255,000
Total liabilities and equities	4,565,000	2,255,000

Income Statements
Year Ended December 31, X7
(in CU)

	Total	Part
Revenues	15,500,000	7,500,000
Cost of goods sold	11,400,000	5,950,000
Other expenses	4,050,000	1,200,000
Profit for the year	**50,000**	**350,000**

Statements of Changes in Equity
Year Ended December 31, X7
(in CU)

	Total			Part		
	Share Capital	Retained Earnings	Total	Share Capital	Retained Earnings	Total
Balance at January 1, X7	3,000,000	1,240,000	4,240,000	250,000	905,000	1,155,000
Dividends		(300,000)	(300,000)			
Profit for the year		50,000	50,000		350,000	350,000
Balance at December 31, X7	**3,000,000**	**990,000**	**3,990,000**	**250,000**	**1,255,000**	**1,505,000**

Additional Information

1) At the date of acquisition, Part's common shares and retained earnings totalled CU250,000 and CU340,000, respectively. The net book values and fair values of the identifiable assets and liabilities assumed were the same except for the following:
   - The fair market value of inventory was greater than book value by CU50,000.
   - The net realizable value of buildings exceeded net book value by CU60,000.
   - The market value of Part's bonds payable was CU460,000 although the net book value was CU400,000. The increase in value is due to a decline in the interest rates since the bonds were originally issued.

> **Additional Information (continued)**
>
> 2) Both affiliated companies use the straight-line method to calculate all depreciation and amortization. The remaining useful life of Part's buildings is 10 years from the date of combination.
> 3) Part's bonds payable mature on December 31, X14, and have a nominal interest rate of 12%.
> 4) Total and Part never engaged in transactions among themselves since acquisition.
> 5) There is also no indication that goodwill has been impaired since acquisition.
> 6) Part elects to measure non-controlling interest as the minority shareholders' share of the fair value of Part's net assets at the date of acquisition.

2   Preliminary Analysis

Exhibit 2 presents the allocation of purchase price (CU800,000) and Exhibit 3, the price differential amortization schedule.

Exhibit 2 • Acquisition of 80 percent of the Outstanding Voting Stock of Part by Total on January 1, X5 - Allocation of the Implied Purchase Price

		(100%) CU	Total (80%) CU
Cost of investment in Part			800,000
Shareholders' equity of Part at the date of acquisition:			
- Share capital	250,000		
- Retained earnings	340,000	590,000	472,000
Price differential			328,000
Fair value increments:			
- Inventory		(50,000)	(40,000)
- Buildings		(60,000)	(48,000)
- Bonds payable		60,000	48,000
Goodwill			288,000

The fair value of Part's net assets (CU640,000) is comprised of the book value (CU590,000) and the full fair value increments (CU50,000). Twenty percent of the fair value of Part's net identifiable assets must be assigned to non-controlling shareholders, that is, CU128,000 (CU640,000 X 20%). Note that no goodwill is allocated to non-controlling interest in the process.

Exhibit 3 • Consolidation of the Financial Statements of Total - Price Differential Amortization Schedule

Items	Price Differential Balance at Acquisition (CU)	Amortization Current Year (X7) (CU)	Amortization Prior Years (X5-X6) (CU)	Unamortized Excess at 31-12-X7 (CU)
Full Fair Value Increments				
• Inventory	50,000	-	50,000	-
• Buildings	60,000	6,000	12,000	42,000
• Bonds payable	(60,000)	(6,000)	(12,000)	(42,000)
Goodwill	288,000	-	-	288,000
Total	338,000	-	(50,000)	288,000

Note that the value of the investment of Total in Part is still shown at CU800,000, that is, the purchase price. This signals the use by Total of the cost method to account for its strategic investments.

3 Consolidation of Financial Statements

The following illustrates the consolidation of the financial statements of Total Inc as of December 31, X7, under, first, the worksheet approach, and second, the direct approach.

3.1 Worksheet Approach

Entries that will be entered into the consolidation worksheet of Total are listed next.

1- Elimination of the Investment Account in the Subsidiary

(1a) To eliminate reciprocal investment and equity accounts at the date of acquisition.

Common Shares (Part)	200,000	
Retained Earnings (Part)	272,000	
Investment in Part (Total)		472,000

(1b) To allocate Total's proportionate share of Part's full fair value at the date of acquisition.

Inventory (Part)	40,000	
Buildings (Part)	48,000	
Goodwill	288,000	
Bonds Payable (Part)		48,000
Investment in Part (Total)		328,000

2- Price Differential Amortization Since Acquisition (see amortization schedule in Exhibit 3)

(2a) To recognize the prior-year realization of the full fair value increment on inventory.

Retained Earnings (Part)	50,000	
Inventory (Part)		50,000

(2b) To amortize the full fair value increment on buildings.

Retained Earnings (Part)	12,000	
Other Expenses (Part)	6,000	
Buildings (Part)		18,000

(2c) To amortize the full fair value increment on bonds payable.

Bonds Payable (Part)	18,000	
Retained Earnings (Part)		12,000
Other Expenses (Part)		6,000

3- Non-Controlling Interest

(3a) To allocate the fair value of Part's net identifiable assets to non-controlling interest.

Common Shares (Part)	50,000	
Retained Earnings (Part)	68,000	
Inventory (Part)	10,000	
Buildings (Part)	12,000	
Bonds Payable (Part)		12,000
Non-Controlling Interest		128,000

(3b) To allocate the subsidiary's net adjusted value since acquisition to non-controlling interest.

Retained Earnings	173,000	
Non-Controlling Interest		173,000

Part's net adjusted value increase since acquisition amounts to CU865,000 as shown below.

Subsidiary's Net Adjusted Value Since Acquisition	CU
• Subsidiary's retained earnings since acquisition (CU1,255,000 - CU340,000)	915,000
• Price differential amortization since acquisition (see amortization schedule in Exhibit 3)	(50,000)
Total	**865,000**

Non-controlling interest's share of Part's net adjusted value increase:
(CU865,000 X 20%) = CU173,000

The following presents the consolidation worksheet of Total Inc for the period ended December 31, X7.

Consolidation Worksheet

	Total (CU)	Part (CU)	Eliminations Adjustments (CU)	Total Consolidated (CU)
ASSETS				
Cash	45,000	80,000		125,000
Accounts receivable	700,000	475,000		1,175,000
Inventory	430,000	300,000	40,000 (1b)	730,000
			(50,000) (2a)	
			10,000 (3a)	
Land	90,000	500,000		590,000
Buildings (net)	1,300,000	900,000	48,000 (1b)	2,242,000
			(18,000) (2b)	
			12,000 (3a)	
Equipment (net)	1,200,000			1,200,000
Investment in Part	800,000		(472,000) (1a)	—
			(328,000) (1b)	
Goodwill			288,000 (1b)	288,000
	4,565,000	**2,255,000**		**6,350,000**
LIABILITIES				
Current liabilities	575,000	350,000		925,000
Bonds payable		400,000	48,000 (1b)	442,000
			(18,000) (2c)	
			12,000 (3a)	
EQUITY				
Common shares	3,000,000	250,000	(200,000) (1a)	3,000,000
			(50,000) (3a)	
Retained earnings	990,000	1,255,000	(563,000)	1,682,000
Non-controlling interest			128,000 (3a)	301,000
			173,000 (3b)	
	4,565,000	**2,255,000**		**6,350,000**

Net impact of the adjustments on the ending balance of RE

Consolidation Worksheet (continued)

	Total (CU)	Part (CU)	Eliminations Adjustments (CU)	Total Consolidated (CU)
Revenues	15,500,000	7,500,000		23,000,000
Cost of goods sold	11,400,000	5,950,000		17,350,000
Other expenses	4,050,000	1,200,000	6,000 (2b) (6,000) (2c)	5,250,000
Profit	**50,000**	**350,000**		**400,000**
Retained earnings	1,240,000	905,000	(272,000) (1a) (50,000) (2a) (12,000) (2b) 12,000 (2c) (68,000) (3a) (173,000) (3b)	1,582,000
Dividends	300,000			300,000
Retained earnings (end)	**990,000**	**1,255,000**	**(563,000)**	**1,682,000**

Net impact of the adjustments on the ending balance of RE

3.2 Direct Approach

Consolidated financial statements of Total Inc for the year ended December 31, X7, are shown in Exhibit 4. Bracketed figures come from the statements of Total and Part. When consolidated balances include consolidation adjustments, a note is added to present the details of the calculation.

Exhibit 4 • Consolidated Financial Statements of Total Inc for the Year Ended December 31, X7

Consolidated Statement of Financial Position of Total Inc
December 31, X7
(in CU)

Assets

Cash (CU45,000 + CU80,000)	125,000
Accounts receivable (CU700,000 + CU475,000)	1,175,000
Inventory (CU430,000 + CU300,000)	730,000
Land (CU90,000 + CU500,000)	590,000
Buildings (net) **(1)**	2,242,000
Equipment (net) (Total)	1,200,000
Goodwill **(2)**	288,000
Total assets	**6,350,000**

Liabilities and equities

Current liabilities (CU575,000 + CU350,000)	925,000
Bonds payable **(3)**	442,000
Share capital (Total)	3,000,000
Retained earnings **(4)**	1,682,000
Non-controlling interest **(5)**	301,000
Total liabilities and equities	**6,350,000**

Consolidated Income Statement of Total Inc
Year Ended December 31, X7
(in CU)

Revenues (CU15,500,000 + CU7,500,000)	23,000,000
Cost of goods sold (CU11,400,000 + CU5,950,000)	17,350,000
Other expenses **(6)**	5,250,000
Profit for the year (7)	**400,000**
Allocation to:	
Total **(8)**	330,000
Non-controlling interest **(9)**	70,000
	400,000

Statements of Changes in Equity of Total Inc
Year Ended December 31, X7
(in CU)

	Share Capital	Retained Earnings	NCI	Total
Balance at January 1, X7	3,000,000	1,652,000	231,000	4,883,000
Dividends		(300,000)		(300,000)
Profit for the year		330,000	70,000	400,000
Balance at December 31, X7	3,000,000	1,682,000	301,000	4,983,000

(1) Buildings (net)	CU
• Parent (Total)	1,300,000
• Subsidiary (Part)	900,000
• Unamortized balance of the full fair value increment (CU60,000 X 7/10)	42,000
Total	2,242,000

(2) Goodwill	CU
Parent (Total)'s share of the subsidiary (Part)'s goodwill at the date of acquisition	288,000

(3) Bonds Payable	CU
• Subsidiary (Part)	400,000
• Unamortized balance of the full fair value increment (CU60,000 X 7/10)	42,000
Total	442,000

(4) Retained Earnings | CU

- Parent (Total) — 990,000
- 80 percent of the subsidiary (Part)'s net adjusted value since acquisition

  - Retained earnings increase since acquisition (CU1,255,000 - CU340,000): 915,000
  - Price differential amortization since acquisition (see amortization schedule in Exhibit 3): (50,000)
  - Total: 865,000
  - 80% → 692,000

Total — **1,682,000**

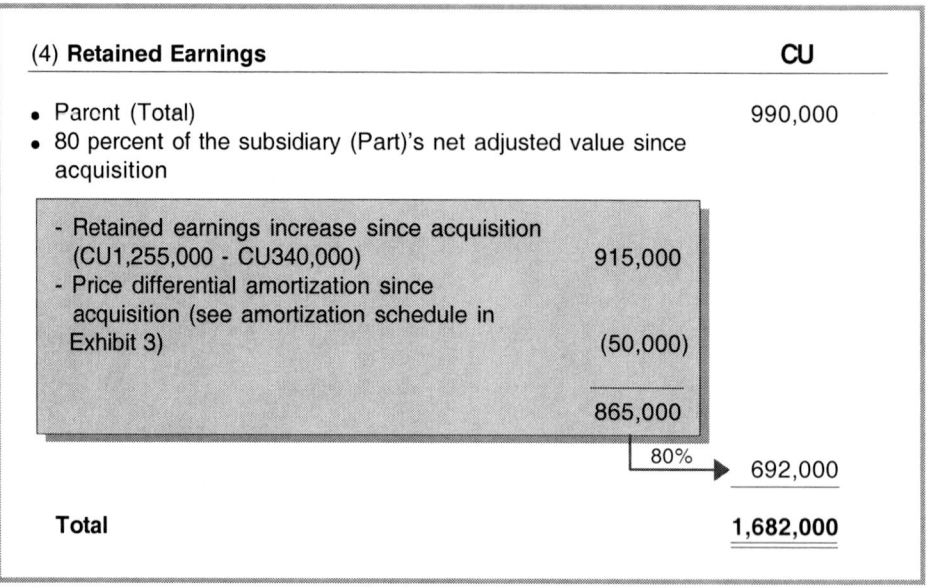

(5) Non-Controlling Interest | CU

- 20 percent of the fair value of the subsidiary (Part)'s net identifiable assets as of January 1, X5

  - Net book value at acquisition: 590,000
  - Full fair value increments: 50,000
  - Total: 640,000
  - 20% → 128,000

- 20 percent of the subsidiary (Part)'s net adjusted value since acquisition

  - Retained earnings increase since acquisition (CU1,255,000 - CU340,000): 915,000
  - Price differential amortization since acquisition (see amortization schedule in Exhibit 3): (50,000)
  - Total: 865,000
  - 20% → 173,000

Total — **301,000**

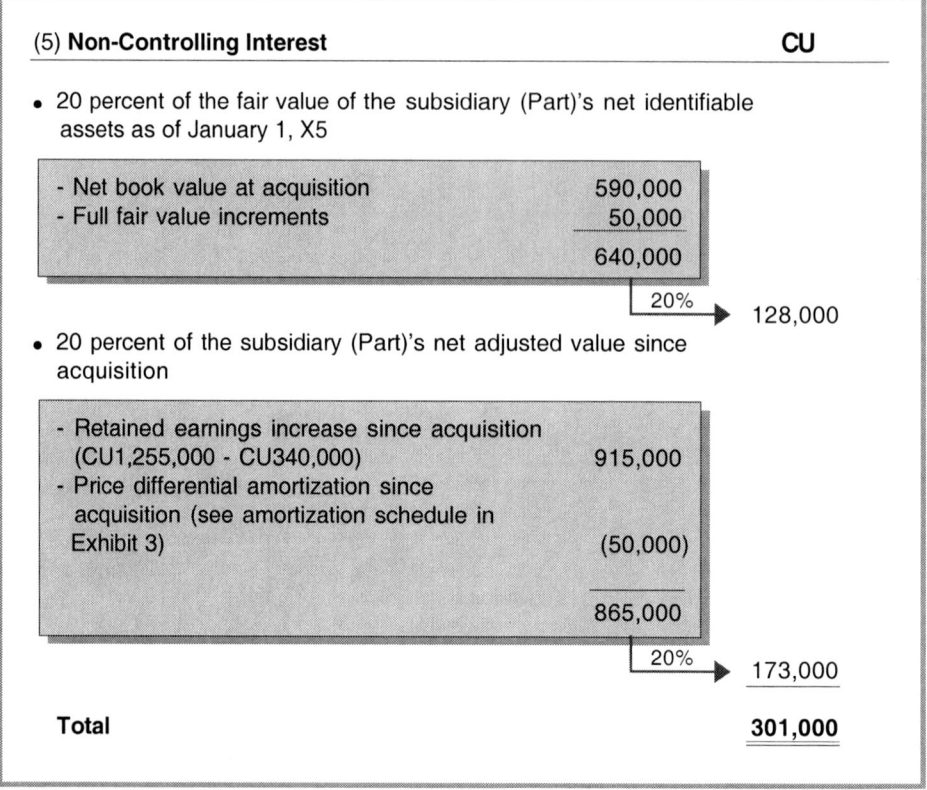

(6) **Other Expenses** (including depreciation expense)	CU
• Parent (Total)	4,050,000
• Subsidiary (Part)	1,200,000
• Current-year price differential amortization (see amortization schedule in Exhibit 3). Includes full fair value increments on:	
- Bonds payable (CU60,000/10)	(6,000)
- Buildings (CU60,000/10)	6,000
Total	**5,250,000**

(7) **Consolidated Profit for the Year**		CU
• Total's profit		50,000
• Part's adjusted profit:		
- Part's profit	350,000	
- Current-year price differential amortization (see amortization schedule in Exhibit 3). Full fair value increments on:		
- Bonds payable (CU60,000/10)	6,000	
- Buildings (CU60,000/10)	(6,000)	350,000
Total		**400,000**

(8) **Consolidated Profit Allocated to Total**	CU
• Total's profit	50,000
• 80 percent of Part's adjusted profit (CU350,000 X 80%)	280,000
Total	**330,000**

(9) **Consolidated Profit Allocated to Non-Controlling Interest**	CU
20 percent of Part's adjusted profit (CU350,000 X 20%)	**70,000**

4 Investment Account on Equity Basis

Assume that the equity method is employed by Total to account for its investment in Part instead of the cost method. The individual financial statements of Total as of December 31, X7, are shown in Exhibit 5. Consolidated information is also reported on a comparative basis.

Exhibit 5 • Financial Statements of Total Inc for the Year Ended December 31, X7 - The Investment in Part is Accounted for Using the Equity Method

Statements of Financial Position of Total Inc
December 31, X7
(in CU)

	Equity Method	Consolidated
Assets		
Cash	45,000	125,000
Accounts receivable	700,000	1,175,000
Inventory	430,000	730,000
Land	90,000	590,000
Buildings (net)	1,300,000	2,242,000
Equipment	1,200,000	1,200,000
Investment in Part	1,492,000	
Goodwill		288,000
Total assets	5,257,000	6,350,000
Liabilities and equities		
Current liabilities	575,000	925,000
Bonds payable		442,000
Share capital	3,000,000	3,000,000
Retained earnings	1,682,000	1,682,000
Non-controlling interest		301,000
Total liabilities and equities	5,257,000	6,350,000

Consolidated Share Capital (CU3,000,000) and Retained Earnings (CU1,682,000) are equal to Total's separate-entity Share Capital and Retained Earnings under the equity method. Moreover, the profit of Total under the equity method is equal to the consolidated profit allocated to Total in the consolidation process, that is, CU330,000.

Income Statements of Total Inc
For the Year Ended December 31, X7
(in CU)

	Equity Method	Consolidated
Revenues	15,500,000	23,000,000
Equity in earnings of Part	280,000	
Cost of goods sold	11,400,000	17,350,000
Other expenses	4,050,000	5,250,000
Profit for the year	**330,000**	**400,000**
Allocated to:		
Total	330,000	330,000
Non-controlling interest		70,000
	330,000	400,000

Statements of Changes in Equity of Total Inc
Year Ended December 31, X7
(in CU)

	Equity Method			Consolidated			
	Share Capital	Retained Earnings	Total	Share Capital	Retained Earnings	NCI	Total
Balance at January 1, X7	3,000,000	1,652,000	4,652,000	3,000,000	1,652,000	231,000	4,883,000
Dividends		(300,000)	(300,000)		(300,000)		(300,000)
Profit for the year		330,000	330,000		330,000	70,000	400,000
Balance at December 31, X7	**3,000,000**	**1,682,000**	**4,682,000**	**3,000,000**	**1,682,000**	**301,000**	**4,983,000**

The approach to computing equity in earnings and investment accounts is shown in Exhibits 6 and 7, respectively.

Exhibit 6 • The Equity Method - Computation of Equity in Earnings of Part

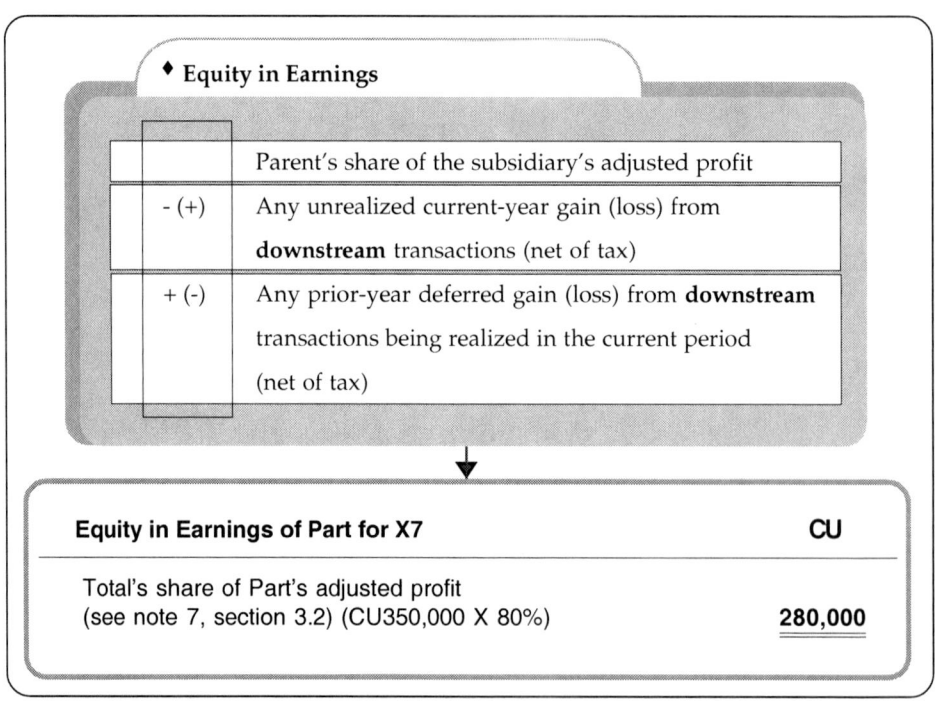

The following presents the journal entry that Total must have recorded in X7 to account for its investment in Part using the equity method.

1- Equity in Earnings of Part

2- No Dividends Have Been Declared by Part

Had Total been using the equity method to account for its investment in Part instead of the cost method, this journal entry should have been eliminated via the following additional consolidation entry.

Exhibit 7 • The Equity Method - Computation of the Balance of the Investment in Part

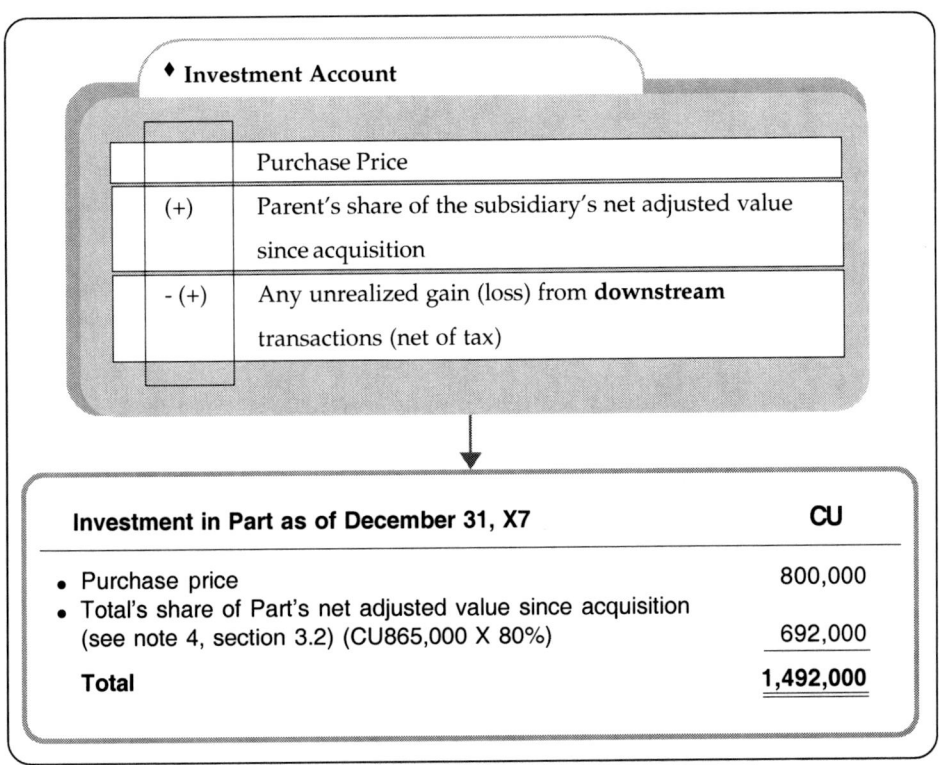

Investment in Part as of December 31, X7	CU
• Purchase price	800,000
• Total's share of Part's net adjusted value since acquisition (see note 4, section 3.2) (CU865,000 X 80%)	692,000
Total	1,492,000

Additional Consolidation Entry #1

Equity in Earnings of Part (Total)	280,000	
Investment in Part (Total)		280,000

To eliminate equity in earnings of Part.

After this entry is entered into the consolidation worksheet, the remaining balance of the investment in Part amounts to CU412,000 as shown next.

	CU
Balance of the investment in Part as of December 31, X7, under the equity method (see Exhibit 7)	1,492,000
• Purchase price (already eliminated via entries #1a and #1b)	(800,000)
• Equity in earnings of X7 (additional consolidation entry #1)	(280,000)
Remaining balance of the investment in Part	**412,000**

The remaining balance of CU412,000 reflects the increase of the investment account from the date of acquisition to the beginning of the current year and must be eliminated with the following final consolidation entry.

Additional Consolidation Entry #2

Retained Earnings (Total)	412,000	
Investment in Part (Total)		412,000

To eliminate the remaining balance of the investment account.

Case 10

Giant Inc

What this Case is About

- ☑ Consolidation of a Non-Wholly Owned Subsidiary
- ☑ One Year Subsequent to the Date of Acquisition
- ☑ With Intercompany Transactions Involving Land, Building and Dividends
- ☑ Illustration Under the Cost and Equity Methods
- ☑ Measurement Basis for Non-Controlling Interest: Fair Value of Subsidiary's Net Assets

Contents

1	Basic Information	380
2	Preliminary Analysis	382
	2.1 Controlling Ownership	382
	2.2 Intercompany Transactions	384
3	Consolidation of Financial Statements	385
	3.1 Worksheet Approach	385
	3.2 Direct Approach	390
4	Investment Account on Equity Basis	394

Giant Inc

1 Basic Information

On January 1, X7, Giant Inc purchased a 90 percent interest in Pratt in exchange for 25,000 shares of its CU20 par value voting common stock. On December 31, X6, Giant's common stock had a closing market price of CU30 per share on a national stock exchange. Both companies continue to operate as separate business entities maintaining separate accounting records with years ending December 31.

You are asked to prepare the consolidated financial statements of Giant Inc for the year ended December 31, X7. Exhibit 1 shows the financial statements of Giant Inc and Pratt Corporation for that period.

Exhibit 1 • Financial Statements of Giant and Pratt for the Year Ended December 31, X7

Statements of Financial Position
December 31, X7
(in CU)

	Giant	Pratt
Assets		
Cash	711,000	150,000
Accounts receivable	860,000	350,000
Inventory	1,060,000	410,000
Land, Plant, and Equipment (net)	950,000	470,000
Investment in Pratt	750,000	
Total assets	4,331,000	1,380,000
Liabilities and equities		
Current liabilities	1,340,000	594,000
Share capital	1,700,000	400,000
Retained earnings	1,291,000	386,000
Total liabilities and equities	4,331,000	1,380,000

Statements of Income
Year Ended December 31, X7
(in CU)

	Giant	Pratt
Net sales	3,945,000	1,500,000
Dividend Income	36,000	
Gain on sale of warehouse	30,000	
Cost of goods sold	2,360,000	870,000
Operating expenses	1,100,000	440,000
Profit for the year	**551,000**	**190,000**

Statements of Changes in Equity
Year Ended December 31, X7
(in CU)

	Giant			Pratt		
	Share Capital	Retained Earnings	Total	Share Capital	Retained Earnings	Total
Balance at January 1, X7	1,700,000	740,000	2,440,000	400,000	236,000	636,000
Dividends	-	-	-		(40,000)	(40,000)
Profit for the year		551,000	551,000		190,000	190,000
Balance at December 31, X7	1,700,000	1,291,000	2,991,000	400,000	386,000	786,000

Additional Information

1) At the acquisition date, the fair value of Pratt's machinery exceeded its book value by CU54,000. The excess cost will be amortized over the estimated average remaining life of six years. The fair values of all Pratt's other assets and liabilities were equal to their book values.

2) At December 31, X7, Giant management reviewed the amount attributed to goodwill as a result of its purchase of Pratt's common stock and concluded an impairment loss of CU35,000 should be recognized in X7.

> **Additional Information (continued)**
>
> 3) On July 1, X7, Giant sold a warehouse to Pratt for CU129,000. At the date of sale, Giant's book values were CU33,000 for the land and CU66,000 for the undepreciated cost of the building. Based on real estate appraisal, Pratt allocated CU43,000 of the purchase price to land and CU86,000 to building. Pratt is depreciating the building over its estimated five-year remaining useful life.
> 4) Both affiliated companies use the straight-line method to calculate all depreciation and amortization as well as a full year of depreciation for the year of acquisition.
> 5) Giant elects to measure non-controlling interest based on Pratt's fair value of net assets at the date of acquisition.

2 Preliminary Analysis

Figure 1 lists the consolidation scenarios that apply to Giant.

2.1 Controlling Ownership

Exhibit 2 presents the allocation of purchase price (CU750,000). The fair value of Pratt's net identifiable assets at date of acquisition amounts to CU690,000 and consists of the book value (CU636,000) and the full fair vlaue increment on machinery (CU54,000). Ten percent of that value must be assigned to non-controlling interest, that is, CU69,000 (CU690,000 X 10%).

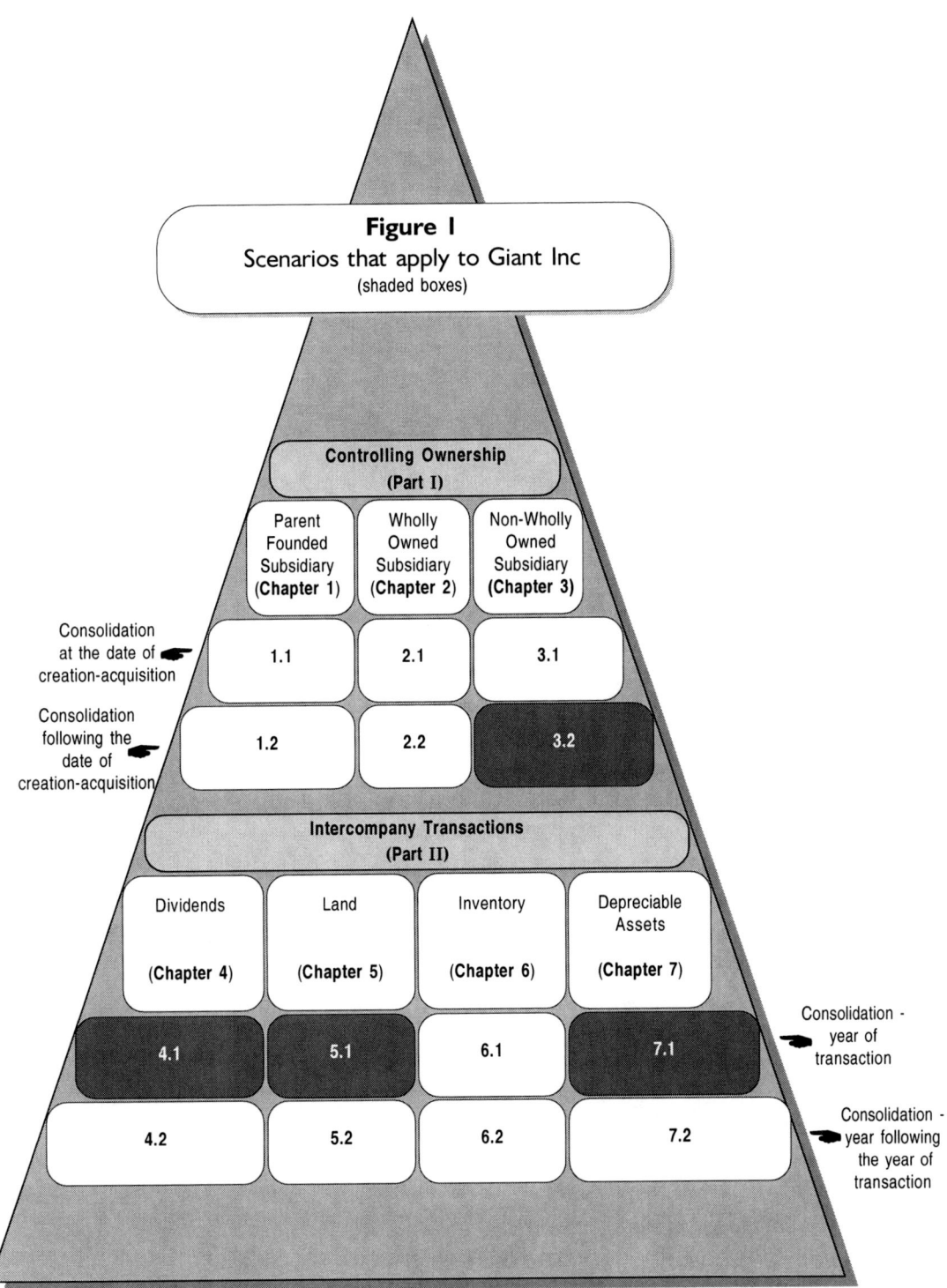

Figure 1
Scenarios that apply to Giant Inc
(shaded boxes)

Exhibit 2 • Acquisition of 90 percent of the Outstanding Voting Stock of Pratt by Giant on January 1, X7 - Allocation of the Implied Purchase Price

			Giant
		(100%) CU	(90%) CU
Cost of investment in Pratt			750,000
Shareholders' equity of Pratt at the date of acquisition:			
- Share capital	400,000		
- Retained earnings	236,000	636,000	572,400
Price differential			177,600
Fair value increment on machinery		54,000	48,600
Goodwill			129,000

The full fair value increment of CU54,000 on Machinery must be amortized over the remaining six years, that is, at a rate of CU9,000 a year so as to adjust for the underdepreciation expense on Pratt's records. In addition, goodwill of CU129,000 must be reduced by CU35,000 so as to account for current-year goodwill impairment. Since no goodwill is assigned to non-controlling interest, the full amount of goodwill impairment is allocated to Giant.

Consistent with the use of the cost method, the balance of the investment of Giant in Pratt as of December 31, X7, is still shown at CU750,000, that is, the purchase price.

2.2 Intercompany Transactions

Transactions conducted between the affiliated companies are analyzed below.

Intercompany Dividends

During X7, Pratt declared dividends for CU40,000. Since there is no indication of reciprocal receivable and payable balances at the end of the year, one can assume that dividends declared by Pratt were fully paid in the current accounting period. Furthermore, since the investment of Giant in Pratt is accounted for using the cost method, dividends received by Giant (CU40,000 X 90% = CU36,000) have been recorded as dividend income in the income statement. To avoid double-counting of Pratt's earnings, intercompany dividends must be eliminated.

Downstream Sale of Warehouse

A warehouse has been transferred from Giant to Pratt in the current period. A gain on sale of CU30,000 has been recognized by Giant which consists of the difference between the selling price (CU129,000) and the book value of the warehouse at the time of the sale (CU33,000 for the land + CU66,000 for the building = CU99,000). The overall gain on sale of CU30,000 can be broken down into the following two components:

(1) Gain on sale of Land of CU10,000 which consists of the difference between the portion of the purchase price assigned to the land (CU43,000) and the book value of the land (CU33,000);

(2) Gain on sale of Building of CU20,000 which consists of the difference between the portion of the purchase price assigned to the building (CU86,000) and the underdepreciated value of the building (CU66,000).

Since there is no indication that the transferred land has been resold to an outside party prior to the end of the current period, the intercompany gain of CU10,000 must be considered as being unrealized from the viewpoint of the economic entity and, as such, must be eliminated. Similarly, since the land now carried on the books of Pratt contains the intercompany gain, this account must be reduced by CU10,000 so as to return its value back to the price originally paid by the selling affiliate.

Likewise, the intercompany gain on sale of Building of CU20,000 must be eliminated. This gain will however be consumed over the estimated five-year remaining useful life of the building, that is, at a rate of CU4,000 a year (CU20,000/5 years).

3 Consolidation of Financial Statements

The following illustrates the consolidation of the financial statements of Giant Inc as of December 31, X7, under, first, the worksheet approach, and second, the direct approach.

3.1 Worksheet Approach

Entries that will be entered into the consolidation worksheet of Giant are listed next.

Adjustments Related To Controlling Ownership

1- Elimination of the Investment Account in the Subsidiary (see purchase price allocation in Exhibit 2)

(1a) To eliminate reciprocal investment and equity accounts at the date of acquisition.

Common Shares (Pratt)	360,000	
Retained Earnings (Pratt)	212,400	
Investment in Pratt (Giant)		572,400

(1b) To allocate Giant's proportionate share of Pratt's full fair value at the date of acquisition.

Land, Plant and Equipment (Pratt)	48,600	
Goodwill	129,000	
Investment in Pratt (Giant)		177,600

2- Price Differential Amortization Since Acquisition

(2a) To amortize the full fair value increment on building.

Operating Expenses (Pratt)	9,000	
Land, Plant, and Equipment (Pratt)		9,000

(2b) To recognize current-year impairment of goodwill.

Operating Expenses (Pratt)	35,000	
Goodwill		35,000

3- Non-Controlling Interest

(3a) To allocate the fair value of Pratt's net identifiable assets to non-controlling interest.

Common Shares (Pratt)	40,000
Retained Earnings (Pratt)	23,600
Land, Plant, and Equipment (Pratt)	5,400
Non-Controlling Interest	69,000

(3b) To allocate the subsidiary's net adjusted value since acquisition to non-controlling interest.

Retained Earnings	14,100
Non-Controlling Interest	14,100

Subsidiary's Net Adjusted Value Since Acquisition	CU
• Subsidiary's retained earnings since acquisition (CU386,000 - CU236,000)	150,000
• Current-year price differential amortization:	
- Full fair value increment on Building	(9,000)
Total	**141,000**

Non-controlling interest's share of Pratt's net adjusted value increase:
(CU141,000 X 10%) = CU14,100

Pratt's net adjusted value increase since acquisition (CU141,000), as computed above, does not include the impairment loss of CU35,000 since there is no goodwill allocated to non-controlling interest. Only Giant's share of Pratt's goodwill (CU129,000) is brought onto the consolidated financial statements. Consequently, goodwill impairment of CU35,000 is assigned only to Giant in the consolidation process.

Adjustments Related to Intercompany Transactions

(4) Intercompany Dividends

Dividend Income (Giant)	36,000	
Retained Earnings	4,000	
Dividends Declared (Pratt)		40,000

To eliminate current-year intercompany dividends. Dividends assigned to non-controlling shareholders (CU4,000) reduces Retained Earnings so as to be consistent with adjustment #3b.

(5) Downstream Sale of Warehouse (Land)

Gain on Sale of Warehouse (Giant)	10,000	
Land, Plant, and Equipment (Pratt)		10,000

To eliminate current-year intercompany gain on sale of land and reduce land to its cost basis.

(6) Downstream Sale of Warehouse (Building)

(6a) To eliminate current-year intercompany gain on sale of building and reduce building to its cost basis.

Gain on Sale of Warehouse (Giant)	20,000	
Land, Plant, and Equipment (Pratt)		20,000

(6b) To recognize a portion of the intercompany gain as being realized in the current period.

Land, Plant, and Equipment (Pratt)	4,000	
Operating Expenses (Pratt)		4,000

Case 10 Giant Inc

The following presents the consolidation worksheet of Giant Inc for the period ended December 31, X7.

Consolidation Worksheet

	Giant (CU)	Pratt (CU)	Eliminations Adjustments (CU)	Giant Consolidated (CU)
ASSETS				
Cash	711,000	150,000		861,000
Accounts receivable	860,000	350,000		1,210,000
Inventory	1,060,000	410,000		1,470,000
Land, Plant, and Equi.	950,000	470,000	48,600 (1b) (9,000) (2a) 5,400 (3a) (10,000) (5) (20,000) (6a) 4,000 (6b)	1,439,000
Investment in Pratt	750,000		(572,400) (1a) (177,600) (1b)	–
Goodwill			129,000 (1b) (35,000) (2b)	94,000
	4,331,000	1,380,000		5,074,000
LIABILITIES				
Current liabilities	1,340,000	594,000		1,934,000
EQUITY				
Common shares	1,700,000	400,000	(360,000) (1a) (40,000) (3a)	1,700,000
Retained earnings	1,291,000	386,000	→(313,100)	1,356,900
Non-controlling interest			69,000 (3a) 14,100 (3b)	83,100
	4,331,000	1,380,000		5,074,000

Net impact of the adjustments on the ending balance of RE

Consolidation Worksheet (continued)

	Giant (CU)	Pratt (CU)	Eliminations Adjustments (CU)	Giant Consolidated (CU)
Net sales	3,945,000	1,500,000		5,445,000
Dividend Income	36,000		(36,000) (4)	-
Gain on sale	30,000		(10,000) (5) (20,000) (6a)	-
Cost of goods sold	2,360,000	870,000		3,230,000
Operating exp.	1,100,000	440,000	9,000 (2a) 35,000 (2b) (4,000) (6b)	1,580,000
Profit	551,000	190,000	(106,000)	635,000
Retained earnings	740,000	236,000	(212,400) (1a) (23,600) (3a) (14,100) (3b) (4,000) (4)	721,900
Dividends		40,000	(40,000) (4)	
Retained earnings (end)	1,291,000	386,000	(313,100)	1,356,900

Net impact of the adjustments on the ending balance of RE

3.2 Direct Approach

Consolidated financial statements of Giant Inc for the year ended December 31, X7, are shown in Exhibit 3.

Exhibit 3 • Consolidated Financial Statements of Giant Inc for the Year Ended December 31, X7

Consolidated Statement of Financial Position of Giant Inc
December 31, X7
(in CU)

Assets

Cash (CU711,000 + CU150,000)	861,000
Accounts receivable (CU860,000 + CU350,000)	1,210,000
Inventory (CU1,060,000 + CU410,000)	1,470,000
Land, Plant and Equipment **(1)**	1,439,000
Goodwill **(2)**	94,000
Total assets	**5,074,000**

Liabilities and equities

Current liabilities (CU1,340,000 + CU594,000)	1,934,000
Share capital (Giant)	1,700,000
Retained earnings **(3)**	1,356,900
Non-controlling interest **(4)**	83,100
Total liabilities and equities	**5,074,000**

Consolidated Income Statement of Giant Inc
Year Ended December 31, X7
(in CU)

Net sales (CU3,945,000 + CU1,500,000)	5,445,000
Cost of goods sold (CU2,360,000 + CU870,000)	3,230,000
Operating expenses **(5)**	1,580,000
Profit for the year (6)	**635,000**
Allocation to:	
Giant **(7)**	616,900
Non-controlling interest **(8)**	18,100
	635,000

Statements of Changes in Equity of Giant Inc
Year Ended December 31, X7
(in CU)

	Share Capital	Retained Earnings	NCI	Total
Balance at January 1, X7	1,700,000	740,000	69,000	2,509,000
Dividends to NCI			(4,000)	(4,000)
Profit for the year		616,900	18,100	635,000
Balance at December 31, X7	**1,700,000**	**1,356,900**	**83,100**	**3,140,000**

(1) Land, Plant, and Equipment — CU

- Parent (Giant) — 950,000
- Subsidiary (Pratt) — 470,000
- Unamortized balance of the full fair value increment on machinery (CU54,000 X 5/6) — 45,000
- Unamortized portion of the gain on downstream sale of warehouse (total gain of CU30,000 - portion being realized in X7, CU4,000) — (26,000)

Total — **1,439,000**

(2) Goodwill — CU

- Parent (Giant)'s share of the subsidiary (Pratt)'s goodwill at the date of acquisition — 129,000
- Portion being impaired in X7 — (35,000)

Total — **94,000**

(3) Retained Earnings — CU

- Parent (Giant) — 1,291,000
- 90 percent of the subsidiary (Pratt)'s net adjusted value since acquisition

  - Retained earnings increase since acquisition (CU386,000 - CU236,000) — 150,000
  - Price differential amortization since acquisition (amortization of the full fair value increment on machinery) — (9,000)
  - — 141,000

  → 90% → 126,900

- Goodwill impairment — (35,000)
- Unamortized portion of the gain on downstream sale of warehouse (total gain of CU30,000 - portion being realized in X7, CU4,000) — (26,000)

Total — **1,356,900**

(4) Non-Controlling Interest — CU

- 10 percent of the fair value of the subsidiary (Pratt)'s net identifiable assets as of January 1, X7

- Net book value at acquisition	636,000
- Full fair value increment	54,000
	690,000

  × 10% → **69,000**

- 10 percent of the subsidiary (Pratt)'s net adjusted value since acquisition

- Retained earnings increase since acquisition (CU386,000 - CU236,000)	150,000
- Price differential amortization since acquisition (amortization of the full fair value increment on machinery - Goodwill impairment not included)	(9,000)
	141,000

  × 10% → **14,100**

Total — **83,100**

---

(5) Operating Expenses (including depreciation expense) — CU

• Parent (Giant)	1,100,000
• Subsidiary (Pratt)	440,000
• Current-year price differential amortization	44,000
• Current-year realization of intercompany gain on sale of warehouse	(4,000)
Total	**1,580,000**

(6) Consolidated Profit for the Year

		CU
Giant's adjusted profit:		
- Giant's profit	551,000	
- Current-year unrealized gain on downstream sale of warehouse (CU30,000 - CU4,000)	(26,000)	
- Intercompany dividends	(36,000)	489,000
Pratt's adjusted profit:		
- Pratt's profit	190,000	
- Current-year price differential amortization (machinery)	(9,000)	181,000
- Goodwill impairment		(35,000)
Total		**635,000**

(7) Consolidated Profit Allocated to Giant

	CU
• Giant's adjusted profit	489,000
• 90 percent of Pratt's adjusted profit (CU181,000 X 90%)	162,900
• Goodwill impairment	(35,000)
Total	**616,900**

(8) Consolidated Profit Allocated to Non-Controlling Interest

	CU
10 percent of Pratt's adjusted profit (CU181,000 X 10%)	**18,100**

4 Investment Account on Equity Basis

Assume that the equity method is employed by Giant to account for its investment in Pratt instead of the cost method. The seperate-entity financial statements of Giant as of December 31, X7, are shown in Exhibit 4. Consolidated information is also reported on a comparative basis.

Exhibit 4 • Financial Statements of Giant Inc for the Year Ended December 31, X7 - The Investment in Pratt is Accounted for Using the Equity Method.

Statements of Financial Position of Giant Inc
December 31, X7
(in CU)

	Equity Method	Consolidated
Assets		
Cash	711,000	861,000
Accounts receivable	860,000	1,210,000
Inventory	1,060,000	1,470,000
Land, Plant, and Equipment	950,000	1,439,000
Investment in Pratt	815,900	
Goodwill		94,000
Total assets	4,396,900	5,074,000
Liabilities and equities		
Current liabilities	1,340,000	1,934,000
Share capital	**1,700,000**	**1,700,000**
Retained earnings	1,356,900	1,356,900
Non-controlling interest		83,100
Total liabilities and equities	4,396,900	5,074,000

Income Statements of Giant Inc
Year Ended December 31, X7
(in CU)

	Equity Method	Consolidated
Net sales	3,945,000	5,445,000
Gain on sale of warehouse	30,000	
Equity in earnings of Pratt	101,900	
Cost of goods sold	2,360,000	3,230,000
Operating expenses	1,100,000	1,580,000
Profit for the year	616,900	635,000
Allocated to:		
Giant	616,900	616,900
Non-controlling interest		18,100
	616,900	635,000

Statements of Changes in Equity of Giant Inc
Year Ended December 31, X7
(in CU)

	Equity Method			Consolidated			
	Share Capital	Retained Earnings	Total	Share Capital	Retained Earnings	NCI	Total
Balance at January 1, X7	1,700,000	740,000	2,440,000	1,700,000	740,000	69,000	2,509,000
Dividends to NCI						(4,000)	(4,000)
Profit for the year		616,900	616,900		616,900	18,100	635,000
Balance at December 31, X7	1,700,000	1,356,900	3,056,900	1,700,000	1,356,900	83,100	3,140,000

The approach to computing equity in earnings and investment accounts is shown in Exhibits 5 and 6, respectively.

Exhibit 5 • The Equity Method - Computation of Equity in Earnings of Pratt

Equity in Earnings

	Parent's share of the subsidiary's adjusted profit
- (+)	Any unrealized current-year gain (loss) from **downstream** transactions (net of tax)
+ (-)	Any prior-year deferred gain (loss) from **downstream** transactions being realized in the current period

Equity in Earnings of Pratt for X7	CU
• Giant's share of Pratt's adjusted profit (see note 6, section 3.2) (CU181,000 X 90%)	162,900
• Unrealized portion of the gain on downstream sale of warehouse	(26,000)
• Goodwill impairment	(35,000)
Total	101,900

Exhibit 6 • The Equity Method - Computation of the Balance of the Investment in Pratt

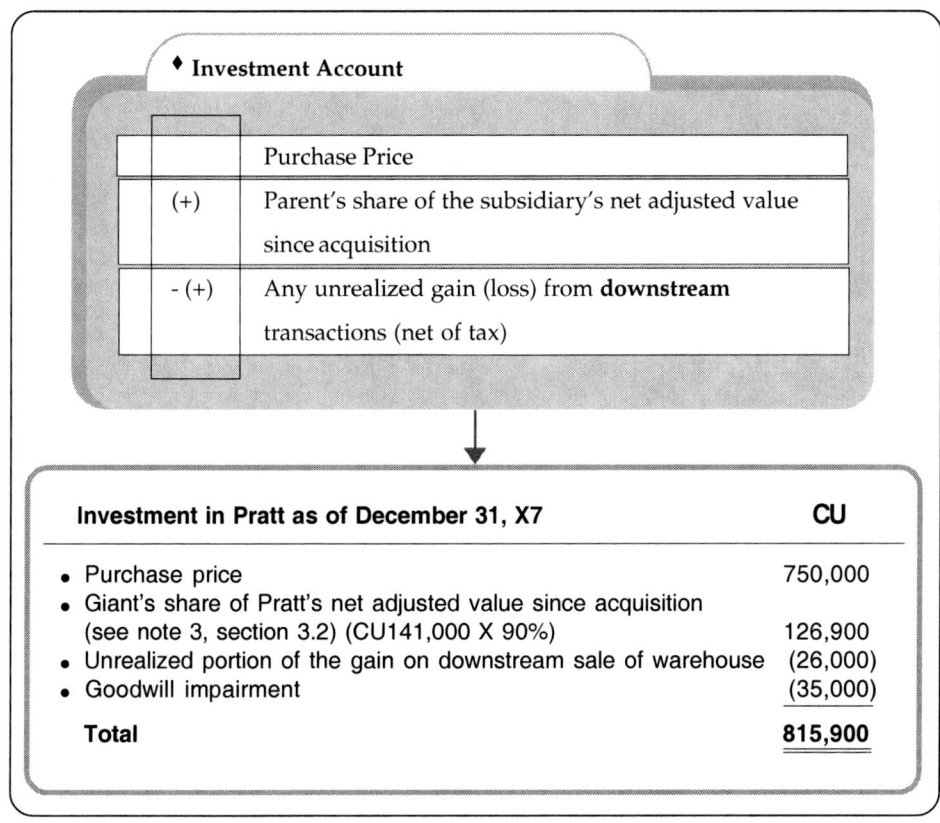

Investment in Pratt as of December 31, X7	CU
• Purchase price	750,000
• Giant's share of Pratt's net adjusted value since acquisition (see note 3, section 3.2) (CU141,000 X 90%)	126,900
• Unrealized portion of the gain on downstream sale of warehouse	(26,000)
• Goodwill impairment	(35,000)
Total	**815,900**

The following presents the journal entries that Giant must have recorded in X7 to account for its investment in Pratt using the equity method.

1- Equity in Earnings of Pratt

Investment in Pratt	101,900	
Equity in Earnings of Pratt		101,900

2- Dividends Declared by Pratt

Cash	36,000	
Investment in Pratt		36,000

(CU40,000 X 90%) = CU36,000

Had Giant been using the equity method to account for its investment in Pratt instead of the cost method, these two journal entries should have been eliminated via the following additional consolidation entries.

Additional Consolidation Entry #1

Equity in Earnings of Pratt (Giant)	101,900	
Investment in Pratt (Giant)		101,900

To eliminate equity in earnings of Pratt.

Additional Consolidation Entry #2 (replacing entry #4)

Investment in Pratt (Giant)	36,000	
Dividends Declared (Pratt)		36,000

To eliminate intercompany dividends.

After these two entries are entered into the consolidation worksheet, the balance of the investment in Pratt is reduced to zero as shown below.

	CU
Balance of the investment in Pratt as of December 31, X7, under the equity method (see Exhibit 6)	815,900
• Purchase price (already eliminated via entries #1a and #1b)	(750,000)
• Equity in earnings of X7 (additional consolidation entry #1)	(101,900)
• Dividends declared in X7 (additional consolidation entry #2)	36,000
Remaining balance of the investment in Pratt	-

Key Concepts

Key Concepts	Chapters
Acquisition Method	2
Building-Block Approach	Intro
Business Combinations	2
Cost Method	1
Direct Approach	Intro and 1
Double-Counting	1 and 4
Downstream Transactions	5
Economic Entity	Intro and 1
Economic Entity Concept	3
Entity Theory	3
Excess Depreciation	7
Fair Value Increments-Decrements	2
Full Fair Values	3
Full Goodwill	3
Full Goodwill Approach	3
Goodwill	2
Goodwill Impairment	2
Intercompany Dividends	4
Intercompany Transactions	4
Implied Purchase Price	3
Negative Goodwill	2
Non-Controlling Interest	3
Non-Wholly Owned Subsidiary	3
Parent	Intro
Parent Founded Subsidiary	1
Partial Goodwill Approach	3
Price Differential	2
Price Differential Amortization	2
Reciprocal Sales and Cost of Goods Sold	6
Subsidiary	Intro
Subsidiary's Net Adjusted Value	2
Unrealized Intercompany Gains and Losses	5
Unrealized Intercompany Profits and Losses	6
Upstream Transactions	5
Visual Approach	Intro and 1
Wholly Owned Subsidiary	2
Working Paper Entry	1
Worksheet Approach	Intro and 1